Death by Drama and Other Medieval Urban Legends

JODY ENDERS

Death by Drama
and Other Medieval
Urban Legends

THE UNIVERSITY OF CHICAGO PRESS / CHICAGO AND LONDON

Jody Enders is professor of French at the University of California, Santa Barbara. She is the author of *The Medieval Theater of Cruelty: Rhetoric, Memory, Violence* (1999) and *Rhetoric and the Origins of Medieval Drama* (1992), the latter awarded the Scaglione Prize for French and Francophone Studies by the Modern Language Association.

The University of Chicago Press, Chicago 60637
The University of Chicago Press, Ltd., London
© 2002 by The University of Chicago
All rights reserved. Published 2002
Printed in the United States of America

11 10 09 08 07 06 05 04 03 02   1 2 3 4 5
ISBN: 0-226-20787-0 (cloth)

The University of Chicago Press gratefully acknowledges the generous support of the John Simon Guggenheim Memorial Foundation toward the publication of this book.

Library of Congress Cataloging-in-Publication Data

Enders, Jody, 1955–
    Death by drama and other medieval urban legends / Jody Enders.
        p. cm.
    Includes bibliographical references and index.
    ISBN 0-226-20787-0 (alk. paper)
    1. Therater—Europe—History—Medieval, 500–1500.   2. Drama, Medieval—History and criticism.   3. Legends in literature.   I. Title.
PN1751 .E48 2002
792′.094′0902—dc21   2002004777

For my husband

CONTENTS

ILLUSTRATIONS

ACKNOWLEDGMENTS

The ineluctability of truth will be a main theme of this book, but one thing is for sure: My intellectual debts to colleagues, friends, and family are real, not imaginary.

I am deeply indebted to the John Simon Guggenheim Memorial Foundation for enabling me to spend an entire year immersed in this project. I also thank the University of California, Santa Barbara, for helping to grant that most precious resource, time.

At a very early stage of this project, Jesse Hurlbut shared resources and bibliography with a selflessness that I have rarely seen in the profession. When the nascent sketch of "Medieval Snuff Drama" was being considered by *Exemplaria*, James Paxson posed penetrating questions. When Karen Sullivan invited me to lecture at Bard College on some of these materials, she and her colleagues engaged me in a spirited debate that altered the course of this book. While I was tracking down obstreperous devils, John Coldewey communicated his own findings with a devilish grin. Three of our most eminent specialists of the French medieval stage were magnanimous with their considerable expertise: Alan Knight, Graham Runnalls, and Darwin Smith. I have also been privileged to have as interlocutors such innovative scholars as Howard Bloch, Stephen Nichols, Geoffrey Parker, Richard Schechner, Virginia Scott, and Bert States. Naturally, if any errors have marred this book, I alone am to blame.

Bett Miller and Cynthia Requardt of the Eisenhower Library at Johns Hopkins University graciously allowed me to borrow the unique U.S. copy of the *Chronique de Metz de Jacomin Husson.* I am also grateful to Annie Rosenkrantz of the Departmental Archives of Seine-et-Marne; and to Layla Lyne-Winkler, Carol Hurley, and the entire staff of the Interlibrary Loan Office at Davidson Library of my home institution, who assiduously helped me secure even the most obscure documents. Additionally, I thank the Aspen Center for Physics, especially Jane Kelly and Deb Pease, for allowing me to use their office equipment during the summer. Suzanne Braswell was a godsend of a proofreader, and Rita Keane was a fabulous resource in my hunt for appropriate images.

For their willingness to lend an incisive ear, I acknowledge William Ashby, David Bevington, Cynthia Brown, Martin Camargo, Julie Carlson, Dorothy Chansky, Robert Clark, Larry Clopper, Howard Enders, William Kibler, Loren Kruger, Carol Lansing, Elizabeth MacArthur, Peggy McCracken, Robert Morstein Marx, Lynette Muir, Emily Odom, Bob Potter, Marya Schechtman, Judy Shoaf, Cynthia Skenazi, Vance Smith, Claire Sponsler, Ronald Tobin, and William Warner, along with the community of scholars at the Newberry Library and the Renaissance Seminar of the University of Chicago.

I offer my heartfelt thanks to William B. Worthen and an anonymous reader, who read the first draft of this book for the University of Chicago Press. Their profound insights were both a challenge and a pleasure to ponder. Randy Petilos has been the ideal editor during every step of this project because of his enthusiasm, intelligence, and unceasing professionalism. Lys Ann Shore's stylistic elegance and deep understanding of medieval texts made her the perfect copy editor, indexer, and reader.

I also acknowledge my father, Howard Enders, for encouraging me lo! these thirty years to pursue the poetry of prose.

Finally, I thank my husband, Eric D'Hoker for playing test-listener time and time again to over a dozen stories in various oral, written, and even musical versions! It is rare that an intellectual project is accompanied by so much joy, so it was all the more special to be able to share it with the man I love.

ABBREVIATIONS

Full citations for works listed here can be found in the list of works cited, at the back of this book.

AD Clément, *Anecdotes dramatiques*

AFS Hawkins, *Annals of the French Stage*

AM Foxe, *Actes and Monuments*

AP Stanislavski, *An Actor Prepares*

BLS *Butler's Lives of the Saints*, ed. Thurston and Attwater

BT Brunvand, *The Baby Train and Other Lusty Urban Legends*

BTA Schechner, *Between Theater and Anthropology*

CBA Brunvand, *Curses! Broiled Again: The Hottest Urban Legends Going*

CD Brunvand, *The Choking Doberman and Other "New" Urban Legends*

CMJH *Chronique de Metz de Jacomin Husson, 1200–1525*, ed. Michelant

CPV *Chronique de Philippe de Vigneulles*, ed. Bruneau

CRCD Hardison Jr., *Christian Rite and Christian Drama in the Middle Ages: Essays in the Origin and Early History of Modern Drama*

CVM *Chroniques de la ville de Metz*, ed. Huguenin

DP Foucault, *Discipline and Punish*

DTT Ryan, *Dramatic Table Talk*

EBTA *The Everyman Book of Theatrical Anecdotes*, ed. Sinden

FA Goffman, *Frame Analysis*

FR Bynum, *Fragmentation and Redemption: Essays on Gender and the Human Body in Medieval Religion*

GCM Darnton, *The Great Cat Massacre and Other Episodes in French Cultural History*

GL Jacobus de Voragine, *The Golden Legend: Readings on the Saints*

GR States, *Great Reckonings in Little Rooms*

GT Rubin, *Gentile Tales: The Narrative Assault on Late Medieval Jews*

HDTW Austin, *How to Do Things with Words*

HF	Bynum, *Holy Feast and Holy Fast: The Religious Significance of Food to Medieval Women*
HM	Carro, *Histoire de Meaux*
HMS	Cohen, *Histoire de la mise-en-scène*
HP	Moreau, *Histoire du protestantisme*
HS	Minois, *History of Suicide*
HTB	Faber, *Histoire du théâtre en Belgique*
HTF	Parfaict and Parfaict, *Histoire du théâtre françois*
HV	d'Outreman, *Histoire de la ville et comté de Valenciennes*
HVP	Felibien, *Histoire de la ville de Paris*
HYL	Greig, *Heads You Lose*
IO	Quintilian, *Institutio oratoria*
JBP	*Journal d'un bourgeois de Paris 1405–1449*, ed. Tuety and Beaune
JBT	*Journal d'un bourgeois de Tournai. Le second livre des chroniques de Pasquier de le Barre (1500–1565)*, ed. Moreau
LC	Suetonius, *The Lives of the Caesars*
LCR	*Le Livre de conduite du Régisseur et Le Compte des dépenses pour le* Mystère de la Passion *joué à Mons en 1501*, ed. Cohen
LM	Petit de Julleville, *Les Mystères*
MAA	Lebègue, *Le Mystère des actes des apôtres: Contribution à l'étude de l'humanisme et du protestantisme français au XVIe siècle*
MES	*Medieval European Stage*, ed. Tydeman
MFI	Runnalls, *Les Mystères français imprimés*
MP	Brunvand, *The Mexican Pet: More "New" Urban Legends and Some Old Favorites*
MPC	Gurevich, *Medieval Popular Culture*
MPV	Konigson, *La Représentation d'un mystère de la Passion à Valenciennes en 1547*
MTOC	Enders, *The Medieval Theater of Cruelty: Rhetoric, Memory, Violence*
MWM	Cavell, *Must We Mean What We Say? A Book of Essays*
PDMA	Rey-Flaud, *Pour une dramaturgie du moyen âge*
PP	Austin, *Philosophical Papers*
RIC	Ozment, *The Reformation in the Cities*
ROMD	Enders, *Rhetoric and the Origins of Medieval Drama*
RPI	Wilshire, *Role Playing and Identity: The Limits of Theatre as Metaphor*
SAF	Brunvand, *The Study of American Folklore: An Introduction*
SB	Fabre-Vassas, *The Singular Beast: Jews, Christians, and the Pig*
SBD	Farel, *Sommaire et brève déclaration (1525)*

SH   *Le Mistere de la Sainte Hostie*
SMA   Murray, *Suicide in the Middle Ages*
SR   Diehl, *Staging Reform, Reforming the Stage: Protestantism and Popular Theater in Early Modern England*
SRT   Pywell, *Staging Real Things*
ST   Kubiak, *Stages of Terror*
SW   Baudrillard, *Selected Writings*
TA   Larwood, *Theatrical Anecdotes*
TEF   Petit de Julleville, *Le Théâtre en France: Histoire de la littérature dramatique*
TGT   Brunvand, *Too Good to Be True: The Colossal Book of Urban Legends*
TMA   Tydeman, *The Theatre in the Middle Ages*
TMB   Kobialka, *This Is My Body: Representational Practices in the Early Middle Ages*
TPF   Sainte-Beuve, *Tableau historique et critique de la poésie française et du théâtre français au seizième siècle*
TRF   Lebègue, *La Tragédie religieuse en France*
VH   Brunvand, *The Vanishing Hitchhiker*
WH   de Certeau, *The Writing of History*

It has been observed that in books of theatrical anecdotes there is probably more unscrupulousness and falsehood to be found than in any other miscellanies. On the other hand, it may be safely concluded that very few stories, however absurd, relative to plays and players, are to be pronounced absolutely incredible. They may have been a little rouged or burnt-corked *secundum artem*, but what of that? Too great a regard for truth has taken the point out of many a good story, and to weigh evidences concerning the "flying words" of a theatrical anecdote is a waste of critical acumen equal to the feat of breaking a butterfly on the wheel.

—Jacob Larwood, "Preface," *Theatrical Anecdotes*, 1882

PROLOGUE

Not all folklore has to be generations old, and . . . part of every legend is true.
— Jan Harold Brunvand, *The Choking Doberman*

In the early 1990s, I remember picking up a copy of *Smithsonian* magazine and being shocked to learn that certain monitory tales I had always believed to be true were only "urban legends." In reality, there were no alligators in our sewers, no dead mice in soda-bottles, no deep-fried rats at fast-food restaurants, and no silly women bringing home rats from Mexico thinking that the animals were Chihuahuas. Instead, those stories were urban legends, examples of the folkloric genre that Jan Harold Brunvand defines as "realistic stories concerning recent events (or alleged events) with an ironic or supernatural twist," stories that constitute "a unique, unselfconscious reflection of major concerns of individuals in the societies in which the legends circulate."[1] Thus, the tale of the alligators would translate into something like: "Don't walk too near the sewer. All those tourists who return from their Florida vacations with baby alligators flush the poor critters down the toilet when they get too big . . . and, from there, the animals wind up in the sewer system, alive and well, huge and dangerous." Meaning: "Our public works are not properly maintained," or "Beware rich people with time on their hands and no ethical boundaries about life and death."[2] "The Mouse in the Coke-Bottle" becomes: "Don't buy that brand of soda-pop any more. Someone found a dead mouse at the bottom of the bottle." Meaning: "Factory mass-production of food is unsafe," or "Beware the need to get those few extra pennies by recycling your bottles: it's an unclean solution."[3] "The Deep-fried Rat" translates to: "Don't eat at that fast-food restaurant. Don't you know the story about the woman who was wolfing down her piece of fried chicken in a moonlit parking lot . . . only to spy the outlines of a tail and to discover that she was eating a deep-fried rat?" Meaning: "Beware the fast-food mentality and the shoddy food-preparation standards that go along with it" (*VH*, 81–84).[4] "The Mexican Pet" would carry this admonition: "Don't bring back any pets from Mexico, lest you mistake a rat for a Chihuahua." Meaning: "Stupid people shouldn't travel to uncivilized places," or, with a certain disdain for other races and classes, "Beware the lower standard of living in Mexico where pets mean pestilence."[5]

I still have the *Smithsonian* article carefully preserved in my files, and I leave it for others to judge what I was doing reading magazines instead of scrutinizing literary theory. The point is that never for a moment did I imagine back then that this discovery would turn out to be pertinent to the history of the medieval French stage.[6] Somehow, though, that is exactly what happened.

If that is where everything began, it was all to begin again when, on 31 January 1995, a jarring bibliographic query was posted to the PERFORM electronic discussion network by Jesse Hurlbut, a friend, colleague, and professor at Brigham Young University.[7] Something was bothering Professor Hurlbut about a particular performance event. Its details had been widely circulated as fact by numerous medievalists, myself included; yet Hurlbut was stirred to write:

> I've read in a couple of places (I'm trying to remember where) that in some instances, condemned criminals participated in medieval mystery plays—their own execution lending dramatic realism to the depiction of martyrdom scenes.
>
> Is this verifiably true? do we have documented instances of this practice?
>
> Are there also other ways in which the very real becomes part of the "play" like this?[8]

What Hurlbut had in mind was the story of a gory performance of the biblical drama of Judith and Holofernes that had supposedly taken place in 1549 in the now Belgian city of Tournai. It is our title story, and it goes like this:

Two especially ambitious producers, Jean de Bury and Jean de Crehan, were said to have concocted something truly special in honor of Prince Philip II of Spain, who was proceeding through their city during his crown-prince tour of the Low Countries. At the crowning moment of the play, when the heroine Judith saves her city from the Assyrian general Holofernes by decapitating him in his drunken sleep, the producers purportedly arranged for two last-minute substitutions. A convicted heretic would step into the role of Holofernes, so that he might be executed on stage by a second convicted criminal playing the avenging Judith. At the moment of truth, "Judith" ostensibly beheaded "Holofernes" to thunderous applause from the audience and restrained appreciation from Philip.[9]

Hurlbut asked his question. Since most medievalists had cited chapter and verse of the story—usually from where *they* had read it in Henri Rey-Flaud's *Pour une dramaturgie du moyen âge*—then what was Rey-Flaud's source?[10] As Hurlbut calmly noted, there was nothing in his footnotes to indicate the source of the story.

Eventually, Hurlbut answered his own question far better than any of his respondents in a generous bibliographical contribution to PERFORM, posted on 3 February 1995. By a tour-de-force of detective work, he determined that Rey-Flaud's unattributed source was Frédéric Faber's *Histoire du Théâtre en Belgique* and that Faber himself had gotten the story from a variety of sources, several of which had been lost.

The tale from Tournai was a postmodernist's dream, and I could hardly wait to write it up as the perfect example of mystification.[11] Each detail exemplified Jean Baudrillard's concept of "simulation." There was no "objective difference" between the real execution, the dissimulated one, and the simulated one because, as Baudrillard speculates of a simulated theft in a department store, "the same gestures and the same signs exist as for a real theft; in fact the signs incline neither to one side nor the other."[12] The story also confirmed Michel de Certeau's definition of historiography as "a play of life and death [which] is sought in the calm telling of a tale."[13] It bore out Kenneth Burke's theory that "the symbolic act of art overlap[s] upon the symbolic act in life."[14] It documented Bruce Wilshire's contention that "life is already, in various ways, theatre-like."[15] And it darkly illustrated Anthony Kubiak's suggestion that "we forget that theatre is the primary condition of life, that life itself is 'always already' subsumed by the theatrical."[16] Indeed, each and every aspect of the tale from Tournai constituted a tantalizing display of indeterminacy, including that surrounding death itself.[17] That indeterminacy would have been reinforced, moreover, by the philology of the French language, where *histoire* still denotes both "story" and "history"; *représentation* denotes both "performance" and symbolic "representation"; and *échafauds*, both theatrical scaffolding and the executioner's gallows.[18]

Then again, invoking Baudrillard—or even that old standby, philology—wasn't solving the problem. Surely, one would need to ascertain whether or not this thing had really happened. It seemed just as verisimilar, believable, and credible as it did *invraisemblable*, unbelievable, incredible. Certain features didn't seem right. There was, for instance, the part about "Holofernes" *pretending* to be asleep just before the decapitation. What were the odds that a convicted criminal about to be beheaded would take the time and trouble to play-act his own death? What were the odds that "Judith," unskilled as an executioner, would get it exactly right the first time, so that the notoriously implacable Philip would be impressed by the morbidly skillful blow of the man in drag? It was all sounding more and more like a sixteenth-century version of a snuff film, the cinematic genre in which a real murder is supposedly filmed in real time and which is itself shrouded in doubts about its existence.[19] In truth, what it *really* sounded like was one of Brunvand's urban legends, "highly captivating and plausible, but mainly fictional, oral narratives that are widely told as true stories" (*CD*, ix). Maybe a phenomenon that has captivated enough present-day readers to ensure the success of Brunvand's eight book-length compilations (and counting) might also have flourished transculturally and transhistorically in early Europe.

Like a shot, the memory of that *Smithsonian* article came back to me. If the so-called true story from Tournai sounded *untrue* and could not be verified because the original sources had been lost forever, then maybe it *was* untrue. Maybe the Tournai tale was an urban legend—a myth that, then and now, would disclose more about what spectators hoped and feared *could* happen in their theater than about what actually *did* happen. "Beware the theater, because it can lead to death." "Beware the imperialistic Philip encroaching on your territory." "Beware the dramatic representation that is so lifelike that it is deathlike." "Beware all those things as Reformation Europe debates the possibility or impossibility of distinguishing between true and false, illusion and reality, reenactment and representation, trustworthy and untrustworthy sources:[20] that executed criminal was a heretic who might burn just like you."

If modern Americans regularly regale themselves with urban legends of terrorized babysitters and lunatics with deadly hooks, or if they flock to a movie like *Urban Legend* to be thus regaled, then why shouldn't early France have had its own urban legends?[21] And if today's legends elucidate the concerns of the "American mentality," why shouldn't yesterday's legends elucidate that notoriously elusive entity known as the "medieval mentality"? Such questions may raise the dreaded specter of the *Zeitgeist* notion of a people's mentality, but folklorists and theater historians have been raising that specter for centuries. For example, when Jean-Marie Bernard Clément in 1775 paid homage to the French national character with a book of theatrical anecdotes, he held that "it is at the theater that a Nation best makes itself known and discovers its spirit without imagining that that is what it is doing."[22] Some two hundred years later, Aron Gurevich's advice had a familiar ring when he urged that the texts related to medieval popular culture expressed a "world-view which their creators could only 'utter' unwittingly."[23] Brunvand remarks of his favorite genre that "we folklorists call them urban legends, although modern legends might be a more accurate term" (*CD*, ix). When it comes to the present treasure trove of tales, so too would be "medieval urban legends."

Everything was starting to make sense, then, as some kind of fascinating reflection of Tournai's hopes, fears, and anxieties. Maybe there never *was* a convicted felon condemned to a horrible ordeal, no last-minute substitution, no performance of *Judith* before Philip. Then reality reared its head: There *was* evidence that Jehan de Crehan existed. He was a contemporary of Pasquier de le Barre, the author of the *Journal d'un bourgeois de Tournai,* a chronicle covering the years 1500–1565.[24] There *were* heretics aplenty in Tournai: historians Gérard Moreau and Geoffrey Parker are explicit on that subject.[25] There *were* plays performed in Philip's honor on the specific occasion of his royal entry into Tournai—*lots* of them.[26] There *was* a real Judith play—several, in fact.[27] There was just no mention in any extant source that *that* particular play was ever fatally performed in that particular year on that particular occasion.

Then again, reality had its own problems: There was no mention anywhere of the decapitation—unless, of course, we want to count an unedited manuscript that burned in a fire in Tournai in May 1940 (apparently unrelated to World War II).[28] Even if we assume that the manuscript burned *after* and not *before* Faber had had a chance to see it with his own eyes, it was becoming more and more difficult to tell whether we were dealing with the relatively common phenomenon of the lost medieval source or with another phenomenon, which is and always has been the hallmark of the urban legend. Its standard narrator is called the "FOAF" (friend of a friend)—the "reliable witness" whom no one can ever seem to find or name.[29]

Suddenly, there were elusive fifteenth- and sixteenth-century witnesses popping up all over the place, each one telling a story that forms a chapter in this book. Each and every one tendered a stunning example of what the historian Natalie Zemon Davis calls "fiction in the archives," and each and every one was about the theater.[30] The question was *why*. Although not *all* medieval legends were about the theater—nor did the medieval theater in every instance give rise to legends—there was clearly something about the genre that caused storytellers to stage it time and time again in their folklore. Specifically, each story staged the tenacious beliefs that lives are changed forever when people go to the theater and that dramatic representations are directly linked to the real actions and real sentiments of real life.[31] Clearly, there was something about the theater that not only reinforced belief but *created* it as it unfolded in real time. There was something about the realities of the experience of representation that made for true experiences, if not necessarily true accounts. The problem facing me was how to tell the stories.

Each story seemed to function as what Erving Goffman terms a "frame fantasy," referring to the special ability of anecdotal evidence to construct imaginary yet en-

during boundaries to experience. Far from detracting from the reality of experience, its fictive nature actually enhances reality:

> What appears, then, to be a threat to our way of making sense of the world turns
> out to be an ingeniously selected defense of it. We press these stories to the wind;
> they keep the world from unsettling us. By and large, I do not present these anec-
> dotes, therefore, as evidence or proof, but as clarifying depictions, as frame fan-
> tasies which manage, through the hundred liberties taken by their tellers, to
> celebrate our beliefs about the workings of the world. What was put into these
> tales is thus what I would like to get out of them.[32]

If I too could press my early stage stories to the wind, then the anecdotal nature of
the evidence would tend to strengthen, not weaken, the case for the "world views"
or frame fantasies imparted by any urban legend.[33] Indeed, the anecdote was a veritable staple of New Historicism.[34]

Few are more accustomed than medievalists to listening to the voices of the
long-dead, with the possible exception of a medium holding a séance or maybe a
classicist . . . or maybe a Stephen Greenblatt, who introduced his *Shakespearean
Negotiations* by proclaiming: "I began with the desire to speak with the dead. . . . It
was true that I could hear only my own voice, but my own voice was the voice of the
dead, for the dead had contrived to leave textual traces of themselves, and those
traces make themselves heard in the voices of the living."[35] With all due respect for
James Wilkinson's intelligent reminder that "not everything in the past has left
traces," there were traces of medieval and Renaissance drama all over the place.[36] It
was a question of how to decipher them or—as Jean-Claude Schmitt declared of
the difficulty of approaching medieval popular culture—a question "not so much
of sources as of cognitive tools for decoding them."[37] The history of the stage
offered one such cognitive tool, especially insofar as each one of our theatrical stories appeared to be pondering the very essence of cognition. Any history of the
Western stage and any historiography of the Middle Ages would have to take into
account the absolutely precocious ways in which early France told, retold, invented, and reinvented stories of the tenuous boundaries between theater and real
life, thereby helping audiences to confront the nature of artistic representation.
There was no doubt that all the stories would be enjoyable on their own terms as
stories. But were they true? Thus began my own dialogue with both the living and
the dead.

Before me was one of the richest casts of characters I had ever seen, with each
personage demanding that the story of his or her identity be told. I began to feel
like the mystery writer contrived by Francis Greig in his appealing short story, "At

Random." When the time comes to name his characters, the author has trouble every time, and expresses his anxiety: "They were spaces in the manuscript, possessing idiosyncrasies, playing parts, becoming victims, hating, loving, interacting, and all waiting to have their names, their identities, filled in."[38] I found myself torn between the desire to interpret the stories and the desire simply to retell them. Should I attempt to resolve their ambiguities or leave them as they were? Michel de Certeau seemed to reply to my question with his elegant statement that historiography "oscillates between 'producing history' and 'telling stories,' but without being reducible to either one or the other" (*WH*, 102). So I hope the reader will pardon my occasional refusal to come down definitively on the side of the "truth" or "fiction," the existence or nonexistence of any given event. More often than not, that is the pleasurable posture our texts themselves seem to favor. More often than not, the only choice was to retain choice—or choices.

On one hand, aficionados of the urban legend would say that the truth doesn't matter. One of the cornerstones of urban legendry is that tellers tend to cling to the "reality" or "truthfulness" of a given story long after it has been proven to be untrue. Thus Paul Dickson and Joseph Goulden point out that "formal refutation does nothing to deter the popularity of a fable,"[39] while Brunvand emphasizes that although urban legends must to some degree be considered false, "the lack of verification in no way diminishes the appeal urban legends have for us. We enjoy them merely as stories, and we tend at least to half-believe them as possibly accurate reports" (*VH*, 2). Similarly, Francis Greig notes that whether or not the events occurred, they "remain relevant to us: have about them something of a basic fear or a particular attraction that finds a universal response. Viewed in that light, the apocryphal story becomes even more intriguing" (*HYL*, x). At that point, what would matter is that somebody believed a story like that of Tournai—or that *somebody else* believed (or needed to believe) that a first somebody believed it.[40] As Brunvand summarizes the situation of the oft-outrageous claims of certain legends, "there are some who would respond . . . that any comments about the truth or falsity of urban legends are moot, since legends are by definition untrue. Others would assert that since we are studying *stories*, not actual incidents, it makes no difference whether any of these stories—or parts of stories—happen to be true."[41] Just as Hamlet once intoned that "the play's the thing," in this book, "the story's the thing": the story *is* the actual theatrical incident.[42] Sometimes it's more, sometimes less.

On the other hand, Tournai was said to have been the site of a snuff death. To claim that the truth did not matter would be to espouse the worst of phenomenological approaches to literature. No matter what the reception, there must be a *moral* difference between real and represented death on stage. There is certainly a difference for the person who dies—or does not die.

On one hand, since each story was situated at that fuzzy boundary between theater and real life, one could scarcely interpret them without phenomenology or history. Each story would show, following a Bert States or a Bruce Wilshire, that nowhere was theater more lifelike or life more theaterlike than on the late medieval stage.[43]

On the other hand, the stories practically interpreted themselves. I did not wish to psychoanalyze my subjects—not that I could—even though we clearly had at least one hysteric on our hands. I was no folklorist; but folklorists' materials were readily available. While Vladimir Propp, for example, had acknowledged the "close ties" between literary criticism and the "verbal art" of folklore, he had also cautioned that "literary analysis can only *discover* the phenomenon and the law of folklore poetics, but it is unable to *explain* them."[44] It didn't seem right that theater history, however different from folklore, would stop short at discovery and be able to explain nothing.[45]

On one hand, the most inspired historians—Natalie Davis, Alain Boureau, and Emmanuel Le Roy Ladurie—had been intrigued by the literary nature of their objects of inquiry.[46] Meanwhile, the literary critic Hans-Robert Jauss had concurred from his own perspective that "in medieval historiography, as in the epic of the Middle Ages, historical fact and significant fiction are often intertwined in an unfathomable manner . . . The historical events referred to are totally unrecognizable because they have been reshaped by the process of legend making."[47] As Davis established compellingly when she reminisced about her early training in "peel[ing] away the fictive elements in our documents so we could get at the real facts," fiction can be *truer* than truth: "the artifice of fiction did not necessarily lend falsity to an account; it might well bring verisimilitude or a moral truth."[48] While historians would surely be tempted to get to the bottom of every detail of every story in the pages that follow, surely *not* getting to the bottom promised to prove just as interesting.

On the other hand, the spirit of the Renaissance and the Reformation fit particularly well with the practices and metaphors of theater. It was one of those critical conundrums in which a literary theorist might try to sift through whether the social and theological struggles of fifteenth- and sixteenth-century France were profoundly theatrical, or whether that theater's metaphorical struggles were profoundly sociotheological. Naturally, the strands would be impossible to disentangle, but, without being a theologian, any theater historian or theater lover would *want to* disentangle them.

On one hand, each one of our stories would encourage a serious interdisciplinary approach to the inherently mimetic propensities of human beings. From Jean Piaget's classic assessment of the theatrical phase of a child's psychosocial development, to contemporary philosophical treatments of mimesis and selfhood, to cultural anthropology, to the biological basis of behavior, and even to theology, there was ample evidence to suggest that human beings are not only natural storytellers but natural performers.[49]

On the other hand, the stories were just plain *fun*. As forerunners of modern urban legends, they were as delectable as the episodes that fill Brunvand's eight books or the short stories into which Francis Greig retransformed his favorites. Although "fun" was not exactly a standard component of humanistic criticism, Brunvand stepped forward to provide an explanation for *that* as well. Analyzing the numerous urban legends devoted to the dangers of carnivals, he argued for a massive cultural ambivalence about idleness, leisure, and pleasure: "Maybe we suffer some guilt for having fun, and that leads us to project stories about accidents onto the amusement parks" (*CBA*, 37).[50] Without oversimplifying the psychological complexities of the guilt, hopes, fears, and anxieties of the tellers of our medieval tales, one thing is evident: One needn't be a Church Father to notice that theater has always been a place of fun and guilt. Lest there be any doubt about that, one need but recall Isidore of Seville's admonition that audiences should shun a theater that does the devil's work, or contemporary conservative objections that the NEH or NEA should not fund artistic projects of questionable morality.[51]

On one hand, *Death by Drama* could be a response to my own unceasing surprise each time I read the lavish praise heaped upon some avant-garde production by a theater critic because of a director's use of real violence, real pleasure, real sex, or real audience participation. The medieval and Renaissance theater had long boasted such spectacular "innovations." Much in the same way that the postmodern theater, cinema, and television stimulate viewers to cross even the fuzziest of boundaries, so too did the medieval stage. There was a veritable treasure trove of such incidents. They weren't even too difficult to find languishing on dusty bookshelves. Far from it: Petit de Julleville had already published the vast majority of them in his magnum opus, *Les mystères* (1880). And yet Raymond Lebègue's complaint of 1929 still seemed to hold true: While studies of early English drama thrive along with the formidable tasks of archival documentation represented by the REED project (Records of Early English Drama), the French "*mystères* of the end of the Middle Ages and the Renaissance have never been studied in depth."[52] Virtually unknown outside the small circle of French medieval drama scholars, they promised to bring today's urban legends and realities into sharper focus. To someone writing from a French Department, moreover, the prospect of imbuing medieval French drama studies with contemporary relevance was tantalizing in and of itself. In one of the great ironies of the New Historicist enthusiasm for the indeterminacies of medieval literature, one French literary genre steadfastly remained too indeterminate even for aficionados of indeterminacy: the medieval theater.[53]

On the other hand, there had to be a better way to capture the substance and spirit of those stories than to house them in a standard work of literary criticism, or even in an imaginative New Historicist brand of anecdotalism. I sought to create a kind of hybrid form, situated somewhere between short stories and literary theory, in which the storytellers could tell their own stories and in which the telling itself would provide the "key" to the interpretation—if there were one. There had to be a middle ground between the two standard credos. The *raconteur*'s credo is: "Never let the truth get in the way of a good story."[54] The historian's credo might be said to be the opposite: "Never let a good story get in the way of the truth." By the same token, there had to be a middle ground between Jacob Larwood's publication of numerous theatrical anecdotes, regardless of whether or not they were "'based on fact,' or a flight of the imagination,"[55] and Pasquier de le Barre's meritorious efforts to conduct historiographical triage: "with regard to the present observations, wishing not to mix in rumors and common knowledge, we have endeavored to uncover the truth of things, as much through written records as through the accounts of those who were present who took charge of such matters."[56] Perhaps *Death by Drama* could occupy that middle ground.

In the end, I could either throw up my hands (with all those "other hands") or buckle down and work with the stories. As with all interdisciplinary projects, the challenge was to transcend the curiously simultaneous refraction *and* diffusion of focus while maintaining the integrity of a single discipline—in this case, drama. The real life of medieval theatricality was itself a great story waiting to be told. I wanted to tell it to medievalists, theater historians, cultural historians, performance theorists, fiction lovers, urban-legend mavens, and general readers. The "specialists" would have a full critical apparatus at their disposal; the readers of foreign languages would have appendices containing the original texts; all the others would be able to "surf" the book without consulting its specialist features. I have thus grappled on every page with the possibility that I will be too much a storyteller for the historian, too much a medievalist for the general reader, too contemporary for the history buff, too historical for the popular-culture enthusiast.

Furthermore, the world of medieval drama would need to be arranged for the telling. There were choices to be made, major and minor. Regarding the more minor decisions, our stories span a time period from the year A.D. 2 to the twenty-first century. For the most part, my sequence of chapters respects their basic chronological order—that is, when a chronology can be determined. Sometimes, though, I have presented materials out of sequence, the better to follow a given theme, structure, or perspective, or to begin with the "happy stories." Since I am a medievalist, I hope that I will be forgiven an occasionally expansive use of the term *medieval*, especially when referring to the myriad theatrical forms of the fourteenth through sixteenth centuries. The term tends to be appropriate in that a play written between the twelfth and fifteenth centuries is "medieval," even when *performed* in the sixteenth century. Indeed, it bears mentioning here that both the delight and the frustration of working with these materials is that narrations and perceptions are generally so confused that we do not always know who is speaking. An elusive sixteenth-century witness to the performance of a fifteenth-century play may be paraphrased by a seventeenth-century manuscript hunter or by an eighteenth-century pioneer whose account is then further mediated by a nineteenth-century giant like Petit de Julleville.[57] I have endeavored to reproduce such complex genealogies as carefully as possible, but complicated they are and complicated they will remain. For what it's worth, I don't think I'll ever be able to use the phrase *as cited by* again without feeling derelict, and such common locutions as *according to* or *in fact* no longer seem so common to me now.

In turn, those complex genealogies created some difficulties in the usually straightforward task of preparing a bibliography. For one thing, the distinction between a "primary" and a "secondary" source had ceased to be clear. Where, for example, did compendia of theatrical anecdotes belong? Were they primary sources? or someone else's secondhand fantasy of what a primary source was? Hoping to err on the side of caution, I have reserved a special section in my list of works cited for "Collections of Theatrical Anecdotes, Folktales, Legends, Memoirs, Proverbs, Dictionaries," followed by more traditional "Primary Sources" (plays, poetry, chronicles, and so forth), and "Secondary Sources" (historians, literary theorists, and so on). Whenever practicable, I refer to frequently cited works by abbreviations, which appear in the list of abbreviations at the front of this volume.

As for the original texts of my sources, I hope to have made the book more readable by retelling the stories in straightforward and sometimes colloquial language and by organizing primary sources as follows: I have tried to keep parenthetical documentation to a minimum so that it does not disrupt the narratives, and with the exception of the isolated technical term, only English translations from French sources appear in the body of the text.[58] All translations are my own unless otherwise indicated, and when a good published translation of a work exists (such as

Rabelais in the able hands of Donald Frame), I do not reproduce the original in my appendix. The same holds true for the Latin sources, many of which are available in the bilingual editions of the Loeb Classical Library. If an original citation is fairly short, I have included it in the relevant note. Otherwise, all original-language documents appear in the appendix, where I have sometimes had occasion to re-mark others' note numbers with asterisks and daggers. As a rule, I reprint the documents exactly as they appear, warts and all, and have only modernized the occasional print convention (such as rendering *v* for *u*). I reproduce in the appendix only the oldest printed source, except when there are several versions that diverge substantially from one another.[59] Petit de Julleville, for instance, tends to cite his material extremely accurately with only minor, "normalizing" variants in spelling, capitalization, punctuation, and other diacritical marks. Therefore, while I indicate any important variants, I do not normally cite Petit de Julleville *citing someone else.* Instead, I return to *his* source or, when possible, to a *better source.*[60] Additionally, when reproducing lengthy stage directions in both the appendix and the main text, I have occasionally dropped the italics of their editors.

A final note on my translations from the French: When a text is vulgar, I have rendered it in vulgar language—just as I have tried to render doggerel as doggerel. Translations are forever open to interpretation and critique, but I have largely favored spirit over strict literalism. I would ask only that my readers believe that my lousy English poetry doesn't necessarily mean a lousy translation: sometimes the French poetry is really just lousy!

In the final analysis, to enter the world of the medieval theatrical legend is to encounter a strange and enchanting mixture of love and lust, desire and repression, fear and delight, pain and pleasure, war and peace, madness and sanity, community and isolation, integration and segregation, kindness and violence, history and fiction. Our narrators are long dead and gone, but their stories do not die. However elusive their testimony, they are clamoring loudly to tell those stories. I hope that my readers will enjoy listening to them as much as I have.

Medieval Urban Legends?

"Now answer me, Sir Isaiah:
Is this a fable, or prophecy?
What is this you've said?
Did you invent it, or is it written?
You've been sleeping, you dreamed it.
Is this serious or a joke?"

"This is not fable; on the contrary, it's all true."

"Make us see this truth, then."

—Jeu d'Adam

In the year 1468 in the city of Metz, a strange thing is said to have happened during a performance of the *Play of Saint Catherine of Siena*. An eyewitness records that one Henry de la Tour conceived a passion for Catherine that was so overpowering that it prompted him to marry the girl who had played the martyr. Barely two decades later, a different sort of "marriage" took place—this time when Saint Barbara was played in Metz in 1485 by a young man named Lyonard, "who was a very beautiful lad and resembled a beautiful young girl." His acting so moved the audience that a rich widow proposed to adopt him and make him her heir. (She lost out to Master Jean Chardelly, *homme de lettres,* who loved the lad so well that he spirited him off to Paris for an ecclesiastical education.) Much earlier, there had been actors who purportedly went mad while playing madness, others who died on stage while praying for death. There were spectators who met their demise when unable to escape the cannonballs of a theatrical line of fire. There were two priests who almost lost their lives on Metz's stage in 1437 when one was left hanging too long as Judas and the other nearly succumbed as Christ to an ostensibly fake crucifixion. In Melun, near Paris—we are not sure exactly when—a certain Languille

(Mr. Eel) was so terrified while playing the flaying of Saint Bartholomew that he started screaming before the other actor touched him and thence purportedly gave rise to a bit of proverbial wisdom along the lines of "jumping the gun"—or the knife, as it were. There were stories of play devils rushing diabolically off the stage to fill real audiences with real terror. There were stories of silly spectators giggling over the traumatic account of the Passion; stories of mystery plays as divine offerings to God but in which the nature of the offering was open to question. Later, sixteenth-century Parisians staged the fifteenth-century *Mistere de la Sainte Hostie,* a play based on a thirteenth-century legend that celebrated the erection of a real church atop an apocryphal Jewish household and urged new anti-Semitic acts. Meanwhile, over in the city of Doué-la-Fontaine, no one could decide if their amphitheater was a Roman ruin, a bourgeois appropriation of a quarry, a populist fantasy, or something else again. By the year 1547 legends were circulating in the city of Meaux to the effect that some of the actors who had played devils on its short-lived wooden stage had died in poverty, while a Satan had been hanged and a Despair had poisoned himself. And Philip II visited Tournai in 1549, where he purportedly witnessed a snuff drama.[1]

Each of these events provides evidence about the social circumstances of early performance practice as it raises questions about the anthropology, psychology, religiosity, phenomenology, and folklore of theater history. Each one forms a chapter of this book because each provokes an extensive meditation about where theater ends and life begins . . . or, sometimes, where life ends and theater begins. Some of the stories are dark and dangerous, some sexy and scandalous, some preachy and perverse. Some are funny, some are scary. Some are good and scary with plenty of gallows humor to go around. Notwithstanding their great variety of tone, however, each is the story about that passing strange moment when it becomes impossible to tell if life is imitating art or art is imitating life. Each story nurtures, and is nurtured by, a profound confusion between reality and unreality, truth and lies, fiction and actuality, imitation and enactment.[2] From politics and religion to learning and law to marriage and social class, each tale incorporates the theater into emerging principles of history and historiography as postfeudal, Renaissance, Reformation, and, eventually, modern France employed its own legends to explain itself to itself.

That, according to Jan Harold Brunvand, is precisely the function of urban legends, which "reflect many of the hopes, fears and anxieties of our time" (*VH*, 2).[3] Thus each of our eminently believable (and eminently circulatable) tales reflects the hopes, fears, anxieties, and identities of the people who told it. Each tale, each chapter asks a pressing question about those who inhabited medieval and Renaissance cultures—a question that *theater* has already answered by leaving an urban legend in its wake about what happens when that genre surpasses any of its so-called bounds of representation. Most significant, theater asked and answered those questions at a time when belief was everything. Especially when it came to the stories of God, Christ, and the saints—the focus of our legends[4]—it would have been most unfitting that such religious drama look like "make-believe." Quite to the contrary, pious subjects demanded an accuracy, a dignity, and a realism that would *make others believe.* In the 1530s, for instance, Jean Bouchet praised the thespian rendition that was "natural and played without pretense."[5] Similarly, in describing a production of the *Acts of the Apostles* in Bourges in 1536, one commentator noted that the performers were "noble men who knew so well how to play-act with signs and gestures the characters whom they were representing, that the majority of those attending judged the thing to be true and not 'pretend.'"[6] Our first seven stories in Part I, "Telling the Difference," reflect such judgments about the truth of pretense.

Chapter 1, "Lusting after Saints," asks what makes for a good wife. It answers that the happy ending for the marriageable girl playing Saint Catherine was perhaps not so happy after all. Chapter 2, "Queer Attractions," asks what makes for a good Frenchman. For the girlish, German-born actor Lyonard, it involves entering the priesthood and abandoning both his cross-dressing theatrical career and his foreign origins. Chapter 3, "Of Madness and Method Acting," examines what makes for a sane person. Here we return momentarily to ancient Greece to meet an actor who learns, to his psychic and professional detriment, that playing madness can awaken real madness. Chapter 4, "Two Priests and the Hand of God," asks which actors may "play" with sacred materials, and answers: certainly not the two priests who narrowly survived their renditions of Christ's crucifixion and Judas's hanging in 1437. Chapter 5, "Dying to Play," poses a legal question: When two men were accidentally killed during two separate, fourteenth-century theatrical productions, was theater liable? and in an indubitably *true story,* how far did that liability extend?[7] Chapter 6 gives us "The Eel of Melun," who serves to ask what makes for a good actor and responds with what he is *not:* a silly soul who runs for his life from his own impersonation of the soon-to-be-martyred Saint Bartholomew. Finally, a series of tales in Chapter 7, "The Devil Who Wasn't There," ask who is the devil. They reply that theater is the devil in the flesh, conjuring the Evil One and urging that demonic personages stay in character long after a given play is over.[8]

If Part I gives us seven examples of theatrical *make-believe,* the seven stories of Part II join with shifting theological sensibilities to *make* sixteenth-century Europe *believe.* It is no coincidence that they take place during the turbulent years of the

Reformation, when Europe was contemplating anxiously the quintessential question of what was real, what was pretend, and what was pretense. Theater captured perfectly a moment of phenomenology that was also a moment of theology, in that any theatrical representation that laid claim to real life assumed powerful metaphorical, political, and religious dimensions. To some extent, the Reformist debate about the nature of the sacrament resembled the debate about the nature of a legendary theater.[9] In general, Catholics believed that when a priest celebrating Mass took the host and cup of wine in his hands and said, "This is my body, this is my blood," a "real reenactment" of the Last Supper occurred. Reformers countered that this was a symbolic, though powerful, act of what had happened to Christ's body during transubstantiation.[10] Against that ideological backdrop, the tales of Part II, "Make-Believe," span a time period of exactly fifty years (1509–59). They pose a new series of questions related to the fear that where *theatrical* uncertainty reigned, so too did theological *uncertainty*.

In one way or another, the first four chapters of Part II ask what happens when religious spectacle falls into the wrong hands: into those of silly children (chapter 8), of Jews (chapter 9), of patron saints (chapter 10), and of the populace (chapter 11). Chapter 8, "The Laughter of the Children," imagines the special, timeless dangers that theater poses to "children of all ages" as it ponders the question of who is capable of belief. Chapter 9, "Burnt Theatrical Offerings," raises the ominous specter of anti-Semitism, focusing on the *Mistere de la Sainte Hostie,* a play that sharpens the perceived differences between Christians and Jews as it attempts to demonstrate that the Jewish faith is nothing but a vile show. Chapter 10, "Theater's Living Dead," asks if religious drama can bring theological history back to life by using actual holy relics as stage props. Chapter 11, "The Mysterious Quarry," worries that theatrical activity will replace labor and foment a dramatic revolution.

Chapter 12, "Seeing Is Believing," considers the more dangerous question of *theological* revolution by inquiring about what makes for a miracle. If the citizens of Valenciennes in 1547 couldn't tell if they had seen one or not during a certain performance, then another question was more pressing still: What makes for a heretic? Chapter 13, "The Suicide of Despair," answers that question by fantasizing what amounts to an ecclesiastical death wish *for* theater: the execution of a heretical actor and the suicide of the actor who played Despair. Last but not least, we reach in Chapter 14 our title story of "Death by Drama," which wonders whether or not "snuff" was possible in the name of theology. In the epilogue, "The Moment of Truth," modern evidence invites us to believe in snuff films and to believe, if not in the specific "realities" of each of our stories, then at least in their very real repercussions. All the stories have a common concern in asking what makes for a culture. Their common answer is that culture is what theater makes it, and that theater is what culture makes it.

In both the legends and the realities of their theater, the early French discovered a psychic and physical space that alternated between hegemonic and populist agendas, concession and rebellion, oral and written transmission, tradition and change, illusion and reality. They also discovered companion subjective issues of perspective, interpretation, interpolation, embellishment, and causation that dominate historiography, folklore, and literary criticism. In their theater, they discovered *themselves* and their culture in much the same way Paul Zumthor understands when he observes that "of all the arts, theater is, without a doubt, the most receptive to changes in the social structure, and the most revelatory of those changes."[11] Likewise, Marvin Carlson asserts that "no other art seeks to absorb and convert into interpretive structures so much of the total human experience as the theatre does."[12] Yet it is not so easy to figure out just what theater was uttering, receiving, revealing, converting, or interpreting in a given time and place.

In the twinkling of a theatrical eye, the pleasure of a story turns into the pain of its possible reality; innocence turns into guilt, comedy into tragedy. Holofernes's execution and the suicide of Despair were horrific. Presumably, Catherine's marriage to Henry de la Tour was not—unless, of course, we start to worry with modern feminists that he intended to martyr her at home. The effeminate Lyonard purportedly experienced a happy ecclesiastical ending in a Paris seminary, but any historian familiar with medieval perspectives about sodomy—or any aficionado of such news magazines as *60 Minutes*—might wonder if the lad could have been the victim of sexual molestation.[13] The late Geoff Pywell was outraged when he witnessed a scripted on-stage assault at London's twentieth-century "Real and True Theatre" (RATT) that left an actress bloodied and unconscious.[14] Few would be outraged today if an actor were to take a bite of a real apple or a puff of a real cigarette during a play. Few would indict theater for having transgressed its boundaries—unless, I suppose, the actor happened to blow his smoke into the face of a self-righteous nonsmoker. In the pages that follow, smoke will get in our eyes.

Can it be that a theatrically inspired marriage is phenomenologically identical to an ancient Greek actor's insanity or the near-deaths of two medieval priests? Or that the bite of an onstage apple is like the decapitation of a heretic? (Would it help if it were a bite from the apple of the Garden of Eden?) In our own day, it has been more natural to focus on the most violent and offensive collisions of art and life, but the phenomenological stakes of the nonviolent or anodine coincidences are also compelling.[15] Even if we insist that phenomenology is not the same thing as morality, morality is no easier to pin down. What one *can* pin down is this: ultimately, the mystery of whether or not our fourteen stories actually occurred is less important than the fact that our narrators believed, hoped, or feared that they occurred—and that they called upon theater to address those beliefs, hopes, or fears.

Robert Darnton has urged that the cultural historian navigate such a "psychic undertow" by holding fast to the two disciplines of anthropology and folklore.[16] In the flood of endless relativity, theater extends a sort of life-raft. More than any other genre, theater is about process. It takes its audiences to a moment in real time during which belief is created, developed, reaffirmed, suspended, denied, or even destroyed.[17] Be it medieval or modern—and we shall see that nearly every medieval urban legend has a modern analog—theater captures both the construction of belief and the reality of the emotional experiences attendant upon that construction. To be sure, many of theater's realities are emotional, but even when a play does *not* lead to such discernible acts as marriages, career changes, persecutions, and deaths, it leaves real traces of hope and fear, faith and skepticism, belief and disbelief. Above all, it leaves traces about the illusion of reality and the reality of illusion, as it asks: To what elusive events are elusive witnesses pointing elusively, and what are the consequences of their own belief (or lack of belief) in what they saw or did not see?

To comprehend our stories, we need to interrogate the credibility of both the witnesses to the events and the events themselves. Given the difficulty of determining who our narrators really were and what they thought they really saw, each event mystifies the possibility of distinguishing between a true or false witness to a true of false event in two genres that have eternally mystified both true and false: theater and the urban legend. Brunvand calls urban legends "Americans' favorite false-true tales" (*CD*, ix).[18] That phrase is not so far removed from what just about anybody has had to say about that greatest of false-true tales, the theater, a genre ever associated with the on- and off-stage pleasures of "true lies." Plato, for example, had sought to cast out tragic poets from his *Republic* because he believed that "the *veritable lie*, if the expression is permissible, is a thing that all gods and men abhor."[19] Aristotle believed that the playwright could be the "maker" of a true story.[20] At the turn of the twentieth century, Ambrose Bierce coined this quaint definition of the imagination: "A warehouse of facts, with poet and liar in joint ownership."[21] Somewhat later, Constantin Stanislavski's "method actors" realized that "in ordinary life, truth is what really exists, what a person really knows. Whereas on the stage it consists of something that is not actually in existence but which could happen."[22] In light of the proverbial wisdom that "there are a terrible lot of lies going about the world . . . and half of them are true," or that "telling stories is telling lies," the challenge of our stories is to make sense of a tissue of true lies.[23]

As far as the credibility of our witnesses is concerned, we read that, on 24 July 1485, spectators turned out at 4 A.M. on Metz's Place de Chambre to take their places for a performance of the *Life of Saint Barbara*.[24] Does this mean that those spectators were the precursors of modern rock-concert goers who secure a place in line by camping out in the street the night before tickets go on sale? Or, if the hour sounds somewhat exaggerated, can we assume that they did *not* show up extremely early—even if they slept as late as the ungodly hour of, say, 6 A.M.? Once their timing has been called into question, should we doubt that the performance was really postponed when "on Tuesday, there came such horrible weather at around two o'clock in the afternoon, that . . . they had to leave off playing?"[25] Should we decide that, in the city of Romans in 1509, God himself did *not* intervene, contrary to what was claimed, to provide the good weather for a performance of the *Mystère des Trois Doms*?[26] Similarly, when the sixteenth-century historian of Berry, Jean Chaumeau, assures us that, in Bourges, there was a fabulous theatrical arena that held between twenty-five and thirty thousand spectators every day, does that mean that there *was* no such theater? Or was there a less impressive edifice holding fewer people?[27] If we cannot trust Chaumeau on the numbers, then must we also disregard his claim that he had never seen "such sumptuous costumes, finery, and graceful acting"?[28] Would he be more or less credible if we compared his assertion to another statement made by the brothers François and Claude Parfaict (1698–1753), the authors of a fifteen-volume *Histoire du théâtre françois?* Citing the *Journal d'un bourgeois de Paris 1405–1449*, they placed nine to ten thousand people—"not counting the clergy!"—at a Paris procession of 1444, which included a performance of the *Mistere de la Sainte Hostie.*[29] And just because the production of a mystery play typically mobilized a community for several days (as in Metz's successful *Passion* of 1437),[30] does that render *completely* incredible another writer's testimony that, in 1539, the *Mystery of the Acts of the Apostles* at Doué-la-Fontaine "lasted for thirty days"?[31] Or does it make it just *partially* incredible?

Certainly, the nineteenth-century writer Jacques Thiboust didn't think so when he went to a great deal of trouble to tell his readers that what they were reading, as a result of what such others as Chaumeau had seen, was true to life:

> And do not think, good readers, that this play
> described below is false in any way,
> or think that the directors of the stuff
> would deem that written truth was e'er enough.
> It's true: everything happened in the play

From A to Z exactly as I say.
If only I could pray that by His might,
Our God would have permitted you the sight:
For then you'd say: "The author of this book
left much more in than ever out he took."[32]

Just as certainly, Gustave Cohen made every effort to accept Thiboust's testimony at face value: "And don't believe for a minute that this is a fantasy or an invention on the part of the faithful narrator who has described these marvels for us: at that time, the stage costumes for the occasion demanded just that much opulence; and he has taken care to anticipate our surprise . . . at the outset of his faithful account."[33] Discounting the entirety of such accounts would be just as unreasonable as concluding that there were *no* corrupt priests living in Metz, for the sole reason that the chronicler Jacomin Husson has spun a delightful yarn about one that reads more like a *fabliau.*[34]

Then again, any urban legend *sounds* true and reliable, normally by virtue of a plethora of precise, authorizing, localized details that are inserted by the individual tellers of oral tradition.[35] What if the medievalist's "reliable source," venerated by Old and New Historicists alike, were merely the urban legend's "friend of a friend" (FOAF) in disguise?[36] What if an "authority" like Rey-Flaud, Faber, the great Petit de Julleville, or even a manuscript were to prove just as fallible as the stock players of an urban legend, the cousin of a coworker or the niece of the people who used to live next door? "The truth factor in urban legends," contends Brunvand, "is most often simply a matter of people not questioning the teller's details while trusting that narrator's supposedly reliable sources. People believe an urban legend because the plot stays within the realm of possibility—no alien invaders, psychic powers, or sea monsters—and the storyteller is someone 'who would never lie' and who can cite the authority of that famous 'friend of a friend' to whom this remarkable thing actually happened."[37] Like Brunvand's storytellers, medievalists also tend to believe that "the true facts of each case lie just one or two informants back down the line with a reliable witness, or in a news media report" (*VH*, xi). But our reliable, if not infallible, source is usually a manuscript, not a newspaper. Contemporary American storytellers relating the story of the decomposed mouse in the Coke bottle, for instance, would customarily warrant that their own narrative is only several times removed from a real eyewitness or a published newspaper report—often one as dependable as the *Washington Post.*[38] Modern aficionados of avant-garde theater would probably tend to believe Geoff Pywell when he says that he witnessed spectacular brutality at London's Real and True Theatre (*SRT,* 21). Medievalists would tend to believe Raymond Lebègue when he renders what

Jacques Thiboust attributes to Jean Chaumeau about Bourges;[39] in the case of the *Sainte Hostie,* they would likely buy John Gatton's rendering of what Petit de Julleville reads in Henri Michelant's edition of Philippe de Vigneulles.[40] The storytellers all *seem* reliable, especially given the medievalist's devotion to that beloved academic convention known as the footnote. But, as Anthony Grafton has written of the those little numbers at the bottom of the page, "footnotes guarantee nothing, in themselves." Instead, "the culturally contingent and eminently fallible footnote offers the only guarantee we have that statements about the past derive from identifiable sources. And that is the only ground we have to trust them."[41]

Urban legends ordinarily circulate among a privileged group whose stories comprise "an integral part of white Anglo-American culture and are told and believed by some of the most sophisticated 'folk' of modern society—young people, urbanites, and the well educated" (*VH*, xi)—but that group holds no monopoly on the truth.[42] Far from it. If, as Darnton puts it, "peasants tell tales" (*GCM*, chap. 1), so too do literary historians: and they tell tales that, in retrospect, look a lot like urban legends. Indeed, once the "friend of a friend" has made his or her entrance onto the stage of literary criticism, we have the possibility of potentially endless mediation. We have what any schoolchild would simply call a game of "telephone" (*CBA*, 19). As an original message becomes so garbled through repetition as to be totally transformed, nonsensical, or unrecognizable by the time it reaches the last speaker, the child's schoolyard play has become the medievalist's historical interpretation.[43] So it was that the brothers Parfaict noticed that a chain of muddled testimony had made it virtually impossible to attain any kind of true sense of what medieval theatrical performances were all about. They resolved their difficulty as best they could, which meant approaching the medieval theatrical admixture of history, legend, and rumor through a critical admixture of history, legend, and rumor: "the obscurity to which these Plays were condemned on the basis of good taste and *politesse* decimated them so in the eyes of the Public that there remained only the vaguest notions of them, which soon became falsehoods."[44] Then again, not everything was just a "story."

Folklorists make room for the "true-true" tale, and medievalists must do the same when faced with the occasional proof that not every legendary occurrence was a legend.[45] As far as the credibility of our stories themselves is concerned, we will do well to recall that real things could and did happen on the early French stage. In theater, real things happen all the time. They still do today during many live events, including theater, filmings, videotapings, and even spectacular sporting events.[46] On the lighter side, actors Warren Beatty and Annette Bening begin a love affair during the filming of *Love Affair* and later marry. Crooner Lyle Lovett falls for pretty woman Julia Roberts on the set of *Ready to Wear*. Ralph Fiennes becomes enamored of Francesca Annis while she plays mother to his Hamlet, offering ample grist for both the gossip and the Freudian mill. On the dark side, an actress is beaten to a pulp on the stage of London's RATT. Actor Vic Morrow dies during the filming of *The Twilight Zone Movie*, and Natalie Wood during *Brainstorm*. As I was writing this book, the wrestler Owen Hart fell fifty feet to his death on 24 May 1999 during what was to have been a spectacular aerial entrance into the Kemper wrestling arena in Kansas City.[47] On both sides, real things are even said to happen *because* of plays, movies, television, or other art forms. Happily, Errol Morris's *Thin Blue Line* instigates a new trial for a wrongly convicted man and restores justice. Soap operas encourage women to request mammograms. *America's Most Wanted* occasionally culminates in the capture of fugitives. Sadly, such reality-based shows as *Cops* are said to prompt copy-cat crimes, just as depressing song lyrics are said to give rise to suicides. A film like *Stand By Me* allegedly inspires teens to lie down on the freeway and jump up just in time to avoid speeding trucks—or not. Perceived causation may even spur perceived "solutions," as when distressed politicians hold out their hopes for the filtering effects of V-chips or for the consecration of special hours devoted to "quality family programming." That was also the case when early French communities engaged in the regulation and censorship of the theater.[48]

The events just listed are not urban legends; they are real events that reflect real anxieties about the interplay between art and life, and they are no less compelling than the anxieties expressed by our medieval stories. If there was at least the *possibility* that theater could lead to true love, marriage, education, and the priesthood, or to terror, destruction of property, rebellion, heresy, madness, torture, punishment, suicide, and execution, then such moments could have been "performative" in the sense understood by the ordinary-language philosopher J. L. Austin. Speaking of certain precise, ritualized settings, Austin argued that when a man utters a phrase like "I bet $50" at the roulette table or "I do" before his fiancé and his rabbi, those are "speech acts" that alter real life: "the issuing of the utterance is the performing of an action—it is not normally thought of as just saying something" *(HDTW,* 6–7). If a medieval saint's play exhorted spectators "to incite the good people here / to do good works that are not feigned," and if its audience then went on to perform such good works, the play was performative.[49] When actors of a *Mystère de la Passion* in Angers protested from *inside* the play that their on-stage words should not trigger accusations of heresy *outside* the play, they too recognized that they were doing considerably more on stage than "just saying something":

> For all the players everywhere
> I make this claim in open air
> Of mysteries just like this one
> So, should there ever be someone
> Who dares against the faith to speak
> Or act, he'll suffer no critique.
> We don't intend, in word or deed,
> To say a thing against our creed.[50]

They were involved in a theatrical genre that did something *in* real life and *to* real life.[51] Although one cannot say that every medieval play was performative, our folklorist friends have shown us that a given event need only happen once—if at all—for its recurrence (or perceived recurrence) to be believable. "Put the facts and the illusions together with the skills of a good narrator," says Brunvand, "and you have believable, and even partly 'true,' urban legends" (*TGT,* 450).[52]

In that sense, what matters is that each one of our stories transmits an eminently believable fear about the believable. Even as the medieval and modern theaters evince striking moral, tonal, and conceptual differences, both establish that we are dealing with two cultures that, although separated by six hundred years, suggest in their varied and spectacular ways that believability is "truer" than truth. Such a mission is the very province of theatrical verisimilitude—and also the province of urban legends. When it comes to the true or false testimony of credible or incredible witnesses, one thing is unmistakable. We are dealing, on one hand, with the historical status of the reliable source as weighed against the unstable pleasures of unstable storytelling. On the other hand, we are dealing with the distinct possibility of real or imagined theatrical performativity in conjunction with the real or imagined apprehensions of legend making. In both cases, urban legends reveal the special power of theater itself to disclose the specificity and also the difference, or "alterity," of the Middle Ages.[53] They do so, moreover, in ways that often surprise us as to who is more "medieval" in their take on theology and theater: citizens of the 1500s or those of the present day.

With tremendous political and theological consequences—consequences that we shall be exploring throughout—theater has always provided a place where audiences have been happy to suspend their disbelief. Should they refuse to, insists Gustave Cohen, they can no longer go to the theater. They cannot go because they can no longer accept its symbolic landscapes, its unrealistic staging, or its impressionistic conceptions of distance: "You're not afraid that the banks of the Rhine are going to overflow and spill over onto your silk hats and your black get-ups, even though the stage looms before you several meters ahead." While he agreed with Petit de Julleville that medieval "techies" were far from perfect, Cohen was emphatic on this point: "Let's be clear about something: the very conventions that we deride over there, we accept here. Isn't everything just a convention in the theater? . . . For heaven's sake, let's be a little less severe, and may he who has never willingly given himself over to the enchantment of the theatrical illusion cast the first stone at the past" (*HMS*, 70).[54] Minus the biblical overlay, it is possible for us to take that approach to each one of our medieval urban legends. Most of our narrators, however, found it *impossible* to do without that overlay. For medieval Christian audiences, the stories staged by biblical dramas, Passion plays, and saints' lives were not *theological* legends—even though they gave rise to *theatrical* legends. They were *true* historical narratives, not "fictions." Indeed, visual and auditory reminders of their religious truthfulness were available everywhere: in paintings, sculptures, and architecture; in relics, at Mass, in books and sermons; in the classroom, in the courtroom, and, of course, in drama itself.[55] What is so tantalizing about our stories is that each one has a way of inviting us to suspend simultaneously both our disbelief and our belief.

Perhaps nowhere is that phenomenon illustrated more irresistibly than in Stanley Cavell's story of the local southern yokel who rushes onto the stage to save Shakespeare's Desdemona from the evil black Othello. "The usual joke," explains Cavell, is "that he doesn't know how to behave in a theater." But anyone wishing to correct the yokel quickly experiences anxieties: "How do we imagine we might correct him?—that is, *what* mistake do we suppose him to have made? If we grant him the concept of play-acting, then we will tell him that this is an instance of it: 'They are only acting; it isn't real.' But we may not be perfectly happy to have had to say that. Not that we doubt that it is true. If the thing *were* real. . . . But somehow we had *accepted* its non-factuality, it made it possible for there to have been a play."[56] Cavell then tenders this conclusion of both the spectacle and the possible audience responses to it: "Neither credible nor incredible: that ought to mean that the concept of credibility is inappropriate altogether" (*MWM*, 329). Since the yokel is an otherwise ignoble racist who has nevertheless felt a noble impulse to save a woman's life, it becomes impossible to sustain simultaneously the three contradictory impulses necessary to correct him: We cannot instruct him that his noble instinct to save a woman's life is out of place at the same time that we correct his ignorance of theatrical conventions at the same time that we teach him about race relations. What it takes to "correct" the yokel is an explicit disavowal of the very "make believe" and "pretending" upon which theater depends (*MWM*, 326–27). We cannot simultaneously exhort him to suspend both his belief and his disbelief. Yet that is precisely what we must do if we wish to decide something about any of our stories. Like Cavell's yokel, we must watch as both realities and illusions appear and disappear before our eyes in a multitude of forever mediated interpretations.

Insofar as our fourteen stories ask us both to doubt and to believe, they tend to be neither provable nor unprovable, neither probable nor improbable, neither credible nor incredible, neither real nor unreal. As Bruce Wilshire lucidly phrases it, "we live on the pivot connecting the fictional and the actual and can never leap off to land solidly on either 'side.' Indeed, in the case of human life, the idea of a purely fictional or a purely actual is a delusion" (*RPI*, 258). Just because somebody claimed that there was a snuff drama in 1549 doesn't mean that there *was* one. Nor does it mean that there *wasn't* one. This latter suggestion parallels the logic of two well-known psychic scenarios. The comic take is that Tournai might divulge that "just because you're paranoid doesn't mean that everybody is *not* out to get you." The serious take is the common nightmare in which a dreamer asks, "Is this a dream or is it real life?"—only to hear within the dream that most terrifying response of all: "No, this is real life." That fearsome answer within the dream impinges upon the dream of real life in ways that are no less frightening than the nightmare of Tournai—and no less glorious than the marriage fantasy of the saintly Catherine of Metz. Dream or nightmare, joke or horror, our chapters do what theater does: they *play* with the creation and destruction of truth. If nothing else, it is possible to know *that*—and to know it about the theatrical genre that is so uniquely equipped to address and enact the dreams and nightmares of believability.

As the slippery relationship between shadowy sources and shadowy events will show, we cannot really authorize what we cannot debunk, and we cannot really debunk what we can never authorize. Why should we do either? Wilshire asks, "Does theatre reveal what is the case or only what we would like to be the case? The distinction enshrined by the question is grossly misleading. For what could be more actual than the dreams and desires we do have? How can we know ourselves unless we know what these are? Theatre is peculiarly apt to reveal them" (*RPI*, 252). Elsewhere, Brunvand points out that it is more difficult to prove an urban legend's grain of truth than it is to debunk the whole thing (*TGT*, 451). So maybe the best way to approach our stories is to say that they are both provable *and* unprovable, probable *and* improbable, credible *and* incredible, real *and* unreal. Here, a modern example will suffice to demonstrate that it is indeed possible to simulate suffering *at the same time* that real suffering is actually taking place.

During the celebration of Easter in 1995, a local California television station aired a news story about the reenactment of Christ's Passion in the Philippines. The smiling anchorman, Dean Mignola, reported that a group of believers carried their "reenactment a step farther" by allowing themselves to be nailed to crosses before a crowd of some five thousand spectators.[57] Fortunately, modernity had seen to it that the thin nails designed for the Crucifixion had been previously soaked in alcohol in order to prevent infection. The bottom line is that a theatrical event was simultaneously real, ritualized, and representational. Whatever we choose to believe about our fourteen stories, the reality of early dramatic realism is that it regularly staged its own capacity to be any or all of those three things at once.

Over twenty years ago, Paul Theiner had some advice about that subject, which he directed to presumably skeptical historians. Almost a phenomenologist in spite of himself, Theiner proposed entry into the seemingly inhospitable hermeneutic circle of medieval studies with this whimsical language: "To put this all into a more literary perspective, albeit a homely one, we are in the position of blind men feeling around the elephant of medieval literature, but with one crucial difference: we have no omniscient narrator to tell us that the elephant is really there."[58] In Metz, Melun, Meaux, Doué-la-Fontaine, and our other stops on the way to Tournai, the entity lurking in the shadows is plainly no white elephant. Nor does that mean that we should not look for the elephant.

We might bear in mind here another blind man who was elegantly conceived for the screen by Lynda House and Jocelyn Moorhouse in their 1992 film *Proof.* This man takes photographs incessantly—true representations of the world he inhabits but has never seen. A profound cinematic inquiry into the nature of skepticism, the film (using imagery to prove its case) stages the blind man's need for absolute proof of what he has photographed but will never see. His proof (and ours) is possible only through mediated interpretation. Just as the blind man in *Proof* must trust someone to look at the pictures and, using language, tell him what was and is really there, so too must the medievalist trust someone. Sometimes the blind man trusts the wrong person. Sometimes the medievalist does too. But there is always something there. That is what an urban legend is for.

PART I

Telling the Difference

C H A P T E R   O N E

Lusting after Saints

TRUTH, *n.* An ingenious compound of desirability and appearance.
—Ambrose Bierce, *The Devil's Dictionary*

Of all the things that might have run through the young girl's mind when she agreed to play Saint Catherine of Siena in the city of Metz in the mid-sixteenth century, finding a husband was probably not high on the list. She was, after all, performing at a convent—a proper training ground for young wives because of its spirituality, not its theatricality. A spinster of the ripe old age of eighteen would likely have been hoping to marry—but the stage was not the normal venue in which a well-brought-up young lady would attract a husband. Yet that is exactly what happened, if we believe the chroniclers of Metz.

By the account of Philippe de Vigneulles, the eighteen-year-old girl was a superb actress, and a certain Henry de la Tour, in attendance that day, a great catch. The lass did such a brilliant job of representing Catherine's martyrdom that the audience wept while Henry fell madly in love:

> In the aforesaid year [1468], there was performed and played in Metz the play of Milady Saint Catherine of Siena, true sister of the Order of Jacobins. And this play was put on in the courtyard of the [convent of the] Great Preachers over the three feasts of Pentecost. . . . And the role of Saint Catherine was played by a young girl of approximately eighteen years of age, who was the daughter of Dediet the glazier [of Four du Cloistre]; and she acquitted herself marvelously well in her role, to the taste and pleasure of everyone there. Moreover, this said girl had 2300 lines of dialogue; and nevertheless, she had every line at the tip of her tongue. And this girl spoke so spiritedly and piteously that she prompted many people to weep; and she was pleasing to everybody. And on account of this, the girl was very well married to a gentleman,

mercenary of Metz, by the name of Henry de la Tour, who fell in love with her on account of the great pleasure he had taken there.[1]

This narrative teems with what Dickson and Goulden call the "semblance of seemingly supportive specific detail," which would tend to reinforce either its historical veracity or its potential status as an urban legend.[2] For example, Philippe is clearly referring to a specific version of the *Play of Saint Catherine*, because only someone extremely familiar with the text could have warranted that the young lady had memorized a full twenty-three hundred lines of dialogue.[3] Henry, armed with his gentlemanly aristocratic particles, had a military record to boot, a combination that might well have enhanced his desirability to the opposite sex or to their families. Most intriguing, the normally bellicose Henry had more than war on his mind that day when he felt such "great pleasure" as a result of the theater that he sought to make it last by marrying both it and *her:* a girl who played martyrdom so well that we don't even need to know her first name. For Henry, for the chroniclers, and for later disseminators and readers, it was presumably more than enough to know that "Catherine" wound up as Madame de la Tour. She had fulfilled one of her social roles by finding a husband attracted to her plight.

So far, so good. Whatever it was that seduced Henry—the beauty of the cloistered setting, the possibility of spiritual edification, the poetry of a dramatized saint's life, the surprise at seeing a young woman on stage at a time when it was less common for women to be there, or perhaps some sort of subconscious recognition that martyrdom was the ideal calling-card for a future wife—the story goes that Henry was completely taken.[4] Who wouldn't want such a wife? No matter how astute medieval historians' insights into the spiritual bond of marriage, an eighteen-year-old who knew how to play a saint might prove equally saintly in the kitchen or, better yet, in the bedroom.[5] Here was no unnamed shrew of a wife from the *Farce of the Wash-tub*, henpecking her poor husband into doing all the household chores.[6] Here was no late-night manipulator crying crocodile tears in bed in order to obtain pretty new clothes from the ensnared spouse in the *Fifteen Joys of Marriage.*[7] Here was no threat of cuckoldry—and Henry had doubtless seen plenty of *that* on stage, not only in farces but in religious theater's giggly renditions of Christ's earthly father, Joseph.[8] Instead, the young girl was the picture of submission, piety, and martyrdom, willing to accept suffering rather than to renounce her belief in Jesus Christ. For any red-blooded medieval man desirous of a gloriously subservient spouse, this girl was the "real thing." For any man of Metz, she was a martyr in a city that had already exalted martyrdom, as when its good-hearted men sacrificed themselves during the siege of 1324: "Our noble men are martyrs true; / And God has raised them up to Him."[9]

Under the circumstances, how could Henry have helped falling in love? He too was playing the ultimate part in a theatrical experience that had traditionally encouraged active audience participation. It had done so as early as the thirteenth-century *Herod,* when actors invited "the people standing around" to come and adore the Christ child.[10] Whether or not Henry's especially enthusiastic participation coincided with the original intentions of the nuns who had lent their dwelling for the spectacle of a saint's life remains to be seen. For the moment, it simply sounds as though the couple lived happily ever after. It sounds as though John Elliott might have been right to conclude from his own reading of the tale that "some medieval reports, like many modern reviews, tell us little more about dramatic interpretation than the fact that the reviewer was smitten by the actress."[11] But the story of "Catherine" and Henry (who is not the reviewer, but one of the subjects) tells us a good deal more.

As we shall see, our first story takes us straight to the heart of theater phenomenology. We might be inclined, for instance, to accept Bruce Wilshire's contention that theater's realities don't matter because they are idealized, symbolic communications: "Actual persons and things are used in the production but their real factual reality is bracketed out so that what they are as types and essences can be revealed" (*RPI,* 137). Our chroniclers were not so kind as to provide the full name of the actress who played Catherine of Siena, but if the story is true, it was not an essence who walked down the aisle with Henry de la Tour. Insistently human, insistently real, it was a woman who was wed to a man. So, was she or wasn't she?

At first blush, we seem happily to find confirmation in another chronicle of Metz by Jacomin Husson, who tenders this substantially shorter testimony:

> Item, in the aforesaid year, the *Play of Saint Catherine of Siena* was performed over the three feasts of Pentecost. . . . A young girl of approximately eighteen years of age played Saint Catherine and acquitted herself marvelously well in her role and in her performance; and she had 2,300 lines of dialogue; and she was most pleasing to many people; and, on this account, she was married to a mercenary by the name of Henry de la Tour, who fell in love with her on account of the great pleasure he had taken there.[12]

Our two chroniclers thus agree on a number of details, including the play's timing with Pentecost, the age of "Catherine," the version of the play performed, the success of the performance, and the actress's subsequent marriage. They also agree on the play's sponsor, a woman devoted in her own way to religious life: "The arrangements for the performance of the play were made by Lady Catherine Baudoiche, at her own cost and expense."[13] For his own part, Petit de Julleville was thrilled by this compelling piece of evidence attesting to the early presence of both a female actress and a female patron, noting of the latter that it was "rather rare" to see a play "performed in a monastery" and a "pious lady who bore the costs of the performance."[14] As for "Catherine," he thought incorrectly that it was "absolutely unheard of" to find an actress on stage in 1468, since we must normally wait until the 1530s for the thespian advent of women in such cities as Valenciennes and Grenoble (*LM*, 2:32). Jacomin Husson even bears him out here by affirming that when another *Play of Saint Catherine* was performed on Metz's Place en Change on 15 June 1434, the title role went to a man.[15] However, when it comes to the other details about the performance, our commentators diverge—and the devil is in those details. They are so confusing that we don't always know where to turn or—to borrow the French expression more appropriate to our subject—"*to which saint* to turn" *(à quel saint se vouer).*[16] Henry de la Tour, of course, knows very well where to turn in order to make sure that *another* proverb does not apply in his case: "the lady is interested in someone else" *(elle est voüée à un autre Saint).*[17]

In this story of heads turned, there are both technical and spiritual uncertainties: the date of the *coup de foudre;* the identity, status, and character of the real "Catherine"; the physical circumstances of the production; and, above all, the moral (or morals) to be drawn from the story (or stories).

First of all, Petit de Julleville (with Huguenin) places the young actress's *tour de force* in 1468, while Jacomin's "aforesaid year" is 1448, twenty years earlier.[18] It seems unreasonable to posit two *separate* performances of the *Play of Saint Catherine* spaced twenty years apart and in which Henry would have had his *coup de foudre* twice! That would oblige us to envisage a distinctly unmedieval scenario in which he swoons over "Catherine" all over again and maybe decides to renew his vows with his wife. Therefore, whatever we may think about cultural difference, it is sensible to assume that Henry and his bride had no hand in the accounts. Surely *they* would not have forgotten the date of their *coup de foudre*—unless Henry was the sort to forget his anniversary. Nor do we know exactly *when* they married or if a brief courtship followed the *Play of Saint Catherine.* Nor does it seem very likely that, if Henry and his nubile bride had married in 1448 (or sometime thereafter), she would have taken to the stage twenty years later to reimpersonate (while pushing forty) the life of a saint whose extraordinary conversion was said to have taken place at a very young age and who died at the age of thirty-three.[19]

It helps a bit to know that there *was* a Henry de la Tour among the "noble lords" in attendance at Metz's ill-fated Passion play of 1437 in which two priests almost died.[20] In that case, he was either eleven years older in 1448 (for Jacomin Husson) or thirty-one years older in 1468 (for Petit de Julleville citing Huguenin). Or he was *not* the same Henry de la Tour. Or there were *two* Henrys, junior and senior. If we make certain assumptions about a man's marriageable age or mortality in the fifteenth century and imagine that, in 1437, the gentlemanly Henry had reached the age of sixteen, then he took his eighteen-year old bride either in 1448 at the age of twenty-seven, or else in 1468 at the more decrepit age of forty-seven. The problem is that the Huguenin edition of the *Chroniques de Metz* tells us that in 1433 there was a gentleman mercenary named Henry de la Tour seeking financial damages from the city of Metz in connection with his recent service—and that he *already had a wife and children.*[21] If his wife died in the intervening fifteen or thirty-five years, the chronicle does not say. But either she *did* and Henry took a new bride or she *did not,* and the story of Henry smitten by a saint is just that—a story—because he couldn't have two wives at once. It is also plausible that the litigious Henry was not the same Henry de la Tour, even though both are listed as gentleman mercenaries.

What is so charming about the story is that it works under any of those circumstances, and it works in the way that legends work. If we believe Jacomin Husson, Henry married "Catherine" at the perfectly reasonable age of twenty-seven or so. If we believe Petit de Julleville, he married her at the more advanced age of forty-seven or so, still a reasonable age at which a man with enough of a career to sport the moniker "gentleman mercenary" might take a young bride. Certainly no modern arms need be twisted into accepting the possibility that older men marry younger women, especially when some kind of stardom is involved. By the same token, any postmodernist would pounce on what appears to be an early enactment of Wilshire's appealing motto that "art is like a vow which we make to each other. In artistic activity we are vowing to each other that it is valuable to do what we are doing" (*RPI*, 220). What could be more valuable than a saintly play inspiring a saintly Christian marriage? As Dickson and Goulden remind us, the truth has never gotten "in the way of a good story," and the tale of Henry and "Catherine" was one good story.[22]

Furthermore, if Henry's existence looks relatively clear, the identities of the two women in our story are rather more ambiguous. Concerning the young actress, we know only that she was the daughter of Dediet, the glazier of Four du Cloistre and, for Jacomin Husson, the daughter of nobody in particular.[23] It would certainly be nice to know a bit more about the young actress, such as how she came to be assigned the saint's role. But the only real Catherine who commands the attention of our commentators is Catherine Baudoiche.

We seem to know that, in honor of her saintly namesake, Catherine Baudoiche assumed the responsibility and costs for a performance in honor of Saint Catherine: "And this lady was laid to rest at the aforesaid [convent of the] Great Preachers inside the chapel which she had founded and had built and which is situated at the entrance of this church and founded in the name of Saint Catherine."[24] This is not a lyric poem like "Belle Doette," in which an imaginary maiden builds an abbey after the death of her *ami*.[25] This is a real historical figure who lived and died a life of sufficient social importance to have been buried at the very site where she had practiced her devotion. Petit de Julleville may well have found it unusual that Catherine Baudoiche had had the funds and the inclination to put on a show at her cloister with a secular actress. Or perhaps the daughter of Dediet was one of the young ladies given over to the place for a religious education—a fate not inconsistent with that of a glazier's daughter. Perhaps the girl was the very model of piety that Henry saw before him, although one must recognize that theatrical expertise would scarcely have enhanced a nice girl's reputation. Perhaps, like the lead character in the miracle play, *The Nun who Left her Abbey*, or in Georges Brassens's much later "Légende de la nonne," she was a novice who abandoned her calling when seduced by the charms of a man.[26] Her presence on stage might thus have heralded such a spiritual downfall. Indeed, we do not know if she fell or not—for anyone but Henry. Our narrators imply only that Henry and his actress-wife lived happily ever after, or as the French say, "they got married and had lots of children."

Did they? And what about Catherine Baudoiche? Was there a happy ending for her as well? Did any of the principals get what they bargained for? Surprisingly, the story contains as many seeds of doubt about a happily-ever-after as it does premonitions for future *un*happiness.

If we believe our story, then something very real happened that day (whichever day it was) when Catherine Baudoiche's choice to honor Saint Catherine theatrically turned out to be performative—but probably *not* in the way that she had planned. She must have begun her theatrical project with the most edifying of intentions, a motive that typically justified numerous communal decisions to move forward with the mounting of a play. For example, in April 1434 the chaplain Jean de Poys of Draguignan helped to subsidize a Passion play "for the honor of God, in memory of his Passion, and for the edification of Christians."[27] The citizens of Montélimar found great merit in the *Play of Saint Catherine* itself when, on 15 May 1453, they sought permission to stage it "for the edification, honor, utility, and profit of the city."[28] On one hand, it is doubtful that Catherine Baudoiche would have deemed matchmaking to be part and parcel of such a spiritual mission. She was a "pious lady," not a matchmaker. On the other hand, if the unnamed actress (novice or not) was not quite firm enough in her faith, then maybe the opportunity of playing Catherine would cement it. The histories of both the stage and the saints had previously hosted such miraculous, theatrical conversions.

As Jacob Larwood later tells the tale, the well-known figure of Saint Genesius had proclaimed as early as the fourth century "his conversion to Christianity publicly on the stage, a piece of 'gag' which so displeased the emperor [Diocletian], that he rewarded him with martyrdom" (*TA*, 230).[29] Also flying in the face of Tertullian's denunciations of the godlessness of the stage was the tale of Ardaleon, another fourth-century pagan actor who "was struck with the truth of Christianity whilst acting in a farce in which he ridiculed the Christians and their religion" (*TA*, 230).[30] Something similar happened to the actor Porphyrius when he "pretended to be a convert to Christianity in order that he might study the Christians and better be able to ridicule them on the stage." He found that going through the theatrical motions of Christianity achieved the real, devout thing. When he allowed himself to be baptized, "the holy water drove the arch-enemy out of him, and though 'he came to scoff, he remained to pray'"—at least until he was beheaded in 362 (*TA*, 230–31). Or maybe Catherine Baudoiche was familiar with the story of Margarita (sometimes known as Marina or Pelagia of Antioch), who left her theatrical life of fame and fortune after a bishop had converted her to Christianity. Larwood dubs her the only "sainted actress" and relates that after "renouncing the stage, its pomps and vanities, she distributed her property among the poor, assumed the garb of a male hermit, and ended her days as such on the Mount of Olives, in A.D. 451" (*TA*, 230).

Then again, our own "Saint Catherine" did not become a nun. She got married—and did so, moreover, after playing a character who had expressed hostility toward the very idea of marriage. "It is useless for you to huff and puff," wrote the real Catherine of Siena, "a waste of time, and therefore I advise you to blow on the wind any idea of marriage because there is no way I intend to accommodate you. I must obey God not men."[31] Our unnamed actress, daughter of Dedict, performed the antithesis of her character's behavior, and she certainly never became a saint—at least, not in the eyes of the Church. If Henry canonized the future Madame de la Tour at home, we will never know. One thing is for sure: it is difficult to imagine him permitting her to continue her acting career once she had moved into the more suitable domestic role of wife.[32] The theater piece that had sainted her in Henry's eyes must eventually have come into conflict with her new social role as his wife. It would *never* have been in conflict, however, with her *acting the part* of his wife.

Perhaps Catherine Baudoiche should have anticipated such a role conversion. After all, it was she who had funded the conversion of a cloister into a theater when spatial considerations necessitated exposing to the elements the noble names and remains of those who had been laid to rest in the courtyard, the better to stage the *Play of Saint Catherine:* "And, in order to put on the play, they tore down the cov-

ered walkways that had been erected all around against the walls and which protected the old epitaphs and sepulchers."³³ It was she who had deemed it "necessary
to disrupt the courtyard of the convent in order to set up a theater" (*LM*, 2:32).³⁴
So, once the space of religious devotion had given way to the space of theater, there
was no way to guarantee that it would inspire spiritual contemplation instead of
terrestrial joys or such "pleasures" as Henry's. Catherine's efforts appear to have
culminated in precisely the sort of lust-driven union that antitheatrical polemicists
had feared. Plato himself had written that "in regard to the emotions of sex and
anger, and all the appetites and pains and pleasures of the soul which we say accompany all our actions, the effect of poetic imitation is the same. For it waters and
fosters these feelings when what we ought to do is to dry them up" (*Republic*, 606d).
Drying up her appetites was what the real Catherine of Siena did best.

One might disagree with Rudolph Bell's verdict that Catherine Benincasa (of
Siena) suffered from anorexia nervosa, but Caroline Walker Bynum notes that
Catherine "withdrew for several years into her bedroom and starved herself to
death" (*FR*, 69). Although Henry de la Tour is cast more or less as weeping for her
along with the rest of the susceptible crowd, let us consider for a moment just what
he saw in the life of Saint Catherine that could have caused him such "great pleasure."

As Plato had warned, Henry might actually have been titillated by the spectacle
of his future bride's suffering.³⁵ What a slap in the face to the pious setting of the
cloister! Under such circumstances, Catherine Baudoiche herself would have been
complicit in soliciting all the earthly pleasures of the pagan "circus" that had been
denounced by the likes of Isidore of Seville; the young actress playing Catherine
would have come dangerously close to the sexuality and magic of Isidore's Circe,
who "was a sorceress and a poisoner, and a priestess of demons, in whose practices
we may recognize both the deeds of the magic art and the cult of idolatry."³⁶
Beware, Henry, lest male spectators wind up lusting constantly after your wife.
Beware lest you wish for something that might come true. Beware, Catherine Baudoiche, lest an earthly husband emerge as a more appropriate and desirable bride-
groom than Jesus Christ. Beware especially, all of you, the process by which
theatrical skills might be translated into domestic ones.

If we believe Jacomin's version, or any of the stories, Henry de la Tour married
a theatrical incarnation of sainthood in a medieval world in which producers *(entrepreneurs)* did indeed believe in what we call today "type-casting." In theater, it
was important to find an actor with just the right "look" so that an audience might
simultaneously believe and suspend its disbelief. A particularly potent example
comes down to us from a later period (the 1530s), when a certain Monsieur Billon

of Issoudun invited the illustrious Jean Bouchet of Poitiers to direct his proposed production of a Passion play. Bouchet declined the offer with this friendly advice:

> Do try to give the characters on stage
> their parts in full accordance with their age.
> And though their borrowed clothing be of gold—
> it matters not how much—you have been told
> that costume must befit each player well.
> It's not a pretty sight when you can't tell
> The difference between learned men, you see,
> And Pilate, lawyers, or a Pharisee,
> Or Herod for that matter. . . .[37]

On Metz's stage, Saint Catherine was one pretty sight, and Henry must surely have believed that she had been perfectly cast. But was that a good thing?

The real Saint Catherine was kind and served her neighbors actively, but she was also quite headstrong, subjecting her body to exhausting fasts, refusing to marry, and "berating the clergy and even . . . dabbling in papal politics" (*FR*, 69).[38] Henry might thus have done well to think twice about becoming conjoined with such a rebellious spirit. If there was such a thing as the fusion of theater with real life—and the story of Henry's own marriage exists to say that there *was*—then his young bride might just as readily have been submissive and doting as audacious and insubordinate. Indeed, there was plenty in Catherine Benincasa's story of steadfast and disciplined devotion to God to hint that any girl emulating her would have been most unlikely to hang, *à la* Jim Croce, on a "Lover's Cross" for her man.

"After protracted conflict over vocation with her family," for instance, Catherine "became unable to eat anything except the eucharist. Ordered by Christ to join her family at table and taste something, she afterward rammed twigs down her throat to bring up the food she could not bear in her stomach" (*FR*, 141).[39] Presumably, what Henry saw on stage was a girl who, as Bynum puts it, "seems to have seen any hunger pangs as 'greed,' to have lost the ability to feel 'cold,' and to have felt panic at the passage of any food down her throat" (*HF*, 169).[40] Heaven knows that Henry would not have been the first man in history to find himself mesmerized by a wafer-thin woman. (Medieval norms of feminine physical beauty were not exactly forerunners of Twiggy, but everything we know about type-casting suggests that Catherine would at least have been played by someone thin.) But the most crassly pragmatic medieval man might have intuited that if a starving wife was inexpensive to maintain, one who wasted her victuals by regularly inducing vomiting was not. As Catherine Benincasa lived in denial and abstinence, her digestive juices dried up, perhaps along with her sexuality. At a minimum, her sexuality was not of this world (although theater had made it so), while Henry de la Tour's was. He was drawn to an actress playing a woman who "abhorred her own flesh, condemning it as a 'dung heap'" (*HF,* 175).

As for the kind of housewife Catherine would have made, the famous pus-drinking incident would hardly have made an appetizing advertisement for her skills in the kitchen. Bynum documents Catherine's "substitution of the filth of disease and the blood of Christ's agony for ordinary food. Several of her hagiographers record that she twice forced herself to overcome nausea by thrusting her mouth into the putrefying breast of a dying woman or by drinking pus" (*HF,* 171–72).[41] Then again, during Catherine's "period of withdrawal into a cell in her father's house," she reportedly "plunged into a combination of fasting, sleeplessness, and hyperactivity, particularly frenetic housework and feeding of others. She did the laundry at night" (*HF,* 170). Henry would never have lacked a clean shirt, but would he really have relished living with the real Saint Catherine's other tendency to fill in for the servants when they fell ill (*HF,* 170)? Additionally, even the fortitude of a gentleman mercenary would have been sorely tested if Henry's bride had started to imitate Saint Catherine by giving away "great quantities of food" (*HF,* 170).

At a minimum, the real Catherine was controversial in that "although many acclaimed her as a saint, some dubbed her a fanatic, whilst others loudly denounced her as a hypocrite, even some of her own order" (*BLS,* 194). Why would Henry have walked into a situation that might bring scandal and gossip to his house? He might well have wept along with the crowd, but did he really want to be married to a miracle-worker? Saint Catherine was a girl who, once having "angered her father by giving away the best wine" (*HF,* 170), purportedly went ahead and performed a miracle. One of her biographers, Raymond of Capua, draws an analogy with "the gospel feeding of five thousand" and when "God miraculously made the cask flow again" (*HF,* 170).[42] Miracles might bring plenty to a household, but they could also bring plenty of trouble. So too could Catherine of Siena.

We read in *Butler's Lives,* for example, that her disenchantment with the "fratricidal struggles" of Christendom moved Catherine to correspond directly with the pontiff and "to throw herself energetically into Pope Gregory XI's appeal for another crusade to wrest the Holy Sepulchre from the Turks" (*BLS,* 195). Nor did she fear male authority when she cautioned in a letter to three Italian cardinals that "[I] write to you in His precious blood, in the desire of seeing you return to the true and most perfect light, of seeing you leave the great darkness and blindness into which you have fallen. Then you will be fathers to me; otherwise you will not be."[43]

If Catherine was fearless against cardinals, kings, and pontiffs, her older husband was not likely to fare any better, unless he too were a friend of Jesus. Beware, Henry, lest your new wife go to live under a stairwell like Saint Alexis and forsake her marital bed. Beware, Henry, lest you wind up not with a saint but with a devil on your hands.

Notwithstanding, then, the sorts of ambiguity that prompt despair in historians and excitement in folklorists, one still divines here the remarkably enduring expressions of theater's anxieties. In terms of the possible message to young ladies, that too was a mixed blessing. Saint Catherine's own choice was marriage or death, albeit a death crowned by the glory of Christian charity. The actress *playing* Catherine had different choices: saintly immortality, if she fused with her sainted character and followed a path of abnegation and starvation; on-stage immorality, perhaps somewhat mitigated by the cloistered setting of the play; or off-stage marital submission. The choice that our unnamed actress apparently made indicates that she was a failed saint and maybe even a failed nun but a successful bride, who had somehow managed to gain a husband through the highly questionable histrionic gift of impersonation.

In that sense, the comments made by John Elliott and Rosamond Gilder on the tale of Metz are somewhat curious. Elliott concurs with Gilder that our story had a happy and familiar ending when "we discover that the glazier's daughter who played St. Catherine in Metz worked her charms so successfully that a young nobleman in the audience named Henri de Latour proposed marriage to her, a proposal which she accepted, thus setting, as Rosamond Gilder has observed, 'a precedent that has been followed ever since.'"[44] For her own part, Gilder provided a lovely translation of our story and concluded that when this special theatrical representative of the fairer sex "made a rich match with a nobleman belonging to the hired troop of Metz," she simultaneously ended, "we are to presume, the brief career of the first actress of whom we have any record, the first woman, as far as we know, ever allowed to raise her voice in public in a religious play."[45] Like Petit de Julleville, Gilder was impressed by the girl's skill—only to deem it fitting that "Catherine" should have given it all up for the more suitable social outcome of marriage. The happy ending to a thwarted acting career is a happy marriage. Meanwhile, theater's end is not so happy after all. A gifted actress, beloved by her audience and particularly beloved by one male member, has vanished from the theater on account of her gifts. Which one of those gifts best served Madame Henry de la Tour or her husband is unknown—for that is the end of the story.

The only group for whom this ending is unambiguously happy is the antitheatrical polemicists. Here was a theater piece that succeeded in removing an otherwise talented and worthy woman from the stage. Whether or not the story is true, whether or not our actress was but an essence, the essence of her story is unchanged. To anyone who grew up listening to Judy Collins songs, the legendary story of "Catherine" mystifies whichever one of love's illusions we care to recall. She really didn't know theater at all.

Queer Attractions

Miss Wossingthon, the famous London actress, after having played with a certain success the role of a man, said upon returning home: "I bet you that half the audience took me for a man." One of her friends responded mischievously: "The other half knows just what to do to set them straight!"

—Victor Cousin d'Avalon

The chroniclers of Metz called it love at first sight. It is not clear for how long an unnamed wealthy lady from Saulnière had been widowed, but the sight of the young Lyonard playing the martyrdom of Saint Barbara in Metz in 1485 was apparently too much for her. On 24 July of that year, she watched the barber's apprentice in his female role for three full days and, along with many audience members, conceived her own passion. Like Christ and his saintly followers, one of whom was being impersonated before her very eyes, the widow of Saulnière became passionate about performing good works—at least as far as this particular young man was concerned. Lyonard's "good acting" was well on its way to fulfilling the standard pedagogical goal of medieval religious drama, to persuade spectators to "act good."[1] By the time the show was over, she was proposing to adopt him and make him her heir.

What moved the wealthy widow of Saulnière? Was it the story of Saint Barbara, the lovely young girl who, as the heroine of several hagiographic and dramatic tales, had gracefully, nobly, and unflinchingly endured ordeals in the name of Jesus Christ?[2] Or did the widow prefer the effeminate young man who was playing the saint? Although it was commonplace for medieval religious dramatists to stir their spectators to lead better Christian lives, how much easier that must have been when the needy appeared in the form of a good-looking boy and not a plain one.

As far as we know, there were no reports of marriage proposals for Lyonard (as there had been, supposedly, a generation or so earlier for the girl playing Catherine of Siena). But there were indeed reports of other types of friendships arising from his impressive performance. It turned out that the widow had competition in her efforts to "do for" Lyonard. That competition came from a man of the cloth, in the person of Master Jehan Chardelly. The story goes that the beautiful young Lyonard, originally a foreigner of Germanic extraction, had to make a choice between protectors. Either choice would assimilate the young man into his adopted community, but, in the happiest of happily-ever-afters, Lyonard made the better choice for the Church (and for its representative).

By now we are familiar with the topos. The citizens of Metz had seen the *Play of Saint Barbara* before, but never like this. Men of all walks of life habitually played the whole gamut of female characters, from the Virgin Mary to Mary Magdalen. A medieval French audience might see a notary playing in drag or a man of laws donning an emperor's crown.[3] They might watch their parish priest take up the mantle of God, the horns of Satan, or the modest clothes of a saint. In Metz in 1485 they beheld Lyonard, a simple working man, a young apprentice, a craftsman, who underwent an impressive transformation:

> On the twenty-fourth day of July [1485], there was played in Metz on the Place de Chambre, the Play of the Life and Passion of Madame Saint Barbara. And it lasted for three days; and it was played the best and the most triumphantly that I ever saw; and it was pleasing to everybody. . . . And it so happened that, at the time, there resided in Metz a young barber's apprentice named Lyonard, who was a passing beautiful lad resembling a young maiden. And he hailed from Nostre Dame d'Aix [Aix-la-Chapelle] in Germany; but he had lived for a long time in Metz in the home of Master Hannes, the barber of Quartaul. And this Lyonard played the role of Saint Barbara; and he did it so well and so honorably that he made over six thousand people cry. For he was a beautiful young lad, as already noted; and, as was also the case for his "ladies," his manner, mien, and gestures were so gracious that they were pleasing to everyone and it was not possible to do any better.[4]

Here, the chronicler implies that both Lyonard and his ladies were so convincing as women that he fails to mention that the other "ladies" were doubtless also played by men. Meanwhile, it is as if Lyonard himself has fused with his character at the level of her very name: the *jonne fils bairbier* is *Barbe* ("beard" in French). The beardless barber is "Barbara."

Lyonard's tale presents various fantasies about love, honor, nobility, sexuality, good works, and the Catholic creed—the ultimate beneficiary of his considerable talents. Notwithstanding a long history of antitheatrical polemic, it seems that toward the end of the fifteenth century, theater and the Church could work together when benevolent citizens helped subsume the former to the latter. The Church could "win out" over the theater—if not necessarily by inspiring noble passions in the crowd, then by stealing away its actors and putting them to better pastoral use in the service of France. In any event, that it is how things first appear.

Even before the stunning performance of July 1485, Lyonard must already have had a reputation, because "people went to take their places there at four o'clock in the morning."[5] This may have had something to do with prior *tours de force* in other performances, or with the interest aroused during the week preceding the July performances: It seems that certain citizens of Metz (Messins) had caught a glimpse of the scaffolding that had been "built in the Place de Vezegnuef and upon which the actors represented for themselves and performed the entire mystery play *without speaking*."[6] By all accounts, Lyonard was blessed with a wondrous mastery of the thespian art of gesture. With the flick of a wrist or the turn of a head, an excellent practitioner such as he could use his body to engage in veritable speech acts—in his case, eventually producing real tears over a dramatic representation of a saint's life.[7]

It was not until 24 July that our wealthy widow made her own entrance. While the chronicler casts the aristocratic and ecclesiastical communities as the first spectators to manifest a desire to take charge of the lad, there was certainly no other woman in the crowd who sought to do as much for Lyonard as the widow of Saulnière: "And so much was the lad in the good graces of everyone that there was no one among the nobility, clergy, or laity who did not desire to take charge of this boy to *nourish and raise him;* among whom there was a rich widow of Saulnière who wanted to have him for her heir."[8]

This is a fascinating turn of events that is rendered by a fascinating turn of phrase. The desire to "nourish and raise" the young Lyonard recalls the kind of familial language extant in feudal oaths, such as an early formula from Tours from the second quarter of the eighth century: "Given that it is known to all that *I am unable to feed and clothe myself,* I have asked your munificence, and by your will, you have agreed, that I may be allowed to deliver myself to you and to place myself in your tutelage *[maimbour].*"[9] Since the young Lyonard had chosen to make his home more than a hundred fifty miles from his native Germany, it is as if the more noble members of the audience in 1485 were reexperiencing the seigneur's vestigial feudal role by welcoming the young German into their midst and caring for him, a social role more befitting to men than to widowed women. Good Christians all, they had ostensibly taken the poor foreigner under their communal wing in an act of generosity that mirrored the Christian charity being exemplified by the barber

"Barbara" who stood before them. In addition, then, to producing real tears, Lyonard managed to do something else that is even more significant. Through his theatrical bag of tricks, the alluring young boy anchored his national identity on the French stage.[10]

This was no small feat. We are in the presence of a culture that so mistrusted foreign presence at the theater that the town council of Mons, for example, mandated in 1501 that during a Passion play a night watch of eight man should "learn what people are entering the city" and "innkeepers shall report each night the names of their guests."[11] Foreigners *at* the theater, however, was not the same thing as foreigners *in* the theater, a genre and a space especially well suited for keeping an eye on people. Indeed, the actor's name, Lyonard, didn't sound foreign at all. He was considerably more assimilated than his more Germanically resonant sponsor, Master Hannes. Furthermore, Lyonard would have seemed all the more deserving of such attentions given the common belief that to perform the prudence and devotion of a saint so honorably, prudently, and piously, an actor must surely have been drawing upon his own personal experience of faith.[12]

Whatever the nature of the wealthy widow's commitment—motherly, amorous, sentimental, or some curious combination of all three—she conceived a feudal (if futile) yearning for the barber as Barbara. She was clearly excited enough by Lyonard's performance to want to do something about *it* and for *him*—a superficially noble mission that handily eliminated any need to clarify the ambiguous nature of her attraction to the beautiful "Barbara." Was hers a silently sublimated same-sex love?[13] Or did she resolve through her proposed financial donation an almost incestuous lust for a girlish lad who might have been young enough to be her son (and a German to boot)? Here, the play itself makes room for any number of answers, for Barbara's life had enough gruesome plot twists to have nurtured thoughts of lust and even incest in the most unsuspecting of vessels.

Whichever version of Barbara's life was staged on that steamy July day—and we shall see below that there is ample evidence that it was the *spoken*, not the silent version[14]—this was a saint's life packed with tortures of a positively perverse sexuality. Members of the audience would have had every reason to weep as Barbara was subjected to the ordeal of being "bound to a stake, beaten, burnt, and deprived of her breasts, rolled in a nail-studded barrel, and dragged over a mountain by the hair before [her] final execution" (*TMA*, 177). One can only begin to imagine their growing sense of pathos as Barbara's fate unfolded in a narrative whose actions spoke louder than words. On Day One the pagan girl converts to Christianity through the intervention of the Virgin Mary. On Day Two Barbara is troubled by the demand of her father, Emperor Dyoscorus, that she marry when (like Saint

Catherine) she has vowed to dedicate herself to a life of virginity. By Day Three Provost Marcian is so frustrated by her having designated his gods as *vaines Idoles* that he orders that she be attached to a pillar and scourged.[15] Nor is this an ordinary beating. With a depravity that rivals anything that the notorious Roman emperor Caligula ever dreamed up (or that the Parisian theater of the Grand Guignol *would* dream up in the 1950s), Barbara's own father Dyoscorus looks forward to the spectacle and asks breezily that his supper be brought to him while he watches.[16]

When the punishment continues on Day Four, a nude Barbara is beaten and, later, endures having salt and vinegar applied to her wounds. Her tormentors lead her to prison, command her to sleep upon a bed of sharpened rocks, and mutilate and burn her body (*HTF,* 2:41–45). Consider, now, the order to "cut off her breasts from her body" and to display Barbara "naked from head to toe" throughout the town.[17] How horrible, how wonderful it must have been for the widow of Saulnière to see the body of the beardless and breastless Lyonard suffering Barbara's humiliation and mortification. Lyonard could rise to the occasion still more beautifully since he had no breasts to begin with, his real body a visible scenic memory of what his character had once undergone. When Barbara's father himself orders on Day Five that she be rolled on the enormous nail studded barrel before her decapitation (which Dyoscorus performs personally, as in figure 1),[18] Metz's audience—unlike the titillated Grand Guignol crowds—was weeping. By the chronicler's account, Lyonard really was *that* good. He was so good that he inspired later critics to rehabilitate some of their harsh judgments about the numbed sensibilities of medieval audiences.

Petit de Julleville, for one, was alarmed that medieval dramatists habitually amplified Christ's tortures to a point that far surpassed his original ordeal (*LM,* 1:375), while Gustave Cohen found that the extremely realistic staging of torture was pathologically enjoyed by all comers (*HMS,* 148–49). Quite to the contrary, Raymond Lebègue thought that our heartwarming tale of Metz redeemed those hard-hearted souls: "These tears may rehabilitate somewhat the episodes that modern readers judge repugnant" (*TRF,* 6).[19] But Lebègue may have missed something in those tears—something of which he might not necessarily have approved. The lovely lady from Saulnière was not the only audience member to have been stimulated by Lyonard's rendition of Barbara, for whose noble maidenhead the Angel Gabriel had been dispatched personally to come to the rescue. Also in attendance was another compassionate soul who devised his own version of how to come to the rescue of the maidenly barber. The widow's competitor came forward in the form of man who was supposedly acting upon the noblest of intentions, a priest: "Nevertheless, there was among the others, a lord canon of the great church

Figure 1. The Martyrdom of Saint Barbara. Munich, Staatliche Graphische Sammlung, Lehrs 163.

by the name of Master Jehan Chardelly, who was also a cantor, and a most learned man of letters. He conceived such a great love for the lad that the boy was delivered to him."[20]

If there were odd dimensions to the widow of Saulnière's excitement about the fate of Lyonard as Barbara, then the sentiments of Jehan de Chardelly are even more difficult to gauge. Barbara's ordeal of Day Four, for example, could scarcely have been more phallic when she was rolled on sharpened sword blades at the same time that Marcian's heart continued to *harden*—and was perhaps not the only bodily organ to do so.[21] It must have been passing strange when Barbara extended her limbs *(membres)* and invited her father to eat of them. *Membre* had several meanings. It denoted synecdochally a *member* (like a right hand) of any feudal community, which is, in a sense, the true subject of Lyonard's story. Eventually, *membre* would also refer unambiguously to the male virile *member:*

> Come, wretch, and take a little bite
> if you have got the appetite.
> My limbs *[membres]* are roasted through and through
> Just right for dipping. Why don't you
> Go have them served up right away . . . ?[22]

Had Henry de la Tour's "Catherine" been playing Barbara that day, who knows what pleasurable dinners he might have imagined being prepared in his kitchen as his wife prepared to serve herself up for dessert?[23] But as far as the wealthy widow and the learned Jehan were concerned, here was a young man, possessed of a virile member, talking about his *membres* as he was tortured while representing a woman. This performance of the *Play of Saint Barbara* thus calls attention to the very thing that the Metz production was meant to hide: the question of Lyonard's questionable sexuality.[24] Just as the widow might have been attracted to "Barbara" as much as to Lyonard, so too might the priest have been attracted to Lyonard as much as to "Barbara."

Our text is silent on the subject of just how Lyonard came to be "delivered" to Jehan Chardelly. Presumably, Master Hannes was involved in the decision since Lyonard had been living in his charge. But Lyonard was indeed delivered to the "man of letters," who then arranged to have him brought up in his own image. Lyonard, gesturally expert in the theatrical art of image making, was to dedicate himself to the priesthood. And there was no place like Paris for an ecclesiastical education, in which Lyonard is said to have excelled in all things: "[Jehan de Chardelly] placed the boy in school where he learned more in one year than others do in ten; and later, he sent him to Paris to study, where, after a short time, he was received and accepted as Master of Arts."[25] Lyonard was given over, not to a mother (lusty or otherwise), but to a spiritual father (lusty or otherwise). If anything, the lonely widow of Saulnière emerges as a potential impediment to his education.[26]

If, however, the widow wanted a son, a lover, or a son *and* a lover, then perhaps

Jehan Chardelly wanted the same thing. His attraction to the barber "Barbara" is just as questionable and just as rife with repressed sexuality as that of the widow. True, he did not produce a marriage in the same way that the perverted Nero did when he reportedly wed his freedman Doryphorus, "going so far as to imitate the cries and lamentations of a maiden being deflowered" ("Nero," *LC*, 2:chap. 29). But Jehan de Chardelly married off Lyonard to Jesus Christ in an atmosphere of sexuality that was just as blatant. He simply called it "education."

Even if we would not go so far as to say that Jehan's attraction to a seductive actor in drag (or the widow's to "Barbara") served as kind of "outing" for all concerned, there is no doubt that, at the end of our story, it is the two men who have bonded. So, to those who might object that it was completely routine for medieval men to recite such speeches, one could still counter that this text mythologizes something that was genuinely unusual: Lyonard's deliverance to a man, not to a woman, as result of his acting. Two men form a couple at the end of this story for having sublimated, if not their sexuality per se, then at least their *theater*, in favor of the Church. Lyonard has distinguished himself in his studies and done his new father (or fathers) proud. Once welcomed by Metz as a German barber's apprentice, and later, by the prestigious intellectual community of Paris as one of its own, he ends his days by honoring his adoptive home with the ultimate role. With the decidedly non-Germanic name of Lyonard, he returns to Germany with all the fruits of his Paris education: "And since that time, I have seen him regent and schoolmaster at Saint-Savior in Metz; and afterward, I saw him become a canon at Notre Dame d'Aix and celebrate the high office."[27] The effeminate lad apparently followed in the footsteps of Margarita, leaving the stage behind to pursue a life characterized by the very "prudence and devotion" he had ostensibly played so well in 1485.[28] "Father" Lyonard not only assimilated to French culture but became a spokesman for it in his original homeland. In other words, if theater helped Metz to colonize Lyonard, Lyonard returned the favor when, as a new member of the French Christian fraternity, he brought a chauvinistically superior French education to Germany's pulpit.[29]

What did Lyonard think about all this? Funny thing—we never even hear his voice. Our chronicler initially leaves some doubt as to whether the Messins *themselves* heard it or if they merely *saw* another mimed version of Barbara's story *sans parleir*.[30] Jacomin Husson never mentions him at all, saying only that the *Play of Saint Barbara* was performed "triumphantly in the Place de Chambre and had been very well played."[31] Lyonard's silence and the narrator's ambiguity are, in many ways, the most interesting aspect of the story. They handily dispense with both the question of language—was it French or German?—and the question of

Lyonard's own sexual propensities.[32] Having forsaken theater for the French Church, what or whom did Lyonard desire more: the widow, the Church, or the priest? (Here the story's logic ensures that any transgressive desires would not have been of French origin anyway: they were German.)[33]

So everyone lives happily ever after—everyone except the widow of Saulnière. Lyonard is a cantor and maybe Jehan has pursued further recruiting efforts for fresh Christian blood for the priesthood at home and abroad. Meanwhile, the story serves up some hearty laughs at the wealthy widow's expense: laughs that targeted the expenses she herself was willing to accrue in order to have a pretty young companion as her heir. *Anything*—even being a priest—was better than her company! The question, as always, is: could any or all of this be true?

Lyonard's life certainly makes sense as one of those great "false-true" tales that would carry an urban legend's admonition along these lines: "Beware foreigners in your town and on your stage, unless you can assimilate them."[34] "Watch out for older ladies with money to spare and with the power to corrupt as much as theater does." "Beware, lest such a woman lead you away from your Christian vocation." There is something else to ponder, though, before we rest on this ambiguously happy ending.

If the story of Lyonard's triumph of July 1485 is true, then what was he doing back on Metz's stage barely one year later, playing Saint Catherine of Mount Sinai?

> In the aforesaid year [1486], during the three feasts of Pentecost, there was performed in Metz on the Place de Chambre, the Mystery of the life and passion of the glorious [virgin and martyr], Catherine of Mount Sinai, daughter of the king of Alexandria. During this play, the previously mentioned Lyonard played the part of Saint Catherine: he had been Saint Barbara in the preceding year; and he acquitted himself marvelously well.[35]

There is no doubt about it: Lyonard was still on stage. His presence there is confirmed in the memoirs of one of our more meticulous commentators, the avid theatergoer Philippe de Vigneulles. Philippe, moreover, still refers to Lyonard as a barber, not a student:

> At this time, the *Play of Saint Catherine of Mount Sinai* was performed in the Place de Chambre; and I had been summoned to be present there when the play was scheduled to be performed during the Pentecost holidays in the year 1486. And this play was very well performed with impressive effects; and our Saint Catherine was played by a young barber's apprentice, native to Notre-Dame d'Aix in Germany, who already, the previous year, had played Saint Barbara in the *Play of Saint Barbara,* and over the course of three days he played his role so well that it was impossible to do better.[36]

If Lyonard had, in fact, run off to Paris with Jehan de Chardelly, then why was he now back on stage? It is dubious that, once in Paris, he would have kept a part-time acting job while commuting back and forth from Paris to Metz, a distance of over two hundred miles.[37] Our story has a perfectly logical answer to this question that, happily, coincides precisely with the chronology of one year.

When the chronicler of Metz noted that Lyonard "learned more *in one year* than others do in ten" (*CVM*, 473), this might not have been hyperbole. Rather, it might well have been the duration of the preparatory education that Lyonard received locally in Metz *before* going on to the University of Paris. Lyonard could easily have played Barbara in the spring of 1485 and Catherine in 1486 before packing up his things to begin his clerical education. Philippe de Vigneulles says he did just that: "The aforesaid Chardely placed him forthwith in the best school in Metz. . . . This lad's intelligence was disposed to all. And at the end of the year, the aforesaid Chardely put him in school in Paris" (*CPV*, 3:114). This implies that Master Hannes must have been one understanding mentor. It is doubtful that Metz's *collège* had a work-study program in acting, so no matter how quick on the uptake Lyonard was at school, he could not have had much spare time to learn his lines *and* work as a barber. Perhaps Lyonard took the widow up on her generous offer for a time, only to dump her later. Perhaps he wanted to make a year's worth of pocket money to buy the occasional ale in Paris. Perhaps, in light of Lyonard's popularity, his local teachers were strangely indulgent about the theatrical career he was meant to disavow. Perhaps, however, he had other reasons to leave the theater behind.

In 1486, there were apparently no more offers for Lyonard, financial, ecclesiastical, or marital. Nothing of the sort. One of the other chroniclers of Metz diverges from Philippe de Vigneulles when he tells us that in 1486 Lyonard's Catherine absolutely paled by comparison to his Barbara. This time, the girlish actor was unable to perform to expectation: "But, nevertheless, this mystery [of Saint Catherine] was not quite so pleasing to the people nor to all the listeners as had been that of Saint Barbara. For the aforesaid Lyonard's voice had already started to change a little bit. And, along with that, neither the speeches nor the rhetoric of his character were as well couched nor as moving [piteable]."[38] First of all, this later account indicates that Lyonard had indeed *spoken* well during the 1485 performance of *Saint Barbara*, since our commentator takes great pains to describe his verbal rhetoric (and it is difficult to imagine rhetorical ornamentation without verbal language). Second, we are now in a position to understand fully why Lyonard would have excelled in his studies. As the second account makes clear, he had had numerous lines to learn as both Barbara and Catherine. He thus possessed that skill so crucial in the life of a medieval university student (or in the lives of actors, liars, and tellers of urban legends): an excellent memory.[39] Yet as this new event resolves several mysteries, it creates others.

If the performance was not up to snuff, then why did Phillipe de Vigneulles praise Lyonard to the skies? It may have something to do with the presence of what Petit de Julleville deemed "curious personal details" (*LM*, 2:53). Philippe delighted in being mistaken in public for Lyonard—so much so that he counted such occurrences: "at that time, I myself resembled this lad so well that people mistook me for him seventeen times, and because of that, this lad loved me well, and always wanted me to be one of his ladies in waiting during this particular play."[40] Born in 1471, Philippe de Vigneulles was fifteen years old in 1486, and young and pretty himself. He enjoyed the homoerotic confusion that attended Lyonard as he too "attended" him and as that confusion carried over into a real life in which Lyonard "loved him well." In fifteenth-century philology, a man "loving another well" was not exactly tantamount to a proclamation of queer sensibilities, even when one of the men was in drag.[41] But Philippe's silence in the *Gedenkbuch* is nothing if not pregnant with possibilities. If he ignored the breathtaking events of 1468, in which Henry de la Tour fell for Saint Catherine, it was with good reason, for Philippe was only three years old at the time.[42] But why did he omit the equally stunning tale of the 1485 *coup de foudre* of the widow of Saulnière and Jehan de Chardelly for Lyonard?

Maybe he was silent because it didn't happen—or because he didn't *see* it happen. Then again, maybe the pretty Philippe was jealous of a man (Jehan de Chardelly), if not a woman (the widow of Saulnière), who loved Lyonard even better than *he* did. Philippe goes on to clarify his feelings in the very passage that Petit de Julleville elects *not* to cite: "my heart was elsewhere; and I had resolved in those days that I would run off with my [other] friend *[mon compaignon]* and that we would leave Metz secretly, as I have already said."[43] As Philippe dreamed during his young and nubile runaway days of his own happy ending with a different male friend, he might have been less interested in a happy ending either *with* Lyonard or *for* him. When the actor presumably *did* leave town, he did so with a man who sported an aristocratic particle just like Philippe's (*de* Vigneulles): Jehan *de* Chardelly.

In the end, Philippe's rosy view reveals more about Philippe than about Lyonard's Catherine, which by our other chronicler's account fell short in the eyes of many. Something went wrong with his pentecostal performance of 1486. Something went wrong, moreover, at a time when training in rhetoric would normally have *helped,* not harmed, his theatrical delivery—unless, of course, he was too distracted by his studies to learn and practice his lines as before.[44] That something lies not in his delivery but in his person.

Anywhere from eighteen to thirty-eight years earlier, the citizens of Metz had purportedly wept with compassion as Henry de la Tour took a skinny wife, an event that could scarcely have been effaced from their communal memory.[45] They later showered all manner of praise and privileges upon the barber's apprentice in 1485. And yet these same Messins who had so warmly praised the lad's Barbara were unmoved in 1486. They were unmoved by the story of Catherine of Mount Sinai, which related tortures so horrible that there was plenty to weep for. A quick glance at her verse Life gives a good idea of what they might have seen:

> The tyrant becomes enraged.
> He calls for his servants
> And orders that she be disrobed.
> Divested of her clothes, naked,
> She is to be whipped with thorny branches.
> The servants obey willingly.
> They tear her tender flesh.[46]

By the same token, the maid's final agony, as preserved in the *Golden Legend*, was rife with any number of potential moments of pathos. A special instrument of torture made of "four wheels studded with iron saws and sharp-pointed nails" was fashioned for Catherine, upon which

> the virgin [was to be] torn to pieces with these horrible instruments, thus terrorizing the rest of the Christians with the example of so awful a death. It was further ordered that two of the wheels should revolve in one direction and the other two turn in the opposite direction, so that the maiden would be mangled and torn by the two wheels coming down on her, and chewed up by the other two coming against her from below. (*GL*, 2:338)[47]

But Catherine's was also the story of a smart and strong-minded lass who was loyal to Christ and who held her own against the tyrannical Emperor Maxentius (*GL*, 2:334–36). In the hagiographic version of her life, for instance, she triumphed over fifty pagan scholars and boldly pronounced: "I fear none of the tortures / That you might make me endure."[48] In 1486 Lyonard held his own against a Christian audience with only partial success. For some of the spectators, Catherine had come to resemble a tad too closely the intelligent *lad* playing her. Habituated to a very high level of realism, Metz's audience found Lyonard's inevitable signs of puberty to be distracting enough to compromise the most broadly suspended disbelief in the service of belief.

Ultimately, if Lyonard's story ended well for the French priesthood at several levels, it had an especially sad ending for theater. Traditionally, both Christian and pre-Christian polemicists had targeted the histrionic and effeminate gestures of actors, orators, and even priests. Tertullian had complained bitterly about the "filth" of the pantomime, and Quintilian before him, about "the lascivious melodies of our effeminate stage . . . [which have] to no small extent destroyed such manly vigour as we still possessed."[49] To the implicit delight of the ecclesiastical community of Metz, a gifted actor left the theater for the Church. He left not because he was too effeminate but because he was too masculine: not because he could impersonate women brilliantly but because he *couldn't*—except when under the passionate scrutiny of the likes of Philippe de Vigneulles. In 1485 Lyonard's histrionic gift was morally suspect to ecclesiastics and delightful to audiences. By 1486 that gift had been compromised by the onset of his virility. Lyonard was no longer effeminate enough to play young women for the pleasure of men and women alike. He was now, however, at the ideal stage to become a *man* of the Church. Forsaking the theater, he could "go straight"—or straight into an ecclesiastical world with queer sensibilities of its own.[50] A foreigner became a job holder, and an effeminate German became a masculine Frenchman manly enough to be a priest.

In the nineteenth century Jacob Larwood arrived at the optimistic conclusion that "the constant acting of female parts does not appear to have in the least destroyed the energy, grandeur, and manliness of the style of these old actors" (*TA*, 38–39). For Lyonard, manliness eventually took over and killed the women inside him. In their stead, it created a priest. But in a world whose lusty crowds had been consistently indicted for poor moral values by ecclesiastics who thought they knew better, Metz's once unanimously appreciative audience lost their favorite actor to the Church. They lost him because of their own intolerance of one very specific intrusion of real life into Lyonard's acting: his virility. They were unforgiving of his new manhood at the same time that the Church welcomed with open arms a real man of the cloth. As Barbara, Lyonard had seduced the widow of Saulnière and the cleric Jehan de Chardelly. As Catherine, he failed with the audience but triumphed with the Church. He could now serve that Church, not with his vice-ridden prior effeminacy but with his new manhood. Lyonard could also take his French-grown manhood back to his native Germany, where he may even have taken other transitional souls under his wing.

Putting aside the emotional state of the rejected widow (as our story does so nimbly), the big loser here is the audience. Theirs was a lose-lose situation that would have been music to ecclesiastical ears. The theatergoers of Metz renounced their favorite son and favorite female impersonator as they simultaneously ratified the Church's self-fulfilling prophecy about the people's attraction to filth, obscenity, and effeminacy. Not only did they forfeit their effeminate charmer, they forfeited him through their own shortcomings and through a rapacity for realism for which they had only themselves to blame. Not everyone was as forgiving as Bertolt Brecht, who wrote of the great variety of theatrical experiences that "we must always remember that the pleasure given by representations . . . hardly ever depended on the representation's likeness to the thing portrayed. . . . Even today we are happy to overlook such inaccuracies if we can get something out of the spiritual purifications of Sophocles or the sacrificial acts of Racine or the unbridled frenzies of Shakespeare."[51] Lyonard's audience was as unhappy as the Church was happy. They lent a queer new wrinkle to the Austinian category of the "unhappy performative," in that not everything was forgiven.[52]

Once again, a happy ending is not so happy after all. Indeed, theater's happily-ever-after had long been associated with the threat of a frightening forever.

Of Madness and Method Acting

If men define situations as real, they are real in their consequences.
—W. I. Thomas

One of the earliest theatrical anecdotes to come down to us is from ancient Greece, recorded by the second-century writer and satirist, Lucian of Samosata. Once upon a time, there was a famous actor who, in the midst of imitating the madness of Ajax, gave every indication that he had actually gone mad. Having longed to dazzle his audience with the ultimate representation of defeat, he was himself defeated during a performance that was both too tangible and too intangible:

> By some ill-luck, I know not what, he wrecked his fortunes upon an ugly bit of acting through exaggerated mimicry. In presenting Ajax going mad immediately after his defeat, he so overleaped himself that *it might well have been thought that instead of feigning madness he was himself insane;* for he tore the clothes of one of the men that beat time with the iron shoe, and snatching a flute from one of the accompanists, with a vigorous blow he cracked the crown of *Odysseus,* who was standing near and exulting in his victory; indeed, if his watch-cap had not offered resistance and borne the brunt of the blow, poor Odysseus would have lost his life through falling in the way of a crazy dancer.[1]

Lucian's is the story of an accidental death that *almost* occurs (that of "Odysseus") owing to an unexpected piece of theatrical psychosis that *does* occur. It is a performance of madness that is so much on the mark that the actor himself winds up off the mark. It is a performance that bears an eerie resemblance to the philosophical scenario imagined by J. L. Austin in which a man pretending to be a hyena overreaches himself by taking a real bite out of someone's leg. Austin comments that "when something claimed to be pretending is ruled out by reason of 'going too far,' this will commonly mean something such as 'going beyond what was socially permissible on that occasion' rather than 'slipping into doing the actual thing'" (*PP*, 213). That is precisely Lucian's point when he complains about the "bad taste" of mimes who "exceed the due limit of mimicry and put forth greater effort than they should."[2] At the same time, however, Ajax "slips." Austin concludes that "this sort of thing in these circumstances will not pass as '(only) pretending to be a hyena.' True—but then neither will it pass as *really being* a hyena" (*PP*, 204; original emphasis). In our present story, "Ajax" seems really to be mad.

Situated somewhere between the illusions and realities experienced by the mad actor and the audience whom he confused, terrorized, or amused, Lucian's story sports a warning about a very special type of "representation anxiety," to say nothing of "performance anxiety" (a term taken over by pop psychologists). If an actor play-acts at anything too well, then his play becomes "the real thing." He does so not for better but for worse—not even for better *or* for worse, as with Monsieur and Madame Henry de la Tour, or for better *and* for worse, as with Lyonard. This is a legend which threatens that an act of impersonation has the power to alter reality so drastically that, quite literally, it may hit an actor, an "Odysseus," or a spectator over the head with it. As "Ajax" runs amok in the senatorial benches, he incarnates the extreme and irreparable dangers theater has eternally been said to pose to actors' careers and to their very lives. "Beware theatrical emotion, lest it become the real thing." "Beware lest theatrical verisimilitude awaken the sleeping germ of madness or, for that matter, plant it." "Beware the actor who ceases to be himself, or who ceases to be altogether."[3]

If this an urban legend—and the evidence below will suggest that it is—it certainly *sounds* believable enough. An unnamed actor is so anxious to resemble the real thing that he mistakenly steps over some kind of invisible line that separates illusion from reality and, in his case, madness from sanity. Nor do we ever learn the actor's name—perhaps because he was so famous that no reminder was needed or perhaps because he never existed. The tale would ring true for any contemporary actor familiar with the "curse of *Macbeth*," long rumored to wreak such havoc with real thespians that they dare not speak the name of "the Scottish play."[4] It would sound logical to anyone familiar with actor Nick Nolte's decision to live on the streets "homeless" for a time, the better to portray a bum in *Down and Out in Beverly Hills*.[5] And, closer to the middle-class home of the typical urban legend demographic,[6] it would seem plausible to any American who had played the 1970s board-game called *Group Therapy*. One player, having been invited by the card she had drawn to "scream 'yes' or 'no'" until it felt comfortable to stop, wound up having what was called in those days a "nervous breakdown," winning the game but losing her mind.[7]

Similarly, our story manages in one fell swoop to bridge any apparent philosophical gulf between classical antiquity, medieval performance practice, and the modern work of J. L. Austin and Stanley Cavell. For example, in the celebrated story of the yokel who rushes onstage to stop Othello from murdering Desdemona (played by Mrs. Siddons), Cavell underscores the insufficiency of any endeavor, critical or otherwise, to separate actor from character:

> You can say there are two women, Mrs. Siddons and Desdemona, both of whom are mortal, but only one of whom is dying in front of our eyes. But what you have produced is two names. Not all the pointing in the world to *that* woman will distinguish the one woman from the other. The trouble can be put two ways; or, there are two troubles and they pull opposite ways: you can't point to one without pointing to the other; and you can't point to both at the same time. (*MWM*, 328; original emphasis)[8]

Nor can Lucian point to one without pointing to the other when he refers to "Odysseus" instead of "the actor playing Odysseus"—although, if we agree with Cavell, he *could not* have done so.[9] Lucian simply states that the life of "poor Odysseus" was at risk—not that of the imperiled actor charged with the role.[10] Nor could spectators at a splendid pretheatrical procession in late fifteenth-century Seurre point to the men costumed as devils without pointing to the devils themselves. For André de la Vigne, the actors were positively "possessed" by their roles well before they took to the stage: "And it must be noted that there was such a great procession that when God and His Angels left the said place riding behind the others, *the Devils were already beyond the prison tower*."[11] Nor can we point today to the mad actor without pointing to Ajax.

In all these cases, however, and despite Cavell's assertion, we can indeed point (with a certain phenomenological discomfort) to both actor and character at the same time. In the story of Ajax, our unfortunate actor *is* both at the same time, fusing two identities that most spectators wish to keep separate. We *can* and we *can't* point to the truth without pointing to a lie because, in this false-true tale, "Ajax" is living a true lie on stage. Almost a millennium later this true lie came to be associated with the technique pioneered by Constantin Stanislavski known as "method acting."[12] Even if there never was an "Ajax," he embodies the very question raised of the Stanislavski Method by Robert Lewis: was it method or madness?[13]

When Stanislavski's *An Actor Prepares* first appeared in English translation in 1936, one of its most striking recommendations was that actors forego "mechanical acting [which] makes use of worked-out stencils to replace real feelings" (*AP,* 29). Instead, method actors were to ensure affective authenticity by living, becoming, *being* their characters. As they tapped their real lives in order to convert and reconvert personal experience into scenic reality, they would also come to believe in the truths that were, for them, *self*-evident because they themselves had *created* them. Theatrical "truth" *seemed* real because it *was* "real," and it *seemed* believable because it *was* believable, having emerged from the truth that was personal memory.[14] A first truth was thus "created automatically and on the plane of actual fact": that of real people engaged in such real activities as looking earnestly for a comrade's lost wallet (*AP,* 127–30). A second one was "to feel and to create a scenic truth in which you can believe while you are on the stage" (*AP,* 128). That scenic truth far surpassed good old Aristotelian verisimilitude, by which "a convincing impossibility is preferable to that which is unconvincing though possible."[15] The emotions behind it were so powerful that actors and audiences alike could all too easily *keep* believing it once they had left the stage.

So far, so good. But why, then, wasn't it so good for "Ajax"?

Stanislavski's was a vision of the actor's total fusion with his or her character— a deliberate effort to create what "Ajax" had created only accidentally. Moreover, one of the byproducts of the Stanislavski method was a legendary fear that when method actors "became" their characters, they had a tendency to move precariously close to the madness that accompanies a loss of self.[16] Stanislavski's very terminology even smacks suspiciously of the dime-store definition of insanity or the inability to distinguish an external "real life" from interior mental life: "Of significance to us is: the reality of the inner life of a human spirit in a part and a belief in that reality. We are not concerned with the actual naturalistic existence of what surrounds us on the stage, the reality of the material world!" (*AP,* 129).[17] More curiously still, it sounds like the condition of insanity set forth by the medieval theologian Jean Gerson (1363–1429). "Abnormal ideas which dwell in the mind," he wrote, "may become so embedded, so deeply rooted by a mania, insanity, or neurosis, that *eventually, they will be considered true;* thus one will think that he hears, sees, or touches something which is not perceived by an external sense."[18] Although Gerson was differentiating between faith and fancy, he effectively described the psychic pathology that may accompany any theatrical suspension of disbelief in favor of "make-believe."[19] In other words, if Bruce Wilshire believes that "art is controlled delirium" (*RPI,* 218), there was nothing so terribly controlled about the boundless delirium of "Ajax."

It was all very well to draw for drama an aesthetic line in the sand that was invisible but believable. Stanislavski drew one to separate true from false, good from bad, theater from life when he urged: "Never lose yourself on the stage. Always act in your own person, as an artist. You can never get away from yourself. The moment you lose yourself on the stage marks the departure from truly living your part and the beginning of exaggerated false acting" (*AP*, 177). But this was the same line that "Ajax" had so tragically or tastelessly crossed. It was the line that Quintilian sought to efface in the law courts when he drew an explicit analogy to the stage: "I have often seen actors, both in tragedy and comedy, leave the theatre still drowned in tears after concluding the performance of some moving role" (*IO*, VI.2.35).[20] It was the line that Geoffrey of Vinsauf blurred in the thirteenth century when he recommended in his *Poetria nova* that a poet wishing to convey anger should "arise a voice full of gall, a face enraged, and turbulent gestures. Outer motion follows the inner, and the outer and inner man are equally moved. If you play this part, what shall you, the speaker, do? Imitate genuine fury."[21] It was the line crossed by Mrs. Siddons herself when she purportedly attributed her success playing the tragic Constance to the power to "*have transfused the mind of the actress into the person and situation* of the august and afflicted."[22] So it was that, centuries before Stanislavski, early theorists had already come to the conclusion that in many kinds of public performance "the prime essential for stirring the emotions of others is . . . first to feel those emotions oneself" (*IO*, VI.2.26). At the most, modernists might fault Quintilian for being concerned with the *appearance of sincerity* (*IO*, VI.2.27) or for espousing a practical agenda (winning the case) over an artistic one. Nevertheless, these various quests for "true appearances" didn't ruffle Stanislavski or his American followers like Lee Strasberg and Richard Schechner. The latter recalls, for instance, that for all its anomalies, the "admirable" goal of Stanislavski's affective memory was "to represent 'real,' true, or 'sincere' emotion on stage."[23]

My own point here is that, if modern aesthetic theory has taken oh-so-seriously the theatrical methodology envisioned by Stanislavski, then early dramatic theory needs to be taken just as seriously. What is respectable in the mouth of Mrs. Siddons ought to be respectable in the mouth of Quintilian. Plainly, we have in "Ajax" a man whose mind is "transfused" with that of his mad character. So, if Wilshire contends of drama that "'broken hearts' neither maim nor mend, but cease to be when the curtain falls and the mind turns from their contemplation" (*RPI*, 262), the damaged mind of the actor playing Ajax could *not* turn away. Completely in sync with his character, he was performing a strictly "true appearance" of madness without artifice. Perhaps he was no longer sane enough to know if he was acting or not, whereas there had doubtless been a more lucid moment earlier that day when he had planned merely to impersonate Ajax. Now, however, "Ajax" had lost his "collective" mind and failed to perceive the consequences of *their* actions. Whatever the truth of the matter, his theatrical situation appears to have been just as confusing for the audience. For if an actor could not be sure of what was happening to *him*, then how was an audience to ascertain what was happening to him or to *them?*

Consider Jean Baudrillard's scenario in which a prankster decides to simulate a theft at a department store. The ersatz thief goes through all the motions, including slipping his booty inside his jacket and preparing to leave the store. The only difference is that he lacks the criminal intent to steal and stops just short of doing so. Baudrillard maintains that observers cannot tell the difference between the real and simulated thefts because "the signs incline neither to one side nor the other" (*SW,* 178). Nor, after 11 September 2001, do they incline to one side or the other when airport security guards seek the signs of terrorism and gallows humor seems bitterly inappropriate. Nor did they incline to one side or the other for Lucian's audience. As Baudrillard puts it, "feigning or dissimulating leaves the reality principle intact: the difference is always clear, it is only masked; whereas simulation threatens the difference between 'true' and 'false', between 'real' and 'imaginary'" (*SW,* 168). Lucian's mad actor threatened so well that his audience could no longer differentiate between simulated madness and real madness, simulated hazards and real hazards. Were they viewing the truth of a dramatic falsehood or the falsehood of a dramatic truth?

Insanity can be moving, thought-provoking, funny, or frightening, as in so many urban legends about escapees from asylums.[24] For Lucian's audience, it was all those things as the spectacle of "Ajax" "caused some to marvel, some to laugh, and some to suspect that perhaps in consequence of his overdone mimicry he had fallen into the real ailment."[25] As far as the gigglers were concerned, they shamefully demonstrated what Plato had once predicted of audience laughter: "if in comic representations, or for that matter in private talk, you take intense pleasure in buffooneries that you would blush to practise yourself, and do not detest them as base, you are doing the same thing as in the case of the pathetic."[26] Meanwhile, instead of chuckling, the spectators in the pit "all went mad with Ajax, leaping and shouting and flinging up their garments; for the riff-raff, the absolutely unenlightened, took no thought for propriety and could not perceive what was good or what was bad, but thought that sort of thing consummate mimicry of the ailment." Other attendees felt themselves to be at risk, including two ex-consuls who "were very much afraid that he would seize one of them and drub him, taking him for a wether!" They were not wrong to be afraid—for "Odysseus," for the actor, and for themselves in that the crazy dancer had compromised any supposed safety of theatrical distance.[27] They were genuinely in danger and not in the *appearance* of danger.

Still other spectators found such histrionic excess to be in such poor taste that they offered up applause to remind everyone that this was *supposed* to be theater. Since "Ajax" seemed an actor no longer, they drew upon their *politesse* to advertise their own superior understanding of a tacky theatrical failure: "The politer sort understood, to be sure, and were *ashamed* of what was going on, but instead of censuring the thing by silence, they themselves *applauded to cover the absurdity of the dancing*, although they perceived clearly that what went on came from the madness of the actor, not that of Ajax."[28] In an interesting reversal of actor and audience, the judicious few correctly judged that an actor had failed in his duty to represent insofar as he was truly mad. Consequently, they themselves provided the playacting by performing not their true feelings but a simulation of appreciation through insincere applause.[29] "Ajax," one of the first method actors (in spite of himself), made nonmethod actors of his audience. As realistic acting becomes real, spectatorship becomes acting.

At this point, the second admonishment of the legend of Ajax makes its most powerful appearance. "Beware a theater that imperils the sanity not only of actors but of audiences." "Beware lest it place *you*, the audience, not only in psychic but in physical danger." This is a legend that, if not going quite so far as to warn that physical violence is contagious, certainly warns that theatrical insanity is catching. It warns very clearly that theater poses a real psychic and physical threat to its audiences—a warning borne out not only by the frightened ex-consuls but by "Ajax"'s fellow actor "Odysseus," who experiences not a perceived crisis but a real one.[30] That is to say that if "Ajax" no longer knew what he was doing on stage, "Odysseus" *did*, believing correctly that a real madman stood before him and surviving his performance only by chance. The allegation that audience response to such potentially lethal effects was mixed only makes matters worse. Things *did* get worse for "Ajax" in the ultimate unhappy ending to his sad story, in which the first legend is ratified by a second one.

According to Lucian, there came another moment when "Ajax" was sane enough to regret his temporary insanity. When his fans later begged him to reprise his role, he responded that "for an actor, it is enough to have gone mad once!" How heartbreaking it must have been when one of his rivals went on to play Ajax's madness "so discreetly and *sanely* as to win praise, since he kept within the bounds of the dance and did not debauch the histrionic art." But, alas, the mad actor's return from temporary madness was itself only temporary. At least, so we learn from that standard opening of so many urban legends, which scarcely inspires confidence in the story's authenticity: "Moreover, the man himself, *they say*, once he had returned to his sober senses, was so sorry for what he had done that he really became ill through distress and in all truth was given up for mad."³¹ An actor's real distress, occasioned by a transient piece of reality-laden theater, became a permanent performance of madness. The insanity he ostensibly play-acted on that fateful day appears in retrospect to have been a woeful reality—in part, because it must already have been there. Had Lucian's actor not experienced some prior mental imbalance, it seems highly unlikely that the theatrical imitation of Ajax would have pushed him over the edge. It seems just as unlikely that theater, by analogy to a hypnotist and his subjects, could have caused him to behave in a way that was completely "out of character." After all, from ancient Greece to off-Broadway, method acting has always been about becoming something that, to a certain extent, one already is. Moreover, storytellers have been remarkably consistent in their portrayals of theater's psychic risks—that once an actor germinates the seed of a genuine emotion, it is difficult to keep it from sprouting. That seed is planted long before a play ever begins, and its persistent offshoots include a slew of legends about theater's madness.

Witness, for instance, the unalterable yet "sudden madness" that allegedly befell the tragic actor Mr. Layfield, who distinguished himself on the eighteenth-century British stage as Iago to Thomas Sheridan's Othello. One night—Jacob Larwood does not say exactly when—he is said to have made this unfortunate slip of the tongue: "Oh, my Lord! beware of jealousy;/It is a green-eyed *lobster*" (*TA*, 107; original emphasis).³² A real-life tragedy immediately ensued: "After this the play could proceed no further. Layfield was at that moment struck with incurable madness, and died somewhat in the manner of Nat Lee, the tragic poet. The above 'green-eyed lobster' was the first instance poor Layfield gave of this dreadful visitation" (*TA*, 107). It might have been the first *visible* instance, but theater clearly crowned years of dormant dementia in a bona fide psychotic episode.

Similarly shrouded in legend is the idiosyncratic life of the actor Junius Brutus Booth (born in London in 1796). "Once while playing Richard at the Park Theatre," reports Larwood, "this lunatic, sword in hand, chased the Richmond of the evening out by the back door of the theatre into the street" (*TA*, 259).³³ On yet another evening in Charleston, Booth is said to have retained the mad rage of Othello after the curtain had gone down. When he returned to his hotel, he apparently mistook his roommate, Tom Flynn, for Iago, intoning "'Villain, be sure thou prove,' with such terrible vehemence that Flynn in self-defence grasped the poker, and struck Booth over the nose, breaking it, and thus marring his noble countenance for ever." But, just as "Odysseus" would not have been wrong to fear "Ajax," Flynn would not have been wrong to fear "Othello" attacking "Iago" (*TA*, 257–59). Larwood then wraps things up with this strange phrase, which suggests that the event was simultaneously improbable and real: "such is one of the improbable versions of this accident, which happened in 1837" (*TA*, 259). Indeed, Booth's own daughter Rosalie was unwilling to confirm or deny it. In her biography of her father, she stated that "the rumours of this melancholy event are so numerous and contradictory, that we never could form a definite conclusion in regard to the occurrence" (*TA*, 259). Presumably, one could look to the marred countenance of Booth himself to prove it, but his distorted features could just have easily proved something else entirely.

Equally distressing was the fate of the eighteenth-century actor, Samuel Reddish, who was reportedly unable to leave behind the hallucinations of Hamlet. Reddish was bald, the story goes, so during the first night of his performance at the Covent Garden Theatre, he was extremely embarrassed when Laertes (played by Whitfield) "made so clumsy a lunge that he struck off the bag-wig of Hamlet, and exposed his bald pate to the laughter of the audience" (*TA*, 214). This accident is said to have caused the unfortunate actor to "wig out," as it were, creating another "lunatic" no longer capable of functioning in society: "The mortification . . . made so strong an impression on his mind that he never appeared on the stage again, and . . . [enter the standard tag-line of urban legends] *I heard*, ended his days in the asylum at York" (*TA*, 214; my emphasis). Again, minus the localized detail that Brunvand has so often touted, this is the same legendary story as Lucian's, whose Ajax never reappeared on stage either and who was also "given up for mad." Furthermore, just as the well-bred theatergoers of ancient Greece simulated their appreciation for "Ajax," so too did a certain journalist from *The Sun* try to assuage the remorse of the poor, dewigged Mr. Reddish. He put on this charitable but perhaps insincere private performance for the institutionalized actor: "In conversing with him in Bedlam, . . . I soothed him by telling him that I was present at the scene, and that, though the accident had a visible effect, the audience knew the fault was wholly to be ascribed to the awkwardness of his competitor."[34] Even that post hoc and verisimilar invention of a possible truth could not restore the actor to sanity.

Is it really plausible that so many actors have carried within their souls the seeds of mental illness? Is it more likely that a large-scale thespian identity crisis has sown those seeds? Or do all these stories amount to one and the same legendary representation anxiety according to which, if one sojourns too long in the world of illusion, the visit will become permanent? The Grand Guignol dramatist André de Lorde thought that "deep down, all of us (or almost all of us) carry inside of us that little grain of sand which, in the twinkling of an eye, can stop dead the entire machinery of reason."[35] But what were the odds that a sane and stable human being with a successful career would move from sanity to perpetual insanity on account of a play? or a silly unmasking or dewigging?

If we believe Stanislavski, the odds were very good. In one of the most affecting sequences of *An Actor Prepares*, he tells the tale of Dasha, who renders hysteria so magnificently that she becomes hysterical. Her director, Tortsov, is unaware of what the improvisational exercise he has planned will induce when he invites the girl to play a grief-stricken mother:

> All during her acting the tears were coursing down her cheeks and her tenderness completely transformed for us the stick of wood she was holding into a living baby. We could feel it inside the cloth that swaddled it. When we reached the moment of the infant's death the Director called a halt for fear of the consequences to Dasha's too deeply stirred emotions.
> We all had tears in our eyes. (*AP*, 151–52)

It is hard to imagine a more apt demonstration of Rainer Maria Rilke's statement that "death is always inside us, like a pregnant woman carrying a dead baby."[36] One of Dasha's comrades was moved by her performance of real emotions to confirm what had previously been only the *rumor* that Dasha herself had lost a child born out of wedlock.

By the same token, another anecdote relates that the actress Mrs. Montford never recovered from her own sense of loss after playing Ophelia for the last time, at the turn of the eighteenth century.[37] Apparently, the lady was quite distressed when a friend of hers, Miss Santlow, married a man whom she had earlier rejected on financial grounds. Mrs. Montford later "gave way to despair, which soon deprived her of her senses" and was taken to London to receive constant medical attention (if not strict confinement). One night, she snuck out of the house to attend a performance of *Hamlet* in which "she had ever been received with rapture as Ophelia." Having hidden patiently in the wings until Ophelia makes her crazed entrance in Act 4, Scene 5, Mrs. Montford "then pushed on to the stage, before the lady who had performed the previous part of the character could come up, and *exhibited a more perfect rendering of madness than the utmost exertions of mimic art could effect. She was, in truth, Ophelia herself,* to the amazement of the performers, and the astonishment of the audience" (*TA*, 55; my emphasis). Here was the perfect type-casting—although it is doubtful that this is what Jean Bouchet had in mind when he counseled the citizens of Issoudun to suit the actor to the role.[38] The lady's madness, moreover, was permanent: "Nature having made this last effort, her vital powers failed her. On going off she exclaimed, 'It is all over!' She was immediately conveyed back to her late place of security, where a few days after, 'Like a lily drooping, she bowed her head and died'"(*TA*, 55).

Judging from these last two stories, one begins to wonder why there is no curse of *Hamlet, Othello,* or just plain Shakespeare. In any event, Mrs. Montford's death is a haunting culmination of any number of insanities with which theater history is replete: tales of actors and audiences who were, literally, "dying to play." Lest the reader fear I am being too dramatic here, a later apocryphal tale provides a handy epigraph—and epitaph—for our next chapter: "Montfleury, a celebrated French tragedian, was one of the greatest actors of his time, for characters of deep pathos. He died of the violent efforts he made in representing *Orestes,* in the 'Andromache' of Racine. . . . 'The man, then, who would know of what I died, let him not ask if it is of the fever, the dropsy, or the gout; but let him know, it is of *the Andromache!*'"[39]

Examples could be multiplied. Jean-Paul Sartre was so moved by the apocryphal life and on-stage death of the English actor Edmund Kean (1787–1833) that he saw in Kean "the Myth of the Actor incarnate. The actor who never ceases acting; he acts out his life itself, is no longer able to recognize himself, no longer knows who he is. And finally is no one."[40] There was the wretched Mr. Jordans, whose "appalling" and "sudden death before the foot-lights" was "too well remembered to bear repetition" (*TA,* 200).[41] And the eighteenth-century British actor Mr. Bond is said to have "closed [his eyes] forever" while playing Lusignan in Voltaire's rather dull *Zaïre,* upon which "the house rung with applause, but finding that he continued a long time in that situation, the audience began to be uneasy and apprehensive" (*TA,* 198).[42] Similarly, when his contemporary, John Palmer, purportedly passed away while playing in *The Stranger,* "the audience supposed for the moment that his fall was nothing more than a studied addition to the part, but on seeing him carried away from the stage, the truth dawned upon them" (*TA,* 199).[43] These audiences were a bit like Lucian's in that there was an instant when both reality and unreality were temporarily held in abeyance. What to do depended on what they were seeing—or *not* seeing.

Did Montfleury really pronounce those words on his sensational deathbed? Maybe, maybe not. Did Kean die on stage? Definitely not. But the lore of urban legends dictates that theater's psychic legacy of fear is real, no matter how apocryphal its origins. And yet, if spectators can sit idly by and watch a play come to an end, presumably they cannot—or *should not*—do so when *life itself* is coming to an end. Indeed, their ability to distinguish a play from the realities of life and death is the very thing that makes it possible for theater and life to continue—or to end. That is the problem posed by our next three chapters, each of which inquires in a different way: What if the Baudrillardian signs *do* incline to one side or the other? What if the difference eventually *does* become clear, but too late? What if perceiving that difference is itself a matter of life and death?

Notwithstanding the elegance of Richard Schechner's definition of theater as "restored" or "twice-performed" behavior, the theatrical behaviors described above *cannot* be restored or repeated. We hope not, at any rate, for the sake of future actors, whose performances would be less encrypted than in the crypt. Meanwhile, the original actors most assuredly cannot repeat their behaviors because they are deceased. Theater has stopped them dead in their tracks at the same moment that another form of ritual repetitiveness arises from their ashes: the urban legend.[44] When theater stops its actors cold, the legends start. It is a jump-start.

Two Priests and the Hand of God

But surly death, offended at his play,
Would not be jok'd with in so free a way.
He, when he mimick'd him, his voice restrain'd,
And made him act in earnest what he feign'd.
        —Pierre Bayle, on the death of Molière

If we are to believe the several chroniclers and numerous theater historians who have circulated the story, a performance of the Passion on Metz's
Place en Change in 1437 was one of the unluckiest events ever. The sultry
days of July ushered in a great day for the city and for its bishop, Conrad
de Bayer de Boppard, who personally oversaw the performance. Since at
that time Duke René (the future king of Sicily) had just been released
from captivity, Petit de Julleville surmises that a distinctive theatrical
effort commemorated his freedom.[1] Noble men and women turned out in
droves to watch. And then it happened:

> In the month of July [1437], there was played in Metz the *Play of the
> Passion of Our Lord Jesus Christ* at the Place en Change. . . . The role of
> God was played by a priest called Father Nicholas de Neuchâtel-en-
> Lorraine who was, at that time, *curé* of Saint Victor's of Metz. And this
> parish priest's life was in grave danger; and he thought that he would
> die upon the wooden cross, for his heart failed him: so much so that he
> would have died had he not been rescued.[2]

If the cases of Lucian's pre-Christian "Ajax" and Cavell's postmodern
yokel have their anxieties (*MWM*, 328), those pale by comparison. Here
was a special effect that, having become standard scenic fare over time,
was now special again. A parish priest impersonating Christ was coming
so close to death that he believed himself to be dying. To borrow a phrase
from Stanislavski, his "true belief" was true: "Truth on the stage is what-

ever we can believe in with sincerity, whether in ourselves or in our colleagues. Truth cannot be separated from belief, nor belief from truth. They cannot exist without each other and without both of them it is impossible to live your part, or to create anything (*AP*, 129)."[3] Father Nicholas was *dying* his part. He could only await the audience's realization of his real jeopardy and hope that it would be seen in time.

What might he have been thinking? Was he so afraid, so moved by incarnating Jesus Christ that he hyperventilated from the challenge? Was his distress due to frenzied piety? to the believability of the story? to its reenactment? Did he fear playing God? or just playing Him poorly? Did his life flash before his eyes as it flashed before those of his audience? Did he fear death—and if so, why? Shouldn't he have trusted more in God than in the props master? Was he worried about confessing his sins and receiving last rites? Would one of those sins have been his presence on stage in the first place? And how could that have been a sin anyway, in a city such as Metz? For Metz would later place such a premium on companion theatrical processions that in 1513 its bishopric would *mandate* the participation of the clergy "under penalty of forfeiting one silver mark" and provide more durable inducements for potential spectators ("forty days of pardons . . . wherefore there was a great crowd of people" [*CMJH*, 285]).[4]

What about the audience? Were they as confused as those who had reckoned with the mad "Ajax"? Were they seeing a flesh-and-blood man—and a priest, no less—who was dying right in front of them? Or was he merely *representing* their dying Savior who, of course, did not really "die"? Nor did Nicholas de Neuchâtel really die: one or more unknown individuals rushed to the scene and saved the priest's life.[5] Unlike his fellow spectators who were watching Father Nicholas die (in all likelihood because they did not *know* he was dying), this unknown savior of the priest and the play peered through the pretense and saw a deadly reality. Accustomed as he probably was to the extensive medieval theatrical repertoire of fake blood, soft clubs, dummies, dolls, and mannequins, he made a split-second decision that he was *not* seeing a special effect. He knew that it was one thing to *represent* a crucifixion. It was quite another thing to *crucify* someone for real—or to *be* crucified.

This was not the *Admont Passion Play*, whose actors were to bring "whips and rods dipped in red paint [so that] when they strike Christ's body it becomes bloody."[6] This was no technical recipe for a good crucifixion, such as that recorded in the fourteenth-century Old Provençal *Quaderno di segreti* calling for "an iron cap, and then some sponges on that iron cap which are all full of vermilion or blood, and then placed atop those sponges will be a false wig."[7] No indeed. This was a more subtle ordeal with nary a mention of bleeding—something that made its deciphement all the more difficult.

Be that as it may, at least one attendee was able to demystify what mystery plays normally take such great pains to mystify: the spectacle of suffering. That was no small feat.

For example, in the Good Friday ceremonies of medieval Brussels, a condemned criminal was ritually pardoned every year in exchange for playing Jesus during a reenactment of his Passion. Frédéric Faber reports that "the imitation even went so far as to simulate the blood that must have flown [from his hands and feet]. That effect was achieved by means of little bladders full of *red liquid* that were attached to his limbs and by which the condemned man was attached to the cross."[8] Then again, Faber's source, Madame Clément, née Hémery, doesn't exactly say that. She refers only to vague "manuscript sources" when invoking the "little bladders full of *blood*" and affirms that "once these were pierced by the nails, they made the spectators believe that the hands and feet of the victim had really been nailed."[9] Modern readers have the luxury of having Faber or Jesse Hurlbut make the determination for them, as when the former concludes that "they simulated the nailing to the cross," and the latter, that "it sounds to me like they faked the nails."[10] The audience on Metz's Place en Change had no such luxury—far from it.

Most likely, the unnamed man (or men) who saved Father Nick in the nick of time held a true belief about the events of the Passion play. But he also held a true belief about its lead actor, and he acted on that belief in a situation that demanded action, in addition to affect. No Cavellian yokel he, this good Samaritan understood that Nicholas was not representing death artfully: he was *dying* artfully.[11] When time was of the essence, this man made correctly the same command decision that the yokel made incorrectly when that yokel assumed that the actress playing Othello's Desdemona was dying. Having earlier suspended his disbelief enough to watch the Passion play, he alone came to the rescue. He alone perceived the urgency with which *somebody*—anybody—needed rapidly to restore a belief in theater's real consequences.[12]

In Erving Goffman's terminology, our good Samaritan was no longer an "onlooker" who "sympathetically and vicariously participate[d] in the unreality onstage" (*FA*, 130). Ordinarily, an onlooker would deem it "perfectly obvious to everyone on and off the stage that the characters and their actions are unreal, but it is also true that the audience holds this understanding to one side and in the capacity of onlookers allows its interest and sympathy to respect the apparent ignorance of the characters as to what will come of them and to wait in felt suspense to see how matters will unfold" (*FA*, 136–37). Refusing to adopt a "wait and see" attitude, he was, instead, a "theatergoer," who is bound to such realities as time, space, money, and, in this case, danger (*FA*, 129–30).[13] When he opted to remove himself from his "organized role" at the theater, he broke frame (*FA*, 350).[14] But his self-removal was the only thing that could remove Nicholas from the cross and ensure the survival of both the priest and his acting career: "And the next day, the aforementioned parish priest of Sainct-Victor was feeling much better, and he accomplished the resurrection and played his role wondrously well. And this mystery play lasted for four days."[15] Furthermore, in breaking frame, he might even have broken an unwritten law about audience intervention. Although he had likely been reared on a diet of theatrical participation, he would probably *not* have expected to participate in quite this way. The twelfth-century audiences of the Fleury Playbook *Herod* might well have been invited *into* the play to adore the Christ child,[16] but the town council of Beauvais issued an edict in 1452 that strictly forbade physical intervention by spectators, especially at a play's opening moments. Specifically, attendees were not to "do anything that is intended to or will have the effect of stopping the players from taking to the platforms and scaffolding."[17]

Critics have usually assessed the tale of Father Nicholas as an example of the rapacious medieval quest for scenic realism, which resulted in an actor being roped too tightly to the cross. That technical error then cut off his circulation and caused mild asphyxia, a heart attack, or sheer exhaustion. Certain medieval roles, infers Petit de Julleville, were "wearisome or even dangerous because of the imprudence of the medieval stagehands [who] were already very bold but still very unskilled."[18] Regardless, however, of whether the events related here occurred precisely as described, this is no simple story of technical ineptitude. It is a complex phenomenological scenario in which a typical special effect gone wrong prompts an atypical behavior gone right. Our good Samaritan demonstrates the limitations of Bruce Wilshire's view that "the actor as artist is living even as he is performing, and he can seek to authentically answer death in his art even if he cannot cancel it" (*RPI*, 225). Someone else—a spectator, for instance—can cancel death *for* him. Except he can only cancel it if he makes the very distinction between realism and reality that both theater and urban legends exist to efface.

Above all, our story poses intriguing problems for anyone trying to make sense of the occasionally unholy alliance between theater and theology.[19] If the events of Metz in 1437 are legendary, it is because they express so poignantly the longstanding anxieties about that alliance, particularly where a histrionic clergy was concerned. While a mystery play presumably promised the hope of an eternal life in recompense for a good terrestrial one, it seems highly unlikely that a priestly actor would expect the arrival of that recompense at the exact moment of his theatrical performance. Yet that is precisely what is at issue. Hans Robert Jauss has argued that medieval Christian literature and art "went about revalorizing the previously negated world of the here and now as a manifestation of God's creation."[20] That "here and now" has always been the province of theater. He further argues that "an art that wished to do justice to the transcendence of the Christian faith had to give the invisible or future and, consequently, unreal truth a degree of certainty in contrast to which all the probabilities of the visible, everyday world would pale into 'as ifs,' if not into delusions." A theatrical performance—especially one staged with graphic realism—was the great "as if." But Father Nicholas's performance was a reality. He survived that day on account of someone's realization that theater was not an "as if" but an "as is." The genre that makes things present presented a disturbing doubt as to whether or not God Himself were also present, presently watching his flock and their shepherds.

For example, when it came time for Christ to speak the words, "My God, my God, why hast thou forsaken me?"[21] there could scarcely have been a more eloquent theatrical exhibition of that abandonment than leaving a priest of Metz to die as God's son. Maybe the kind of priest Nicholas had been on earth had been insufficient to secure him a place in the great hereafter. Maybe it was indeed his priestly heart, and all the heart signified, that failed him because it was in trouble.[22] Maybe, as the citizens from nearby Mons would discover in 1501, there was something profoundly incongruous about putting a priest on stage. One clerical thespian, the learned Jehan de Neelle, had been "a brother in Saint Francis's cloister in this city of Mons." Having accepted the role of God in their *Mystère de la Passion*, he found himself compensated on 22 April for "having thus occupied his time learning the said role, neglecting his usual preaching and other duties, etc.; for which he was duly dispossessed of this said role with just cause, and his part was remanded to Jehan le Francque," another priest.[23] From that standpoint, the story of Father Nicholas would have suited clerical mistrust of the theater very well. In a world where ecclesiastics were suspicious of theater's influence on terrestrial and eternal lives, the legend of Metz was living proof of its dangers to all.

First and foremost among those dangers was the apparent scenic resolution of the theological question of divine embodiment: theater displays mere mortals incarnating the Incarnation.[24] Bert States contends that "the ritual in theater is based in the community's need for *the thing* that transpires in theater and in the designation, or self-designation, of certain individuals who, for one reason or another, consent to become the embodiment of this thing" (*GR*, 157). What happened in Metz in 1437 was not a phenomenologist's metaphor. Spectators witnessed a literal, corporeal, and, most important, a man-made and man-powered embodiment of

Christ's own embodiment as a living—and dying—body. When Nicholas almost died on the cross, he came as close as any man could get on this mortal coil to representing Christ, who almost "died" in his own way. In the beginning, Nicholas might have intended only to *play* at martyrdom. In the end, he was in real danger of being martyred on theater's cross. He too was "forsaken" by God the Father, unless we are to assume that God was acting through the citizen or citizens who came to Nicholas's rescue.

Perhaps those noble citizens even dared to think, as they were hustling Nicholas down, that God was working through *them* to save his priest. Perhaps they were working *against* the will of God by *not* sacrificing Nicholas to His devices. Perhaps they thought nothing of the sort or weren't thinking at all. After all, it was in no way preposterous to imagine that God Himself might be a key player in the production of a religious drama. Jean Bouchet surely thought so when he wished the citizens of Issoudun godspeed on their proposed Passion play: "All goodness comes from him and him alone. / Without his help, man falters on his own."[25] But we are talking here about a *play* put on by men, not by God. This was *Deus*—not *Deus ex machina*. So there is considerably more at stake here than the topos of the poet-creator who mimics divine *logos* by fashioning verses. At stake is the ability of theater or its entrepreneurs to rival God in his power over life and death.

So far, the incidents of Metz in 1437 blatantly contradict any number of contemporary critical commonplaces about the medieval theater. For instance, Gustave Cohen remarks of the entrepreneurs' representation of death that "at the moment of the execution, their habitual method is to replace the actor with his *feinte,* that is, with his fake image or by a simple dummy destined to represent him."[26] No dummies stood in for Father Nicholas in Metz. Elsewhere, William Tydeman asserts more pointedly that when stage directions called for "beheadings, mutilations, burnings, drownings, and other bodily sufferings. . . . human lives plainly *could not* be put at risk."[27] Plainly, they *could* be. More noteworthy still, the Passion play at Metz complicates Cavell's already complicated assertions about Desdemona. "What mistake has the yokel in the theater made," asks Cavell, when he tries to stop Othello?

> He thinks someone is strangling someone.—But that is true; Othello is strangling Desdemona.—Come on, come on; you know, he thinks that very man is putting out the light of that very woman right now.—Yes, and that is exactly what is happening.—You're not amusing. The point is that he thinks something is really happening, whereas nothing is really happening. It's play acting. The woman will rise again to die another night. . . .
>
> You tell me that that woman will rise again, but I know that she will not, that

she is dead and has died and will again die, die dead, die with a lie on her lips, damned with love (*MWM*, 328).

In medieval Metz, Christ will always rise again—but, minus the intervention of some yokel, Nicholas de Neuchâtel will not. Sometimes, a "Desdemona" really *does* desperately require deliverance. Jacob Larwood tells us as much when he relates that that eccentric Junius Brutus Booth once "bore down so heavily with the pillow on the Desdemona that she was in danger of her life, and was only rescued from suffocation by the other actors, who rushed upon the stage to save her" (*TA*, 259). And if readers are skeptical, let them consider the fact that Nicholas's accident was followed by a *second* accident during the same play.

Father Nicholas was feeling much better, thank you. But his colleague playing Judas, one Jehan de Nissey, was about to feel much worse:

> In this same play, there was yet another priest who was called Father Jehan de Nissey, who was a chaplain at Mairange, and he was playing the role of Judas; but because he was hanging too long, consequently, he lost consciousness and was almost dead, because his heart failed. For that reason, he was taken down in great haste [unhanged] and taken to a nearby place so that he could be rubbed with vinegar and other things[s] to casc his pain.[28]

The chronicler doesn't miss a beat. He simply continues his narrative, mentioning in the same breath the *additional* special effects that had no noxious consequences: "The Hell-Mouth of the said play was very well done; for, by means of a device, it opened and closed all by itself when the devils wanted to enter or leave. And this particular face [of the Hell-Mouth] had two great eyes of steel that shone marvelously."[29] This is the same tone he adopts after describing Nicholas's unfortunate accident—following which, from the ranks of the play's torturers and tyrants, another priestly actor was summoned to the stage as a substitute. Our commentator dispassionately discloses that the replacement Christ pulled off the remainder of the scene without a hitch—so calmly, it seems, that it was not worth mentioning his name: "And so it was decided that another priest would be put in his place to complete the role of God; and that priest was at the time one of the executioners and tyrants from this play. But anyway, his role was given to somebody else and he completed the crucifixion scene that day."[30]

Sandwiched between two highly eventful scenes of near-death is a perfectly *uneventful* scene, which almost suggests that a stage effect gone awry is no more and no less interesting than one that hasn't. While, at first glance, this narrative appears to confirm the widespread modern belief that jaded medieval crowds were inured to the ubiquitous sight of death, there were at least some spectators in Metz in 1437 who were not so jaded as to fail to intervene to save the lives of not one but two imperiled priests.[31] Two men of God were struck down and cast out in a play presumably performed in his honor. Two questions remain. If it is reasonable to think that Metz's Passion play featured one potentially fatal mischance, is it also reasonable to accept that the play was jinxed to the point of housing *two* such accidents, one befalling the priest impersonating Christ, the other happening to the one representing his betrayer? Isn't this the stuff that urban legends are made of?

Not really. Urban legends are characterized by numerous localized details, but this Passion play boasts a precision not often seen when it lists the full names of such identifiable people as Nicholas de Neuchâtel, Jehan de Nissey, and all the noble lords and ladies in attendance. True, there are a small number of conflicting details, but these are limited to such minor concerns as variant spellings of the protagonists' names or the presence or absence of vinegar used to ease Jehan's pain.[32] It does indeed seem that the events happened as described: all the more so in that there is additional evidence that such accidents were not isolated occurrences.

It was common practice, for example, to render realistically the abyss of Hell, from which Lucifer emerged "breathing fire and smoke through his gaping mouth."[33] But André de la Vigne introduces us to one Satan who got along with theater like a house afire. During a performance of the *Mystery of Saint Martin* in Seurre in 1496, de la Vigne saw the whole thing and described in painstaking detail how the Devil's *derrière* caught fire, as one might easily imagine from the proximity of pyrotechnics in figure 2:

> Next Lucifer began to speak, and during his speech, the man who was playing the part of Satan was preparing to emerge from his underground hiding-place; and, as he did, fire broke out on his clothes near his buttocks, so much so that he was seriously burned. But he was rescued so quickly, undressed and redressed, that, as if nothing had happened, he came back to play his role; and later went back home. Many of the players were much horrified by this thing; for they thought that any thing which begins badly must also end badly. Nevertheless, thanks to my lord Saint Martin, who took matters into his own hands, things went fully one hundred times better than one could ever have expected.[34]

This crafty "devil" even managed to turn his theatrical misfortune to his advantage. He later reappeared with a bang and with a joke suited for the occasion—one that, as Gustave Cohen warns, makes up in relevance for what it lacks in poetic splendor: "May death nip your life in the bud, / You sleaze, son of a bitch, I swear! / When I stirred up your devil's blood, / I fried my own ass everywhere."[35] As in all

Figure 2. A magician works with fire before spectators. Drawing in *L'Ancienne France*, based on a fifteenth-century manuscript.

urban legends, something more frightening lurks beneath the surface—or, in the case of our unfortunate Satan, on the surface of his ass.[36] Something about theater's flame was deadly and likely to spread as rapidly, as rabidly, as wildfire, madness, or the flames of Hell.

If the tale of the Devil's grilled bottom has tended to elicit mockery, the fates of Nicholas and Jehan offer up a social commentary about the interplay of theater and the divine that is no less searing. Raymond Lebègue once commented that, "unfortunately, we have no way of knowing the impression that the death and Passion of the Savior made on the public."[37] Thus, we may never know the dominant emotion of the crowd in Metz in 1437. But fear and distress were doubtless present at the very moment when the promise of the great hereafter should have been most strongly characterized by more sure and certain hope. If the dying Nicholas had been struck down by God Himself, then the mad rush to save him was *God's* business with his eternal life, not the *audience's* business with his terrestrial one. Metz's Passion play would have accomplished the antithesis of what religious theater was supposed to do. Instead of inspiring humility, it would have created a situation in which spectators rightly believed that they themselves were capable of doing things that God could not (or would not). Therefore, for all the explicitly expressed edifying ends of religious drama, maybe it was not such a good work after all—in which case it was perilous to perform it, as perilous as the improbably jinxed Passion play at Metz suggests.[38] If God was the one to assail Fathers Nicholas and Jehan, then not all the documentation in the world about faulty special effects could kill off the potent and believable fear that God did not like the theater.[39]

By the same token, as Jehan de Nissey mimed the suicide of the despairing Judas, he demonstrated that he, Jehan-the-actor, did not *want* to die. At a minimum, his neighbors did not want him to die, and—notwithstanding Cavell's later stipulations—they had no trouble at all pointing to the priest they wanted to save and not to the betrayer who supposedly deserved his fate (*MWM*, 328). Yet by saving the man's life, they ruined the New Testament story in a way that is identical to the eruption of Cavell's yokel at *Othello*. When they perceived correctly that both Judas *and* Jehan were dying, the Metz interlopers saved the character as well as the actor. Our chroniclers do not say whether Jehan was replaced, and normally a dead man wouldn't *need to be*. But such Passion plays as Jean Michel's actually have Judas's soul return after his suicide to deliver more lines about his eternal damnation.[40] Regardless, this would have been a Passion play in which the audience, having come so close to seeing the accidental death of Jehan, never saw to completion the suicide of Judas. They saw a *mystère* in which Judas (hastily unhanged) *did not die*. The theatrical rescue of Jehan de Nissey compromised a story in which the character of Despair is supposed to "unhang" Judas's body and deliver his soul to a diabolical escort.[41] The nature of that compromise may help to explain the highly ambiguous and unattributed version of our story that was later circulated by Frederick Hawkins.

Although Hawkins presents it as a true story, he finessed the details to such an extent that it is unclear whether Jehan de Nissey survived his performance of Judas at all. "Distressing accidents occasionally happened," he notes, as when "an actor who had the courage to impersonate the Saviour nearly died on the cross, and *a Judas was found to have hanged himself only too effectually*."[42] It can scarcely be irrelevant to determine whether or not the man actually died. Nevertheless, theater historians don't always provide the needed clarity.

For example, J. M. B. Clément traced the threats of theater all the way back to the aerial acrobatics of ancient Rome. He neglects to tell us, though, whether another endangered actor outlasted his stunt:

> The ancients had machines of all types for their theater pieces. [There were those] . . . in which the gods descended all the way down to the stage; others, finally, that were employed for raising up and holding in the air persons who seemed to be flying. Insofar as [the devices] in this last category were in every way similar to those of our own flights, they were subject to the same accidents. Thus

we see in Suetonius that an actor who was playing the role of Icarus, and whose machine unfortunately met with the same fate, wound up falling near the place where Nero was situated, and he covered with blood those who were standing around him.[43]

Clément's silence may strike one as shocking, but it is nothing compared to the actions attributed to a much later audience at Madrid's Teatro del Circo. "Some time in 1880," begins Larwood as he invokes the urban legend's standard caveat, "*if newspaper reports may be trusted,* a madman armed with a hatchet made his way on to the stage." Far more menacing than Lucian's mad "Ajax," he slays "one of the attendants who attempted to seize him," upon which "the inconvenient supernumerary swung the hatchet about his head with such desperation that the municipal authorities dared not approach him." Initially, a squad of soldiers give a simulated performance of their own: "under the instruction of their officer, [they] fired at the madman with blank cartridge, in the hope of frightening him into surrender." When pretense fails, they proceed to the successful use of real ammunition and "the intruder, his antics all over, lay upon the stage a corpse, with three bullets in his head and body" (*TA*, 284; my emphasis).[44] A real madman has broken the theatrical frame with a real murder—only to die on stage because he fails to respond to simulated gunfire. But in a horrible dénouement that bears a certain resemblance to the events of Metz, the proverbial show went on: "so soon as it was known that the man was dead, the audience returned to the places they had quitted in terror, and the performances were resumed at the point at which they had been interrupted by this little episode" (*TA*, 284).

If confusion, nonchalance, or even comedy in the face of death appears farfetched today, nothing could be further from the truth. Larwood's tongue-incheek account is no match for comedian George Carlin's quips about shootings in elementary schools. Should a gunman have opened fire on his generation's classmates, he jokes, the class would have "gone on with our arithmetic: 23 classmates minus 2 equals . . ."[45] Then again, no one was laughing when the wrestler Owen Hart plunged to his death in Kemper Arena. When ABC's Peter Jennings reported the story on 24 May 1999, he clarified that, at first, it was necessary to announce that Hart was not acting and that his lifeless body was "not a part of the entertainment here tonight."[46] Also, in a remark that should give pause to anyone who witnessed the aerial ascents and descents of Broadway fare from *Peter Pan* to *Jesus Christ Superstar*, NBC's Tom Brokaw declared that "after Mr. Hart's body was carried from the ring, the show went on."[47] It went on just as it had in Metz and Madrid. All that was required was the removal of the bodies of the dead from the theatrical arena.

In all these theatrical moments of extreme jeopardy, the pleasures, perils, and pains of pretense are suspended as the audience determine whether or not they have witnessed—or *are witnessing*—real death, whether or not any given spectacle is imitating or enacting performativity. What all our stories underscore so anxiously is the dreaded moment when theatrical events are not quite representation and not quite reality. Given that perspective, it is just as difficult to accept the postmodern meditations of a Baudrillard as it is the grumblings of a William Gruber, who complained that "so frequent nowadays is disparagement of writers on ethical grounds that one sometimes feels as if a generation of scholars is attempting—perhaps in desperation—to convince themselves and their students that literature has a more than parenthetic relationship with real life."[48] For Nicholas de Neuchâtel and Jehan de Nissey (as for Owen Hart today), the relationship between theater and real life was much more than parenthetic. Their stories have perpetually suggested that this is *the* relationship to investigate.

As we have just seen, various instances of madness, fire, and death bear out the eternal tendency of theater to "spill over" into real life and "real life" to spill over into theater.[49] Indeed, there is a way in which theater itself has been said to have been born of such spillage.[50] Sometimes, this was a perfectly simple matter of the heavy rains that postponed the *Play of Saint Laurent*, just as they did Lyonard's performance as Saint Barbara.[51] Sometimes, this was a happy spillage, as it presumably was for Madame Henry de la Tour and for the French-assimilated Lyonard. Sometimes, when theater and real life collided, the dark side was all too clear. In a fascinating (if sobering) letter of remission of 1395, for instance, we learn that a theatrical performance in Chelles near Paris brought to town a seamy group of men who gang-raped a woman.[52]

As all the acts described here have shown, drama really can be dangerous. Devils' *derrières* do catch fire. Priests almost hang and suffocate while speaking of death. A murderous lunatic is gunned down on stage. Do those realities lend greater or lesser credence to the apocryphal on-stage deaths we reviewed in chapter 3 of Montfleury, Edmund Kean, or John Palmer (*TA*, 198–99)? No matter how tempted we might be to conclude that most of the stories in this book are urban legends, no matter how compellingly each one speaks to deep-seated apprehensions about the hazards of imitation, sometimes reality rears its ugly head.

Having become impatient with the Stanislavski method, Robert Lewis reproached its practitioners as follows for their self-indulgence: "You constantly hear, in rehearsal, 'I don't feel it.' . . . When I hear that I want to say, 'Who cares? It's the *audience* which is supposed to feel it!'"[53] As we shall see, the audience was never supposed to feel it like this.

CHAPTER FIVE

Dying to Play

We struggle with dream figures and our blows fall on living faces.
—Maurice Merleau-Ponty

When Jehan Hemont left his job at the bathhouse on 27 March 1380 for a pleasant outing at the theater, little did he suspect the fate that would befall him. Going to see the Passion plays in Paris was always an adventure. Such massive, sprawling spectacles. Crowds coming in from everywhere, raucous shouting at the actors, noisy applause and participation from the spectators. This particular Passion play promised, moreover, to boast wonderful special effects; and word was already spreading throughout Paris about the use of a real cannon to simulate thunder in the most jarring possible way.

Jehan Hemont did not return home that day. He died at the theater, the accidental victim of a special effect gone horribly wrong. Nor was Jehan the only one to suffer such a fate. Just over four years later in the Parisian suburb of Aunay-lès-Bondy, one Perrin Le Roux was killed on 19 June 1384 while attending a rehearsal of the *Miracle de Théophile*. On both occasions, theater was performative. On both occasions, theater was deadly.

These are not urban legends. Jehan and Perrin are survived by their stories, extant in two separate letters of remission granted by kings Charles V and VI to Guillaume Langlois and Fremin Severin. Both documents were published in *Romania* in 1900 by A. Thomas.[1] They are riveting enough to merit extensive excerpts, but not without the following precisions.

Despite all the apocrypha we have been and will be exploring, it is discomfiting to observe that Jehan Hemont and Perrin Le Roux force us to believe in an actual theatrical death threat. They thus enhance the believability of all those other stories, from Lucian's mad "Ajax" to the curse of

Macbeth. They plant the kiss of death upon theater's safe distance, which collapses under the weight of performativity. They obliterate Bruce Wilshire's seemingly logical pronouncement that in theater, "*the violence is not really happening*" (*RPI,* 250; my emphasis). And they bear out Brunvand's contention that even the most preposterous-sounding urban legends could have happened to someone at some time somewhere down the line (*SAF,* 91). For something to seem true enough to trigger the chain of storytelling, there need only be a good-faith belief that if a given thing genuinely happened, it might happen again.

In these cases, the evidence is not elusive, not deconstructable, not invisible. Two tangible documents stage two citizens who, whether on or off the stage, are caught in theater's crossfire. If theatrical death had a nasty way of spilling over into real life in such a way as to shorten suddenly the lives of actors, such spillage posed an analogous threat to audiences. Above all else, our two letters of remission investigate the mortality of a theatrical moment that Bert States otherwise finds endearing when he ponders the presence of working clocks or dogs on stage: "the floor cracks open and we are startled, however pleasantly, by the upsurge of the real into the magic circle where the conventions of theatricality have assured us that the real has been subdued and transcended" (*GR,* 34). On 27 March 1380 and 19 June 1384, that upsurge was distinctly *unpleasant.*

Jehan Hemont and Perrin Le Roux challenge from beyond the grave any postmodern pleasure that has been taken in the ideology, theatricality, and phenomenology of death.[2] While I am by no means suggesting that death *cannot* be symbolic, it is indubitable that what Jehan Hemont and Perrin Le Roux experienced at the fourteenth-century theater was not a theory or a symbol. They died. But for the theater, they would have lived.[3] Much in the same way, then, that Elaine Scarry has sensitively demonstrated that "pain is pain and not a metaphor of pain," death is death and not a metaphor of death.[4] If ever we stood ready to revise Peter Brook's statement that the deadly theater contains "often tantalizing, abortive or even momentarily satisfying flickers of a real life," it is now.[5] We cannot help but notice that the performances of Paris and Aunay-lès-Bondy offered dissatisfying, though strangely satisfying, flickers of real death. There would be many others. There always had been.

As the city of Paris prepared for the highly instructive and commemorative performance of Christ's Passion, Guillaume Langlois's duties were clear. He had been "charged, asked, and assigned by the actors playing the roles of the enemies and devils" to detonate the glorious cannon that had been specially selected to render fire and brimstone for the crucifixion. That scenic feat of realism "would ensure that [the actors] would play their roles better." It was a big job, requiring no fewer than ten pieces of heavy artillery, so Guillaume's friend, Jehan Hemont, apprentice in the bathhouses *(varlet d'estuves)*, kindly came along to "help him with the play and with the firing of the ten cannon at the right time and place, as was the custom in days of yore."[6] Two heads were better than one and four hands better than two when it came to ensuring that actors and audience alike would suspend the disbelief necessary to *believe* in the portrayal of Christ's Passion.

Our letter of remission is silent on the subject of who placed the red-hot rammer into one of the cannon the two men had carefully primed for "just the right moment" of the show-stopper. But it fired unexpectedly and prematurely in such a way that, quite literally, all hell broke loose. Jehan Hemont was mortally wounded in the leg. (In a grimly ironic twist, the man who spent his days surrounded by water at the baths was unable to put out the fire.) Meanwhile, Guillaume suffered severe burns about the face, his own condition touch-and-go there for awhile:

> And so it was that they arranged and prepared the aforesaid cannon for detonation and blasting at the specific time and place of the crucifixion, which is the customary practice in these plays in remembrance of the death and Passion of our lord Jesus Christ. And because, upon the place where the aforesaid complainant and Jehan Hemont were standing, there had been placed a hot rammer *[broche]*, which was stuffed into one of the cannon standing at that site, the plug *[cheville] of the aforesaid cannon [mis]fired and exploded earlier and otherwise than the aforesaid plaintiff and Hemont had anticipated or expected.* [It happened] in such a way that the aforesaid Hemont was struck and, by chance, wounded by this said plug in one of his legs; and *from the strength of the explosion and the flames which broke out, the aforesaid Guillaume was also burned and charred all over his face;* and there was great doubt as to whether or not he would die from the adventure or be fatally wounded.[7]

Even J. L. Austin could never have imagined anything like this when he described the performative utterance that fails to reach fruition as a *misfire*. When participants in a speech act do not conform to the agreed conventions in the proper setting, "then the act that we purport to perform would not come off—it will be, one might say, a misfire. This will be the case if, for example, we do not carry through the procedure—whatever it may be—correctly and completely, without a flaw and without a hitch. If any of these rules are not observed, we say that the act which we purported to perform is void, without effect" (*PP,* 225).[8] The performance of 1380 did *not* come off without a hitch, and the only thing voided was Jehan Hemont.

Likewise, contemporary philosophers have meditated on the problem of "moral luck" in such scenarios as a drunk driver who, after running a stop sign, luckily kills no one. Regardless of the lucky outcome for the potential victim, the drunk is no less guilty. Sometimes, however, the victim is *unlucky* enough to die, a level of performative "unhappiness" that far surpasses Austin's original definition.[9] In Paris in 1380 no one was more unhappy than Jehan Hemont. Guillaume had enlisted his friend's assistance to effect a performance that was true to life. Instead, it was true to death. Later, in 1437, two medieval priests would *seem* to be representing death artfully as they were really dying. In 1380 we have two individuals who were not meant to participate in the world of theatrical seeming but, to their own detriment, were engulfed in the boundlessness of its lethal reality.

From a modern standpoint, this event provokes a deadly dilemma that drastically complicates Erving Goffman's normally sensible definition of the spectator's two roles as physical theatergoer and psychic onlooker.[10] None of it was so sensible in fourteenth-century Paris. Jehan Hemont's family would not have been much comforted to learn that it was Jehan the theatergoer who had died rather than Jehan the onlooker. By the same token, his death makes it difficult to endorse Bradley Butterfield's comments about the Baudrillardian accident, which initiates a "postmodern symbolic exchange with death where one signifying system *breaks through* into another and thus ruptures the *semiotic wall* between self and other, life and death, real and imaginary." "Whether real or imaginary death initiates the exchange," concludes Butterfield, "is beside the point."[11] It was scarcely "beside the point" for Jehan Hemont or for the loved ones he left behind. Furthermore, the medieval theater had never been characterized by any such "semiotic wall." Far from it. Modern readers might tend to imagine such recognizable edifices as the Lillian Gish on Broadway, the Mark Taper in Los Angeles, or even Shakespeare's Globe. But the medieval theatrical scene that provides the backdrop for our legends was not a specific building at all. It had no fixed dwelling, no proscenium stage, no *théâtre vitrine* to separate its stories from everyday life as though behind glass.[12] Rather, it was a place that changed the meaning of ordinary spaces by investing and reinvesting them with meanings old and new.[13] From the earliest liturgical dramas, it had long come close to quotidian existence, alive and in motion as it paraded itself through time and space before the eyes of spectators. Medieval theater required only an agreement, a communal accord for actors to represent and for audiences to watch its stories in some sort of ritually designated space: a public square, a *temenos*, the stairs of a church, a marketplace.[14]

Nor was the apparently simple matter of delineating its bounds so terribly simple. For example, in the richly documented performance of the *Mystère de la Passion* at Mons in 1501, town officials took great care to draw the same dividing line that had functioned so poorly in the sad case of Lucian's mad "Ajax." They too grappled with the problem of specifying where real life stopped and the Passion play began. The problem was that the wooden bleachers for the spectators had extended so far that, had proper measures not been taken, the play threatened to block everyday physical access to the dwellings on the square:

> *Item,* regarding the playing area or stage *[parcq],* which seems too small and whether or not bleachers *[hourts]* will be fashioned [and placed] at the outer edges of the stage *all the way to private homes* [on the square]. It was concluded that the bleachers should be placed in such a way as to occupy the space *extending from the edge of the stage to the houses, preserving the entrances to the same,* and also to keep wide-open the entrance to City Hall, without enclosing it inside the confines of the stage.[15]

Given what happened in 1380, such anxieties were justified at the level of public safety alone.[16] Later on, they would bespeak many of the metaphysical anxieties of the Renaissance. As Deborah Shuger has argued, "the problem of boundaries touches almost every area of Renaissance culture, from the organization of the arts curriculum to the respective limits of Crown and Parliament, but particularly the relations among the sociopolitical order, the self, and God."[17] It also touches on drama's role with regard to those relations.

For the moment, believe it or not, our story has a happy ending. Although Jehan Hemont passed away, Guillaume Langlois was later able to explain his intentions satisfactorily enough to justify the issuance of a princely letter of remission that absolved him of all criminal wrongdoing.[18] It helped a great deal that Jehan Hemont himself, being of sound mind if not body, had proclaimed his friend Guillaume "entirely, truly, and absolutely innocent of the deed which had thus been committed and of any [other] legal cause of action that might justly ensue on account of that deed at some future date, saying and confessing that the two of them had always been good friends."[19] Moreover, one of the most compelling pieces of evidence attesting to Guillaume's good intentions was, tautologically, his participation in the very play whose special effects had precipitated his friend's death. Since Jehan had pardoned Guillaume on his death bed, and since Guillaume had led a good life (as verified by his participation in the useful, instructive, and godly theatrical commemoration of the life of Christ), he could be forgiven: "in consideration of the aforementioned deeds, and acknowledging that the plays in which he was engaged were designed to signify and represent an example of goodness, and that the aforesaid petitioner has led a good life, has a good reputation, and has been forthright in his dealings with others, we have forgiven, acquitted and pardoned the supplicant."[20] Additionally, there was a happy ending for Guillaume's family and their heirs, all of whom would be protected from the blame, shame, and stigma of having a convicted killer in the family. The story even has a happy ending of sorts for Jehan Hemont who, cast as a good man, would doubtless have gone to heaven.

The ending for theater is rather more complex. We now know that ever since ancient Greece, theater audiences have been on speaking terms with the illusory, the real, and the hyperreal. Whatever the result—be it violent or nonviolent, nightmarish or phantasmagoric, welcome or unwelcome—once theater and reality have coincided, their interplay is tricky to stop. It is true that stopping it has been at the root of innumerable philosophical crises from Plato to the Middle Ages to contemporary American litigation that attempts to hold various art forms liable for criminal acts committed in real life.[21] In 1380 and 1384 theater got off scot-free. Instead, *individuals* faced liability for their actions and not—at least, *not yet*—the entire genre of theater, whose good intentions were ruled to be beyond reproach.[22] And yet, that was not the end of it.

Despite the purity of its own edifying intentions, despite its implicit absolution by Charles V on account of its capacity to set a good example, this Passion play set a *terrible* example. Rituals in general, as Miri Rubin has observed, can "go wrong; wrong, that is, for their planners."[23] This yearly event most definitely went wrong. After all, it was a Passion play, and not the 1980 Ringling Brothers Circus, in which accidents became "in a Kafkaesque way part of the ceremony" (*BTA*, 120).[24] Accidents weren't a *part* of the Passion play any more than was Jehan de Nissey's *unhanging* as Judas. But accidents seemed to keep happening anyway. Indeed, a scant four years later, a strikingly similar accident befell another spectator. One may recall here the witty definition of the term proposed by Ambrose Bierce: "ACCIDENT: an inevitable occurrence due to the action of immutable natural laws."[25] Perhaps what happened on 19 June 1384 was also inevitable.

If there were any superstitions to arise from the death of Jehan Hemont—some kind of "curse of the *Passion*" along the lines of the latter-day curse of *Macbeth*—then their echoes and lessons had yet to reach the citizens of Aunay-lès-Bondy, just outside of Paris. A certain Perrin le Roux died at the theater, prompting an intervention, now by Charles VI, after a new investigation. This time, the letter of remission absolved one Fremin Severin of wrongdoing in Perrin's accidental death during the *Miracle de Théophile*, "a play in commemoration of the miracle which was performed for Theophilus at the request of the Virgin Mary."[26] By now, what occurred has a familiar and deadly ring: "At this play there was someone playing a character who was charged with firing a cannon," and it apparently happened that, on the Sunday before the aforesaid holiday of Saint John just past, the aforementioned townspeople [of Aunay] were at the church of the aforementioned city.[27] . . . The aforementioned Fremin, who was charged with operating the said cannon, apparently filled the mouth *[bouete]* of the said cannon with paper alone, without placing there any iron or wood. And at the moment when he was supposed to fire this said cannon, the aforementioned Fremin apparently said to the people who were standing around there: "Get back! You've got no business being so close! It's too dangerous!"[28]

Fremin's insulating admonition was insufficient: "Nevertheless, the late Perrin Le Roux happened to place himself in front of the aforementioned cannon as it was going off, so that, while the aforesaid cannon was firing, the paper, which was in the barrel of said cannon, hit him in the eye . . . [and he] passed from life to death the following Friday."[29] In an irony that rivals that of the bathhouse attendant lacking water to put out a fire, we have before us a play that celebrates the triumphant intercession of the Virgin Mary into the life of the fallen priest Théophile—but during which Fremin's own intercession is unsuccessful. Good-hearted though he may be, he is just a man, and he is unable to save the life of Perrin Le Roux.

Were the same events to take place in the twenty-first century, we would doubtless be talking about Guillaume's "good faith" effort to save his friend's life. Good faith is what the *Miracle de Théophile* was all about. Today, Perrin's insurance company would probably refuse to pay out on his distraught family's claim, calling his death an "act of God." In the Middle Ages, an act of God meant a little bit more. God Himself may well have saved Nicholas de Neuchâtel and Jehan de Nissey, the imperiled priests of Metz.[30] Mary may well have gone to Hell and back for Théophile.[31] But she did not intervene to save poor Perrin Le Roux or, for that matter, Jehan Hemont. Did the Virgin object to the miracle play being performed in her honor? or to man's audacity in representing her? We will never know more than that Fremin deemed it necessary to rescue his own reputation from beyond Perrin's grave. He was helped in that regard by none other than Perrin himself who, like Jehan Hemont before him, took responsibility for his actions and forgave his unwitting assailant on his deathbed: "the aforesaid deceased Perrin said that he [himself] was to blame for the aforesaid blow and not the aforesaid Fremin."[32] Given Perrin's own admission that he had hovered too close to the special effects, and given that Fremin had always been "of good reputation and character," Charles VI purported to resolve the affair to the satisfaction of all the parties.

There now remains to be considered a final crucial detail, which I have thus far elided from the discussion. Perrin was killed not before a full house during the actual performance but at that special "in-between" or liminal moment that is the rehearsal, *not yet* intended for an audience. He met the Grim Reaper during a representational event that was, at the time, a work-in-progress: the participants were at church *"in order to rehearse their roles."*[33]

Things *can* and *do* go wrong during a rehearsal. There are dropped lines, staging snafus, accidents, and a host of other unintentional peccadilloes that, if repeated on opening night, would threaten the delicate balance of spectators' suspension of disbelief and hurl them back to the reality they would presumably have left behind. That is one of the reasons to have a rehearsal: to find out what *can* go wrong in order to prevent it from going wrong again or, on the brighter side, to find out what goes right so that it can be repeated. A mortal accident would certainly qualify as unrepeatable. But are there other qualifications to be made as well?

If one were to be a cold-hearted phenomenologist about the theatrical events of 19 June 1384, one might say that Perrin's death "didn't count" as theater, since rehearsals always keep one foot in reality (albeit with Perrin's other foot in the grave). One might even argue of 27 March 1380 that, if no spectators happened to notice Jehan Hemont's leg going up in smoke, then there was no deadly spectacle. Such statements are as inappropriate as they are inhumane. No contemporary critic, whether liberal or conservative, New or Old Historicist, postmodern or structuralist, can possibly contend that there was anything "liminal" about Perrin Le Roux's death (unless, of course, one were to include unspeakably the progressive act of dying itself).[34] Like Jehan Hemont, Perrin Le Roux really died. He died from real injuries to his real body from real effects. He did not die from any *theory* of the *rehearsal* of real effects, even though those effects were really being rehearsed at the time.

This is not to deny the fascinating nature of the phenomenological problems of theater. We would probably agree with Wilshire, for instance, that "weird things happen in theatre, and not just in pornographic or violent enactments; they are particularly arresting as they are discovered in rehearsal, and most particularly in improvisations in rehearsal" (*RPI,* 251). A fatal accident is more than just "weird" in that, if medieval Christian life was but a rehearsal for death and its hereafter, then life itself was arrested when the rehearsal of the *Miracle de Théophile* snuffed out Perrin's own life-in-progress. Furthermore, when Wilshire goes on to assert that both pornography and extreme violence are not art because the "artists cannot achieve the level of control of the subject matter necessary for such art" (*RPI,* 251), his statement tends to reinforce the conclusion that the Paris Passion play of 1380 and the *Théophile* of 1384 were no longer "plays" when two men died. And that, once Lucian's "Ajax" had lost his mind, audiences similarly lost their theater. And that, in one of the most notorious theatrical stories of all time, the *Eumenides* of c. 460 B.C. ceased to be a play when various spectators were struck dead with terror.

In one of the earliest known examples of death by drama, Aeschylus is said to have introduced his chorus into the orchestra in such a horrendous way that some of the spectators were literally scared to death: "children died and women suffered miscarriage."[35] While A. M. Nagler cautions that "we must be aware . . . that the anonymous biographer compiled his account from rather spurious sources," the inauthenticity of the tale in no way bothered André de Lorde, who cited it as fact while championing the violent realities of the Grand Guignol. De Lorde even went so far as to proffer fresh details, which had never been invoked by the ancient commentator: "*It is reported* [by whom he doesn't say] that, during a performance of the *Eumenides* of Aeschylus, around the year 460 B.C., the entrance of the hideous goddesses provoked a veritable panic in the crowd. Women aborted, children died, and *several spectators were struck by madness.*"[36] In all likelihood, de Lorde was simply filling in the psychic blanks of some published edition of Act 1.1 of the *Eumenides*, in which the vengeful ghost of Clytemnestra awakens the twelve sleeping Furies (and in which there is no particular mention of madness). Even so, his embellishment is nothing compared to the earlier effort of J. M. B. Clément, who recirculated the tale in 1775. Without giving the slightest clue about his sources, Clément speaks not of dead fetuses aborted but of older children who died. There is no implication that the premature newborns failed to survive their premature birth, induced by theater's terror:

> In the tragedy of *Eumenides* by Aeschylus, Orestes appeared in the first act, surrounded by the Furies who had been put to sleep by Apollo. They were wearing black and bloodied garments and holding, in one hand, torches that cast a pale and flickering light, while, in the other hand, they held whips made of snakes. Their heads were covered with furious grass-snakes. Their faces were so horrible, so pale, and so terrifying that, at the moment when they awakened, and began to walk tumultuously about the stage, pregnant women gave birth from terror, and children died of fear.[37]

Were these dead children real enough to have died? Or was the suspiciously spurious tale meant as *advertising*, designed not to traumatize but to publicize? In light of what happened to Jehan and Perrin, do the spontaneous abortions of the *Eumenides* seem more or less likely to have occurred?

It is clear that within the framework of medieval and Renaissance drama, the threats of fire and brimstone would not *always* be enacted literally (be it accidentally or on purpose), but it is equally clear by now that genuine pain was a definite possibility. Once reality has attacked as irrevocably as it did in the cases of Jehan Hemont and Perrin le Roux, not all the phenomenology and reception theory in the world can refute what two men have confirmed definitively: the very real prospect of a performative death by drama.

On one hand, Jehan and Perrin have delivered with their demise a death blow to any avant-garde phenomenological contention that real violence on stage (assaults, medical procedures, bodily mutilations) is a symbol, a sign of itself, a mere "story."[38] Jehan's and Perrin's are real stories of real deaths, and neither man died because of any politics of representation. So this is no time to revel in any Baudrillardian confusion about the signs inclining neither one way nor the other (*SW*, 178). Even the most hardened habitués of phenomenology must acknowledge that there simply has to be a difference between a special effect, a close call, a lethal accident, and a murder.

On the other hand, reception theory fares no better. It is plainly inappropriate to ask, "How did the audience feel?" without also asking, "Did the two men die?" It is just as inappropriate to validate the position expressed by the conservative commentator George Will about the 1976 exploitation film, *Snuff*. As if buying into the marketing strategy that created "confusion over the film's generic identity and the appropriate social response to it," Will declared that "the final murder, *whether real or fake*, is repulsive enough to convince the dismal viewers who want to believe it is real, which includes most of the people who shell out $4 to see it."[39] We cannot discount Frank Rich's wariness that some of those viewers might verifiably have been dismal enough to want to "believe that *Snuff* will offer an actual murder as entertainment."[40] Nor can we discount the importance to the snuffed-out actress of whether her murder was real or fake. Similarly, it mattered a great deal to Jehan Hemont and Perrin le Roux whether their deaths were real or fake. It mattered a great deal to the audiences who, notwithstanding any initial confusion akin to the recent grisly spectacle of Owen Hart's death, must eventually have realized that Jehan and Perrin had truly been mortally wounded.[41] For all parties, theater was a matter of life and death.

So it is that the true peril of Jehan and Perrin casts a pall over each one of our stories, to which it lends credence. As "legendary" as Jehan's or Perrin's deaths might have been in their day, there was nothing apocryphal about them. Consequently, maybe women really *did* miscarry at the *Eumenides*. Maybe Lucian's "riffraff" were not wrong to fear the mad "Ajax." Maybe a group of thirteenth-century spectators in Riga did indeed flee a prophet play, terrified that the pugnacious looking actor-soldiers were about to attack *them*.[42] Maybe it was totally reasonable for William Prynne in the seventeenth century to allude to God's wrath against the theater in the form of "the various tragicall ends of many, who in my remem-

brance at London, have been slaine in Play-houses, or upon quarrels there commenced."[43] Maybe Gosselin was right to say that

> it was rare that such numerous [theatrical] assemblies failed to give rise to some
> sort of commotion or some dramatic scene. One could scarcely leave a mystery
> play without having been a witness to or an actor in "a wounding and bloody
> battle." Fist-fights were more rare than fights with daggers, swords, and sticks,
> after which one was obliged to go and explain oneself before the judge and tell
> him all about these incidents, which were unpredictable but always assured by a
> mystery play.[44]

In the strictest possible sense, Gosselin has described a *coup de théâtre.*

Were Jehan Hemont and Perrin Le Roux still with us today, they could testify to
theater's threat of violence. So too could the fifteen spectators at the Old Haymar-
ket Theater who were reportedly "trampled to death" on 3 February 1794.[45] So
could the nine concert-goers who met a similar fate in the summer of 2000 while
patronizing a Pearl Jam concert in Roskilde, Denmark. So could any contemporary
spectator familiar with the dangers of festival seating or mosh pits at theatrical, musical, or sporting events.[46] So could any town council trying to legislate crowd control in the Middle Ages with a flurry of edicts designed to protect their city and
citizens from the excesses of the stage.

For example, in 1483 municipal officials of Troyes sought to safeguard their *res
publica* by placing paid guards at the gates of the city during the performance of a
Mystère de la Passion: "for the security of the city and the public good and during
the days on which the *Mystery of the Passion* will be represented, the gates of the
city shall be guarded by four men instead of two, and the gates of Madeleine and
Comporté will be closed."[47] Three years later, as the city of Angers prepared for
Jean Michel's *Passion* of 1486, its town councilmen also passed extensive security
measures. They were moved on 12 August to permit access to their city through
two gates only, of which "only one portal will remain open for the duration of the
aforesaid plays," while a constable would be on hand with the keys.[48] They en-
joined innkeepers to make inquiries into the identity of their lodgers: "Item,
innkeepers of the city and surrounding areas will be required to take very good care
what people will be arriving in their homes."[49] They forbade the carrying of sticks:
"Item, it will be announced and ordered to the sound of trumpets that it is forbidden to carry throughout the city sticks for fighting and aggression, with the sole exception being those who are thus ordered for the safekeeping of same, under threat
of prison and a fine."[50] And they reinforced their police corps, calling for "twenty

well-armed men per day, each taking his turn to watch the gates of the city," for re-inforcements to the nightwatch, and for twenty-five men "in good battle-gear" to patrol the streets in order to "prevent disturbances from rabble-rousers [cro-cheteurs] and other evil folk, for the protection and safekeeping of the whole city and its inhabitants."[51] Without such reinforcements, audiences might run wild.

If any of this were truly *un*believable, if audiences never risked their lives for the sake of theatrical pleasures,[52] none of our stories could have circulated at all. In that sense, Raymond Lebègue was wrong to invoke the "*unbelievable* realism [with which] Christ or the martyrs are abused, slapped, beaten, tortured in a thousand ways."[53] The opposite was true. It was all too believable, all too "credible" in the threats it appeared to pose and *did* pose. Indeed, the notion of credibility still en-dures today, as when a group of social scientists released the findings of their na-tional study of television violence. They defined violence as "any overt depiction of the use of physical force—or the *credible threat* of such force—intended to physi-cally harm an animate being or group of beings."[54] Pity for theater, though, that credible doesn't always mean true. Or that it does. Or that actors and audiences *think* that it does.

The Eel of Melun

THE ACTOR: "Talk, talk, talk! I can tell you exactly what you mean by art. It's the
art of making copies, copies of what you choose to call reality. Sir, art *is* reality.
Art is so far above ordinary reality that it'd be fairer to call reality a copy of art.
A very incompetent one, at that."

—Bertolt Brecht, *Messingkauf Dialogues*

The story struck Petit de Julleville as so untrustworthy that he relegated
it to the final footnote of his two-page treatment of the ill-fated theater of
Meaux.[1] It is a companion legend, which he admits to finding "too legendary" for inclusion with the other legends—but which he includes
nonetheless.

Once upon a time, there was an actor named Languille (The Eel), who
lived in Melun, located some thirty miles southeast of Paris in the region
of Seine-et-Marne.[2] While Languille was playing the gruesome scene
that called for Saint Bartholomew to be flayed alive, he was reportedly so
terrified by the special effects that he began to scream before the actor
playing his torturer could lay a hand on him. Whence an enduring bit of
proverbial wisdom about "putting the cart before the horse," "jumping
the gun," "borrowing trouble," or, as Hamlet might have said, being
"frighted by false fire."[3] We have no specific information about the date or
occasion of the performance, but here is the Eel's story:

> I would not dare to mention anywhere but in a footnote a legend that
> is well known but vague and hardly authentic. A resident of Melun,
> named "The Eel," was playing the role of Saint Bartholomew in a
> mystery play. At the moment of the ordeal, he started screaming be-
> fore the actor playing the executioner could even touch him. Whence
> the proverb: "He's like the Eel of Melun: screaming before you skin
> him!"[4]

In this quaint approach to that beloved entity known as the footnote, Petit de Julleville has reversed contemporary conventions. Today, we hasten to the footnotes to revel in documentation that is the *least* questionable and the *most* authoritative. The venerable critic has instead placed in his footnote his *most* questionable and *least* authoritative reference: the entire story of the Eel of Melun.[5] He has blazed a proverbial trail of proverbs that can prove definitively only that the story is "vague and inauthentic." The Eel himself, however, has proved something else: an actor can provide acting so good that it's bad.

Here is an individual who has bought the whole story of death by drama hook, line, and sinker. He is an actor who thinks that theater is a matter of life and death when it is not. He is the thespian version of Cavell's yokel, but he is the yokel who seeks to save his *own* life and who believes so well in theater's realities that he becomes *unbelievable* as an actor, succeeding only in making a comic spectacle of himself.

As we follow his less-than-illustrious trail, we arrive at Petit de Julleville's source, M. Le Roux de Lincy's nineteenth-century *Livre des proverbes*—only to find that Le Roux de Lincy had, for his own part, borrowed the tale from Fleury de Bellingen's seventeenth-century *Etymologie ou explication des proverbes françois*. Citing a variety of etymologies for the legendary Eel, Le Roux de Lincy also called the story into question, noting that while Fleury de Bellingen's "is the most widely accepted of etymologies, nothing proves that it is true."[6] Like Petit de Julleville, he too reproduced the story anyway, with both additional information and additional humor. For Fleury de Bellingen, the Eel is a bad actor, whose gaffe would be akin today to that of the thespian who picks up a telephone before the props master has caused it to ring. Fleury de Bellingen seemed so amused by his entry on *L'Anguille de Melun* that he placed Saint Bartholomew in a *comedy!* (Despite the plethora of terms that denoted early theater pieces—*ordo*, miracle, mystery—Bartholomew's story was no "comedy" even by medieval standards.)[7] He had a good chuckle over skinning the Eel by the tail—or was it the tale?

> SIMPLE. And don't forget to skin that Eel of Melun!
> COS. I've got him by the tail. In Melun, which is a city in the province of Brie located on the Seine River about nine or ten leagues above Paris, there was a young man named The Eel who, during the public performance of a comedy, was playing the character of Saint Bartholomew. As the executioner came toward him, his knife in hand as if to skin him, he began to shriek before he could even touch him: which gave rise both to great laughter in the audience and to this proverb: *He is like the Eels of Melun: He screams before you skin him.*[8]

As if there were any doubt, Le Roux de Lincy makes these clarifications. The person who approached the Eel with a knife was not "the executioner" but "*the man who was playing the executioner*," and the proverb "henceforth, is applied to all those who fear misfortune before it happens."[9]

The pedagogical message of the Eel's story is clear: "Don't complain about bad things that have not yet come to pass"; "Don't be like the child who says 'ouch' before the doctor administers the shot"; or in the less charitable idiom, "Don't be an idiot!" Nevertheless, if we attend uncompromisingly to that moral, it is difficult to have theater, the genre that excels in tragic foreboding, hysterical anticipation, and the solicitation of real emotions (comic or tragic) from events that may never have occurred and never will.[10] It is difficult to retain the very genre that has given us the Eel of Melun, who exists to lobby for the opposite message: martyrdom is so clear and so present that we have every duty to anticipate its realities.

For our purposes, then, the proverbial problem of the Eel of Melun is a problem of theater phenomenology, which we need to resolve before exploring the rest of his considerable legacy—one that spanned popular song, the works of Rabelais, French-language dictionaries, and even nineteenth-century French vaudeville. In cutting the figure he does (the figure who fears cutting), Monsieur Eel has stepped over the same line in the sand that Lucian's mad "Ajax" had once traversed. But he has prompted laughter instead of tears—and not the confused mélange experienced by Lucian's audience. To adopt Michael Bristol's well-turned phrase, the patently untheatrical conduct of Languille has helped his audience treat "death as a laughing matter."[11] While I am not calling into question here the long-standing tradition of comic relief in the most macabre of violent scenes, the martyrdom of Saint Bartholomew was not a story that lent itself to giggles, and the Eel of Melun has made a fool of that saint. Saints suffer their ordeals with patience and piety. The Eel of Melun couldn't wait long enough to take the chance of even *feigning* patience and piety. However, that he *has* solicited inappropriate laughter may help to explain why the critique of Languille has been unflinching even if Languille himself was not: he is incompetent.

If an actor—even a bad one—believes himself to be legitimately threatened by theater's reality, then he isn't really acting at all, whatever the subsequent derision of his poor performance. When the Eel starts to scream, he is not playing terror: he is terrified that his life is on the line. True, it was way too early for him to line up Constantin Stanislavski on his behalf. But, like Fathers Nicholas and Jehan, he too evinced a true belief in what he encountered on stage. Unfortunately for him and for his audience, he became the perfect method actor whose perfection was uncalled for: "Everything that happens on the stage must be convincing to the actor himself, to his associates, and to the spectators. It must inspire belief in the possibility, in real life, of emotions analogous to those being experienced on the stage by the actor. Each and every moment must be saturated with a belief in the truthfulness of the emotion felt, and in the action carried out, by the actor" (*AP,* 129–30). The Eel of Melun is good and saturated. His audience simply thinks him *bad* and saturated. Because the Eel is so convinced by his colleague's impending death blow that he screams, his real fear of ruin ruins the true story of Bartholomew. Again, he could not have known that, centuries later, Bruce Wilshire would describe the phenomenological situation of theater in language weirdly relevant to his own case:

> Make-believe is always involved in the theatre, but only to the extent that the artist makes-believe for himself as character that the only time that matters is the time in which the character exists in his "world." *Even if the character is depicted as anticipating his own imminent death,* for example, it is just now—in that "world's" time—that he is doing it. *Unknown to him, factors may be at work within that "world" which will prevent that death from occurring.* (*RPI,* 107 [my emphasis])

Unknown to the real historical figure of Bartholomew are the factors that might prevent his death. Unknown to the Eel are the factors in his "real world" that might *hasten* it. The question is: was his questionable life really in danger? To answer it, we must do what his story asks us to do: consider whether he has broken the theatrical frame because he is unfamiliar with theatrical conventions or because he is all too familiar with them.

We have already seen that on the medieval French stage, things looked real because they *had* to look real. We have seen the highest praise accompany the performance that was true to life and the lowest esteem accompany improprieties that spoiled the show.[12] The Eel of Melun was more afraid that something might spoil his life. But, like Jehan Hemont, Perrin Le Roux, Nicholas de Neuchâtel, and Jehan de Nissey, perhaps he was not wrong to be afraid or, at the very least, to be bewildered.

No stranger to life on the planks, L'Anguille would surely have been aware of the countless instances in which the very language of medieval scenes of extreme violence tended to heighten the confusion between reality and representation, which he was feeling so acutely. In one *Mystère de la Passion,* for instance, Christ's torturers actively address the question of authenticity when they proclaim that their blows upon Jesus must be true, not imitated: "Now take your lance and stab away / On his right side, a good hit, eh? / And take care that this is no play! / You get that thing in all the way!"[13] In the *Geu Saint Denis,* the brutal Fescennin assures his partners in crime that the price to pay for a fake beating will be real death—for *them, not* for their victim: "I pray Mohammed to hang him / Who only fakes his forceful blows."[14] Elsewhere, in an inversion of the theories of Lucian and Aristotle, the torturers of the Mons Passion play imply that the pleasure of watching imitated pain is nothing compared to that of watching the genuine, no-holds-barred article. As they engage in a competition for the best bloody stroke to Christ's body, Gadifer and his crony Rabanus taunt, "I see you faking!" and "you're just gaming."[15] There is every reason, then, to attribute the Eel's confusion to the play's confusion.

So, what did he do that was so terrible? He wrecked the show because, like a yokel, he believed in its sheer truthfulness—to say nothing of its *shear* transparency. In that sense, though, he sounds more like the ideal spectator than the poor actor of religious drama. He is a "true believer" much like those to whom the Passion play of Amboise is addressed. "I believe in you without pretense," says one of the faithful to Christ in that play, devotedly determined to maintain the indivisibility of belief and reality—the very essence of which the Eel, as actor, is now so comically committed to.[16] If the mission of religious drama was belief without pretense, then one needs to imagine the delicate performance situation in which theater—the genre of pretense—must feign "belief without pretense" in a way that should simultaneously seem to be without pretense. The genre of seeming must not *seem* but *be*. But it must not be too much, lest being seem like seeming. To provide anything more (or anything less) was to resemble not a believer but a nonbeliever.

For example, in Jean Michel's *Mystère de la Passion*, performed in Angers in 1486, the most ardent nonbelievers are the very persons who believe most ardently in theatrical pretense. Especially, with the anti-Semitism that is the disturbing hallmark of such plays, Michel implies that it is the diabolical Jews who exalt the possibility of pretense.[17] It is they who endeavor to dismiss as stage trickery or false-seeming the "true miracles" performed by Christ. Here, they express their skepticism about the resurrection of Lazarus:

My Lords, how can you think it so?
To stand in such transfixion
Before a piece of fiction?
In truth, do you believe the section
On Lazarus's resurrection?
Nay, nay! 'Tis just a fantasy,
'Tis black magic, necromancy,
With devils pulling all the strings.[18]

By contrast, our Eel of Melun sounds like a very good Christian indeed. He's a believer. Then again, he also sounds like the defeated pagan demon of Bartholomew's own story who cried out, "Stop, you poor fools, stop sacrificing to me, or you may suffer worse torments than those I am suffering. I am wrapped about with fiery chains by an angel of Jesus Christ . . . !"[19] He fears the real performativity of real martyrdom, and the kicker is that he too will face an audience who are more than indifferent to his real fear about his real plight—they are angry about it.

When it comes to justifying what the Eel might or might not have rightly or wrongly believed—if he existed at all—the possibilities seem endless. Maybe he was acquainted with the countless stage directions calling for bloodshed, and feared that his own blood would be spilled.[20] Maybe the fake executioner on Melun's stage that day was also an authentic executioner. If we can believe Rey-Flaud, the citizens of Arles once imported a professional executioner from Avignon to play one on stage, thereby lending immediacy to the torture scenes of one of their Passion plays.[21] Maybe the Eel didn't trust the actor playing the torturer, anticipating the fears of Petit de Julleville about the rudimentary skills of early stage-hands.[22] Maybe his fellow actor was the ancestral kindred spirit of the "lunatic," Junius Brutus Booth, who gave chase to "Richmond" armed with a real sword.[23] Maybe the actor playing the torturer happened to be Languille's real-life rival in love, eager to exact a bit of folk vengeance through the theater. Maybe Languille knew a bit more about Bartholomew than it might seem from a text like the *Golden Legend*, which casts doubt on the saint's actual mode of death. Jacobus de Voragine recalls that "there are various opinions about the kind of death Bartholomew suffered. Saint Dorotheus says that he was crucified. . . . Saint Theodore says that he was flayed. In many books, however, we read that he was beheaded. This disagreement can be resolved by saying that he was crucified, then, before he died, taken down and, to intensify his suffering, flayed alive, and finally had his head cut off" (*GL*, 2:112–13). In other words, one wasn't necessarily crazy to fear crucifixion, beheading, or flaying when one could fear all three at once. Maybe the Eel of Melun thought that the whole of those doubts was infinitely more terrifying than the sum of its parts.

Once we acknowledge that the apprehensive Eel of Melun might have been justified in his believable fears, his legacy is assured. For even if his fears were complete fantasy, the anxieties that subtended them were not. He scarcely needed to anticipate Antonin Artaud's "theater of cruelty" to worry that "once launched upon the fury of his task, an actor requires infinitely more power to keep from committing a crime than a murderer needs courage to complete his act."[24] Furthermore, a bit of experience at the marketplace could have amplified Languille's anxiety, instilling in his mind even what the most flawless performance by Bartholomew's executioner could not. Perhaps on that fateful day, Languille's fellow actor bore a suspicious resemblance to a real fishmonger getting ready for the job of skinning a real eel. Perhaps Monsieur Eel recognized the stance, the position, the shape of the knife poised to prepare the celebrated delicacy of Melun, a town that, Donald Frame tells us, was "famous for its eels."[25] Those culinary techniques endure today and do not present a pretty picture. Hoping not to offend vegetarian sensibilities, I quote David Forrest on the subject of eel preparation and capture:

> In the preparation of kabyaki, live eels are pinned through their heads to a wooden board, slit open down the side of their backs and their guts and backbones removed. This is all done very swiftly, *as one would hope*. A number of European eel merchants skin live eels once a customer has made a selection. An insertion is made just behind the head, extended round the head, the skin raised and then pulled back down the body (rather like taking a stocking off). The skinned eel then dies slowly.[26]

Forrest even comes close to the definition of murder when he refers to "the *actual intentional killing* of eels" by two primary methods: death by salt and death by electrocution. The former seems cruel and unusual in that "the eels thrash around together for up to two hours, gradually absorbing more and more salt, and eventually die."[27] Given Forrest's implication that the tasty prey truly suffer in the process, it is thus reasonable to ask if one might imagine them *screaming*.

Le Roux de Lincy thinks not, and he veritably deconstructs his own story of the Eel of Melun to tell us so. Citing another eminent medievalist, he states that "Monsieur Fournier . . . thinks that the proverb derives from the customary calls of merchants."[28] But Monsieur Fournier goes further than that when he specifies that the protagonist of another work is the "son of Jacques Bonhomme, and not the son of the man who used to scream in olden days *like the eels of Melun and who complained for nothing*."[29] Fournier affirms that

> the origin of the saying: *He screams like the eel of Melun, before you skin him* is uncertain. However, we are no longer in a position to believe that it refers to a man by the name of Languille, resident of Melun, etc. I shall spare you the story. What is more probable is that one should only see an allusion to the cries of fishwives, selling completely fresh, before skinning them, those famous eels of Melun. *Melun Eel, before the skinning*, they shrieked, in their loudest possible voice; and it barely took much more for the people to come up with their saying.[30]

Are we then to conclude that eels don't scream any more than any Eel of Melun ever did?

Although twentieth-century fishmongers report that their catch is silent during the ordeal, we learn from C. L. Deelder's biological synopsis of eels that the beasts find certain visual stimuli to be "highly repellent."[31] He doesn't exactly mention the sight of a knife, but he does cite "objects drawn over the bottom of the water, as is the case with eel trawls," and points out that this "obviously causes a spreading terror among the eel stock, resulting in diminishing catches."[32] Yet even science is not without legends of its own. When Léon Bertin, "Professor at the Museum of Natural History in Paris," introduces his biological study of eels, he includes an entire section, "Truth and Legend." There, he bemoans the perpetration by Pliny of "observations [that are] more or less correct, mixed indiscriminately with legends"; he is even more incensed by the absurdities attributed to Aristotle about the so-called spontaneous generation of eels.[33] "The truth," he concludes, "emerges but fortuitously." So too does that of the Eel of Melun, who shares many features with the real zoological creature.

Since Languille managed to escape his perceived danger, his behavior was in keeping with that of the *anguilla*, notorious for its "slipperiness." A thirteenth-century proverb warns that "Holding an eel by the tail's no closed deal."[34] No indeed. Folklorists have regularly encountered eels, such as those stolen by a corrupt priest who is himself the slippery one: "a certeine sir *John* [who], with some of his companie, once went abroad a jetting, and in a moone light evening robbed a millers weire, and stole all his eeles."[35] Our own Monsieur Eel was also a slippery fellow, slipping in and out of his role of Bartholomew. If we are polite about his performance, we can say that he "put the cart before the horse" or that he "borrowed trouble." If we are impolite, we can say that he went about his duties "ass-backwards."[36] And if I have chosen a more vulgar proverb here, it is for two good reasons. First, Forrest points out that the actual gutting of an eel occurs "ass-backwards": "To gut an eel, a slit is made in its belly an inch or so beyond the anus vent, and the knife is passed up through the belly to the head."[37] Second, the Eel of Melun turns up again in one of the most entertainingly vulgar writers of all time, François Rabelais (1494–1553).

We meet the Eel for the first time in *Gargantua* during the violently farcical Picrocholine War. On the verge of defeat, the obstreperous King Picrochole is busy inflicting horrible tortures upon his disloyal man, Blowhard. Granted, the ordeal is not the flaying alive to which Saint Bartholomew was subjected, but it was no less horrendous: "Then he ordered his archers to cut him to pieces, which was done on the spot so cruelly that the whole room was covered with blood."[38] When his cowardly men start to rise up against him, Picrochole shrieks: "Shit, shit! . . . You're like Melun eels, you scream before you're skinned. Just let 'em come!"[39] Rabelais's Eel next comes forward in the strange land of the *Pantagruel* in which some men "were flaying eels by the tail, and the said eels were screaming before being flayed, as the Melun eels do. Others were making great things out of nothing, and making great things return into nothing."[40] As far as making something out of nothing is concerned, it's hard to imagine anyone better placed than the Eel of Melun. Even so, Rabelais's French editor Guy Demerson found the screaming of the eels perplexing. Despite Fournier's earlier wisdom on the subject, Demerson remarks in a footnote that "the pun derives from the ambiguity of the subject: we do not know whether it is the improvised calls of the fishmongers 'screaming' 'eels for sale'; or if it is the fish themselves that are screaming."[41] Our legend tells us that a real, live Monsieur Eel gave one heck of a yelp, capturing the potent fear that it is *theater* that makes something out of nothing. That fear saved his proverbial life, which was long and healthy.

Just as Clarice Starling could never forget the screaming lambs to the slaughter in *The Silence of the Lambs,* France has not forgotten its squealing Eel. No less an authority than the 1694 *Dictionnaire de l'Académie Française* records his specific existence: "One also says, 'he resembles the Eel of Melun, screaming before you skin him,' to mean that he is complaining of a misfortune that has not yet occurred."[42] Earlier, in 1640, Antoine Oudin had carved out a place for him—or rather, *them*— in this list of six eely expressions:

Anguille de haye, a type of grass-snake.

Eels elude even a good fisherman: even a skilled man can miss his opportunity.

There are eels beneath the rocks. Danger or evil lurks beneath the surface.[43]

To skin an eel by the tail. To go about a thing the wrong way around. And to undertake a difficult task.

To break an eel on your lap. To take up a difficult matter that has no hope of succeeding.

He resembles the Eels of Melun, screaming before he gets skinned. He complains before he has suffered any pain (vulgar).[44]

Le Roux de Lincy further instructs that the shrieking Eel of Melun went on to enter the realm of popular song in such tunes as the "Coq-à-l'Asne": "The simple folk say / That we hear all the squeals / Coming from Melun's Eels / Before they can say 'Flay!'"[45] Finally, the *pièce de résistance:* by the beginning of the nineteenth century, the stage would play host to another eel—another Eel of Melun, to be exact.

Thanks to the pen of Georges Duval, our timorous protagonist reappeared in a vaudeville under Napoleon I. In a play that bears his name, he graced the stage for fifteen performances at the Parisian Théâtre Montansier in Messidor (June/July) of the year XII (1804 of the republican calendar). *Languille de Melun, Vaudeville-Poissard en un acte* is completely obscure today, but it resurrects the slimy antihero in a curious love story. Languille is on his way to meet his intended, Javotte, who is already in love with another suitor. He hopes to impress her with his good breeding, style, and, above all, his fame as an actor: "If you want to get to the bottom of that, then you must be apprised that we have in Melun, on *rue de la Savaterie,* we have us a spectacle that is, like, really *traaaaay distingué and traaaaayze* appreciated by the bourgeois fans. You can even get in *gratis,* provided you pay at the door a little something for the costs. And, *entray nous,* you should also know that I, myself, am one of the best and most expert subjects of this spectacle."[46] It is unclear why Javotte would be impressed with the story of a performance in which Languille's audience turned against him, but he proceeds nonetheless to tell her all about his hallmark narrow escape:

> There lives right here in our fair town
> An author, young, who, buckling down,
> Of late composed a tragedy.
> One night inside the sultan's harem
> A man was found: they tried to scare 'im.
> Some sort of tragedy, you see,
> It all took place out in Turkey.
> Courageously, he fought and fought
> Until such time as he was caught,
> As is the custom—one, two, three-
> They sent him on a torture spree.
> And so I was assigned the role
> Of this poor fellow, oh so droll.
> I even played him happily,
> But then, while playing well, I see
> That, lo! by me a soldier nears;
> His horrid skewer stokes my fears.
> Immediately overtaken,
> I start to shriek 'cause I am shaken.
> I break the rope that's binding me
> And, lickety-split, I am free.
> And if I'd not managed to split
> Then I was boy-food on a spit.[47]

Duval's Eel is just another coward running for his life, running *from* his performance, his role, his lousy acting, and all their consequences, real or imagined. He hot-foots it to a distant coach with whatever belongings he can quickly snatch up, chased all the while by "a band of thirty little good-for-nothings who were screaming: 'Arrest the Eel of Melun, who screams before . . . '"[48] His audience is furious with him for having jumped the gun of representation and for having spoiled their enjoyment of the torture scene.[49] As Languille is about to learn, however, there is more than one way to skin an eel.

Having fallen victim to Javotte's charms, he makes some unsuccessful attempts at romantic badinage in which he can envisage no better seduction than the transformation of his own story into a love song:

> When I'm near you, my lust
> So transports me, my dear,
> I can't help it! You're near
> And my heart wants to bust.
> I now burn on your fire
> I'm cooking, I feel,
> Grilling here on love's pyre,
> M'lun's Eel.[50]

Duval's play seals a happy ending for Monsieur Eel. He and Javotte get married after various obstacles and live happily ever after. Again, the ending for the theater of Melun is more ambiguous.

Gustave Cohen once made the following comment about the typical scenic use of dummies, which were brought on stage at the last minute to replace the actors who were playing roles that called for torture or death: "one can readily imagine that these substitutions were carried out with great technical skill, so as not to lead to too great a feeling of *disillusionment* in the spectator within whom the exposure of fiction would have forestalled the desired emotional response."[51] Contrary to what Cohen thought, the squealing Eel of Melun provided the ultimate *dis*-illusionment. He was so disillusioned by the prospect of death by drama that his terror *dis*-illusioned the audience. No matter who screams or jumps before being touched—the Eel, the audience, or the twentieth-century reader—it was not always possible to make a clean getaway from theater's clutches. Verily, it was frequently impossible to escape the genre so frequently associated nowadays with escapism. Theater could make no guarantees that one could make a literal or figurative escape from *it*.

In 1437 in Metz, two priests narrowly avoided a staged terrestrial death. In the

1380s near Paris, two unfortunate citizens did not succeed in avoiding an unexpected theatrical death. In the timeless story of the Eel of Melun, two Messieurs Languille apparently *did* beat a hasty retreat from the theatrical site of their pretend demise. When Duval's Eel high-tails it away from those thirty good-for-nothings, he eventually gets married. Not so our medieval Eel of Melun who, like Lucian's mad "Ajax," kills off his performance of a character along with his own reputation. He has made a nincompoop of himself and of Saint Bartholomew, and has left a legacy of laughter, disgust, and even vengeful fury from his audiences. How could a mystery play have occasioned such unsympathetic responses to the misfortunes of others?

Drawing on literary and aesthetic theories of the Enlightenment, David Marshall has suggested that such unsympathetic responses to the spectacle of cruelty arise because "battles, accidents, and public executions . . . *feel like theater.*"[52] Medieval commentators had another explanation: the Devil made them do it.

Jean Michel had intimated that the Devil was pulling the strings of religious drama. Was he? A vast cast of characters comes forward to demonstrate that, while the Eel's terror seemed ridiculous, there was nothing ridiculous at all about an audience's outright panic at the threats that one particular character posed to their real lives. Could it be Satan?

The Devil Who Wasn't There

> By this tale ye may see that men fear many times more than they need—which
> hath caused men to believe that spirits and devils have been seen in divers places,
> when it hath been nothing so.
>
> —*A Hundred Mery Talys*

Immediately after Lyonard wowed the citizens of Metz with his Saint
Barbara of 1485, the chronicler of Metz tells a remarkable story—one
that, to my knowledge, has gone completely unnoticed by theater historians:

> It next came to pass that, at this same time, there was performed in
> Bar-le-Duc a play in which there were several men playing the parts of
> devils. Among them was one who, in that get-up, wished to enjoy con-
> sortium with his wife. And she was putting him off and asking him
> what he was trying to do; and he responded: "I wish," said he, "to make
> the beast with two backs *[faire le dyable]*." And, hard as she tried to re-
> sist, she was forced to obey him. It then came to pass that she was preg-
> nant and brought the child to term. But it came to pass that she gave
> birth and was delivered of *a body* that was, from the mid-torso down,
> the form of a man, and, from the mid-torso up, the form of a devil. People
> were much astonished by this thing. And no one dared baptize the
> child until a trip had been made to Rome in order to determine what
> was to be done with it.[1]

This incredible tale is credible for two reasons. First, it does *not* come to
the expected symbolic conclusion that the baby's nether regions constitute the diabolical half. Second, it speaks to a medieval fear that was as
ubiquitous as the Devil himself.

There was good reason to fear the Devil. He was everywhere under
many names: in art, literature, and architecture; in historical chronicles,

proverbial wisdom, jokes, folklore, sermon stories, superstitions, criminal behavior, and the theology of learned and popular cultures.[2] For our purposes, he was all over drama as early as the twelfth century. In the Anglo-Norman *Jeu d'Adam*, for instance, Petit de Julleville claims that "the demons—that is to say, the individuals charged with representing that infernal role—ran among the rows of spectators, creating a levity mixed with fright."[3] In drama, the Devil embodied multiple fears that spanned the realms of crime, punishment, economics, and religion, each with legends attached to them. We shall see in this chapter that they all amount to a single primal fear that theatrical costuming meant diabolical conjuring. Citizens worried that the role of the Devil would stick permanently and performatively to whoever played him (as Ajax's madness had once stuck to Lucian's actor). Presumably, they also panicked at the prospect that a stage devil would place their lives in physical and spiritual jeopardy. Most of all, they feared drama's mystical capacity to invite the real Satan to put in an appearance. It wasn't always clear who exactly was appearing: a man in a devil costume, a truly devilish man, or the Devil incarnate. Nor has it always been clear to theater critics, many of whom have seen the Devil where he was not. He is "the little man who wasn't there," or who probably wasn't. But once the smoke has cleared, there linger traces of all the anxieties that had summoned him in the first place: first and foremost, the fear that theater does his work.

BY THE TURN of the sixteenth century, actors who were lucky enough to snag the roles of Satan and his cohorts were said literally to have taken their devilish behavior "to the streets." In what resembles today's Mischief Night, the actors playing devils in the "expiatory pardon parades" of Chaumont apparently took such a liking to their *diableries* that they began to play them in earnest. Just as Lucian's mad "Ajax" must have already possessed a seed of madness, these fiendish fellows must have been prepossessed of a seed of evil:

> For three months before the plays, from Palm Sunday to the Feast of Saint John, they had authorization to run about the city and surrounding countryside in their costumes in order to announce the festivities: those playing Saracens in the company of Herod's pageant joined them. These parades led to strange abuses: devils and Saracens—enough for an army—began to steal . . . from the villages and marketplaces. Their monetary tolls caused them to be feared and hated, and contributed greatly to the suppression of the mystery plays.[4]

Like our friend the Eel of Melun, the Devils of Chaumont are even credited with the birth of a proverb that "confirms their bad reputation": "If it please God, the

Blessed Virgin, and Saint John, I too will be a Devil and pay my debts."[5] In Chaumont, to play a devil meant to be a thief, on and offstage. Moreover, a peculiar incident of 1539 demonstrates that such stories were nightmares that came true.

Preserved by an *arrêt du Parlement*, this is the story of a family of ne'er-do-well
actors: the Montléon brothers and their cousin Hamel who played Satan. By the
time the *Play of Saint Barbara* began on 10 August in the parish of Tirepied near
Avranches, at least two of the Montléons already "had a record." A warrant had
been issued for their arrest on charges of theft. But since the slippery duo had thus
far evaded capture, the complaining party, the Lord of Vaulevrier, decided to get
them "where they lived"—*during the performance itself,* and not once but twice.
Play or no play, the accompanying officer experienced no Cavellian difficulty in
pointing to the "Montléons" whom he wished to arrest as opposed to the unidentified characters they were playing (*MWM*, 328). That was not to be. On opening
day the Lord of Vaulevrier showed up early:

> Having learned that they each had roles in the mystery play . . . [he] appeared
> there with Officer Dufeu [Firebrand, as it were] in tow. But his timing was no
> good. Since the Montléons had guessed the motive for the presence of Vaulevrier
> and Officer Dufeu, they made it known to all their fellow players and, each and
> every one of them "armed with swords and small daggers, bearing knightly clubs
> and crossbows of various forms, all bearded and banging their drums," received
> Vaulevrier so effectively that he promptly retreated without so much as looking
> back.[6]

Nevertheless, the Lord of Vaulevrier was a persistent fellow. One week later, on 17
August 1539, he returned to the scene of the crime with Officer Firebrand. This
was the second of the four consecutive Sundays that had been booked for the play
of Saint Barbara. This time he came in the middle of the show: "'He had said to
himself that it would be much easier to seize and arrest the Montléons while they
were busy playing.' But he hadn't banked on the *Devil,* who was none other than
the cousin of the Montléons! This cousin, by the name of Hamel, was as nasty as a
devil; and inasmuch as he was the main person in charge of the play, he had chosen
for himself the role that best suited his nature: that of the devil."[7]

The dastardly Hamel intervened on behalf of his cousins with chaotic results.
Loyal to his family and disloyal to the law, he "interrupted the mystery play, rallied
all the actors, and, leading the charge in his devil-costume, rushed Vaulevrier and
his hapless officer, who could think only of retreating as rapidly as possible and 'returning whence they came without *waiting for the closing act.*' For their own part,
Hamel and his trigger-happy troupe, 'each armed with loaded crossbows,' followed

tenaciously in hot pursuit."[8] With a stunning histrionic gesture, Hamel then cast his devil's suit upon the ground, amply showing that he didn't need it. He *was* the Devil, a fact not lost on the police, who had broken no "theatrical frame" since Hamel's iniquity had rendered him one with his part.[9] Only now he was playing a real-life game of cops-and-robbers in which the roles were reversed. Armed criminals were giving chase to the representatives of the law: "Hamel, whose devil-garb was hindering his running, ripped it off and, armed with a sword in both hands, eased off on the chase only when the escapees had put the River Sées between himself and them. After that, the victors returned to Tirepied and resumed the action where they had left off in this most unfortunately interrupted play."[10]

In the end, the reversal of roles was only temporary. Obviously, there could be no letters of remission for such a bad lot.[11] Instead, as Petit de Julleville puts it, "the *affaire* ultimately reached its dénouement before Parliament."[12] The devils, quoth Gosselin, "were not to have the last word. There was an Act V of this *mystère*, which played out before Parliament. Montléon was condemned to be flogged and banished; and Hamel to pay damages—and sent back to testify against his accomplices.[13]

In a positively prescient way, the Montléons' arrest was as theatrical as any modern episode of *Cops*, *Rescue 911*, or a host of voyeuristic television shows depicting the law in action. True, medieval dramatic events had long drawn on the innate spectacle of jurisprudence.[14] But it was something else again to see the play of law playing out legally *within a play*. Tempted though modern theorists might be to invoke Baudrillard, the Montléons' penalty would refute his notion that simulation is dangerous because "it always suggests, over and above its object, that *law and order themselves might really be nothing more than a simulation*."[15] Law and order eventually triumphed over Hamel and his diabolical kind, not on stage but in life—but not before they finished off *Saint Barbara*. Indeed, one wonders if Hamel even bothered to put his costume back on. Hamel's diabolical kind was theater's kind. Witness the fruit of the Devil's theatrical loins in our opening story. Witness the spookier appearances still of the Devil in the flesh.

One might say that it was the nature of a sacred play to call up Satan each time drama arranged to represent him. Superstition had it that there could be no "playing around" when it came to speaking his name, lest the Devil manifest himself in person with deadly consequences. His pointy ears were always listening, always ready to parse someone's words or to give a binding contractual meaning to any smug or careless utterance. With its own propensities toward performativity, drama had always been well placed to review precisely such utterances. So too was the beloved *Miracle de l'enfant donné au Diable*, performed in Metz, for example, on

10 October 1512. "As well played as had been seen in a very long time," according to Jacomin Husson, this play told another tale of domestic sexual abuse like that of Bar-le-Duc. A husband forces his wife to submit to him sexually, even though they have agreed to a life of chastity. She blames the Devil, to whom she pledges any fruit of the coerced union: "The angry wife said that the Devil had played his part in this, and that if she were to conceive a child, that it would be the Devil's and that she would give it to him. And this was ill-advised, for at that very hour, she conceived a son: whence she cursed the evil hour more than one hundred thousand times."[16] Having thus invoked his name, she and her beautiful, pious son are poised to pay the price for her thoughtless words (if not for her husband's thought-less actions). Enter the Virgin Mary when the lad turns fifteen, the appointed time for Satan to collect his debt. She receives leave from God to "go into Hell to take him back."[17] When the child returns from the underworld, he tells "how the thing had played out, and related the great and horrible torments of Hell that he had seen."[18] That was drama's job too: to show and tell anew "how the thing played out." More important, it confirmed tangibly for the audience that, in theater as in life, the Devil was all too close. So close that Jacomin's chronicle of a *miracle play* sounds more like the chronicle of a *miracle*. So close that, in that same month of October 1512, the Devil pulled a similar stunt during a card game with equally dramatic results.

This time, in a motif well known to folklorists, a different sort of "player" paid a stiff price for taking the Devil's name in vain: a card player.[19] During a rough night of gambling, Blanctrain, a habitué of the tables, was heatedly arguing with a fellow player when he made the ominous mistake of swearing not only to "God and his saints" but to the Devil that "never again would he play cards or any other games with that man."[20] "In his fury," he even went so far as to state that "he gave himself over to the Devil, and that the Devil should twist his neck if he were ever to play with the man again." Unfortunately for him, the Devil was listening as Blanctrain entered into a mortal contract, which he foolishly ratified several times. Once the two hotheaded card players had cooled off and resumed playing, up jumped the Devil: "But, by God, listen to the miracle which then showed itself evidently and evidentially *[evidentement]*! For this same Blanctrain, who had thus foresworn and called for the Devil's help, as if someone had clubbed him over the head, dropped to the ground, and while falling, he began to cry and scream, saying in a loud voice: 'Ha! The Devil is taking me away! The Devil is taking me away!'"[21] Having spoken and misspoken the Devil's name, the glad-handed card player now resembled the dummy in the film version of *The Exorcist,* with his head twisted around 180 de-grees: "And upon saying those words, he lost half of himself; and he had his head twisted from front to back; and so he remained, frozen in various grimaces, so that he was taken for dead; nor could he ever speak perfectly again."[22] For a second time, half a body is targeted by the Devil, whose very theological existence symbolized the corporeal duality between good and evil. Too late and too literally, Blanctrain has acquired, exactly where he needs them, "eyes at the back of his head." Actors don't need eyes at the back of their heads in order to watch their backs. Actors "cheat front."[23] The problem underscored by all these stories is that actors and players *cheat*. But they can cheat neither death nor the Devil, as hard as drama may try.

Perhaps nowhere in the history of the stage was that fear more firmly entrenched than in the belief that the Devil might materialize at any time in theatrical company, unintentionally conjured by thespians. "As early as 1594," reports John Cox, "stories surfaced that an extra devil appeared in a production of *Dr. Faustus* at the Theatre, terrifying actors and audience alike."[24] William Prynne affirmed in the *Histriomastix* (1633) that *Doctor Faustus* had rousted "the *visible apparition of the Devill on the Stage at the Belsavage Play-house, in Queene* Elizabeths *dayes, (to the great amazement both of the Actors and Spectators)*."[25] And as if that weren't enough, the same thing supposedly happened again during another *Doctor Faustus* at Exeter. A certain J. G. R. claimed in 1850 to have discovered the following story in a manuscript note "on the last page of a book in my possession printed by Vautrollier in 1585":

> As a certain number of Devels kept everie one his circle there, and as Faustus was busie in his magicall invocations, on a *sudden* they were all *dasht*, every one harkning other in the eare, for they were all perswaded there was one devell too many amongst them; and so after a little pause desired the people to pardon them, they could go no further *with this* matter: the people also understanding the thing as it was, every man hastened to be first out of dores.[26]

Prynne's claim to have heard the "truth . . . from many now alive, who well remember it" has given rise to J. G. R.'s lost manuscript note, which in turn gives rise to the stuff of folklore or, rather, FOAF-lore.[27] If, however, one believed in the Devil (a reasonable assumption in the Middle Ages), then it was as natural to believe in the dangerous performativity of *Doctor Faustus* as it was to buy the stories of Hamel, Blanctrain, and the Devils of Chaumont. But did the Devil really turn up in any of those venues? Or do all these alleged events simply carry the urban legend's usual admonitions about the dark side of pleasure along the lines of "Death in the Funhouse" (*CBA*, 37): when there is work to be done, one should not be out gallivanting at the amusement park—or the theater.

A nineteenth-century version of the story sheds some light on the matter. In 1824 the characters have changed, but the scary situation is the same in *The Sorcerer*, a "celebrated pantomime" played at Lincoln's Inn Fields. As if reviving the snaky goddesses of the *Eumenides*, Richard Ryan relates that twelve devils danced, "represented in dresses of black and red, with fiery eyes and snaky locks, and garnished with every appendage of horror" (*DTT*, 3:189).[28] And then there were thirteen, for suddenly, in their midst, there stood another devil who was, "if possible, more terrific than the rest": "His fellow furies took the alarm; they knew he did not belong to them, and they judged him an infernal, in earnest. Their fears were excited; a general panic ensued, and the whole group fled, different ways; some to their dressing rooms, and others, through the streets, to their own homes, in order to avoid the destruction which they believed to be coming upon them for the profane mockery they had been guilty of" (*DTT*, 3:190). It turns out that the producer, Mr. Rich, had contrived with his friend, Mr. Bencraft, to play a little joke on his theatrical company "without reflecting on the serious consequences."[29] Those consequences included the mantra of any urban legend: "never let the truth get in the way of a good story."[30]

The audience at Lincoln's Inn Fields believed so fervently in the Devil that they clung clumsily to their collective hallucination despite his rapid disappearance and despite the subsequent issuance of an official disavowal:

> The *odd* devil was *non inventus*.[31] He had invisibly fled away, through fears of another kind. He was, however, seen by many, in imagination, to fly through the roof of the house, and they fancied themselves almost suffocated by the stench he had left behind. The confusion of the audience is scarcely to be described. They retired to their families, informing them of this supposed appearance of *The Devil*, with many of his additional frolics in the exploit: so thoroughly was its reality believed, that every official assurance which could be made the following day, did not entirely counteract the idea. (*DTT*, 190–91; original emphasis)

From Lincoln's Inn Fields to Mrs. Fields' Cookies, this is standard urban-legend fare. Mrs. Fields may well have fought the legend that she was charging the exorbitant sum of two hundred fifty dollars for her famous recipe with "a disclaimer that was printed on cookie bags and on a poster displayed in her outlets" (*TGT*, 261). The cookie legend lives on. The satanic hallucination sticks: like "Ajax" 's madness, like Blanctrain's neck. Our bedeviled audiences were the ultimate theatergoers, respectful to the end of drama's special task of creating illusions so convincing and so credible that they were indistinguishable from the truth.[32] Whether or not Satan himself was present that day to twist and corrupt their perceptions is less important than that they *believed* him to be there. Or did they?

Returning now to Petit de Julleville's widely circulated claim about the devils of the *Jeu d'Adam* running among the spectators and "creating a levity mixed with fright" (*TEF,* 3), we discover several irregularities. Although no one has doubted its veracity, this account does not appear to be based on any extant eyewitness corroborations. Rather, in the history of the medieval stage, its wisdom about audience trepidation has become a composite of several sources: the stage directions of the *Adam* itself, plus various postmedieval interpretations of those directions by François Rabelais; the Renaissance poet Clément Marot (1495?–1544); Victor Luzarche, a late nineteenth-century editor of the *Adam;* and Marot's early twentieth-century editor, Georges Guiffrey.

The shadow play begins when Marot uses the expression *pour iouer ung grant Lucifer,* loosely translatable as "to play a devilish prank":

> It seems that we are all aflame
> For we are here tied up in chains
> Fashioned in iron and we're bound.
> It seems that to this place we came,
> Were brought for someone's special aim
> Of *dev'lish monkeying around.*[33]

The diabolical allusion so intrigued Marot's editor, Guiffrey, that he endeavored to prove in a very long footnote that Marot's "little scene is not purely imaginary. It was certainly copied from nature."[34] What has virtually disappeared from the afterlife of that seemingly authoritative footnote, however, are Guiffrey's leaps from various postmedieval fantasies of *diableries* to the presumed realities of medieval theatrical performance and, more troublesome still, to the likely reception by spectators of those fantasies and realities.

Guiffrey states that "when the King of Hell appeared, surrounded by his infernal *cortège,* on the stage of the *confrères de la Passion,* there was always a *noisy explosion* of chains, sobbing, and gnashing of teeth . . . imbuing their diabolical exhibitions with a *terrifying appearance.*" He also creates the impression that he is referring to actual performances of *Misteres de la Passion* in Paris, Poitiers, and Angers, which he backs up with a reference to the edition "published in February 1512 by Michel Le Noir."[35] Nevertheless, closer inspection suggests that Guiffrey has based his opinion almost exclusively upon the prior judgment of Victor Luzarche, from whom he borrows "a little tableau" that he is content to "transcribe word for word." Not really. Here is Guiffrey's paraphrase of what Luzarche had been careful enough to call an *imitation libre* of the *Jeu d'Adam:* "Satan appears in the middle of a troupe of demons, of whom three or four are carrying irons and chains, which they attach to the necks of Adam and Eve. Some of the devils push them, others lead them toward Hell; another group of devils occupies the gate to Hell and *they make a horrible racket* as they attend to the Fall of the two pitiable sinners."[36] The problem is that Luzarche, whom Guiffrey has not even copied verbatim, has already done little more than transcribe word for word the play's stage directions. In David Bevington's translation from the Latin, the *didascalia* that accompany the expulsion of Adam and Eve from Paradise read thus:

> Then the devil will come, and three or four devils with him, carrying in their hands chains and iron fetters, which they will put on the necks of Adam and Eve. And certain ones will push them, others drag them to Hell; still other devils . . . *will make a great dancing and jubilation* over their damnation; and . . . *they will bang together their pots and ca[u]ldrons,* so that they may be heard outside.[37]

Didascalia are directions *to actors* about what to do on stage. While there is no reason to assume that the learned men performing the *Jeu d'Adam* did *not* endeavor to follow such directions as faithfully as possible, there is also no reason to assume that the mere presence of didascalia guarantees that directions were executed successfully, unsuccessfully, or at all.[38] By the same token, there is no reason to endorse the subtle critical interpolations that have relied on a single piece of didascalic evidence about diabolical noise, dancing, and jubilation in order to shift the stakes of the *Adam* from play text to performance to reception. Even Petit de Julleville seems to engage in a similar operation when he alludes to the audience's "levity mixed with fright" (*TEF,* 3). The stage direction says only: "Meantime let devils run to and fro through the *platea,* making appropriate gestures. . . . Then let the Devil withdraw; and he will go to the other demons, and make a foray through the *platea.*"[39] From there, Guiffrey generalized the response by *the medieval public at large* to the "frightful racket" of any Passion play's *diableries.* Relying on none other than the sly Rabelais, he asserts that "Rabelais has preserved for us several details about the *performance* [of Passion plays], which always succeeded in making a vivid impression on the popular imagination."[40] Those details do not exactly inspire confidence.

Once upon a time in the *Pantagruel,* a group of actors avenged themselves on the stingy Friar Estienne Tappecoue, "sacristan of the cordeliers," by putting on their costumes and taking "black sticks full of firecrackers" to frighten him.[41] The story goes that the real poet, François Villon, had retired to Saint-Maixent in Poitou, where he had undertaken "to put on the Passion in Poitevin ways and language." But Villon locked horns with Friar Estienne when the latter refused to lend some priestly vestments (his cope and stole) to the actor playing God.[42] (Apparently, he had yet to hear Panurge's famous speech in the *Tiers Livre* about the pleasures of lending!)[43] An indignant Villon resolved that there would be hell to pay and enlisted his devil crew to mete out the friar's just deserts.[44] The "devils" lay in wait on the roadside, prepared to give Friar Estienne the scare of his life—which was also the scare of his death. It turns out that Tappecoue should rather have been dubbed Tappe*cul* ("beat his ass!"). Unable to disentangle his sandal from the horse's mount, the friar was dragged "flayass" by his filly, torn to pieces, disemboweled, and "de-brained" in what Petit de Julleville calls an "amusing and lugubrious account" (*LM*, 1:381).[45] It is pertinent to our analysis because of its noise. Not only were the devils "girt with great leather belts from which hung big cowbells, and mule-jangles *that made a horriflc racket*," but when they spied their prey, they again made "*a frightful racket*, throwing fire from all sides onto him and his filly, banging their cymbals, and howling like devils."[46]

A *frightful racket* implies that somebody is *frightened*. Finding out who is no easy task. This time, even the brothers Parfaict were skeptical, cautioning that "we dare not ensure that the adventure which Rabelais reports . . . is very reliable."[47] Petit de Julleville agreed and made several efforts to debunk the "famous but doubtful anecdote": "nothing proves that this anecdote is false; nothing confirms its legitimacy."[48] Yet this apocryphal incident has long passed for a trustworthy rendition of the realities of stage devils. Maybe the racket of those cymbals was what Henri Chamard heard when, two years after the publication of Petit de Julleville's *Théâtre en France* in 1923, he rendered one of the stage directions of the *Adam* in his "new translation" as the "*frightful racket* of cauldrons and pots."[49] Since we have yet to encounter the word *frightful* in any of the didascalia of the *Adam*, it is just as plausible to surmise that medieval audiences were not frightened at all when and if the devils rushed among them. If anything, that infernal "racket" seems to have been reconstructed based on intuition, fictional sources, and various proverbs, such as *faire le diable à quatre* (to make a hell of a racket), *un bruit de tous les diables* ("enough noise to raise the dead"), and the ever popular *que diable* ("what the devil . . . ?")[50]

So, what the devil was going on?

Just who was it that was seeing things that were not there—early spectators? ecclesiastical and municipal officials? theater historians? some strange combination of them all? Given the readings, rereadings, and misreadings discussed above, we may wish to speculate that early spectators were no more and no less apprehensive than their modern descendants. Perhaps there never *was* a panicked audience who fled the menacing soldiers of that prophet play in Riga in 1204.[51] Perhaps there were no collective audience hallucinations at *Doctor Faustus* or *The Sorcerer*. Perhaps postmedieval critics have proudly abandoned "medieval" superstitions that might never have played out.

What about the Devils of Chaumont? Their exploits might seem proverbial, having given rise to proverbs. But their *diableries* don't sound like mere superstition. Their abuses would ring true for anyone who has witnessed the spectacular excesses that mark (and mar) New Year's Eve celebrations in Times Square or postparade wilding attacks in Central Park. So too would the deviltry of the Montléons in Tirepied when they broke loose from their thespian engagement to perform real diabolical acts—unless, of course, someone was pulling not just our *foot* (*tire-pied*) but our leg.

Religious drama was meant to instill divine certainty, not diabolical uncertainty. Be that as it may, there reigned one devil of a confusion. For example, when the inquisitor Heinrich Kramer opines that witches cast their spells with the Devil's help, their satanic work bears an eerie resemblance to the work of theater and urban legends. Witches, he explains, cause apparitions "by changing the mental images in the imaginative faculty, so that when men thought the devils were present in assumed bodies, they were really nothing but an illusion."[52] Theater casts its own spell by bringing tangible illusions before the eyes of an audience. Just as Kramer believed that the Devil drew out such illusions from the memory, so too do urban legends *about* the Devil draw out their own mnemonic cast of characters from the collective memory.[53] If a witch can cause a man "to think that he sees with his external eyes" such a creature as a beast "when there is actually no such beast to see," then the Devil's beastly business was theater's business.[54] And that theatrical business was itself the business of legends and legend-making.

We shall see in Part II that as Europe was gripped by the Reformation, the theatrical problem of seeing things that weren't there took on haunting new dimensions. Whatever the later objections of a Calvin, a Luther, or a Foxe (who ridiculed worshipers for "imagin[ing] a body were they see no body"), theater had always been in the business of giving carnal form to imaginary bodies on stage.[55] Where Jean Michel had dramatized the widespread fear that the Devil was pulling the strings of religious drama,[56] so too did the Protestant Reformer Guillaume Farel address the subject, and in remarkably similar language. His section on incredulity in the *Sommaire et brève déclaration* (1525) reads almost like the Devil tale of Lincoln's Inn Fields. Absent a divine anchor to steady them, warns Farel, a credulous people will find it impossible to tell the words and works of God from those of the Devil, a truth from a falsehood, a divine miracle from a piece of black magic:

> Full of inconstancy, [Incredulity] fears where there is nothing to fear, trusts in that which is unsure. With no certain purpose or resolve, it is as changeable as the moon, subject to all manner of trickery and deception. For there where there is

not the light of faith, the bright clarity of the word of God, *there reign the princes of darkness*, there are the missteps and falls into the abyss. Instead of the good path, one chooses to take the path of evil; for the will of God, the dreams of man; for things that are pleasing to God and to his holy doctrines, the diabolical doctrines which He abhors.[57]

In the theatrical world of fictive realities and tangible insanities, one man's faith was another man's fetish; one man's stagecraft, another man's sorcery; one man's folly, another's true wisdom; one man's religion, another's Reform.

Between the years 1509 and 1559, religious drama sought to make present *true* illusions. Its mission was less *make-believe* than *making* audiences *believe*. It was difficult for them to believe anything at all, though, when, by all accounts, the Devil had them doing something else: something that forces a revision of Petit de Julleville's timorous crowd at the *Jeu d'Adam*. They were *laughing*. Laughing like children. Laughing at the Devil. Laughing at God. The Devil now takes us by the hand into Part II, where he demonstrates that, if incredulity was as credible as true belief, and faith as incredible as diabolical magic, then fear and trembling were just as likely as grins and giggles. Or were they?

PART II

Make-Believe

The Laughter of the Children

The first task of the dramatist is to gather us and then to silence
and immobilize us.
　　　　　　—Stanley Cavell, *Must We Mean What We Say?*

According to Frederick Hawkins, "roars of laughter filled the air when
holy men spat in his [the Devil's] face, when liberties were taken with his
tail, when a stalwart anchorite brought him to the dust with a well directed blow, and, above all, when St. Dunstan seized him by the nose with
the traditional red-hot pincers."[1] Richard Ryan agreed—especially when
it came to the fifteenth-century French mystery cycles—that devils were
a "particular favourite with the audience" but "instead of inspiring horror, such was the taste of the day, laughter prevailed."[2] We have every reason to believe that laughter prevailed in the contemporaneous *Farce
nouvelle à troys personnages*, the flip side of the *Enfant donné au diable*, in
which an adulterous wife arranges to have her *curé* lover disguise himself
as the Devil and appear the moment her husband cries, "The Devil take
you!"[3] Laughter still prevails today in Norm MacDonald's comedy routine in which the Devil commands a man to kill his wife and children.
When the man obeys and reports back to the Prince of Darkness that he
has executed his satanic will, the "Devil" rips off his Halloween costume
and reveals himself to be the novice killer's neighbor playing a practical
joke. Meanwhile—oops!—the imaginary wife and children are dead, as
the audience chuckles.[4] Sixteenth-century audiences also chuckled when
reading the terribly amusing tale told by Nicolas de Troyes in the *Grand
parangon des nouvelles nouvelles* (1535–36). To rid herself of three sex-
crazed suitors, a virtuous young lady makes a date with all three in a ceme-
tery, but asks each to wear a different disguise. One is Death; the second,
the Devil; and the third, a policeman. Suffice it to say that the *galant* in the

Death outfit is frightened off by the *galant* in the Devil outfit, who, in turn, scares the bejesus out of the *galant* in the gendarme outfit.[5] The young lady has successfully rid herself of three unwanted suitors by transforming their "suits" into their costumes, while revealing simultaneously *her* true and *their* false identities. Indeed, Nicolas's story is itself based on a play: the delightful fifteenth-century *Farce nouvelle de trois amoureux de la Croix à quatre personnages,* in which a married coquette dupes her three lovers in an identical prank (the only substantial difference being her coquettishness as opposed to the later lady's virtue).[6] As a silly farce becomes a comic prose tale, the medieval theater's legends of pity, fear, and comedy endure in print culture in much the same way that urban legends endure in Brunvand's compilations or theatrical legends in collections of anecdotes. A dangerously delightful story from across the Channel makes that evident.

In the *Hundred Mery Talys* (1526), we make the acquaintance of one John Adroyns, an actor who has just played Satan in Suffolk but who has forgotten a change of clothes.[7] He is thus obliged to retain his Devil costume while returning to his village some two miles away. On the way home, John comes upon a "real devil" in the form of a corrupt parish priest who is busily stealing coneys (rabbits) from the traps of a wealthy landowner. Since the priest is hardly cut from the right cloth, it is really *he* who should be wearing the Devil's costume, and not John Adroyns, who is not *acting the part* of the good guy but actually *is* the good guy. When the inappropriately garbed ecclesiastic and his consorts spy the inappropriately garbed Devil—whom they believe to be absolutely *appropriately* garbed as the Prince of Darkness—they flee the scene. John attempts to set matters right by returning their ill-gotten gains to the rightful owner. But when he arrives at the manor house, still dressed as Satan, he petrifies master and servants alike. Eventually, John understands their confusion: "nay, *feare not* me; for I am a good deuyll; I am John Adroynes your neyghboure in this towne and he that playde the deuyll to day in the playe."[8] He *is* a "good devil," and not an assassin like Villon's men, who also characterize themselves as "good devils" as they are killing Friar Estienne.[9] Our narrator then concludes that "so all the foresayd feare was turned to myrthe and disporte." John Coldewey, however, argues that that unmistakably anticlerical laughter is "not entirely innocent." Commenting adroitly on Adroyns, he notes that a bad priest is the real "poacher of *souls,*" while John's "*false* raiment" is the "secret but *true* 'raiment' of the poaching priest."[10]

This "merry" tale forcefully discloses that theater is second only to religion as a venue for disguise, pretending, and false pretenses. It is the ultimate venue for unmasking the truly hypocritical priests who hide behind their ill-fitting costumes: those who steal coneys or geese, who hoard their copes and stoles, or who have sex with parishioners.[11] Here, theater does precisely what the likes of Saint Basil feared it could *not* do: it reestablishes the proper "harmony between profession and life."[12] It also points out presciently that Cavell's point about pointing is wrong. The story of John Adroyns neatly distinguishes the actor from the Devil and wittily demonstrates that one *can* "point to one without pointing to the other" and that one *can* "point to both at the same time" (*MWM*, 328). More important, the tale makes perilously clear that, on stage or off, theatrical conventions assisted audiences in pointing the finger directly at religion. For clerical and municipal authorities alike, that was cause enough to try to put a halt to such laughter—that is, if audiences were laughing at all.

Long before Umberto Eco ever conceived an exquisite monastic murder mystery that posits the birth of laughter as the death of religion, Eustace de Mesnil of the Paris Faculty of Theology had spoken out vehemently in 1445 against theatrically inclined priests who "rouse[d] the laughter of their fellows and the bystanders in infamous performances, with indecent gestures and verses scurrilous and unchaste."[13] In 1516 the attorney Bartholomew Chassanée was grateful to God Himself for preventing ridicule during a splendid rendition of the *Life of Saint Lazarus* in Autun: "God, moreover, saw fit that, on this occasion, there were no hisses, no commotion among the people, no mockery or derision."[14] In England, the beating of Fergus in the Corpus Christi cycle reportedly "used to produce more noise and laughter than devotion."[15] In the 1530s the humanist Juan Luis Vives voiced his disgust at theatergoers' unseemly frivolity:

> Here, they *laugh* at Judas who boasts of the most inept things in the world while he betrays Jesus Christ. There the disciples flee policemen in hot pursuit, not without a *big yuck* on the part of both the players and spectators alike. Here, Saint Peter cuts off Malchus's ear as people dressed in black applaud him—as if the captivity of Jesus Christ were avenged in that way. And, a little while later, this very man . . . denies his Master while the multitude *laughs* at the chambermaid who questions him and boos Saint Peter who denies Him.[16]

In 1542 the procurator general of Paris concurred that low-brow crowds were taking pleasure in all the wrong things. Far from leaving the theater still drowned in Quintilianic tears, they hot-footed it off the stage while deriding the divine personages whom they had just incarnated: "Returning from these plays, the players would make fun noisily and publicly throughout the streets, imitating some piece of improper language they had heard in the play or some other poorly done thing, shouting derisively that *the Holy Spirit didn't wanna come down* and other sorts of mockery."[17] So it was that, as fifteenth- and sixteenth-century actors and audiences laughed at life and death, believing and disbelieving in their realities, they were cast as too silly, too foolish, too rustic to comprehend the very plays that were presumably being performed for their benefit. After all, only ignorant children would laugh simultaneously at God and the Devil.

There is more at stake here than the subversive function of laughter, as elaborated in the pioneering work of Mikhail Bakhtin.[18] At stake is the actual legislation engineered by clerical and municipal authorities to silence, discipline, and punish audiences for improper responses.[19] The motto of fifteenth- and sixteenth-century French antitheatrical polemic seemed to be: "If audiences behave like children, they will be treated like children." Enter now a critical topos that has itself endured as one of the medievalist's favorite urban legends. In the medieval infancy of humankind, snickering simpletons were so childlike that they couldn't tell the difference between dramatic illusion, theatrical reality, and Gospel truth. Their laughter, it seems, was so hard to fathom that a very old apprehension was new again: theater posed special dangers to children.

Perhaps nowhere is the ecclesiastical angst about laughter better reflected than in the classic tale of Jehan de Pontalais, a loud-mouthed, sixteenth-century actor and *enfant sans souci*.[20] His story comically exhibits that if the conduct of renegade actors was deplorable, then that of audiences and clergymen was even worse. It comes down to us from Pontalais's near contemporary, the author Bonaventure des Periers (1500–1544).[21] But we begin with the version disseminated by the brothers Parfaict, as translated verbatim into English (and without attribution) by Hawkins. It was Pontalais's custom, he writes,

> to sally forth into a public place, execute a short but noisy fantasia on a drum [as we see, in general, in our figure 3], and, having brought around him a large crowd, give forth the name and expatiate upon the good qualities of the next pieces to be played by his brother Devil-may-cares. One Sunday morning, in the middle of sermon time, the congregation at St. Eustache, hearing the sound of his drum in the adjoining square, rushed out to hear what he had to say. The officiating priest followed, naturally in no very amiable mood. "It is like your impudence," he hotly told the farceur, "to make your announcements while I am preaching." "And it is like your impudence," was the reply, "to preach while I am making my announcements." The priest having reported the incident to the magistrates, Pontalais was kept in durance vile for six long months to learn better manners. (*AFS*, 1:26–27)

The moral of the story? The church wins this round. The brothers Parfaict are sure of it, noting that the magistrate "had Pont-Alais put in prison" and that "it was only at the end of six months that the latter obtained his freedom and the permission to continue with his Plays."[22]

Figure 3. Preparations for a play, including an announcer with his drum. Drawing in *L'Ancienne France,* based on a painting by Van Bons (sixteenth century).

Pontalais's punishment sounds real enough. We have it on the authority of the Archives de la Seine-Inférieure, for instance, that in 1462, in Bouafles near Rouen, the Lord of Vieux-Pont spent two days in prison for proceeding with some *Miracles de Notre-Dame* without ecclesiastical permission.[23] Meanwhile, Hawkins has delightfully captured the spirit of the tale, especially in his devilish selection of the term "Devil-may-cares" for the *enfants sans souci* (literally, "children without worries"). But Hawkins is a bit of a Devil-may-care himself, having "plagiarized" a version that had already diverged from what Bonaventure des Periers originally wrote.[24] The *Nouvelles récréations et joyeux devis* contains no mention whatsoever of prison time for the obstreperous actor. That being the case, the question is: who was really laughing at whom and at what real cost?

If possible, the original story is even funnier than its descendants and more trenchant in its unmasking of theological pretense. While the events leading up to the priest's confrontation with Pontalais are more or less identical, Nouvelle 30 by Bonaventure des Periers offers no moral imperative, implicit or explicit, to bow to the will of the Church. Quite to the contrary, *the priest* is punished, even though

Pontalais culpably baits him by deliberately trying to "shut up the preacher, so that the public might come to his plays."[25] The priest is understandably frustrated when his parishioners leave the church en masse. They have departed not to "go shut up that drum" but to hear what Pontalais has to say. The priest gets into the act by descending from his pulpit, making his way to the square, and initiating the famous repartee. Instead of going for the magistrate, he physically attacks Pontalais and destroys his drum, only to acquire a farcical costume of his own:

> Then the preacher, angrier than before, took the knife from his nearby *famulus* and made a great slash in that drum with his knife; after which he went back to the church to complete his sermon. Pontalais took his drum and ran after the preacher and, as if it were an Albanian hat, put the battered drum on his head, costuming the priest with it on the side where the drum had been broken. Then the preacher, finding himself in that state, wished to regain his pulpit so that he might display to the congregation the insult which had been inflicted upon him and show how the word of God had been vilified. But the congregation was laughing so hard at the sight of him with the drum on his head, that he was barely able to be heard. And he was obliged to withdraw and to be quiet about it; for it had been demonstrated to him that a wise man does not take on a fool.[26]

As in the tale of John Adroyns, the priest is the true hypocrite, the true *farceur* in the theater of the Church.[27] Theater, battered but not broken, has unveiled who he really is. Moreover, a *legend* about the theater has disclosed that in this version of the bout, Pontalais is the winner and the Church the loser. As ecclesiastics suited up for the next round, were they responding to genuine events or to works of fiction?

We don't know if the procurator general of Paris knew the story or not. But he griped in 1542 that priests and parishioners were eliminating worship altogether in favor of getting to the show early enough to snag the best seats: "For as long as these plays have lasted, the common people, as early as eight or nine o'clock in the morning—on holy days—would leave off the parish Mass, sermons, and vespers to go off to these plays in order to save their places and to be there until five o'clock in the evening. Preaching stopped, because there would only have been preachers to listen to them."[28] Worse yet, even the shepherds were abandoning their flocks—perhaps because their flocks had already abandoned them. They were neglecting their priestly office for the "box office": "And more often than not, the parish priests, to have the leisure to go to these plays, have left off saying vespers, or have said them all alone toward the hour of noon, not the canonical hour; and even the cantors and chaplains of the holy chapel of the palace, for as long as these plays were going on, said vespers on holy days at the noon hour; and, moreover, they said them hastily and carelessly in order to be able to go to these plays."[29] To be sure, the town council of Amiens believed that to be the case when, on 19 March and 23 October 1550, its *échevins* permitted performances of the *Passion* and the *Acts of the Apostles*, so long as there were "no farces nor impediments to sermons or vespers."[30] Similarly, by the year 1559 Tournai's neighbors in Mons were maligning audiences who "spent all the time they could on plays and banquets. . . . After dinner, instead of going to vespers or to a sermon, they spent their time watching plays, comedies, and farces."[31]

There is nothing uncommon about an urban legend prompting a real response, even a legislative one. Consider a modern individual's decision to stop buying Pop Rocks candy or fast food, to stay off the carnival's merry-go-round, to cease babysitting, or to believe that the U.S. government has concealed the presence of alien beings among us.[32] Foucault's whole point in *Discipline and Punish* is that frightful social dangers are often invented, the better to regulate and scapegoat what may not exist (*DP*, 46–69). Certainly Catholic ecclesiastics believed the threats of theater to be as real as the legendary power of laughter to make real things happen. They thus laid at theater's doorstep a host of sins and social ills, such as heresy, prostitution, avarice, immodesty, spying, theft, violence, wantonness, debauchery, and drunkenness.[33] And they were particularly incensed by the laughter of the "little people." It was laughter that occasioned the objections by Vives and the procurator general to the "cessation of the divine office, a cooling off in charity and alms, infinite adultery and fornication, scandals, derisions, and mockery."[34] It was laughter that motivated the civil authorities of Mons to condemn theater's nefarious effects on theology and politics: "[Participants in the theater] spoke—often in derisive and mocking ways—in the presence of the little people, who were ignorant and indiscreet. They spoke about matters of theology and of the affairs of state, which are the concern of princes and republics. This brought about a disdain for things holy and for good princes."[35] Above all, it was laughter that provoked a flurry of medieval edicts designed to silence silly spectators. Laughter was childlike, but it was also performative, as when, in a later day, poor Mr. Reddish lost his wig and his mind after an audience chortled at his Hamlet.[36] Spectators would need to be protected from theater and from themselves, lest their laughter—be it sympathetic or subversive—perform power instead of submission.

The more powerful (or seemingly powerful) the theater, the more disempowered its audience was required to be. As efforts multiplied to keep spectators safe, silent, and in their seats, a strange pseudo-dialogue was established in which a childlike audience was eliminated from active participation at the same time that its presence was never more compelling. For example, on 29 May 1452, a group of Beauvais clergymen announced bright and early at 8 A.M. that "for the duration of the time, space, and days of these mystery plays of Saint Peter and all things related to them," it was "forbidden to those who are and who will be in the aforesaid public square . . . to make any trouble, noise, or ruckus . . . under threat of whatever fines and punishments shall be deemed appropriate."[37] Likewise, when the town officials of Angers anticipated the performance of Jean Michel's *Passion*, they ruled on 12 August 1486 that an impressive group of civil and ecclesiastical officials would be duly appointed to ensure the imposition of silence: "*Item,* and under threat of similar punishment [i.e., fines and imprisonment], let each and every one be silent and obey those who are commissioned to be present at the play for the purpose of imposing said silence."[38] Silence, remarks Jodogne, was meant to "prepare the spectators for a salutary reflection upon their souls and upon their city."[39] But, by all accounts, French religious drama regularly failed in that mission because silence was so hard to come by. Whence the standard opening plea of such *mystères* as Arnoul Gréban's:

> Open your eyes and look ye here
> Devoted folks, waiting to hear
> Of things salubrious your fill.
> For your salvation, keep ye still
> And give your silence lovingly.[40]

Childish theatergoers refused to sit still and shut up.

In a sense, the story of their disruptions may be traced all the way back to Plato, who had cautioned that public comedy might transform an honest citizen into "a comedian in private." He saw in theater the ultimate metaphor for anarchy, in that "theatre-goers became noisy instead of silent, as though they knew the difference between good and bad music, and in place of an aristocracy in music, *there sprang up a kind of base theatrocracy.*"[41] Plato countered with the interesting proposal that since "the contempt for law originated in the music," then it was music (or theater) which could be marshaled to restrain and retrain an unruly people while reorienting them into a more orthodox theater of the world.[42] As an imitative representation of moral character,[43] theater could then symbolize both the threat to sociopolitical order and the means by which to bring disorder back under control. Such theatrical refashioning was to begin, moreover, with a community's youngest citizens.

One of theater's principal functions was to shape a community's character by ensuring that children would "not become habituated to having pains and pleasure in contradiction to the law." To that end, Plato championed "penalis[ing] the disobedient" by means of a disciplinary option that would prove near and dear to the

Middle Ages: "the children and their ushers and the general crowd were kept in order by the *discipline of the rod.*"[44] However, a theatrical performance for the proverbial sake of the children had its work cut out for it. Even Rabelais declared that Villon's devils on the prowl had made their appearance "to the great satisfaction of the people and great terror of the little children."[45] Much later, André de Lorde advised dramatists and producers for the Grand Guignol: "as for a public who is ready for all manner of jokes and who is disposed to latch on to the slightest subject of ridicule, you must transport them into an atmosphere of pain, of mystery, and of death and hold them there by force. This is not as easy as it sounds."[46] Nor was it so easy in early France, where municipalities sought to protect their children from the theater.

When the councilmen of Mons ruled on 26 June 1501, concerning an impending performance of a Passion play, that "no children under the age of ten shall enter nor any senile old people nor any pregnant women," they revived an urban legend of theater that had struck fear into audiences' hearts ever since that ominous incident from the *Eumenides.*[47] We have already seen that, when women purportedly miscarried in 460 B.C., theater endangered children not only after but *before* their birth.[48] The council of Mons also confirmed that because rhetorical games, comedies, and farces had "incited the youth (sons and daughters alike) to nastiness and immodesty—aside from the fact that these pieces had heretical content—the principal bourgeois of this city have strictly forbidden their children to attend such performances."[49] Although the Mons legislation is virtually unknown today, its message is identical to the contemporary rhetoric that demands that the influential media make artistic concessions "for the sake of the children." Centuries before movies and television programs were rated for sex, violence, nudity, and graphic language, different hegemonies expressed their own misapprehensions that certain spectators—especially women and children—were incapable of distinguishing representation from reality. Consequently, they were not to be exposed to art.[50] As antitheatrical polemicists faced the cognitive dissonance of protecting the very children whose blood was shed so graphically during such a play as the *Slaughter of the Innocents,*[51] they infantilized theater's "ignorant" audiences. In that way the audience's defective mental status might help the Church to regain what theater had lost: control over the flock. Even the Church could not have anticipated who would take up that call.

In the end, it did not matter very much whether or not our fifteenth-and sixteenth-century ecclesiastics were responding to the fictions of Pontalais's outburst or to the realities of crowd control. Nineteenth- and twentieth-century commentators often accepted their assessments uncritically, ruling that rustic spectators were as ignorant about the difference between realism and reality as they were about the moments when to laugh or to cry at a comedy or tragedy—even though there was no such thing as a *tragedy* of the Passion.[52] The brothers Parfaict complained that the inappropriate applause of the early public had compromised the very taxonomy of the sacred theater: "One convincing proof that the *Mystère de la Passion* is only crudely known *[vulgairement connu]* is that many people say the *Comédie de la Passion*, a designation that this poetry has never received except from the ignorant and the impious."[53] Here, it is as if the entire medieval audience has become an *enfant sans souci*, a child without worries, or, as Hawkins chose to translate it, a "Devil-may-care" (*AFS*, 1:26). Religion is for children; yet it is not for children. The naive or the childlike have special protections from God; yet they do not. Simple folk should not dabble in the divine; yet their laughter is ubiquitous and contagious, albeit frequently at their own expense, even among such great friends of the medieval drama as Petit de Julleville, Gustave Cohen, and Raymond Lebègue.

Petit de Julleville, taking a page out of Vives's book, found that "from the most refined to the most vulgar," spectators suffered from what we might call a peculiarly medieval brand of bipolar disorder in their quest for catharsis:

> Such, we believe, were the diverse and complex sentiments that filled the souls of medieval spectators during the representation of the mystery plays. They laughed at the vulgar jokes of the executioners, beggars, and servants; they cried when they saw the Savior of mankind the butt of so many jokes, horrors, and cruel tortures. *They laughed and cried at the same time, alternatively and sometimes almost at the same time in the way that children do.*[54]

His solution to the historical problem of audience response was a hopeful recourse to one of the great teleologies of literary criticism: medieval people were children, while the critic and his peers are adults.[55] By infantilizing his ancestors, Petit de Julleville is able to preserve both his God and his relationship to the immature past that sired him, as he distances himself in a critique dressed up as kindness. Lebègue also trumpeted modernity's superior psychological faculties as opposed to medieval playwrights' paltry "experience of the human soul." Suffering from an arrested state of affective development, "they were mediocre psychologists. They knew how to define the cardinal virtues and mortal sins, but they were ignorant about the systems of feeling and its complex forms."[56]

For real kindness—or at least a kinder explanation of early laughter—we might rather look to Clément Marot's poetic epitaph honoring Jean de Serre, "Excellent Player of Farces." When the actor died during the reign of Francis I, mourners had a tough time shedding tears for him because of the vivid memory of his comic life on the stage:

What do I say? They mourn him not?
They do indeed; they mourn a lot.
The whole point is they laugh so loud
That tears well up inside the crowd.
They cry for him with laughter deep
Just as in laughing, so they weep.[57]

If it was easy to attribute terror to credulous medieval and Renaissance spectators, it was difficult to hear their diabolical laughter. Rabelais's grisly tale of death by *diablerie* was one big joke, designed to prompt not terror but laughter. Yet there is evidence that the joke had already waned by the end of the eighteenth century. When J. M. B. Clément included the story of Estienne Tappecoue in his book of theatrical anecdotes, he sanitized its brutal conclusion, telling a kinder, gentler version in which Villon's devils intend "to give him quite a scare, *if not to hurt him in any way.*" Their prank leaves Friar Estienne only "*half-dead* and all broken from his fall."[58] Under the circumstances, it is ironic that Clément introduces his story with the catch-phrase, "*if we are to believe Rabelais*" (*AD*, 2:568). He has not even circulated Rabelais's version.

Early laughter was so hard to hear, it seems, that Gustave Cohen was offended by the close proximity of comic relief to such violent episodes as the slaughter of the Innocents. Of a childish and effeminate crowd whom he deemed "as excessive in its laughter as in its tears," he speculated that

> in this rapid passage from laughter to tears, we catch a glimpse of the entire soul of the early Middle Ages. Like children, they laugh loud and long with a big guffaw at the slightest thing: at a raised stick, a talking ass, a Jew shaking his head and kicking; and then they cry and swoon with equal ease. So it was for those primitive warriors of the time who, even though their bodies were encased in iron, had weak and childlike souls and fainted like women.[59]

One might readily criticize Cohen for his prejudices about laughter, gender, and theatricality. But today's tendency to suppress medieval laughter in favor of an excessive sophistication is no less problematic. For example, Richard Homan concludes of the slapstick humor of medieval crucifixion scenes, "I doubt that the original audience laughed at the difficulties with which the soldiers do their work."[60] Why wouldn't they have laughed—any more than learned academic audiences alternatively laugh or groan when they first hear the story of Tournai? any more than most readers do the first time they read the stories of the insane "Ajax" or the wigged-out Mr. Reddish?[61] any more than most moviegoers do at the song-and-dance number of the Spanish Inquisition in Mel Brooks's *History of the*

World? The simultaneity of audience fear and laughter appears to be as firmly entrenched as it is in "The Alligator in the Sewer" or "The Mexican Pet." So we might also ask if it was really so childish to be afraid, or unafraid? Was it reasonable to laugh, to cry, or to laugh and cry at the same time? If anything, all of our tall tales suggest that we are no more ready for theater's lessons than medieval audiences were.

Consider this philosophical outing to the theater with Stanley Cavell. This time, we do not attend with a yokel, although our escort does hold a childlike conviction that someone is in danger. Instead, we accompany a terrified tot who is too young to understand the theatrical event to which he has been taken. As adult chaperones, we must attempt to soothe the distraught child with a speech that may be untrue. The child must come to believe the very thing that those two priests at Metz, the Eel of Melun, or Lucian's "Ajax" would *never* have believed: that it's all just pretend: "'They are only pretending' is something we typically say to children, in reassurance. . . . The point of saying it there is not to focus them on the play, but to help bring them out of it. It is not an instructive remark, but an emergency measure. If the child cannot be brought out of the play by working through the content of the play itself, he should not have been subjected to it in the first place" (*MWM*, 329). Faced with the conceptual emergency of late medieval religious plays that are staged on the tenuous borderlines between fiction, the "nonfiction" of Christ's Passion, and real life, we too are being "helped out" of the theater. Ultimately, though, that the Church—and, eventually, *churches*—tried to *help* audiences *out* of the theater is precisely what helps us back in.[62] Since the truth had been ruled elusive to childlike audiences, then spectators would need a hand with what and whom to believe.

Whether the spectators were naive or learned, whether the threat of theological uncertainty was real or unreal, theater audiences were presumably God's children. The problem was that they were *children*, into whose dangerous hands both theater and theology might fall. Therefore, it was important to prove that childlike audiences were intellectually incapable of pondering complex theological arguments about realism, reality, and the interpretation of signs. In that respect, even Protestants and Catholics could occasionally agree as they denounced one perceived peril that stood out above all the rest. Ecclesiastics expressed their terror—itself terrifying—that immature spectators would be unable to distinguish between Christianity and Judaism.

When that enraged procurator general, a Catholic, sought in 1542 to deny a request from the *confrères de la Passion* to stage the *Mystery of the Old Testament*, he justified his acrimony by proclaiming that "there are certain things in the Old Testament that it is not expedient to declare to the people, ignorant folk and imbeciles whose lack of intelligence might motivate them to convert to Judaism."[63] When the Reformist polemic of the *Farce des Théologastres* was staged in the early 1520s, the allegorical character of Faith accused Catholic theologians of "mistaking for true piety / a Judaic ceremony."[64] When Albert Babinot, a Protestant, published in 1559 a poetic collection known as the *Christiade,* he imparted a special repugnance for theatrical godlessness: "The comic, pancake smeared all o'er his face/Does mock the Gospel up there on the stage/As would a Jew or Pagan."[65] Elsewhere, Vives grumbled that the plays that celebrated Jesus Christ were "barely distinguishable from those old stage performances of the pagans";[66] while Farel compared pagans to Jews and renewed the oppositions between Jews and non-Jews. Farel urged Christians to eschew "pagan bacchanals," "Jewish hypocrisy," and "Jewish traditions and obligations [that trample] Christian liberty under foot."[67] In other words, if all the threats, all the injunctions, all the commitments to censorship, all the promises of punishment, all the dismissals of public naïveté wouldn't work, then maybe something else would. After all, not all the censorship efforts in the world have ever extinguished the dramatic impulse.[68]

Maybe *theater* would work. Like Platonic *mousike,* maybe theater could repair what theater had broken. Maybe a play could be enlisted to destroy the very resemblances that drama seemed to propagate between Christian and non-Christian cults. Maybe the right play could certify that the Jewish religion was mere spectacle. One such play enabled sixteenth-century Paris to revisit one of the most notorious anti-Semitic legends of all time: the tale of the tortured, bleeding, resurrected Host. The *Mistere de la Sainte Hostie* does a harrowing job of showing that in any theatrical ministration to God's children, belief itself was at stake. Or at the stake.

CHAPTER NINE

Burnt Theatrical Offerings

The dead souls resurge, within the work whose postulate was their disappearance
and the possibility of analyzing them as an object of investigation.
—Michel de Certeau

Once upon a time, something happened in thirteenth-century Paris that
was so startling and so violent that a Carmelite church was built to honor
the site where it had taken place, and a play was written to chronicle both
the miracle and the formation of a theater guild *(confrérie)* to celebrate it.
At least, so goes the legend of the Jew and the sacred Communion Host.

Most historians of the medieval French stage come to the tale by way
of Petit de Julleville, who presents with great interest the mediated testimony of two historians of the city of Paris, Michel Felibien (1665–1719)
and his eighteenth-century editor, Guy-Alexis Lobineau. Petit de Julleville confirms that "there is no doubt that this *confrérie* existed; and it is
perhaps on its account and upon its orders or at its expense that the
Mistere de la Sainte Hostie was composed and performed."[1] The anti-
Semitic story of that fifteenth-century play is immediately recognizable
to medievalists, who have increasingly evaluated the Croxton *Play of the
Sacrament* as a notorious landmark in English cultural studies.[2] But before we ascertain what Felibien really said, it is worthwhile to review the
French version of the play, which is much less known and much less ac-
cessible than its English analog.[3]

The plot of the *Sainte Hostie* revolves around the Jew, Jacob Mousse,
who exercises economic mastery over a fallen Christian widow. She
wishes to don her best dress for Easter (her *pâques* and the Jew's Passover
or *pâque*), but she must first buy back her surcoat, which she has previously sold to him for cash. Designated only as "La Mauvaise Femme," the
unnamed widow strikes a deal with Jacob Mousse. She agrees to fake

Communion at church, to *pretend* to swallow the Host, and to deliver her Communion wafer to Jacob. Jacob then subjects it to a series of tortures in order to determine whether or not the Host is the true embodiment of a resurrected (and eternally resurrectable) Christ. So gruesome and bloody is the ordeal and so persuasive its transformation into the ascending figure of Christ that Jacob's wife, son, and daughter convert at the sight (and the site) of it. After Jacob's son has spread word of the miracle throughout Paris, local authorities arrive at Jacob's home and retrieve the Host. Judgment is exacted upon Jacob, who is burned at the stake in a town square normally reserved for the buying and selling of pigs.[4] His wife and children are baptized, and his private Jewish home is converted into a public place of Christian worship, the Église des Billettes: "And let this be our legacy / That here inside our own Paris / Inside the home of that damned Jew / A monastery be founded."[5] At that point, there remains only the delayed retribution against Jacob's accomplice. La Mauvaise Femme has escaped to Senlis with a new identity as a chambermaid in a wealthy household. During her seven-year service there, she is subjected to the graphic sexual advances of a valet, who rapes and impregnates her. When the child is born, she murders it, for which crime she dies at the stake after a public confession.[6]

With blatant intolerance, Jacob's story warns a Christian community about the menace posed by Jews, while the widow's story issues an equally powerful warning against consorting with the enemy, miscegenation, infanticide, or what one might call "ritual murder by proxy."[7] Once Jacob's house has been refashioned through violence into the Église des Billettes, it enters the "vast topology of French symbolism" that Pierre Nora terms *lieux de mémoire* (places of memory).[8] The legend of Jacob and the Evil Woman is literally "monumentalized" by a church, an architectural site constructed over the razed home of a Jew.[9] The question is: what have the place and the play enshrined?

Like all the legends we have reviewed thus far, the play speaks volumes about the anxiety-driven and anxiety-provoking superstitions experienced by any given community. Like modern urban legends, it captures and commemorates a scary story that, whether true or false, appeared believable enough to anyone hearing or circulating its anti-Semitism. In its day, the tale would have seemed all too believable in a culture that advocated surveillance of the Jews. In that great theatrical city of Mons, for example, Jews were "tolerated" after 1321 on the riverfront (today the Rue des Juifs) so long as they allowed four Christian "crusaders" into their synagogues to monitor their activities.[10] Fifty years later, an "Inquisitor of the Jews" was appointed to investigate "the sacrilege that several of their nation had committed in Brussels by stabbing the sacred Hosts, whence there issued a miraculous blood that is still preserved till this very day."[11] And yet, if the Jews did *not* kill and cannibalize innocent Christians, then where was the proof of the *Sainte Hostie*?[12] Historiographically speaking, we find ourselves at the same critical impasse that Ronnie Po-chia Hsia, Miri Rubin, and David Nirenberg have confronted in their own work on medieval anti-Semitism.[13] Surely, in a post-Holocaust world in which revisionist history has threatened the realities of the Shoah, the truth or falsity of the story must matter a great deal. It must also matter whether or not any Jews really committed the violence that supposedly justified the Christian retaliations acclaimed by the *Sainte Hostie.*[14]

More explicit and more frightening than the Croxton *Play of the Sacrament,* the *Sainte Hostie* forges a conceptual bond between drama and real life whose virulence far surpasses the apparent bounds of any stage play. Each time a Christian audience gathered together in the old familiar places of theater to designate Jews as evil and to self-designate their fellowship as virtuous, they reenacted a drama that demanded that Jacob's effort to disembody the embodiment of Christ be avenged by the disembodiment of the Jews.[15] As we shall see, they also saw and heard that such vengeance was to be exacted by all manner of "conversions": the appropriation of Jewish property, surveillance, prosecution, persecution, and extermination. I suggest below that when Host desecration legends became intertwined with actual performances of the *Sainte Hostie,* they built upon the architectural foundation of the Église des Billettes renewed conceptual foundations for the real and imaginary eviction of Jews from the city of Paris.[16] Indeed, the legend's legacy appears to owe as much to theater as it does to folklore. Just as the stage directions for deviltry had a way of seemingly authenticating histories that never occurred, the power of prevarication was even more persuasive when cloaked under the apparent authority of genuine performances.[17] The old anti-Semitic legend seemed more real because of theater.

THE TEXT OF THE *Sainte Hostie* contains various self-conscious attestations to its historical reality, as when a priest warns the audience, directly before Jacob is sent to the slaughter, that they have seen "a great miracle, not a play *[non pas jeu]*."[18] Moreover, various aspects of the Paris legend were confirmed by Felibien, who reported that with the official permission of Pope Boniface VIII, a Parisian bourgeois called Rainier Flaming had built in 1294 the Chapel of the Miracles "upon the very site . . . where the Jews had pierced the Holy Eucharist with a knife and had thrown it into a cauldron of boiling water which was miraculously converted into blood."[19] Additionally, we have the assurance of the another *bourgeois de Paris* that the *Sainte Hostie* was known to Parisians by the mid-fifteenth century. On 15 May 1444 there was a splendid procession of "nine to ten thousand people, not counting the clergy" in which the faithful went "most reverently to fetch the little knife *[canivet]* with which the false Jew had cut up our Lord's flesh. . . . After the holy relics came the whole Mystery of the Jew; he was shown bound in a cart with thorns in it as if he were on his way to be burned; next came the judge; then his wife and children."[20]

There also survives an exceptionally detailed account of a performance of the *Sainte Hostie* in Metz in 1513, recorded by the meticulous Philippe de Vigneulles.[21] He was in attendance on the first day of Pentecost when the play's violence came to life. His account is corroborated by Jacomin Husson as well, who is considerably less loquacious but who notes that, on that same day, the *Sainte Hostie* was played in the Place de Chambre, and that "it was a most beautiful miracle and very well played."[22] Furthermore, the dramatization of the legend must have appeared all the more real to Philippe in that in 1504 Metz had been the site of an actual infanticide committed by an unnamed "mauvaise femme" in service. Both Philippe and Jacomin chronicle the fate of this mother, who paid for her crime with her life on 9 December: after giving birth, "she took her child and threw it into a well at the house of Clément d'Oultre Seille in Porsailly; and the aforementioned girl was in service in the house of the aforementioned Clément."[23]

What has *not* survived, however, is the legend's bedrock: the Église des Billettes itself. The expiatory Chapel of the Miracle, recalls Jacques Hillairet, "was demolished and buried toward 1410 when the entire street was raised."[24] Naturally, one still finds in modern Paris an Église des Billettes. It is situated at 24, rue des Archives, near the old Jewish quarter, the Marais. But inside there is no sign of any Host desecration legend, although Hillairet takes readers of his walking tour directly to that address and retells the whole harrowing story. Something has changed, though. His protagonist is no longer Jacob Mousse but Jonathas, like the character in the Croxton *Play of the Sacrament*. Further, he begins with the standard opening gambit of the urban legend:

> *They say that*, in 1290, a miserable woman was unable to buy back her clothes, which she had pawned—except on the condition that she bring to Jonathas the Host that she would receive at Communion. Once she had received it at Saint-Merri on the day of Easter, the miserable woman hastened to turn it over to the Jew. . . . The neighborhood was outraged. Jonathas was arrested and condemned to be burned alive. His possessions and his house were confiscated to the advantage of Philippe-le-Bel.[25]

Since it is unlikely that the names in this piece of pseudo-history have been changed to protect the guilty, it is helpful to return to Felibien's version in order to sort out fact from dramatic fiction—once we can find it, that is.

As it happens, Petit de Julleville proves an ineffectual conduit to this source, for he fails to provide so much as a page or volume number to the five considerable tomes of the *Histoire de la ville de Paris*. Fortunately, the brothers Parfaict come to the rescue by referring us to Felibien's description of the Paris procession of 1444, where the historian states that he has already spoken of the *Mystery of the Jew* "in its proper place."[26] That "place" turns out to be his entry for the year 1290: *The Story of the Sacred Host profaned by a Jew. And the Convent des Billettes.* Notwithstanding Hillairet's later guided tour, Felibien locates the miraculous events on the Rue des Jardins (in the same quarter several blocks away). His lengthy account is teeming with the sort of localized detail that would authorize any urban legend. It tells us virtually everything but the Jew's name:

> At the beginning of the pontificate of Simon Matiphas, there came to pass in the *rue des Jardins* the *miracle of the Eucharist which has since become so famous.* A woman had pawned for thirty sous—that is, for approximately a half-mark of silver—her most beautiful clothes to a usurious Jew. Toward the Easter holiday of the year 1290, this woman went to ask the Jew for her clothes back and she prayed him to lend them back to her for that day only, which, in that year, fell on the second day of April. The Jew told her that if she would be willing to bring him back the bread of the Eucharist which the Christians call their God, he would give her back her clothes for keeps and without any money. The woman accepted the deal, and come Easter Day, she presented herself for Communion at the Église Saint Merri of her parish. She received the holy Host, took care to conserve it whole, and delivered it to the Jew.[27]

The Jew's name does not matter. He is all Jews. But as the famous miracle runs its course, something else also matters. Felibien has melded so many voices and so many versions that it becomes difficult to tell whether he is reporting a *legend* with spectacular features or a *spectacle* with legendary features.

When Felibien arrives at the part about the gruesome tortures inflicted upon the Host, his blending of verb tenses substantially clouds the issue of whether the narrative is unfolding in the characters' past, his present, or our future. As he proudly declares that the story is "still preserved to this day" in yearly processions and that the Reformed Carmelites still honor it by showing "the kitchen knife that the Jew used for his crime," Felibien does for his readers what any good drama does.[28] He renders them witnesses to a scene that he explicitly casts as theatrical and that even includes pieces of dialogue:

> Receiving the Host, [the Jew] said, "I will know soon if this is the body of Jesus Christ, as the Christians teach in their books." Upon which he puts the Host

upon a strongbox and pierces it with several blows of his knife. *They say* that blood gushed out immediately and in abundance, as if from a living body. Initially surprised, the Jew calls his wife and his children, *who were dumbfounded by this spectacle.* . . . Struck by so many prodigious things, [his wife] retired to a separate chamber so that she might cease being a *spectator* to her husband's fury.[29]

The vocabulary of *spectacle* is crucial. Consider, for instance Jacomin Husson's remarkable account of the *Enfant donné au diable* of 1512.[30] It almost sounded as if he were relating a historical event when he was describing a play. What if the same holds true for Felibien? What if he is describing not a legend but a performance of the *Sainte Hostie?* What if parts of the legend are *based on* that performance? That possibility seems more and more reasonable once we compare the striking similarities between Felibien's "history," the Metz performance of 1513, and the stage directions of the play itself.

The Paris legend undoubtedly lived long before the *Sainte Hostie* ever restaged it. So it is possible that the stage directions reprised a sequence of tortures that was already circulating in oral tradition. But it is also possible that the converse occurred: that certain aspects of an actual *performance* attached themselves to the original story (or stories). In other words, it is possible that *theater* materially informed and transformed the legend's afterlife. For example, although Robert Clark and Claire Sponsler cautiously contend that "no records of a Parisian performance of this remarkable play have survived,"[31] Felibien (and the brothers Parfaict who follow him) leave no doubt about it. What Parisians saw in the *Mystery of the Jew* of 1444 was "*a dramatic representation* of everything that had happened in the thirteenth century when they took to his death the sacrilegious Jew."[32] Indeed, the *bourgeois de Paris* seems to reinforce that notion by suggesting the prospect of pageant wagons: "There were two platforms put up in the streets with very touching mysteries on them and the streets were decorated as they are at Corpus Christi."[33] One may thus ask: Did Felibien know the play, the legend, or both? And what about Petit de Julleville, or Hillairet? The last-mentioned pledges that "Jonathas took [the Host] and stabbed it several times with a kitchen knife, upon which blood immediately gushed out from it in abundance. Jonathas then threw it into a cauldron full of boiling water, upon which the Host immediately became red as blood as it rose up above the cauldron."[34] Have all these presumably reliable sources done precisely what so many legend-mongers do? Have they confused history with the believable, living spectacle of theater?

The didascalia of the *Sainte Hostie* graphically depict a progressive ordeal during which Jacob "takes the Host and nails it with a nail upon a column and blood runs out upon the ground." Next, he "casts it into the fire, where it will not stay." He then takes a lance and smites the Host against the fireplace, after which he takes a kitchen knife and chops up the Host; upon which "there appears a crucifix in the cauldron against the hearth."[35] (Compare to figure 4.) When Felibien reprises this new crucifixion, he supports its veracity with an unidentified legal document as the scene reaches its dénouement at the fireplace:

> But, instead of stopping, the Jew drove in a nail with a hammer into the sacred Host, which continued to spill blood. His wife, sore afraid, tried to stop her husband; but, full of rage, he takes the Host and throws it into the fireplace. *The act recorded on this subject* attests that the Host rose up without having been harmed, and began to fly about the room. The Jew tried to hurl it into *the filthiest place in the house [le lieu le plus infect de la maison]*, and wound up throwing it into a cauldron of boiling water. *They say* that the water turned red, that the Host came out whole, and that the wife saw upon it the representation of Jesus Christ attached to the cross.[36]

This grotesque allusion to the "filthiest place in the house"—probably the chamber pot—starts to make sense only when we read it in light of that actual performance of the *Sainte Hostie* of 1513.

Although Philippe de Vigneulles never forgets that he is talking about *a play*, praising on several occasions its marvelous special effects, he does make this curiously vulgar comparison (which exists in none of the extant versions of the play): "Wanting to test [the Host] to see if it were God, the traitorous Jew took the aforesaid Host and put it on a table and stuck a knife through it. Then, *by means of a special effect [secret]* that had been fashioned, there emerged a great abundance of blood and it shot upward from the aforementioned Host, *as if it were a child pissing. And the Jew was all soiled and bloody and played his part very well.*"[37] Felibien's version, which has the Jew trying to hurl the Host into the "filthiest part of the house" is more logical in light of Philippe's "child pissing," which might itself have derived from yet another version of the legend that went on to inspire the Metz production.[38] Meanwhile, that the bloodthirsty Jacob has progressed from a pot of excrement to a pot of food (the cauldron at the hearth) is—to coin a phrase that the *Sainte Hostie* would doubtless sanction—disgusting beyond belief. Belief is what the play is all about.

It is not mere happenstance that in at least three versions of the Paris legend (Philippe's, Felibien's, and the play's), the stabbing violations of the Host culminate at the fireplace, the symbolic heart and hearth of any home. When Philippe tells us that the Host "rose up out of the fire and affixed itself upon the fire-guard of

Figure 4. The Paris Host Desecration. Detail of altarpiece by Jaime Serra
(c. 1400), Barcelona, Museum of Catalan Art.

the hearth *[contre-feu]*," its ascendancy coincides with Jacob's own family rising up against him.[39] It is at Jacob's *mantelpiece* that his family is *dismantled*. The linguistic resonances of the *contre-feu* are as saturated with meaning as the technical effects of the play. The *contre-feu* was a metal plaque that, like modern fire-screens, was designed to protect homes from fire damage. In the *Sainte Hostie*, it belies other connections to faith, incredulity *(contrefoi)*, play-acting *(contrefaire)*, and counterfeiting *(contrefaire)*—whether by actors or by Jews.[40] Philippe has narrated an incredibly credible scene in which Jacob's incredulity *(contrefoi)* is both represented and undone *(contrefaite)* at the *contre-feu* by actors doing what they do best: *counterfeiting (contrefaire)* real emotions and real things. In the end, it is the Jew who is vanquished time and time again by actors who celebrate and relive an ostensibly real historical event by impersonating Jews, the false practitioners of a false faith. He loses his home, his life, and his family (to baptism) because, among other things, his Jewish wife abjures the spectacle of his perfidy just as sixteenth-century audiences welcomed it.[41]

If ever there were a medieval demonstration of what Brunvand calls the folkloric process of "communal re-creation," this was it. "People in a folk community," he writes, "absorb new material into their oral culture, then remake it through repetition and creative retelling" *(VH,* 14). In a powerful false-true tale of the true-true assimilation of Jewish property, the *Sainte Hostie* provides a rationale for persecution. That message may then endure long after the actual church honoring the apocryphal story has disappeared. It may endure even more readily in that the *trustworthy* details of a *trustworthy* account of a theatrical performance might be forever muddled with the *untrustworthy* account of supposedly true yet *untrustworthy* historical events. Therefore, as ecclesiastics continued to launch anti-Semitic objections against theater,[42] the real theatrical performances of a fanciful subject like the *Sainte Hostie* tended to ground the reality of their anti-Semitism in the reality of performance. The *Sainte Hostie* doesn't seem *as true* as history; it seems *more true*. So too would the insidiously enduring stereotype that it perpetuates—the financially rapacious Jew.

In a manner worthy of the *Merchant of Venice,* the *Sainte Hostie* connects dishonesty and faithlessness with Jewish usuriousness and economic power. It was not only vanity but poverty that had caused the Mauvaise Femme to agree to Jacob's terms, his own wife chiming in to say, "About this act no one will ever know;/At least you'll be dressed up and, I daresay,/With no interest or principal to pay./For someone in such straits, it's a great deal."[43] Soon enough, Jacob's daughter predicts her family's reversal of economic fortune when she warns: "And thus before midnight/The one whom my father did smite/Will give him payment back in kind."[44] Local authorities within and without the play then urge that the public ensure its own payback, declaiming that

> Ladies and gents, your lesson's made
> As he has lent, so he is paid.
> He's come apart, the Jewish liar,
> He and his book, burned in the fire.
> We curse his arts upon that pyre.
> As he has lent, so he is paid.[45]

From the so-called miracle of the sacred Host, there lingers a Christian community, a tabernacle to its triumph available for visitation, an admonition about the physical, theological, and economic dangers of Jews, and a Christian brotherhood of actors to rehearse inexorably the violent origins of both church and community with the didactic offering of the *Mistere de la Sainte Hostie.*

Be that as it may, founding goes with funding, and the *confrairie* needs money.[46] Nor were such tangible financial realities of spectacle lost on Philippe de Vigneulles, who wraps up his account of the Metz performance by stressing that he himself was a key financial player in the theatrical proceedings. As if he were composing a modern-day urban legend (or reporting to the IRS), he implies that we can believe his version of the events because he has his receipts: "And I, Philippe, know all this to be true, because I was one of the entrepreneurs; and I raised . . . thirty-three francs for the platforms and scaffolding used during all three days of all three of the aforesaid plays."[47] In Mons, the Jews had been required to turn their cult into a spectacle under the watchful eye of Christian "crusaders" who policed them for profit with "some kind of wages . . . that were regulated by the town's *échevins.*"[48] Now, on the stage of Metz (and perhaps of Paris as well), spectators paid to see a literal Christian conversion of the spectacle of Judaism—on their own dime. As Jacob's story comes to a close, the priest of Saint Jean-en-Grève comes forward to proclaim that the best way to preserve the legacy of the event is to preserve the play.[49] In that way, true Christians may replace the false faith that is hypocritically enacted by false Jewish usurers with their own supposedly sacred spectacle of true faith. More significant, that mission may be most profitably enacted when citizens lend economic support not to Jewish moneylenders but to the *confrairie* charged with putting on the play:

> And what is more, ye good folk here
> Another duty does appear.
> You've seen before your eyes today
> A great miracle, not a play.

Remember it good-heartedly
By maintaining our *confrérie*.
Serve Him by serving us, you see,
For we have the authority
To play upon the very site,
If it please God in all His might.
Amen.[50]

As we shall see, in the name of economics and theology alike, there would be other fears about what happens when theater falls into the hands of other "others": not only Jewish, but Protestant and populist. Notwithstanding the many differences between those groups, each the subject of its own legends, the common denominator is theater itself. For now the *confrérie* troupe dramatically redisseminates the legend of the dangerous Jews, keeping its legacy alive and contributing, through the reality of performance, to the apparent reality of the legend. It is by means of theater that the *Sainte Hostie* proposes to prevent theater, life, and the theater of life from falling into Jewish hands.

Why is it important that, in all probability, it was a fictive Jew who was burned at the stake in thirteenth-century Paris? After all, our sources can't seem to get anybody's name straight but a bishop's. It is important because when Jacob goes down in flames, he kindles and rekindles the flames of anti-Semitism. Certainly there is evidence that conventions of preaching in Metz would have inflamed anti-Semitic thinking, as when Jacomin Husson describes the sermonic *tour de force* on Good Friday of 1515 by one Brother Oliver. In a performance evocative of today's most frenzied Pentecostal performances,

> he did something that no one had ever seen before: for he showed a sacred Host and had the people cry out for mercy when he showed them the Host. And when Pilate wanted to read the sentence, he began to cry out with all his might: "Give him death! Give him death!" and, thus crying out, the trumpet of the City also began to sound in time with "Give him death! Give him death!" And when our Lord died on the cross, he showed a crucifix, again calling out "Have mercy!"; and the people also cried out loudly.[51]

Just as many modern scholars now refuse to ennoble the extermination of six million Jews by referring to the "Shoah" instead of the "Holocaust" (the term reserved for a "sacrificial" burnt offering), so too might we reject the interpretation of such fiery visions as the *Sainte Hostie* as noble sacrifices worthy of that name. Although the Paris legend would have portrayed Jacob's consumption by flames as a juridical "punishment"—not a "sacrifice"—there remains a very real way in which theater gives up his burnt body as its own sacrificial offering to the anti-Jewish cause.[52] This is not a purely "medieval" phenomenon.

Percy Fitzgerald, for instance, tells the tale of "The Jew and Mrs. Siddons," in which the celebrated actress has just brought the house to hushed attention during her exquisite rendition of the stage-whispers of "Mrs. Beverley." A Jewish spectator breaks the silence by asking loudly who has spit in his eye. Regardless of whether or not he speaks, the mere presence of the unnamed man ruins the performance.[53] His resentment at being victimized is transformed into the theatrical community's resentment *of him* for being where he doesn't belong in the first place. Elsewhere, however, modern readers have often passed judgment on early anti-Semitism by attempting to silence *it*. Even the brothers Parfaict tried confusedly to explain what was so "playful" about the "*Play* and Mystery of the Sacred Host," footnoting the word *jeu* with a purportedly simple résumé of the historical context of the *Sainte Hostie:* "Since the title of this Work might mislead the uninstructed, it is worthwhile to point out that it was composed only in order to perpetuate the memory of an authentic Miracle which occurred in Paris in the thirteenth century, and which occasioned the founding of the Carmelite Church of les Billettes of that City."[54] That memory is as stained with blood as was the Metz stage in 1513, and its theatrical mission as ominous as any "blooded thought" that Herbert Blau could imagine.[55]

Peter Haidu would call this operation the "emptying out" or "hypocritical disguisement" of violence by modernity.[56] Such disguisement might not be surprising in the eighteenth century, but one hardly expects to encounter it in enlightened twentieth-century critics. Even so, Henri Rey-Flaud assigns to the "unheard of sadism" of the medieval stage the lofty motivation of the Christian "price to pay for collective salvation." He hastens to assure us that "it is not complicity which medieval men bring to the theater, it is faith."[57] But such high-minded sensibilities have excised some of the venom of anti-Semitism. For his own part, Victor Scherb professes skepticism about the critical tendency to view violence as part of the affective piety of the late Middle Ages—only to conclude of the relentless mutilations of the Croxton *Play of the Sacrament* that "violence is de-ritualized and given bloody form once again so that the action of the play can in effect both mirror and heal the divisions within the contemporary Suffolk community."[58] If torture, bloodshed, and anti-Semitism somehow heal Christian communities, they do so upon the burned bodies of Jews and Jewish sympathizers who are all deemed deserving of their ordeals.

To be sure, these assessments constitute a vast improvement over the earlier tendency to dismiss medieval anti-Semitism as a topos devoid of meaning. Yet one cannot help but wonder if the contemporary emphasis on the *making* rather than the *unmaking* of communities has obscured what Nirenberg terms the resemblance that "the nightmares of a distant past bear to our own."[59] Despite any "mirroring or healing" that might or might not have taken place in fifteenth-century Paris, sixteenth-century Metz, or in a turn-of-the-eighteenth-century history of Paris, the formation of the *Sainte Hostie*'s Christian community depends on the extermination of another (an *other*) Jewish community, which it *unmakes* as it remakes itself. In terms of our medieval urban legends, theater does both.

The spectacle of the *Sainte Hostie* warrants that Jews ruin the spectacle of life at the same time that the play's myths, performances, and mythic performances invest the debate about credulity and incredulity with a clear and present danger.[60] Be it on the streets, in a building, or in the rubble of a demolished Jewish home, theater was a space that brought everything back to life.

Theater's Living Dead

He who cures lives. He who lives is present in his relics.
    —Victricius of Rouen, *De laude sanctorum*

The *Mystère des Trois Doms* was staged in Romans on 27–29 May 1509, the year John Calvin was born. There is no doubt about it. The play itself is extant and comes in at over eleven thousand verses. We know that it was authored by the Chanoine Pra of Grenoble and that after having been lost for many years, it was romantically recovered in December 1881 in the attic of one Madame Sablière des Hayes of Romans.[1] We know that the 1509 performance was motivated by the most pious of intentions to honor the city's three patron saints, because an epilogue tells us so: there was "played and made manifest . . . the life and saintly story *[ystoire]* of the glorious martyrs, friends of God, Saints Séverin, Exupère, and Félicien, commonly known as the *Trois Doms.*"[2] We know that the financial arrangements of that performance were recorded by Jean Chonet in a highly detailed *Accounting (Compte de sa composition)*. We know that Paul-Émile Giraud discovered the manuscript of that accounting "in a private home" in Romans and published it independently in 1848 as Chonet's *Composition, mise en scène et représentation du mystère des Trois Doms.*[3] And we know that Petit de Julleville rightly elegized that document, which "contains details that we possess about no other [performance]."[4]

With so much information available, how can the remarkable story of a remarkable performance still be so ambiguous?

It all starts with an anonymous eighteenth-century commentator who made a most controversial remark about the 1509 production. His words come down to most of us courtesy of Petit de Julleville: "*the relics of these [three] holy martyrs were also carried on stage during these performances.*"[5] Were they or weren't they? Why was their presence so fraught with cantankerous feeling? And if the saintly relics really *were* integrated into a theatrical performance, then whom did that prospect bother more: Catholic ecclesiastics? Protestant reformers? anonymous eighteenth-century commentators? or Petit de Julleville?

The effort to answer those questions takes us on a dizzying historical expedition through a tale of manuscripts lost and found, of commentaries made over a period of three hundred years, and of polarized and polarizing theological views about the "real presence" of the divine, theatrical or otherwise.[6] Although our 1509 performance predates Martin Luther's famous posting of his Ninety-Five Theses in Wittenberg in 1517, it apparently promulgated the same sorts of sensibilities to which reformers so strenuously objected. By the very questions it posed about relics on stage, it enmeshed spectators in ways of thinking that would inflame theological polemic about the worship of saints, the veneration of their relics, the nature of divine intervention, and the distinctions between realism, reality, representation, and reenactment.[7] As the Reformation approached, the presence or absence of relics on stage would come to be connected to the presence or absence of credulity or incredulity—and to the legendary ability (or inability) to tell the two apart.

Mystery plays were meant to elucidate truth, not to mystify it. And yet, if Catholic audiences had a sure and certain hope about the resurrection of Christ and the saints, that was precisely what the *Trois Doms* rendered unsure and uncertain. As we shall see, the 1509 production transformed a question of *theatrical* performativity into a question of *theological* performativity, a very dangerous game.

IN A SENSE, our story begins in ancient Greece, where relics had long had the power to reanimate theatrically the realities of body and soul. It seems, for instance, that in 4 B.C. the celebrated Athenian actor Polus brought as a prop to his role in *Electra* the funeral ashes of his recently deceased son. During the scene in which Electra carries her brother's remains, Polus "took from the tomb the ashes and urn of his son, [and] embraced them as if they were those of Orestes."[8] Another method actor *avant la lettre*, he has returned prematurely to the stage with a pre-Christian "relic" of sorts. He "filled the whole place, not with the appearance and imitation of sorrow, but with *genuine grief and unfeigned lamentation*. Therefore, while it seemed that a *play* was being *acted*, it was in fact *real grief* that was enacted."[9] Almost a millennium later, the citizens of Romans (Romanais) were also seeking to enact something real: an affective and effective intervention by their three patron saints, the Trois Doms themselves.

It turns out that, in 1509, the Romanais had good reason to call theatrically upon Saints Félicien, Exupère, and Sébastien. In 1442, 1446, 1494, and 1505, their city had been decimated by various outbreaks of plague, which had finally died down in

1507. While Petit de Julleville is certain that they wished to "render thanks to God for the cessation of this scourge *and to prevent its return* through some sort of pious work," it is just as certain that their theatrical thanksgiving was also designed to prevent future epidemics.[10] As such, it aimed for more than the scenic gratitude expressed later, in 1535, by the citizens of Issoudun. Articulating their "holiest desire" to "play, show, perform, and put forth the tragedy of the slain Christ, a sure and certain story," they proclaimed: "For this good Christ has given us this year / Such bounty, which he spreads all over here. . . . / That we now bring together all the faithful, / on stage, lest we appear to be ungrateful."[11] With the *Trois Doms*, the Romanais thanked and honored three holy martyrs who had previously interceded at least twice on their behalf, and prayed fervently that those saints would keep on interceding.[12] The preface to the *Accounting* confirms those motives explicitly:

> Earlier, these [saints] demonstrated themselves to be *our intercessors* and friends with God the Creator. During the year of the great drought, which was 1504, we received permission to carry their relics during a general procession and they suddenly gave us rain. . . . And since then, when a plague was ravaging this city in 1507, a *confrérie* was founded . . . which *confrérie* addressed a prayer to these same [saints] and the aforesaid plague immediately ceased. . . . Wherefore, taking this into consideration and motivated by fervent devotion—not without cause—to both the will of God and the saints' manifest daily miracles, the aforesaid mystery play was commissioned.[13]

The play was a prayer to the city's patrons. As such, it problematized one of the most fiercely debated issues of Reformation theology. Some two decades later, for example, Guillaume Farel would take grave offense at the popular belief in the very intervention upon which the citizens of Romans were banking when they mounted their *Trois Doms*. "The worship, adoration, and prayers addressed to saints and to all others who are out of this world," he reprimanded, "is a thing done without faith and against the word of God." By that logic, the play was blasphemy in that "those who say that the saints are our intercessors, advocates and mediators between God and ourselves, our way, our life, and our hope: they blaspheme, perpetrating an outrage against the saints and a dishonor to our Lord Jesus. He alone is our mediator, who intercedes with the Father on our behalf."[14] By the midsixteenth century, the reformer Pierre Brully added that the saints themselves had instructed that good Christians should "imitate their faith and virtues" rather than "invoke them as intercessors, given that that honor belongs to Christ alone."[15]

Stephen Ozment points out that when Protestant reformers first came on the scene, there was a "booming business at local shrines. Pilgrims gather[ed] there by the hundreds, even thousands, many sick, some dying, all in search of a cure or a miracle, but many also out for some needed diversion and entertainment."[16] The *Trois Doms* purportedly provided both. While such historians as Brown, Bynum, Rubin, and Sharon Farmer have refocused our attention on the curative and even festive communal functions of relics, the resonances for theater phenomenology have yet to be explored.[17] When the Romanais ostensibly arranged to integrate the genuine relics of Séverin, Exupère, and Félicien into their spectacular bid for intercession, a theatrical quandary was about to become a theological quandary. Regardless of whether the relics ever made it into the play itself, the Romanais had asked for and received not a simulated cure but a real one.

So it was that the reliquary-based prayer of the *Trois Doms* found itself on the horns of a theological dilemma about saintly intercession on behalf of humankind. What could it mean when a performative theatrical request veritably provided a cure—or failed to provide one? Was the Romanais' continued respite from the plague attributable to real relics, fake relics, or no relics at all? Could fake relics deliver real protection?[18] Whom and what did they protect more: the city, the players, or the play?

Consider this: if the Romanais were healthy enough to tender a theatrical offering to their patrons in 1509, that was not the case in 1510 in nearby Avenières. According to Guillaume le Doyen, the sensational advent of an epidemic of the flulike *coqueluche* so compromised their *Mystery of Saint Blaise* that the thespian ranks of the bad guys were thinned to barely one-quarter of the original cast:

> The Mystery of our Saint Blaise
> Was played out in the very place
> For four full days to our delight
> In Avenières: that was the site
> Where this good lord was born and bred.
> But there was trouble up ahead.
> During the play, before you knew,
> Came suddenly, a raging flu
> From the hills into our town
> And struck a good lot of us down.
> It took from many as it spread
> Their brains and kidneys; they lay dead.
> With one fourth of the tyrants left
> I'm not the only one bereft.[19]

Perhaps the citizens of Avenières had not made the appropriate theatrical offering to their own saints. Or perhaps the cessation of the plague had nothing whatsoever to do with saints and their relics. After all, theater productions had long raised public health concerns, which such municipalities as Angers believed themselves to have addressed effectively. For instance, in preparation for Jean Michel's *Passion* of 12 August 1486, town officials admonished that innkeepers were not to "receive any people from Brissac nor from anywhere else where there is plague."[20] Centuries before Antonin Artaud ever pondered the metaphysical connection between theater and the plague, medieval and Renaissance communities had ruminated about the *physical* connection, reasoning correctly that the disease might spread more rapidly among large concentrations of people.[21] Indeed, for Artaud, the plague was liable to produce the very kinds of social disorder that fifteenth- and sixteenth-century municipalities were religiously trying to regulate. In *The Theater and Its Double,* he mused that "once the plague is established in a city, the regular forms collapse. There is no maintenance of roads and sewers, no army, no police, no municipal administration."[22] An epidemic also threatened psychic collapse, inasmuch as "the plague takes images that are dormant, a latent disorder, and suddenly extends them into the most extreme gestures." Here Artaud saw the connection to theater, which "also takes gestures and pushes them as far as they will go: like the plague it reforges the chain between what is and what is not, between the virtuality of the possible and what already exists in materialized nature." What was dormant in late medieval France was an ideological pestilence of far greater consequence, which would later spread like the plague: heresy.[23] And while Romans appears to have resisted both sorts of pestilence,[24] the role of the relics of the *Trois Doms* in that resistance caused quite a critical commotion among postmedieval commentators.

In a ridiculously complex genealogy of sources, Giraud was the first to come across the curious contention about the relics of Séverin, Exupère, and Félicien being paraded on stage. It was published in an unsigned article in the *Affiches du Dauphiné* of 1787, the title of which reads more like an eighteenth-century novel than a medievalist's archival evidence: "Analysis of a most curious and little known manuscript, which exists in Romans in the Dauphiné, written by Monsieur *** of that same city." That article was reprinted twice that same year: once in the *Journal de Paris* and once in the *Esprit des journaux* (although the former is itself an excerpt that makes no mention of the relics).[25] The author of the original article, reports Giraud, was "a resident of Romans" who had taken the liberty of composing several unflattering pages about the play "under the veil of anonymity."[26] Later, Petit de Julleville agreed with Giraud's assessment of Monsieur ***'s "marked intention to ridicule the drama of the Middle Ages," citing such zingers as this one: "*Human Solace, Divine Grace,* and *Divine Comfort* provide assistance to the heroes of the play and boredom to those who read it."[27] Nevertheless, both gentlemen cited the article anyway. At the time, the avowed anonymous enemy of medieval drama was the only "friend of a friend" to whom Giraud and Petit de Julleville could turn for a sense of how the *Accounting* compared to the actual text of the *Trois Doms*. When Giraud was writing in the 1840s and Petit de Julleville in the 1870s, the manuscript of the play had temporarily disappeared, and both scholars assumed that Monsieur *** had at least had the integrity to base his remarks on the relics before—and not *after*—the manuscript had been lost. Thus Giraud excerpted Monsieur ***, and Petit de Julleville excerpted Giraud, who remains our best conduit to the anonymous claim that lies at the root of the trouble.[28]

Petit de Julleville was skeptical about the relics being part of the action of the *Trois Doms*. The transfer of relics (festively or otherwise) from one site to another was a perfectly standard ecclesiastical practice called *translation*. But it was *not* a standard theatrical practice to "translate" relics onto the stage: "It seems uncertain to us that the relics of the saints were really paraded on the stage. In truth, Romans possessed these relics: but it seems more probable that they were not brought on to the theater and that what was performed was *only the simulation [simulacre]* of their translation."[29] Were they or weren't they? The plot thickens.

Under ordinary circumstances, Petit de Julleville would be right. By all accounts, the relics of the three saints in question really *were* housed in Romans, where no expense was spared to commemorate their dramatic story on a regular basis. In support of that statement, he cites the "slightly vague" and slightly erroneous but contemporaneous testimony of Aymar du Rivail (c. 1490–1557), which he finds largely credible. Legend had it—or was it history?—that Saint Bernard had personally placed the relics of Séverin, Exupère, and Félicien inside the very church he had founded, which relics were thereafter memorialized in theater pieces.[30] But was it legend or history that the relics became part of the dramatic performance of the *Trois Doms*?

At this point, it is Giraud who comes forward to resolve the mystery. Or that is how it seems at first. "Monsieur Petit de Julleville wrongly speculates," he submits, "that the relics of the saints were *not* brought to the theater."[31] Giraud's corroborating evidence from the neighboring town of Valence is irrefutable. "During the performance of the *Mystery of Saint Felix, Fortunatus, and Achilles* of 1500," he affirms, "the citizens of Valence asked the clergy to bring their reliquary *[triarchum]* onto the stage.*" He cites the statute of 3 July to that effect from the Archives of Valence: "As is fitting, it was decided that the lords of the church, 'out of the utmost reverence and honor due to these three aforesaid holy martyrs,' would be asked *to bring upon the place of the stage the receptacle containing their relics.*"[32] If relics were brought onto the stage of Valence, it is plausible that the citizens of Romans authorized an analogous scenic effect for their *Trois Doms*. At a minimum, medieval entrepreneurs would have had to decide on such a prop because, as Monsieur ***, Giraud, and Petit de Julleville all confirmed, there also existed a "one-act play" devoted to the precise subject of the ecclesiastical translation of the relics of Félicien, Exupère, and Sébastien.[33] That play is the *Translacion*, a kind of epilogue to the *Trois Doms*. It contains such speeches as this one by Archbishop Pascase, who directs three clergymen to transport "the reliquary in which three holy bodies make their home [Troys *corps sains* y font tenemant]":

> You'll carry it now, if you please—
> The vessel is not too heavy—
> And present this reliquary
> To Saint Romans; and you shall see
> That its safekeeping has pleased God.[34]

Just as it starts to appear that either actual or simulated relics were on stage during the performance of the *Trois Doms*, a problem arises.

The passage just cited appears in the *Translacion*. But Jean Chonet states explicitly in the *Accounting* that, in May 1509, the *Trois Doms* was performed *"without* the *Translacion*, which could not be played on account of the great length of the principal *mystère.*"[35] Except for the *Translacion*, none of the three days of the *Trois Doms* calls for the display of holy relics at all. This annoying fact makes one wonder in what possible context the relics could have appeared on stage when none of the scenes performed in 1509 would logically have staged them.

Trying to find out what really happened in Romans is like trying to find an alligator in the sewer. Indeed, we encounter a section of the *Accounting* that tells us exactly what happened—but philologically, the passage is so ambiguous that one hesitates to draw conclusions. The passage presents various linguistic difficulties, but may still be translated roughly:

> Et en la fin dudict mistere furent retournées *les chasses desdicts corps sainct et chief* a ladicte esglise en procession generale, *que la avoient estez* durant ledict mistere, avesquez gros chierges, en chantant . . .
>
> And upon completion of the aforesaid mystery play, *the reliquaries containing the aforesaid holy bodie[s] and head[s] were returned* to the aforesaid Church [of Saint Bernard] during a general procession, there *where they had remained* during the aforesaid mystery, and with big candles and singing.[36]

In the first place, the phrase "there where they had remained during the aforesaid mystery [que la avoient estez durant ledict mistere]" prompts us to ask: What is the meaning of *there* there? Certainly, if the reliquaries were being *returned* to the church, then they must, at some earlier point, have *left* the church. Furthermore, since Chonet tells us that the weather was especially beautiful, it is easier to envisage a setting safe enough for the actual relics to have been ceremonially transported back and forth from the playing space.[37] So does "*there*" mean "on the stage"? Or does it simply mean that the relics remained in the custody of the ecclesiastics who had carried them during the general processions that opened and closed the play?[38] Either reading is possible.

In the second place, the phrase that I have translated as "the reliquaries containing the aforesaid holy bodie[s] and head[s] [les chasses desdicts corps sainct et chief]" is mystifying. Even Giraud's seemingly straightforward translation into modern French is anything but clear. He renders *sainct et chief* in the plural as *saints et chefs*, even though the terms are not marked by a final *s*,[39] and his translation has two possible meanings. Either *saints et chefs* are plural nouns, in which case the phrase means "the reliquaries [containing] the aforesaid bodies *[corps saints]* and heads *[chefs]*," or else *saints et chefs* are plural adjectives, in which case the phrase means "the reliquaries [containing] the aforesaid bodies, which are holy *[saincts]* and esteemed *[chiefs]*," the latter reading unattested philologically.[40] In any event, what does *not* make sense is to read the phrase as "the reliquaries containing the aforesaid *holy body and head*" because the reliquary contains not one but *three* holy bodies. In other words, the textual "answer" to the question of on-stage relics only begets more questions. These may be answered nonetheless, for, fantastically enough, all the answers are *not* mutually exclusive in the worlds of legend and theology. It is *because* they are not that we may finally be able to understand why the legendary tale of relics might have circulated in the first place.

What has occurred here, it seems, is one of three things.

1. Chonet (to say nothing of his later expositors) has confused what happens at the end of the *Mystère des Trois Doms* with what happened during the performance of 1509. Let us recall that at the end of the play's Third Day, it would indeed be appropriate to speak of "holy bodies and heads" because the three patron saints of Romans are decapitated, their saintly bodies separated from their holy heads. When Félicien, Exupère, and Sébastien are laid to rest in their coffin, however, a hermit takes great care to reunite correctly each of the three severed heads with the proper one of the three severed bodies. The play draws to a close with the saintly man praying that the faithful Christian audience remember the Trois Doms because he has re-*membered* them.[41] He has put their bodies back together again and placed them side by side in their shared final resting place.[42] Therefore, it was reasonable for Giraud to posit the presence of a single vessel that contained "holy bodies and heads."[43]

2. Our commentators have confused the *Trois Doms* with the *Translacion*. The former locates the holy bodies and heads of the three saints in a coffin *(tumbeau)*. The latter locates only their remains in a reliquary *(chasse)*.

3. Our commentators have confused both the *Trois Doms and* the *Translacion* with the two festive processions that framed the 1509 performance. Truly, the tripartite reliquary or *triarchum* was carried during those processions. But it played no role in the *play* of 1509 because the *Translacion,* which called for it scenically, was not performed.

The beauty of the story is that in Catholic theology all three readings are possible at the same time. The holy bodies and heads that fit into the hermit's coffin at the end of the *Trois Doms* are the same holy bodies and heads that fit into the Romanais reliquary (on stage or off) because, as Bynum tells us, the part is as complete, as living, as resurrectable as the whole.[44] "There is nothing in these relics that is not complete," proclaimed Victricius of Rouen.[45] Likewise, Thomas Aquinas had explained that "a relic, although not identical to the living body of the saint . . . *is* the same by identity of matter, which is destined to be reunited to its form."[46] What remains to be reunited are the theatrical and theological ramifications of the medieval performativity of relics—something that has been torn asunder in the afterlife of the story of Romans.

Did real or simulated relics ever appear in the production of the *Trois Doms?* and to what real or imagined end? Thanks to a conclusion that only an urban legend could provide, we will never know for sure. Actually, that conclusion is provided by *two* urban legends.

The witnesses are long dead and buried, so we can scarcely cross-examine them. Nor can we examine the evidence, for the relics themselves have vanished. Giraud reports that, on 4 May 1562 during the dark days of the wars of religion, Ennemont Odde, Lord of Triors, ordered that the sacred treasures of the Church of Saint Bernard (including the relics of the Trois Doms) be transferred for safekeeping. After that transfer on 12 June, they "disappeared forever."[47] Moreover, before their disappearance, a second legend informs us that the relics had already been contaminated in connection with a processional event. After so much fuss about the dangers posed by relics on stage, it turns out that those dangers were just as great *off* stage. Rich with the hallmark localizing detail of urban legendry, Giraud melds past and present as he recounts the terrible mishap:

Alas! there came a day when this pious practice of carrying triumphally the relics of the three saints during a procession would instill bitter regret within the hearts of the Romanais. On 23 January 1524, Saint Bernard's Day, the customary procession took place. Four young people were carrying the triple reliquary *[tri-archum]*, which contained the remains of the martyrs. All of a sudden, in the rue Saunerie, between the houses of the canon Francois Odde and the noble Guillaume Tardivon—so say the capitularies, which spare no detail—the young people, not out of any malice but simply exhausted, drop their precious burden on the ground and it breaks in two.[48] The relics contained in the middle reliquary are scattered on the earth,[49] to the great shock of both the clergy and the people, and there arises a sort of cloud of dust. In great haste, the saintly debris is collected and brought back to the Church of Saint Bernard.[50]

Although the four hapless youths performed an expiatory procession on the following Tuesday, 26 January, the disastrous contamination could not be corrected. Nor can medievalists correct definitively the contamination of our sources. On Thursday, 24 March, says Giraud, *"what remains of the relics* of the Trois Doms" was finally deposited at the great altar underneath the reliquary of Saint Bernard.[51] Only the remains of the remains remained; the moral of the story could hardly be more blatant. Quite literally, it is dangerous to put the life's blood of religion in the hands of the people.

Most of Brunvand's books have a whole chapter devoted to what he terms "dreadful contaminations." These include such perennials as the "Kentucky Fried Rat," the "Mouse in the Coke Bottle," and the "Alligator in the Sewer."[52] Urban legends all, they stage such distasteful mishaps as the accidental consumption of rats, human flesh, cats, urine, poisonous plants, and so on. As far as we know, there are no medieval legends about people *eating* holy relics,[53] but the conclusion to the confusing case of the contaminated evidence remains unaltered. As far as on-stage relics are concerned, the part is as powerful as the whole, the absent as powerful as the present, the false as powerful as the true. After all, a mystery play was a genre that, while simulating the sacred with bodies real and false, stimulated in audiences all the pleasures and pains associated with the ability or inability to tell the difference.

But something else has happened in all the confusion. It turns out that Monsieur *** was not really quite as intolerant of the performance at Romans as later commentators have made him out to be. True, he does grumble about various historical inaccuracies, the lack of unity of time and place, the devils' "foul language *[propos orduriers]*," and the simultaneous scenic representation of Africa, Europe, Asia, Heaven, and Hell.[54] But he adds that "such license is tolerable in light of the fact that we have never demanded that theater pieces follow history as faithfully as it is followed in *Rodrigue.*"[55] He gripes about Hell's devils, who "have only nonsense to say to the goddess Persephone, who, in a singular mélange of fable and true religion, also takes her place on the stage."[56] But he goes on to conclude more generously that since the play was "followed by a general procession and finished with a *Te Deum*," "we may doubtless presume that our good ancestors believed themselves to be sanctifying their pleasures by incorporating religion into all their entertainments. Their naïveté in this matter deserves praise rather than blame."[57]

In a new version of the myth of the medieval children, Monsieur *** does *not* blame them. On the contrary, in a comment that both Giraud and Petit de Julleville omitted from their excerpts, he maintains that naive medieval audiences were far better equipped than their modern descendants to handle "this mixture of the sacred with the most odious and the most indecent of profanities." Although he grants that the plays might well have "corrupted public morals and faith," he also deems it "reasonable to suppose that, in those days, impressions of evil were less dangerous. Today these spectacles would be rightly seen as quite scandalous."[58] Then again, the most scandalous thing—the parading of relics on stage—is precisely what the *Journal de Paris* version omits. Even then, it is likely that on-stage relics would have scandalized no one but potential Protestant reformers—or the likes of Farel, who felt that cupidity "explained the introduction of the cult of the saints, its immense power of seduction, and the invention and accomplishment of so-called miracles."[59]

Monsieur ***'s today is our yesterday, and our today has problems of its own. Initially, he seems to give voice to the standard complaint about the French mystery cycles, as disseminated, for instance, by Richard Ryan in 1825 with his claim that sacred histories were "acted upon the stage, *mixed with a thousand gross and ridiculous fables.*"[60] But what is an urban legend, if not just such a mélange of history and fiction? What is it if not the very mélange that motivated in our own day the pious John Williams to debunk, in God's name, a slew of Christian legends that "still persist today despite the fact that they are not true."[61] Williams has in mind such favorites as the Russian discovery of the gates to Hell, the homosexuality of Jesus, and the fear that atheists will silence Christian programming.[62] But his message is clear: "hoaxes, urban legends, and false predictions, as well as our own gullibility, have affected our proclamation of the gospel of truth." Therefore, he resolves, "we must learn how to recognize the popular legends, myths, and fallacies that litter our cultural landscape," the better to restore "our desire to uphold God's truth."[63] Medievalists have a different question to resolve: if modern objections to the mixture of fable and religion have fabricated a scandal of the relics of Romans when there was no such scandal, then why have such fabrications proved so enduring?

We have seen that in the Middle Ages questions of performance promptly become theological, especially when such pieces as the *Trois Doms* announce their spiritual intentions. Modern theatrical events would scarcely begin with similar pretensions—yet the two are not as dissimilar as one might think. In modern times, questions of performance promptly become political in a contemporary politics that is often positively theological.

Medieval people would have denied the assertion that they valued believability more than truth, but belied it in the utter indeterminacy of their representational practices. Modern Americans would affirm the indeterminacy of belief but belie a curious need for transparency in their very insistence on "getting to the bottom" of the fiction vs. reality debate.

The medieval religious theater exalted its moral center by staging the "true lives" of Christ, the saints, and other martyrs at the same time that its scenic flights of fancy subverted that "truth" in favor of believability. Conversely, the modern media—one of our own equivalents of the medieval theater—tend to exalt a secular center and secular subjects at the same time that a kind of deism occasionally lurks just beneath the surface—or on the surface, in such religiously inclined television shows as *Touched by an Angel* and *Mysterious Ways.*[64] It's almost as if the media have been enshrined, for better or for worse, by the belief that they wield all the power that the medieval Catholic Church did in its own day—a conclusion that pricks the conscience of both the firmly devout and the firmly secular. I am suggesting here that it was just as easy for the Middle Ages to politicize theology as it is today for modern times to "theologize" politics. Especially in the academy, the politics of Right vs. Left have taken on all the dimensions of a crusade in which the righteous moral fervor on both sides is, to put it bluntly, *medieval.*[65] People from all walks of life have regularly participated politically not just in legend-making but in theater-making.

The Mysterious Quarry

If you think something is "true," no matter how obscure that "truth" seems to be and no matter how specific to you alone, somewhere, someone else thinks it now and at a different time someone had already built a monument to it.
　　　　　　　　　　　　　　　　—Joseph Chaikin, *Presence of the Actor*

The year is 1539, the same year that real devils were pulling the proverbial leg of the citizens of Tirepied.[1] Imagine that there is a special place where a tired populace might go at the end of a long day of labor. Imagine that it is a workplace, a place for stonecutters. Imagine that it is a natural arena— an amphitheater to be exact—where the locals put on their own plays in their own space. Imagine the words of Romain Rolland, who wrote in 1903 that "the theater of the people should share the bread of the people, their worries, their hopes, their battles."[2] Imagine now the story of the mysterious quarry of Doué-la-Fontaine, situated some thirteen miles southwest of Saumur—although, truth be told, it is a story that Raymond Lebègue had difficulty imagining.

"Near the village of Doué (Maine-et-Loire)," he reports, "there was a quarry that was redesigned in the shape of an amphitheater in the fifteenth or early sixteenth century: mystery plays were performed there, to which Rabelais alludes in chapter 3 of the *Tiers Livre* and chapter 13 of the *Quart Livre*."[3] No sooner does he utter those words, though, than he calls the assertion into question: "Is this tradition a faithful account? Or is it, rather, a legend based on the performances of the *Passion* at Saumur and Angers or of the *Acts of the Apostles* at Bourges? The details are precise and inspire confidence; but, in spite of the fact that the story of this amphitheater has been studied in depth and the archives of Maine-et-Loire explored, no other mention of this event has ever been found."[4]

For a scrupulous medievalist such as Lebègue, the extant evidence amounted to a single reliable source. The great humanist scholar, Justus Lipsius (1547–1606), had recorded a fantastic historical event based on the testimony of an unnamed friend. Lebègue's doubts notwithstanding, he recirculates in French translation the story he has gleaned from the *De amphitheatro liber*. This is Lebègue speaking:

> *They say* that in 1539 the great king Francis I allowed the actors in the region who were playing the *Acts of the Apostles* to use this amphitheater. They cleaned it up, decorated it, and a crowd of spectators arrived. This performance, *which lasted for thirty days*, garnered the peasants *[paysans]* a considerable profit. So it was that they asked the king to forbid any future extractions of stones within a radius of 30 *perches* from that place. For, owing to numerous excavations, if this measure had not been taken, then ruin would not have been far behind.[5]

Unless we fancy that Doué's performances were Passion play precursors to Esther Williams movies, the internal logic of the story demands that we assume that the site was still functional as a quarry and had not yet undergone its more natural (if protracted) metamorphosis into a wonderful swimming pool.[6] Francis I, patron of the arts, has saved the day by dramatically curtailing the workload and the work space of the quarry in favor of the theater. Presumably, once his edict was in place, then the layered "seating" that quarrying had presumably provided was protected—and, presumably, it wouldn't have *needed* protection, unless there was still some hope of extracting more stones that would have threatened the haphazard theatrical space.[7] One might even assume that the noisy, dusty task of extracting stones was similarly restricted on days that hosted great spectacles. In a tale of social change, the lives and livelihoods of the rustic locals were altered at the same time as they altered a physical site. Having "garnered considerable profit," the fortunate country folk transformed to their advantage a place of labor into a place of leisure, a work space into a theatrical space.[8] Somehow, the workers had learned an invaluable lesson of economic empowerment from the theater.

But could the story be true? And what would it mean for theater history if it were? On the face of it, the story of Doué-la-Fontaine functions as a curious counterpart to the *Sainte Hostie* of our chapter 9. Both are legends about the expropriation of space. The *Sainte Hostie* commemorates an ecclesiastical site (the Église des Billettes), and its associated *confrérie* reenacts triumphantly the downward economic spiral of a Jewish moneylender who perishes at the stake. The mysterious quarry of Doué-la-Fontaine bids us to believe in theater's transformative initiation of an upward economic spiral for "peasants," laborers, and the bourgeoisie. Both stories monumentalize the anxieties about who shall be empowered to profit financially from the theater. Both are *lieux de mémoire.*[9] The problem lies in what the quarry memorializes.

As in all good legends, here fiction and history come together. From one vantage point, workers, actors, and future populist sympathizers must have seen in the quarry's conversion a veritable Cinderella story in which theater was as powerful as any fairy godmother. Although a town's bourgeois typically involved themselves quite heavily in theatrical representations, the quarry-theater of Doué-la-Fontaine looms large as a tribute to the social and theatrical ascendancy of a different group who threatened civic, ecclesiastical, and even bourgeois authority: the people.[10] We shall see, however, that the nature and origins of the "considerable profit" of the "peasants" are unclear. Among other things, what is distinctly absent from this narrative is the reaction of the person or persons who were in the business of stone-cutting and whose own livelihoods would have been affected by restrictions on their work-related activities. Additionally, one has to wonder if the common people didn't stand to make more money from retaining access to the *entire* space of the quarry than from the frenetic, but only occasional preparations for theatrical festivals (which would normally have been associated with holidays).

From a second vantage point, aristocrats and ecclesiastics must have seen in the amphitheater quite another story. For anyone who believed that the populace should be toiling away as stonecutters, the presence in the quarry of idle theatricality would doubtless have inflamed Catholic polemic—to say nothing of Protestant affirmations of a work ethic. *Before* the show went on, labor had been hard and diligent. *After* the *Acts of the Apostles* of 1539, stonecutting was curtailed—that is, it could take place when the workers weren't too busy fixing up the site for theatrical productions. Maybe those who opposed the theater might find a way to destroy it. Sixty years later, in 1599, over in Esne, a bishop was hell-bent on doing just that. He was so enraged that he had not been consulted about some upcoming farces, comedies, and tragedies that he appeared before his local government and, likening himself to Christ in the Temple, threatened "with great anger, fire, and gall, on several occasions, that he would not permit the aforesaid plays and, moreover, that if the actors played, he would pull them off the stage and would knock down the aforesaid theater, praying that God give him the strength to do so."[11] In Doué-la-Fontaine, such a mission was complicated by the monument's extensive and concrete tenacity: unlike the Parisian home of Jacob Mousse, it is still standing today.

The city's Office of Tourism has produced a flier about the quarry, which invites us to buy a ticket to visit "the amphitheater of Doué-la-Fontaine, which possibly dates back to Merovingian or medieval times, [and which] was built upon the site of old quarries cut into the conchiferous stone. A one-of-a-kind monument . . . , the amphitheater is today the setting for the 'Days of the Rose,' a floral exposition, held each year since 1959, in mid-July."[12] As it happens, that information is ratified not by the Holy Bible but by the tourist's bible known as the Michelin *Guide Vert*. In the hierarchy of worthiness that is the hallmark of that series, the Doué amphitheater is well worth the trip, even though it earns only one of three possible stars in the *Châteaux de la Loire* guide: "Situated in the Quarter known as Douces, this [amphitheater] is, in reality, an ancient open-air quarry, whose tiers *[gradins]* were refashioned in the fifteenth century. Theatrical and musical spectacles, along with botanical expositions, are held there. Under the tiers, there are vast subterranean spaces that were long inhabited: kitchens, common rooms."[13]

Anyone opposed to Doué's theater thus had his work cut out for him. Unlike Jacob's home, the quarry could not be razed. But perhaps its proto-populist origins *could* be done away with. Perhaps they could be razed at the site at which theater had long built dangerous monuments of its own: the human imagination. And, what better way to do that than to call into question the veracity of the origins of the quarry-theater?

Finally, there is a third vantage point, which makes for an additional archaeological layer to the ambiguities of an apparently proto-socialist daydream for theater. Even in the twentieth century a people's theater was not necessarily the populist entity that one might imagine. Loren Kruger, for instance, has argued that for all his leftist pretensions, Rolland was actually committed to a theater that *contained* the people and "depend[ed] on the audience's passive enclosure face to face with the spectacle, not on their own participation in its making. By crowding the people into this confined space, his theatre ends up by crowding them out of an effective public sphere."[14] We too have seen that medieval municipalities took numerous legislative measures designed to supervise, constrain, and contain theater audiences by imposing silence, engaging in surveillance, and regulating public spaces.[15] If this language of confinement seems over the top, then let us recall that in Doué-la-Fontaine, the flip side of liberty has always been imprisonment.

This is no metaphor. Ambiguous though the quarry's purported theatrical origins might be, it is indubitable that the site was once used as a prison. The Michelin *Guide Vert* states that "prisoners from the Vendée were locked up there,"[16] while the town's own Office of Tourism never camouflages that fact in its brochure: "Of uncertain origin, the amphitheater might date back to the medieval era. Its subterranean region and the eleven hundred places in its amphitheater were cut into conchiferous stone. Its cellars served successively as an inn, *a prison*, and a munitions dump."[17] Indeed, quarries had a long historical relationship to prisons, punishment, and even torture. Isidore of Seville had invoked the theatrically resonant context of pain and fear *(dolor et metus)* for the *latomia (quarry)*, which is "a type of ordeal suitable for scourging that was invented by Tarquin the Great as a punishment for the wicked."[18] Therefore, a beautiful fantasy of liberty is not immune from the double-edged sword of social change and the specter of imprisonment. The mysterious quarry stands as a monument to the social insecurity of theater because it concretizes the anxiety about what happens when theater is wrested from the hegemony and delivered—even partially—to the people. If it were really true that theater might fall psychically, physically, and permanently into the wrong hands, then a people's theater might need protection *from* the people.

Clearly, the quarry exists. It's just not so clear exactly what it is: a Roman ruin? a remade quarry? an alligator in the sewer? a Bermuda Triangle? None of the above? All of the above? Turning now to the extant evidence relating to the amphitheater of Doué, we confront first the testimony of the gregarious Rabelais. On two occasions, he alludes specifically to "a more confused deviltry than that of the Doué plays" and to "the devil-crew of Saumur, Doué, Montmorillon, Langeais, Saint Épain, Angers, or indeed, by God, of Poitiers with their great hall."[19] But, when Lebègue commented of the quarry that "mystery plays were performed there" ("*on y* donna des représentations de mystères") one is moved to ask anew: What is the meaning of *there* there?[20] Since Lebègue was speaking of the quarry-turned-amphitheater when he made that remark, it is natural to infer that *there* means *in the quarry.* Presumably, what was interesting or surprising to Lebègue was not the notion that mystery plays were performed in Doué but that they were performed in a quarry. And yet, Rabelais makes no mention whatsoever of a quarry. So much for that.

It is harder to disregard the testimony of Justus Lipsius, who had understood Doué's edifice to be not a quarry at all, but a Roman ruin. Its story appears in the final chapter of the *De amphitheatro liber,* entitled "The Book of Amphitheaters outside Rome" ("De amphitheatris quae extra Romam libellus"). Sometime in the sixteenth century, Justus Lipsius had ostensibly dispatched an unidentified friend to investigate the situation. Later, Lebègue found himself attracted to the mediated testimony of that friend, noting that "by the time a friend of Justus Lipsius explored the amphitheater at the end of the sixteenth century, the performances had stopped." It is unclear whether Lebègue—or Justus Lipsius for that matter—ever visited the site in person. Lebègue is simply pleased to state, in a further piece of mediated testimony, that "this amphitheater was restored in 1924 and . . . traveling actors perform there."[21] Since his "friend of a friend" was unavailable for comment, Lebègue was unable to weigh in definitively.

As he channeled the voice of Justus Lipsius channeling that of an anonymous friend, Lebègue changed the story ever so slightly. Closer inspection of his account of the peasants' theatrical labors of 1539 reveals, for example, that Lebègue omitted the last sentence of Justus Lipsius's account, which is in many ways its most provocative feature. "This much I have learned," proclaims Justus Lipsius, and "this much I have heard. If it is otherwise, then I may have spoken an untruth, but I have not lied."[22] Unless we wish to tag one of the fathers of humanism a liar, then we had better heed Lebègue's call that we accept the anecdotal evidence as offered—even though he has made a minor transcription error in quantification, rendering Justus Lipsius's "36 perches" as "30 perches."[23]

The great humanist needn't have been a liar to have made a mistake. After all, he was writing at a time when the poet Joachim Du Bellay (1522–60) had stood in ecstasy before the ruins of Rome during his sojourn in that city in 1553. Transfixed by the vestiges of a lost civilization, Du Bellay had conferred glorious praise: "Judge! as these ample ruins you behold, / What hurtful Time has eaten all away / Since our assiduous workers of today / Still take a page from all these fragments old."[24] Seen from that angle, it is not inconceivable that when Justus Lipsius fantasized, perhaps through his friend's eyes, that he was there at Doué, he too romanticized the architectural remains of Rome.

There are additional romanticizations as well. Justus Lipsius does indeed disclose that the performance "lasted for thirty days."[25] But thirty days was a long time, even for a massive theatrical undertaking like the *Acts of the Apostles*. In Bourges, however, the same play reportedly commenced on Sunday, 30 April 1536, and lasted *forty* days.[26] As far as early modern number-crunching goes, a calculation of thirty days' duration is relatively mild. Modern readers needn't believe those numbers any more than we believe the details of the *Song of Roland*, which transforms a minor border skirmish of 778 into an epic loss to a hundred thousand pagans on the battlefield at Roncevaux.[27] Nor is it any more shocking than the rhapsodic description of another amphitheater constructed in 1516 in Autun (about seventy-five miles from Bourges). The description appears in the *Catalogus gloriae mundi*, penned in 1649 by Bartholomew Chassanée and reproduced by Petit de Julleville.[28] According to Chassanée, what occurred in Autun was a "perfect performance" of the *Life of Saint Lazarus* in an "excellent and magnificent amphitheater." "There was nothing comparable in all of France," he gushed, noting that "in this amphitheater, eighty thousand men could gather with no difficulty." Furthermore, "since the spectacle had been announced in the neighboring towns, spectators came pouring in, in almost infinite numbers."[29] Bourges's impressive figure of twenty-five thousand to thirty thousand spectators pales by comparison to Chassanée's figure of infinity. So do the paltry eleven hundred spots of Doué-la-Fontaine.

Still, the example of the *Acts of the Apostles* of Bourges is pertinent because that city had supposedly been the site of an interesting agreement between a monarch and his people about a play. According to the sixteenth-century historian Jean Chaumeau, Louis XII, nicknamed "the Father of the People," frequently spent time in his residence in Bourges during his reign (1498–1515). On the occasion of a Passion play near the end of his reign, he is said to have "made an arrangement with the bourgeois of Bourges that the history of the Passion be played at Bourges with great pomp and circumstance over the space of several days at the theatrical site known as the *fosse des Arenes*, which contained every day twenty-five thousand to thirty thousand people. I venture to affirm that I never saw such sumptuous costumes, finery, and acting or a loftier treatment of the subject and more admirable special effects."[30] Regardless of whether or not we discard the occasionally hyperbolic flights of Chaumeau's *Histoire de Berry,* the story of Bourges bears a highly positive message concerning what happens when bourgeois take charge of an amphitheater. The story of Doué-la-Fontaine is no more preposterous. If Louis XII had bestowed such a privilege upon the bourgeois of Bourges, then it is plausible to envisage a similar arrangement in 1539 between the artistically inclined Francis I (1515–47) and the actors and workers of Doué. Certainly the monarch was not shy about recording his theater-related rulings.[31] The problem lies in sorting out whether or not analogous tales lend more or less credence to that of the mysterious quarry.

Nor is that the end of it. If the legend of the quarry of Doué-la-Fontaine seems to have concretized popular conquest of the theater, why was the Latin of Justus Lipsius's original text so circumspect about who was doing what for whom?

In his French translation of the passage, Lebègue merely observes that "they" (the peasants) asked the king to forbid "any future extractions from that place of stones from within more than 30 [sic] *perches.*"[32] But the Latin sentence is less precise. To make a long philological story short, here is a literal translation of the passage from Justus Lipsius that we reviewed above in Lebègue's voice:

> After they [the *histriones*] had cleaned it up and decorated it and had attracted a great crowd of spectators, it is said that, from this festival, *which lasted for thirty days,* the *paganos* [peasants, rustics, or locals] garnered a considerable profit. [It is said that] they were induced by this fact to get the king *[impetrasse]* to forbid any future extractions of stones that were nearer to the amphitheater than 36 *perches* away. Because of such frequent excavations, the destruction of that site was imminent.[33]

The passive verb *impetrasse* indicates that some kind of agreement was obtained or accomplished. But there is no specific designation of *who* obtained that agreement:

the actors *(histriones)* who were *performing* in the quarry or the rustic laborers *(paganos)* who were *working* there. On one hand, it *sounds* as though the *peasants* were the ones to seek regal permission to carry on (*peasants* is the subject closest to the verb). On the other hand, it was the *actors* who had originally requested permission to use the quarry for their theater pieces. It was *they* who had purportedly arranged to refashion the quarry so that it might house the *Acts of the Apostles*. The question is: How did the *peasants* make their "considerable financial profit"?

Even if we believe the story, which is by no means a given, is it rational to posit such a financial windfall from a play? Justus Lipsius does not tender an exact financial figure, but other estimates are extant from companion spectacles. Much farther north, in Valenciennes, for instance, a later performance (1547) would prove such a hit that "the receipts reached the sum of 4,680 *livres*."[34] Were the peasants hired by the actors? Or were the peasants themselves the actors (a most unlikely scenario for such a learned and literate play)?[35] It would not have been revolutionary for a town's bourgeoisie to control a theatrical production. That was the norm. What *is* revolutionary about the mysterious quarry of Doué-la-Fontaine is that the bourgeoisie would have at most expropriated and at least compromised a work space by cordoning off a part of it for their theatrical goals. The year 1539, of course, was still a far cry from the so-called socialist sentiments of Rolland, who launched this accusation against the theater critics of his day: "you have felt that the people's theater would rise up against you; so you hasten to the offensive . . . in order to give the people your 'bourgeois theater,' which you baptize 'theater of the people.'"[36] But Lebègue, writing at the end of the 1920s, was doubtless familiar with Rolland's writings and with the class tensions that had always been present in French theater.[37] Those class tensions between the people, the bourgeoisie, and the church are very much at issue in Doué-la-Fontaine.

So far, then, we have questionable testimony about a performance of undetermined length and undetermined attendance, which netted undetermined revenues for an overdetermined social group because of a play that was performed at a site that, while geologically stable, was a monument to social instability. Fortunately, a picture is worth a thousand words. Then again, maybe it isn't.

Lebègue found himself intrigued by "two curious drawings dating from 1584" that were appended without attribution at the end of Justus Lipsius's chapter on amphitheaters outside Rome.[38] He proceeded to enumerate the interesting features: there were "six round openings through which the actors made their way to the two underground rooms on the right, and a central opening upon which there was affixed a pole [mast]; an awning was held up by cords that were attached to the pole" (fig. 5).[39] Indeed, Chassanée had described in almost identical terms the awning devices of the amphitheater at Autun: "Crowds of people sat there, sheltered by linen sheets that protected from the rain both the actors and the spectators, whether they were standing or sitting."[40] Given the function of such awnings, the two images would seem to lend credence to the story that a quarry was refashioned into an amphitheater. To the modern viewer, the sail-like awning of figure 5 looks more like a ship of state than an umbrella, but it would certainly have protected actors and audiences from glaring sun or pouring rain. Meanwhile, the personages in both images seem busily engaged in laborious preparations for theater work: inspecting the entrances to the subterranean rooms, checking the seating, perhaps cleaning (figs. 5 and 6). Although one is tempted to guess that the persons depicted in the second image are spectators hastening to the show, that is unlikely. There would be little point to having an awning if it were *not* in place precisely when theatergoers were actually present.

Be that as it may, neither image does much to reinforce the notion of a working quarry. Even if we assume that the quarry workers normally stashed their stones in the subterranean passages before hauling them out via the clearly depicted openings in the earth, the chambers in the images look far too pristine to have stored many stones. The presence of a picture has not adequately answered the many questions at hand, and walking through the site today, unprotected from the sun, does little to improve the interpretive situation.

At this point, it seems impossible to confirm or to repudiate Justus Lipsius's twice-told tale about the people's sixteenth-century triumph over their workplace. Faced with yet another tale in which the Baudrillardian "signs incline neither to one side nor the other" (*SW,* 178), we are left nonetheless with these elusive yet strangely satisfying conclusions.

Whoever participated in the theatrical transformation of Doué's social structure, both actors and workmen appear to win out, inasmuch as their spatial expropriation is the story that has survived. As far as the *histriones* were concerned, they had long been fighting an uphill economic and theological battle for the right to perform where and when they saw fit. From Plato's expulsion of actors from his ideal republic, to a Roman edict of the praetor forbidding "comic and satirical actors" from bringing lawsuits, to medieval provisions regulating the legal and theatrical conduct of *histriones* and *scurrae,* to Thomas Aquinas's suggestion that *histriones* should not receive wages, to the great injunction against the mystery plays of 1548: their struggle for social justice and recognition had been long and arduous.[41] With their apparent victory of 1539, our sixteenth-century revolutionaries would thus have marked a new beginning for alternative social collaborations in the theater. All that, with the blessing of a princely patron, who issued a partial death

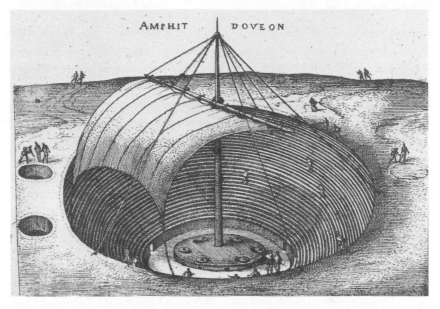

Figure 5. The Amphitheater at Doué-la-Fontaine (with awning). Justus Lipsius, *De Amphitheatris* (Antwerp: Plantin, 1585).

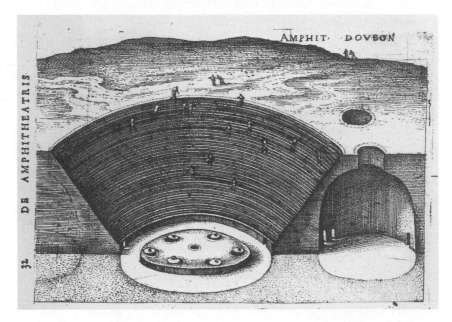

Figure 6. The Amphitheater at Doué-la-Fontaine (with detail). Justus Lipsius, *De Amphitheatris* (Antwerp: Plantin, 1585).

warrant for the quarry while ostensibly enhancing the livelihoods of both actors and peasants. Modern skeptics might counter that until we can find the piece of parchment to validate Francis's royal blessing, the story of Doué-la-Fontaine is but a dream. But by the time Lebègue revisited it in the nineteenth century, he probably enjoyed the pleasantly projected proto-socialist daydream that there really had been such an agreement about the quarry-theater.[42] As for what Justus Lipsius recorded regarding what his anonymous friend thought he saw, that was a different day for a different daydream of Rome. The daydream endures, for as Bruce Wilshire has mused, "art can begin to comprehend through fantasy the role of fantasy in existence. . . . We encompass the present and past only in a new stance of commitment and openness toward the future" (*RPI*, 218).

For their part, the peasants appear to have won something too. The long-lost agreement of Doué-la-Fontaine had an entirely different resonance than, say, the charming accord of Châlons-sur-Marne (3 May 1507) in which bourgeois entrepreneurs graciously provided gratis a costume to a "poor devil" of an actor playing Lucifer.[43] Instead of the Church, the aristocracy, and the bourgeoisie collaborating to bring theatrical edification to the people, the bourgeois were cooperating with the *paganos* (we are told) in order to bring theater to themselves. Before that, rustics had been, at best, the objects of pity and charity (like the poor Lucifer) or, at worst, the subject of countless silly jokes and farces. They might try to walk the walk and talk the talk of their social superiors, but no dice. Their failures at both had been the stock in trade of theatrical anecdote books of all ages.[44] In Doué-la-Fontaine, the peasants' "role," which had been eternally scripted *for* them, was rescripted *with* them into a conclusion that was presumably as tantalizing to actors as it was to workers.[45] Instead of being economically weakened by their association with thespians, the *paysans* were strengthened by it in *someone's* populist fantasy of the assimilation of theatrical property, be it intellectual or physical. Once the proverbial "people" had consorted with the bourgeois, they had found a way to turn theater to their advantage—quite literally *at the expense* of whoever owned the quarry and would lose by the deal.[46] If, in reality, the peasants were exploited by the bourgeoisie, we will never know. Fixing up a quarry must have been a huge job, so although none of our sources says that spectators were accommodated comfortably, they were accommodated nonetheless on what were stone "benches" of sorts, not rock piles. Or perhaps the workers never received any life-altering earnings at all while toiling for their new masters or collaborators. Their bona fide social situation has been subsumed by the story.

In the final analysis, the mysterious quarry-theater may not represent the triumph of the masses, but its vestiges definitely concretize a belief in that triumph. It would be many years before Charles Nodier would call the French Revolution "the greatest drama of all time," a "bloody play" in which "the entire people" would rise up and "enact in the streets and on the public squares the greatest drama of all time."[47] Likewise, it would be many years before "the people" would take by force things like land, property, or the heads of monarchs. In Doué-la-Fontaine, the theatrical revolution apparently took place peacefully. Proof or no proof, it was waged with money, and that was problematic enough in and of itself.

"Whether consciously, preconsciously, or unconsciously," writes Victor Turner, people "take on roles which carry with them, if not precisely recorded scripts, deeply engraved tendencies to act and speak in suprapersonal or 'representative' ways appropriate to the role taken."[48] The workers of Doué were off message and off script, but the script was familiar enough to ecclesiastics concerned with theater's potential for social change. If the moral of all our Devil stories was something on the order of "the Devil made them do it," then sixteenth-century antitheatrical legislation lays the blame squarely at the doorstep of theater and cites economics to buttress moral objections. For example, such reformers as Calvin worried publicly about the potential for spiritual corruption when financial need coincided with theatrical need. He commented on 30 May 1546 that while there was nothing sacrilegious per se in a proposed performance of the *Acts of the Apostles*, it was preferable to "spend one's money on one's brother than on vanities."[49]

On the other side, Catholic clergyman often blamed that very corruption on Protestant theology. The town council of Mons evinced such a view when, in 1559, its members posited a direct connection between money, heresy, and the self-interested "simple folk" who could be bought by charismatic preaching (to say nothing of theater). In a long speech against various spectacular abuses from satire to *lèse-majesté*, the council made the bitter complaint that the underclasses constituted a promising market at which heretics could be bought:

> When it came to pass that pastors and other theologians preaching at their pulpits would refute and blame their errors and abuses, they would say of them in one voice that they were rabbis and Pharisees who were stopping the populace from seeking Christ and drawing near him. In short, during the wars between the emperor and the king of France, the merchants of the Low Countries, who were trafficking in neighboring countries where there were heretics, brought Lutheranism from Germany, Calvinism from France, and Anabaptism from Westphalia and Frise-Orientale. They wound up inciting the poor people so much to become heretics—through gifts and through other means—that some of them wouldn't even do business with them, *except on the condition that they attend the sermons of Huguenot ministers.*[50]

Vinchant's credibility on the subject is not exactly reinforced by his urban legend–like wrap-up: "This account is true; for *I have heard trustworthy older people attest to having seen most of the aforementioned things* take place in the city of Mons during their youth."[51] Since he doth protest too much, one wonders about the rest of the "things"—and about what the experience of Doué might have procured for its own rustics. As with each of our stories, there arise numerous questions about mistaking half-truths for whole truths.

The rock-bottom line of the quarry of Doué-la-Fontaine is the universal (if not univocal) threat of theater to which fifteenth- and sixteenth-century francophone communities responded religiously. It is a tale that tells us that we can barely sort out the truth when it's standing right in front of us—or, after we buy a ticket today to the ruins at Doué, when *we* are standing right in front of *it*. Similarly, fifteenth- and sixteenth-century audiences frequently found it difficult to discern what was before their very eyes. Plus or minus any proto-revolutionary status of the people, things theatrical were getting out of hand.

CHAPTER TWELVE

Seeing Is Believing

The difference between true and false religion is the presence of theater.
—Stephen Greenblatt, *Shakespearean Negotiations*

The mystery begins with Petit de Julleville, from whom we learn that there exists a manuscript of the Valenciennes Passion play that enumerates an impressive series of special effects *(beaux secrets)*.[1] The manuscript does indeed exist in different versions: Bibliothèque Nationale, Fond français 12536 and Rothschild I.7.3, the latter of which is unique in prefacing each of its twenty-five Days with what Elie Konigson terms "either an announcement or a description" of its principal scenic effects.[2] But if the careful Konigson was unable to differentiate between a desired didascalic directive and an actual piece of scenic action, then how on earth are we to understand what happened in 1547 during the miracle of the loaves and the fishes?

"Item, another wonderful special effect for the miracle of the five barley loaves and the two fishes, which Jesus multiplied without [anyone] seeing how this was done, so that [bread] was given to over one thousand persons from among the spectators and twelve full baskets were collected."[3]

Was this a miraculous performance, or the performance of a miracle? And what was the significance or insignificance of the event or nonevent? What was a miracle, anyway—and what was theater?

The plot thickens as both Konigson and Petit de Julleville endeavor to fill in the blanks by looking to Henry d'Outreman's detailed account of these events in the *Histoire de la ville et comté de Valenciennes* (1639).[4] "Barely a year old at the time of the performance," warns Konigson, Henry must have gotten his information from his father, Henry Senior, who had supervised the production of 1547.[5] In his mediated testimony, d'Outreman denies that various biblical miracles again came to pass, postulating instead that the Passion play's dazzling effects only *resembled* the real thing:

> During the Pentecost holidays of 1547, the *principaux* bourgeois of the city per-formed at the theater of the house of the Duke d'Arschot (where the home of the author is at present located in the rear court), the life, death and Passion of Our Lord in twenty-five days; during each of which days, strange and wondrous things were made to appear.[6] The special effects for Heaven and Hell were truly prodigious, and *could really have been taken by the populace for magic spells.* For one could see Lady Truth, the Angels, and various other characters descending from on high, sometimes visibly, sometimes as if invisibly, and then appearing all of a sudden. Lucifer arose from Hell, without anyone seeing just how, carried by a dragon.[7] Of a sudden, Moses's staff, dry and sterile, sprouted flowers and fruits;[8] the souls of Herod and Judas were taken up into the air by devils; and the devils were chased from the bodies of hydropics and other sick people who were cured—all of it done in a remarkable way. Here, Jesus Christ was lifted up by the Devil, who was climbing the length of a palisade over forty feet high; there he made himself invisible; elsewhere, he was transfigured on the Mountain of Thabor.[9]

As if all that weren't impressive enough, something even more remarkable hap-pens when d'Outreman arrives at the Rothschild enumeration of the effects of Day Eight: "Item, [many *beaux secrets* were also seen] at the wedding of Architriclin, where, before everybody, the water that was poured into the jugs was transformed into wine, and more than one hundred persons from among the spectators drank of it."[10] Henry renders the miraculous mutation of water into wine as the *desire* of more than one hundred people to drink—not as the *fact* that they have actually drunk:

> One could see the water changed into wine, but so *mysteriously* that *one couldn't believe it;* and more than one hundred people in the audience *wished to taste the wine.* The five loaves and two fishes were similarly multiplied there, and distrib-uted to more than one thousand people, and even so, there were still twelve bas-kets left over. The fig-tree, cursed by Our Lord, seemed dry, with its leaves withering in an instant. The eclipse, the earthquake, the shattering stones, and *the other miracles* occurring at the death of Our Savior *were themselves represented anew and miraculously.*[11]

We have a problem here. No matter how special an effect, it takes a lot of bread to feed the thousand people of d'Outreman's head count and a generous amount of wine to quench the theatrical thirst of a hundred. Realistically, it is unreasonable to

Figure 7. The Miracle of the Loaves and the Fishes. Valenciennes *Passion*, Paris, Bibliothèque Nationale, Rothschild I.7.3, fol. 162v.

presume that even the most ambitious and well-funded theater troupe would have had the budget to break bread and drink wine with so many people. Yet it is indubitable that during Day Twelve of the *Passion,* something believable *must* happen, in order for the following scene to make sense. Andrew says:

> There is, within the company
> A child of young and tender age.
> To make his meager living he
> Has five barley loaves, seems to me,
> And similarly two fishes.
> But what is all that, I pray thee,
> When we need more?[12]

Furthermore, one of the magnificent miniatures of the Rothschild manuscript depicts a small child holding his basket before Jesus (fig. 7). When Jesus asks shortly thereafter, "Have you now enough, my children?"—and when the company responds, "Yes, Lord"—some kind of scenic happening must make it reasonable for Jesus to send his men into the crowd to collect the remainder of the bread and for Andrew to report that "we have filled twelve baskets."[13] The trick is to determine

whether that "something" was real or imagined—or whether we simply have another scenario in which critics have substituted didascalia for the realities of performance.[14] The *beaux secrets* seem to guard their secrets centuries later.

What happened in Valenciennes in 1547? Before we figure that out, let us take a
moment to ponder the early perils of asking that question. If nothing else, it fore-
grounds our second story, of Tournai in 1559, in which it was perilous to ask such
questions during a performance itself. In *mystères*, *miracles*, and *moralités*, seeing
(combined with hearing) was believing. That was scarcely a new idea. Lucian of
Samosata ascribed it to Herodotus, who had noted that "what is apprehended
through the eyes is more trustworthy than hearing; but dancing [that is, pan-
tomime] possesses what appeals to ear and eyes alike."[15] Arnoul Gréban later
seemed to agree, when he opened his fifteenth-century *Passion* with an expositor
bidding the audience to lend both their eyes and ears.[16] Then, in 1534, Jean
Bouchet similarly saluted receptive Christians who prepared themselves for the
sights and sounds of the Passion play at Poitiers:

> I have been pleased to see the Passion play
> Performed three times, I'm old now anyway;
> I find in daily prayer that my *esprit*
> The *Acts of the Apostles* longs to see.
> For of the prosecution 'tis the story
> Of the sweet fruits of Christ in all his glory:
> His passion true to form, the joyous seed
> As planted by the Church that is our creed.
> Although we see it written, hear it preached,
> Our spirits through the eyes are better reached.
> The thing is far more joyous when it's seen
> And heard, its message easier to glean.[17]

These were noble goals, to be sure. But we have already seen that as early spectators
faced theater's realities, hyperrealities, illusions, special effects, accidents, and
mythologies, they were obliged to make certain judgments about what they were
seeing and believing: facts or fantasies, happy illusions or sad truths, God's miracles or the Devil's deceptions, performance or performativity. In the sixteenth century that obligation enmeshed them in a complex theological controversy about the
representation versus the reenactment of miracles. Theater re-formed and *re-
formed* both the questions and their answers.

It's not a very medieval position to say that the spectators of Valenciennes
couldn't possibly have witnessed a miracle. Nor is it innocent to say that they *did*.
On one hand, the model for reenactment—be it theatrical or theological—was

transubstantiation itself.[18] The transformation of the sacred Host and wine into Christ's body and blood was real enough to the town councilmen of Angers when they made this ruling in 1486 before the performance of Jean Michel's *Passion:* "the better to begin and to have silence, if it be deemed expedient, a Mass shall be said at the play on a properly placed altar."[19] It was also real enough to Michel, whose Jesus blesses the Host at the Last Supper by using that exact term: "This is my body everywhere. / And henceforth, you'll do as I've said: / You'll *transubstantiate* the bread / into my sacred self divine." Thereupon, his Apostles are humbled by their ability to "*transubstantiate* the bread / Into Himself."[20] In Michel's *Passion*, to question a miracle, such as the resurrection of Lazarus, was to be a pagan or a Jew like Jacob:

> He never was raised from the dead.
> It was enchantment, just a scheme,
> An apparition, but a dream,
> A phony dummy, fake confection
> Of what you think the resurrection
> Of Laz'rus, whom you celebrate.[21]

On the other hand, by the time the citizens of Valenciennes saw their Passion play in 1547, Francis I had just ended his reign. Originally sympathetic to Reformist ideas, he had hardened his position after the *Affaire des Placards* of 1534; the situation was to become even more explosive during the wars of religion under his successor, Henri II (1547–59).[22] The reformer Guillaume Farel had warned that "miracles and other things that have come to pass should in no way move us to the point of pulling us away from the word of God and taking on another faith or belief other than one in accordance with the word of God."[23] As the new theological controversies took hold, questioning the nature of miracles also came to be the province of Protestants. In an accusation that resonates with Michel's words above, the reformer Pierre Brully denounced not only Jews and pagans but Catholic priests as idolaters and diabolical magicians: "this muttering with which priests attend the bread and the wine is better suited to witches and enchanters than to Christians."[24]

How, then, was the Valenciennes audience to know what to see and believe? Perhaps, as in our Devil tales, they believed precisely what they had *never* seen.[25] Perhaps, as our two endangered priests of Metz learned almost too late, they failed to believe what they *did* see—or, as the expression goes, they could not believe their eyes and ears.[26] Perhaps they didn't know what to believe at all, a situation that might cause them to forget that the reality of Christ's story was never meant to be uncertain. Perhaps they confused true history with theatrical make-believe. One need only recall the deep ecclesiastical anxieties regarding the introduction of apocryphal materials into religious drama. In 1456, for example, clerical authorities of Angers rejected Jehan le Prieur's *Mystère de la Résurrection* as "not in conformity with the Scriptures" because the players had proposed several additions that were "irrelevant to the subject."[27] In 1542 the procurator general of Paris refused to allow the *confrères de la Passion* to stage the *Mystery of the Old Testament* on account of their tendency to introduce into scriptural narrative "apocryphal materials, lascivious farces, and mummeries."[28] And later, d'Outreman fulminated that "the Devil even sought by this nonsense to *open the doors to the sacrileges of Luther and Calvin,* stuffing these comedies and spectacles with *entr'actes* and profane farces that compromised the dignity of holy things and of the ministers of the Church."[29]

By the same token, French Protestant reformers often launched related objections, as when Luther approved of schoolboys performing biblical plays so long as there were no satirical interludes or errors.[30] Calvin, in 1546, feared that while the text of the *Acts of the Apostles* was "most holy and in keeping with the divine word," a performance of it would create "great confusion."[31] And in 1566 Jacques Grévin prefaced his *Trésorière* (1559) with a poetic and theological critique of the theatrical communion of poetry and religion:

> For it is not our intention
> To mix up our Religion
> With subjects that are make-believe.
> His Scriptures God did not conceive
> So that He e'er should see the day
> That men would turn them into play.[32]

Long accustomed to suspending their disbelief, sixteenth-century spectators might now stand ready to suspend their *belief*—or to change their beliefs, or to lead different lives based on those beliefs. One thing was clear: Regardless of what they were seeing or hearing, mis-seeing or mis-hearing, or were *thought* by theologians to be seeing, hearing, mis-seeing, or mis-hearing, it was dangerous when they believed what they saw or what they *thought* they saw, or when they believed nothing at all. It was also dangerous when they *dis*believed what they saw or what they *thought* they saw, or when they disbelieved nothing at all. Ultimately, if theater audiences couldn't tell the difference between history, illusion, and reality, if the Catholic Church actively *discouraged* them from seeking clarification on those matters in printed Protestant Bibles,[33] then they might just as well have been watching "urban legends" unfold before their eyes—or have believed that they were. They might just as well have believed that *mystères* and *miracles* were merely legends about religion. Worst of all, they might have reckoned that religion itself was nothing more than an "urban legend"—just one of many of what Brunvand would later call "somewhat bizarre unverifiable stories, plausible nonetheless because they are grounded in certain verifiable facts."[34]

In the presence of the theatrical story of God, the certainty of theological uncertainty was intolerable to Catholics and Protestants alike, a situation that was especially dire in Valenciennes in 1547. As in Romans in 1509, a question of *theological* performativity became a question of *theatrical* performativity to which any number of answers were possible and which we explore below:

1. There was no miracle of 1547, but, instead, there was a marvelous special effect whose scope has been exaggerated.

2. Such exaggeration was encouraged and enriched by citations from the Gospel.

3. The Valenciennes spectators were a bit like those who had accommodated Lucian's mad "Ajax" with polite applause:[35] they provided what they deemed an appropriate response by *pretending* to eat the feigned miraculous bread and to drink the feigned wine.

4. A new miracle occurred in 1547 when God intervened to reprise his earlier one of the loaves and the fishes during the Valenciennes Passion play.[36]

5. The Devil wrought a new miracle instead of God.

We shall examine each of these possibilities in turn, in the paragraphs that follow.

1. As far as the first possibility is concerned, Konigson deemed it a simple matter of staging. The miracle of the loaves and the fishes was a matter of technical wizardry: "The baskets of food should appear from trapdoors. The apostles serve the crowd *(and the spectators)*."[37] Unanswered, though, in Konigson's reading are further questions: Were those baskets full of *real* bread or *pretend* bread? and how much bread was distributed during the play (if distributed at all)?

2. Our second possibility—that of scriptural interpolation—responds partially to those questions by providing a model for large numbers. Indeed, the Valenciennes miracle parallels quite closely the Gospel narrative in which Christ instructs his disciples to feed the masses:

And one of his disciples, Andrew, Simon Peter's brother saith unto him,
There is a lad here, which hath five barley loaves, and two small fishes: but what are they among so many?

And Jesus said, Make the men sit down. Now there was much grass in the place. So the men sat down, in number about *five thousand.*

And Jesus took the loaves; and when he had given thanks he distributed to the disciples, and the disciples to them that were set down; and likewise of the fishes as much as they would.

When they were filled, he said unto his disciples, *Gather up the fragments that remain, that nothing be lost.*[38]

Therefore they gathered them together, and *filled twelve baskets with the fragments of the five barley loaves, which remained over* and above unto them that had eaten. (John 6.8–14)[39]

Both scripturally and theatrically, twelve baskets constitute a plausible prop. Five thousand pieces of bread probably do not. Nor do the drastically diminished *thousand* pieces to which both d'Outreman and the Rothschild manuscript of the *Passion* commit.[40] Nor does anything remotely like a thousand fishes! Those fishes are never mentioned in the afterlife of the Valenciennes play, although the sight—and, above all, the *smell*—of such a stinky prop would have been as unforgettable as it was financially prohibitive to a theater company. Therefore, either our narrators are off by four thousand people, or they have readjusted the biblical account to suit the performance account.

Nevertheless, if biblical authority were insufficient to support the numbers, our story fills in the blanks with its own internal logic. "There was such a huge crowd there on account of the arrival of outsiders coming in from France, Flanders, and elsewhere," reports d'Outreman, "that the receipts reached the sum of 4,680 *livres,* even though the spectators paid only a *liard* or six *deniers* apiece."[41] Furthermore, if we recall with Konigson that the apostles served both the crowd *and the spectators,* and with Petit de Julleville that some of those spectators had paid double to be seated *upon the stage,* then perhaps the only audience members to be served *anything* in 1547 were the ones whose higher priced entry fee had bought them a breadcrust.[42] After all, there are no outrageous numbers in Jean Michel's version of the same miraculous distribution, addressed by two stage directions: *"Here six of the apostles sit down and divide numerous loaves into quarters. And the other six serve bread to the people and serve from several plates of fishes . . . Here all the people and all the apostles partake."*[43] For Michel, it simply sounds as though a scaled-down feeding was limited to the bodies on the stage. Some of them were actors, and others might have been spectators. But both seem to have been engaged in the ultimate mission of a *mystère:* they *symbolized* Christ's massive following. Numbers don't matter so much in a metaphorical head count.

3. We have no way of knowing how the audience responded to these real or imag-

ined events. It is possible that they were overjoyed to break bread with the actors, disappointed not to get any, pleased to play along and *pretend* that they did, or confused about the whole distribution process. One thing is for sure: Whether they had just experienced a fantastic effect, a miracle, a collective hallucination, or a delicious snack, they could not have responded unanimously.

4. A miracle occurred, a dicey matter in that, while Christians believed in the scriptural miracle of the loaves and the fishes, there was no miracle of the *Valenciennes loaves and fishes*. Medieval theater audiences were, of course, accustomed to watching plays that celebrated the many miracles of Jesus and the saints. During the spectacular public ordeal of Saint Barbara, for instance, the martyred maiden prays for her torturers to regain their sight and "Many miracles occurred:/Deformed people were cured,/Many dead came back to life/And the blind saw again."[44] That doesn't mean that each single spectator believed that miracles regularly recurred during their dramas. Nor, however, does it mean that spectators would doubt the possibility of a new miracle of 1547. As preposterous as a modern audience might find a Valenciennes miracle of the loaves and the fishes on stage, they might wish to think twice about casting the first stone. They might instead take a closer look at any number of contemporary urban legends about miraculous distributions. It suffices to reconsider such favorites as the dollar bills floating in the East River or the cash free-for-all that falls out of the back of a wayward armored truck.[45] Just as people today may hope and believe that a sudden windfall may come their way, so too might our spectators at Valenciennes have hoped and believed that if their God could perform a miracle once, He could do it again—and do it in the context of a play. Legend already had it that He had done something of the sort when the fourth-century actor Saint Genesius "proclaimed his conversion to Christianity publicly on the stage."[46]

But was it rational to think that God Himself would be kind enough to perform a miracle that was perfectly timed to the play performed in his honor? He was God, not the props-master, and his capacities as the greatest *metteur en scène* of all time would normally have far surpassed the stage. So maybe the Devil was the *metteur en scène*.

5. Finally, the position that the *Devil* wrought a miracle in 1547 is consistent with the teachings of Farel, whose Reformist critique of miracles amounts to a critique of theater. On both theological and economic grounds, he feared that a miracle-maker (theatrical or otherwise) was liable to be the Antichrist: "Jesus certainly warned us about the miracles to be performed at the time of the Antichrist. . . . For anyone who looks closely, he will find no true miracle: only trickery and deception designed to make money."[47] In Valenciennes, the performative powers of the Devil were, at least theatrically speaking, indistinguishable from those of God.

In the end, sixteenth-century spectators might have believed in *all* those possibilities, but not in all of them at the same time. And if modernists delight in the Baudrillardian signs inclining "neither toward one side nor the other" (*SW*, 178), then, theologically, there was nothing delightful about that. Nor were there only two sides. Add to that mix the philosophical attachment of Renaissance humanists to the relativity of truth, and one needn't be clairvoyant to anticipate the theatrical consequences of such mystifications.[48]

Some dozen years later in the city of Tournai, the site of our snuff story, audiences wanted answers. So too did the Catholic Church. But they sought answers to a related question: what makes for a heretic?

On 26 November 1559 there began a series of performances that took place over three consecutive Sundays at the usual locales of the *hostellerie* called La Teste d'Or and the Halles de Saint-Brixe.[49] By that time, reformers seemed positively to control Tournai's successful theaters, while a bishop of Lille had protested in 1560 that the city was "infected by Reformist thinking."[50] On 21 January 1553 religious authorities had succeeded in establishing their right to deny theatrical productions.[51] On 29 December 1556 the council of Tournai had received a complaint that "the players of the Teste d'Or perform plays that defame the clergy and the legal profession."[52] And by 26 January 1560 Philip II prohibited "theatrical performances dealing with questions of religion."[53] Indeed, the bishop of Tournai had previously grumbled that his directives were being violated by the Chambers of Rhetoric, whose biblical plays "were engendering in Lille and its neighboring towns discussions about the Scriptures."[54] Still, not even the most dogged reformer could have anticipated the theological success (and Catholic distress) that accompanied the events of winter 1559.

Thus far, we have seen that ecclesiastics deemed drama dangerous because of what it made spectators *fail to do:* keep silent, go to church, live chastely, worship with humility. It was just as dangerous because of what it made them *do:* think independently, read books, lose control, engage in physical violence (or in this case, in perilous *verbal* violence).[55] Whatever their specific reservations, however, both Catholics and Protestants came to realize that a good play, like a good sermon, might "act upon the crowd and reach all the way out to the illiterate."[56] Nor, as men of the cloth debated theater's merits, were they the only ones doing the talking. As sure as Pontalais's drum beats from beyond the grave, audiences were talking back, acting up, and acting out. Or were they?

Decidedly, that is how it appears when, as Gerard Moreau tells the tale, the winter theater season incited disorderly thoughts of heresy. The first play, a farce, boasted a jokester who tells *The World* that he would like to become a priest so that he might have a "grand old time frequenting girls and the theater." Such anticlerical humor paled by comparison to the very serious intervention by a boisterous spectator in the subsequent performance of the Old Testament episode of Elijah and Jezebel.[57] Despite Lebègue's acknowledgment that between comedy's suitability for polemic and biblical drama's goal of moral edification, "spectacle was the auxiliary of preaching" (*TRF*, 290), there remained the problem of how to practice what one preached or how to interpret what one thought one heard preached. When an *on-stage* prophet chastised his listeners for worshiping, like Jezebel, golden idols instead of adoring one God, this particular *off-stage* attendee heard an invitation to a heretical discussion. No Cavellian yokel he, the man interrupted the performance not physically but intellectually.[58] He responded to the character's speech with a speech of his own, bespeaking a conviction, later seconded by others, that theater's frame—like theology's frame—was meant to be broken.

Both speeches—within and without the play—are preserved in the deposition of Antoine Playart and Sébastien Plouquet by an act of 14 December 1559. The speech in the play went like this: "You have abandoned the living God in order to worship the god Baal along with your idols, which have no power to cure any type of illnesses that exist. You fashion gods of wood, stone, plaster, [and] brass; and you [fashion] images. They have eyes, yet they do not see; and their other body parts *[membres]* offer no assistance. You light candles against the commandment of God, who wishes to be worshipped as one God."[59] At that point, our obstreperous attendee rushed headlong into the theatrical fray. Reformist thinking, it seems, had substantially altered his theological and theatrical consciousness—enough, at any rate, for him to plug into the debates about idolatry, miraculous cures, and three other controversial questions (the nature of purgatory, the consumption of meat on Friday, and the possibility of hearing Mass in the vernacular):

> After the actor had repeated several times the words, "to be worshipped as one God," one of the spectators cried out: "Right on! That's the whole point"; while others began talking heresy, declaring, for example, that "there was no such thing as Purgatory and, indeed, weren't we all living in a purgatory in this world when you couldn't eat meat any time you wanted—as long you did it in moderation." And then they added that "if the Church would just do the Mass in French, then people would be more willing to go."[60]

In a city like Tournai, their familiarity with those five topics was hardly surprising. Before his execution in 1545, Pierre Brully had articulated the major tenets of Reformist thought while under interrogation by Catholic theologians: "the Holy Sacrament at the altar, the Mass, the consecration, the adoration of the sacred host, purgatory, the veneration of the saints, free will, good works, justification, images, baptism, wishes, auricular confession, [and] the virginity of the Virgin Mary."[61] As to the specific issue of idol worship, our belligerent spectator would surely have been cognizant of the biblical injunction of Exodus 20.4, reiterated by Calvin as "Thou shalt not make unto thee any graven image, or any likeness of anything that is in heaven above, or in the earth beneath, or in the water under the earth."[62] Indeed, his intervention mirrors Calvin's own objections to the worship of images that "neither speak, nor see, nor hear, nor walk," and which, although they possess "neither sense nor life . . . affect weak minds just as if they lived and breathed."[63] His sensibilities might have been further honed through such Catholic hagiographic narratives as that of Catherine of Alexandria, which says that

> The gods that your people adore
> Are handmade out of gold and silver.
> They are not gods, but devils
> That belong to Hell.
> Your honoring them is foolish.[64]

It is even conceivable that the heretics of Tournai knew to disparage idol worship because they had seen a play of the life of either Saint Catherine or Saint Barbara. Attendees of Lyonard's landmark performance some two hundred miles away in Metz, for instance, had seen the pope himself commission an "imagist [Ymager]" to fashion Barbara's likeness for worship at the end of the play.[65]

Regarding purgatory, Calvin had called it "a horrible blasphemy against Jesus Christ," while Brully argued that a good Christian neither "knows nor seeks any other purgatory than the blood of Christ."[66] In the case of fish on Fridays, Farel had maintained that "Our Lord gave no laws and no times for fasting, but rather, commands us to live soberly in His service and to help our neighbors."[67] To that end, he advocated the use of the vernacular during Mass because "when the holy people came to the table of Our Lord, it used to be that there were readings from parts of the Holy Scriptures in a language that everyone could understand, and prayers were offered that could be understood by all, with great passion. And during the Mass, everything is said in a language that the people do not understand."[68] Our vociferous Tournaisian spectators might also have known that in nearby Mons in that same year of 1559, nervous parents were seeking to forbid their children to use French while saying grace at table, inasmuch as rhetoricians and heretics used the vernacular in their own festivities.[69]

Most significant, Brully had linked the question of the Mass in the vernacular to that of transubstantiation. When the faithful took the Host on their tongue, he submitted, "the true body and blood of Christ were received at that moment not by the mouth but rather, through faith, by the spirit, while the substance of the bread and wine were in no way changed." In other words, what was important during Mass was that Christ be accessible not merely *on* the tongues of the simple folk *(en langue vulgaire)* but *in* their mother tongue *(en langue vulgaire)*: "[when] the Sacrament is distributed to the assembly of Christians in the vernacular so that all may understand its use and profit, at that point, the bread and wine are truly consecrated, to wit by the word of Christ."[70]

So did the noisy fellow and his colleagues really speak up boldly enough to consecrate their theater? On one hand, we have seen all too well and all too often that appearances can be deceiving: as deceiving as the so-called jail time to which Pontalais was sentenced. On the other hand, to use the contemporary turn of phrase, just because the Catholic Church was paranoid, that didn't mean that theater was *not* out to get it. The fact that Tournai's heretical eruption is preserved in a legal deposition would tend to give it greater historical weight—although, as almost any court watcher has noticed, nothing prevents a deponent or a witness from lying under oath. Additionally, the story gains in credibility from so many earlier invitations that audiences participate (admittedly less aggressively) in such dramas as the Fleury Playbook *Herod*.[71] It is more believable in light of our earlier acquaintance with the charismatic preacher, Brother Oliver of Metz, who appears to have taught dramatic intervention *inside* the church.[72] It would be believable to anyone familiar with the tumult associated with opening night of Victor Hugo's *Hernani* (25 February 1830) or with the post-theatrical eruption of the Belgian Revolution that same year in Brussels.[73] Likewise, it is believable today to any spectator who has ever thrown popcorn at the screen during the *Rocky Horror Picture Show*, responded to actors' invitations that they solve the murder in *Shear Madness*, or voted on the final love song of *The Mystery of Edwin Drood*.

Regardless of what truly happened in Valenciennes in 1547 or Tournai in 1559, what matters is that vehement clerics believed the dangers they saw before them (or thought they saw before them) to be real, and they responded with real repressions. Heretical speech would have to be silenced. The metaphorical response to those heretics in Tournai was "bite your tongue." In 1546 the actual response to eight heretics in Meaux, the setting for our next story, had been to have "their tongues cut out before being taken from prison to their execution for fear that they would confess too indiscreetly before the people for whose beliefs they were dying."[74]

If ancient Greece had its legends of contagious madness and spontaneous miscarriages, the French Middle Ages had legends that were just as deadly. Lucian's legendary actor and Melun's legendary Eel were not alone in having paid a terrible price for acting. Sometimes, moreover, the blow was self-inflicted. In any event, the Catholic Church might have every reason to hope that it would be.

CHAPTER   THIRTEEN

The Suicide of Despair

A murder, a suicide, or an ordeal terrify less on stage than the anticipation of that
ordeal, that suicide, or that murder—as necessary nonetheless to the plot as the
final chord of a symphony.

—André de Lorde, *Théâtre de la mort*

Apparently, anyone who was able to catch a performance at the wooden
theater of Meaux in the 1540s saw something quite special. But they had
to act fast: Meaux's theater lasted only two years, built in 1547 and torn
down by 1549. So said the nineteenth-century historian A. Carro in his
Histoire de Meaux; and so said Petit de Julleville when he quoted him.[1]
According to Carro, early chroniclers attributed the theater's short life to
the sad demise of some of its actors, whose deaths proffered these ominous examples of life imitating art:

> After two years of performances,[2] and in spite of their success, the the-
> ater was demolished and its land sold off. One does not see that stage
> plays in Meaux were taken up again for a long time. Perhaps the miser-
> able end of several people who had taken part in them was the cause of
> this—an end that, *in the account of the chronicler, seems to impinge some-
> what on the legendary.* In fact, according to this account, those who had
> played the roles of devils died in great poverty; the man who had played
> the role of Satan, a certain Pascalus to whom the nickname "the Devil"
> had stuck, was hanged; and the man who had played Despair [Dés-
> espoir] poisoned himself.[3]

Here were representations so lifelike that they were deathlike. And yet, it
all made sense. Terrible happenstance had been associated with the theater as far back as ancient Greece. Perhaps "Despair" killed himself due
to the same kind of acute histrionic distress that Lucian of Samosata had
ascribed to the mad "Ajax," or Quintilian to actors who habitually left the

stage still "drowned in their own tears."[4] If so, then Meaux presents yet another story of early "method actors" who carried with them the rage, poverty, madness, disease, or despair of their characters long after the play-acting was over. Or did they?

Lucian himself had noticed that mythology had a way of embellishing and transforming even the simplest theatrical situation. He went so far as to surmise that the mythic Proteus was no human chameleon at all but merely an actor: "It seems to me that the ancient myth about Proteus the Egyptian means nothing else than that he was a dancer, an imitative fellow, able to shape himself and change himself into anything. . . . Mythology, however, on taking it over, described his nature in terms more paradoxical, *as if he became what he imitated*."[5] That moment of Protean *becoming*, that great *as if*, signals the quintessential *birth* of theater. In Meaux, it signals the *death* of both theater and its actors. We shall also see that it signals an ecclesiastical death-wish *for* theater. What initially sounds like an urban legend designed to panic actors into thinking that they will die at theater's hand makes more sense as the Catholic Church's wish that theater itself should die.

Situated chronologically at a moment of intense antitheatrical polemic, Meaux is the ultimate tale of theater's ultimate peril. If one or more of the legends are true, then theater was a most dangerous place. If they are false, then sixteenth-century Meaux was the dangerous place. If true, the moral of the story (or stories) would have this familiar ring: "Avoid the theater, or it will destroy you." If false, the moral would be: "Avoid the theater, or *we* (the Catholics of Meaux) will destroy *it*." Either way, theater stands center-stage at somebody's vision of poetic justice, exemplifying what Brunvand calls the "quintessential urban-legend plot twist—the poetic justice, or got-what-he- (or she-) deserved, ending."[6] But the legend of Meaux has woven so many different voices together that it is difficult to ascertain who deserved what according to whose justice—and when that justice was meted out by whom.

In multiply mediated testimony, Petit de Julleville cites Carro, who was citing the eighteenth-century Dr. Rochard, who was citing the manuscript testimony of the sixteenth-century prosecutor L'Enfant and the seventeenth-century *curé* Janvier.[7] Rochard, moreover, liked the passive voice, which is notorious for rendering agents unclear. He doesn't mention Pascalus by name, but we can thank Mademoiselle C. Lebert for quoting Rochard directly in a lecture of 1 June 1955 (instead of quoting Carro quoting Rochard): "the most unique thing that *has been observed* of them was that those who played the roles of devils died in great poverty; the man who played Satan was later hanged, and the man who portrayed Despair poisoned himself."[8] For his own part, Carro has no trouble *interpreting* the story:

Without wanting to depoeticize the legend too much, one might note that those who played the demons were "poor devils" *[de pauvres diables]* in whom the passion for play-acting had occasioned a distaste for the daily grind of their real jobs, as the author himself insinuates. As for Pascalus, we shall see him later during the [times of] religious and civil unrest [of the Reformation]. He is playing for keeps *a dangerous role* that sometimes could (and, in his case actually did) lead straight to the gallows, in spite of his devilish connections. (*HM*, 212–13)[9]

Although it is no longer standing, the theater of Meaux stands for a great deal. It symbolizes the classic worries that impersonation could be as permanent as the madness of Lucian's "Ajax"—or as dastardly as the roles that stuck to those thieving Devils of Chaumont or to the Montléon brothers.[10] We have a proverbial "poor devil *[pauvre diable]*," defined by Antoine Oudin as "a man who is unhappy or in great need. Item, one deserving compassion."[11] And we also have Pascalus, whose life and death confusedly embody another proverb: "*le Diable s'en pende*" or "May the Devil hang himself on account of this!" an expression employed "when we regret something or when some sort of misfortune has befallen us."[12]

But something is missing and something is wrong. First of all, the devilish Pascalus does not hang *himself:* he is executed. Our story doesn't come right out and say that he was a Protestant heretic, but he was indeed put to death in a city that had a penchant for the spectacular execution of Protestants. Barely one year before Meaux's theater went up, sixty religious dissidents went down. They had been arrested on 7 October 1546 for having assembled illegally "to pray to God in their own way, and to read the Bible in French." Fourteen were later burned alive at the Grand Marché.[13] In the lugubrious closing act of the legend of Meaux, the theatrical scaffolding upon which Pascalus once trod *(échafauds)* is historically, symbolically, and philologically identical to the hangman's gallows *(échafauds)*. If we suspect, however, that his execution is best elucidated by such modern theories as Foucault's "spectacle of the scaffold" or Kubiak's "theater of punishment," we might miss the message of an urban legend like Meaux.[14] Any reader of Foucault knows that the scaffold is a stage. Pascalus transforms the stage into a shroud.[15]

Second, and more important, the suicide of "Despair" is the only subject that Carro is unwilling or unable to depoeticize. From the same historian who had so readily advanced a socioeconomic explanation for the deaths of those poor devils, and a politico-theological one for Pascalus, there is complete silence on the subject of "Despair"'s decision to take his own life with poison. Silence from Petit de Julleville as well. At the risk of echoing Joseph Bédier's enraptured observation about the second horn scene of the *Song of Roland*, I would venture to say that that silence is the most sublime aspect of the story.[16]

No matter how dark and depressing modern drama may get, there is a very real way in which one might argue that, metaphorically speaking, one of the great aesthetic functions of the theater has always been to hasten the death of despair. Theater's spell, mused Lucian, "is so potent that if a lover enters the theatre, he is restored to his right mind by seeing all the evil consequences of love; and one who is in the clutch of grief leaves the theatre in a brighter mood, as if he had taken some potion that brings forgetfulness and, in the words of the poet [Homer], 'surcease from sorrow and anger.'"[17] Indeed, in a strange antithesis to some of the stories we have already reviewed, Lucian suggests that theater *cures* audiences of the very maladies it *inflicts* upon actors. An "Ajax" leaves the stage madder than when he arrived; a "Polus" leaves more grief-stricken.[18] So if the dream of theater was to effect the metaphorical death of despair, it was not supposed to facilitate the suicide of the man *playing* Despair. Instead of a restorative magic potion, "Despair" has imbibed a theatrical poison that kicks off the grand finale of his theatrical, physical, and eternal lives. "For Catholics, Lutherans, Calvinists, and Anglicans alike," notes Georges Minois, suicide was an unforgivable and diabolical act.[19] When "Despair" snuffs out his God-given life and takes his theater along with him, he has no final resting place. He has only an epitaph in the form of a legend.

Does anybody have doubts about these events? On the face of it, the theatrically inspired suicide of Pascalus shouldn't seem any less plausible than the suicide of the modern actor "Pete," who played the Hunchback during that brutal RATT performance in London.[20] Nor is it any less plausible than the "accidental" suicide of Jon-Erik Hexum, who died on 12 October 1984 while filming the short-lived television series *Cover-Up*. As a joke, Hexum had fired a pistol charged with blanks at his temple. The force of the detonation was sufficient to disturb a dormant aneurysm and kill him. He died from feigning suicide.[21] Furthermore, should readers still have doubts about Meaux's dead devils, Pascalus, or despairing "Despair," the legend offers a stunning rationale to quash them. The fact that the theater is *no longer there* actually authorizes the stories. Its *absence* reinforces their *presence*. As real life and theatrical imagination coincide in death, nowhere do these characters seem more real than when they are real enough to die and disappear.

Let us get acquainted with our victims in the same order as they appear in the narrative: the impoverished devils, Pascalus, "Despair," and, last but not least, theater itself.

Who were those poor working stiffs who, by our commentators' accounts, could never have returned peacefully to their menial jobs after having tasted the thrill of impersonating devils? Maybe the "poor devils" of Meaux died in poverty because they started out poor and would always be poor.[22] Rochard implies that the devilish thespians were so taken by their roles that "they preferred such experiences to their daily work; whence many became idle *[gueux]*."[23] Or maybe they died in poverty while waiting for that big break, a situation that would be credible to anyone on friendly terms with a struggling actor—or to anyone who has ever ascribed to actors the trademark desire to be more than they are. Doué-la-Fontaine had monumentalized that ambition in its mysterious quarry. Meaux destroyed it.

Then again, Gustave Cohen insinuates, with a curious choice of verb tenses, that the devils of Meaux might never have made it onto the stage at all. Medieval spectators, he submits, were so superstitious that they "take pleasure in noting that the actors who *are to play* the devils in Meaux in 1547 died in great poverty."[24] But maybe, as was the case in Châlons-sur-Marne, there was the distinct possibility of encountering not just a proverbial "poor devil" but a real one. Witness the case presented by another friend of Petit de Julleville concerning an impoverished soul who received special assistance from his community so that he might incarnate the satanic master during a *Mystère de la Passion*. In a long-lost communication by one Monsieur Pelicier, "archivist of the Marne region," we learn that the town council issued this ruling on 3 May 1507:

> *Item,* there was a request made by the man who is to play the part of Lucifer and who is indigent, that several of our gentlemen who are not playing might wish to assist him by providing his costume. . . .
>
> Our lords the abbots . . . and several wealthy persons of the aforesaid Châlons, who will not be playing, have come forward and promised to costume the man playing the part of Lucifer at their own expense *because he is a poor man and a good actor.*[25]

Given this true *pauvre diable* in the flesh, it is reasonable to imagine another one: the diabolical Pascalus, who purportedly retained his thespian sobriquet during heretical activities that were to prove even more diabolical.[26]

Our commentators may well have exhibited the proverbial compassion recommended by Oudin for the other "poor devils." No such compassion was extended to Pascalus, who wound up "playing straight" during the great political drama of the Reformation. We know nothing about the precise nature of his role or religion: indeed, there is no proof that Pascalus did anything the least bit heretical.[27] It is conceivable, however, that, if Rochard, Carro, and Petit de Julleville are correct about Meaux's penchant for Old and New Testament dramas,[28] then that repertoire might have begun to nurture an intellectual crisis substantial enough to transform performers into reformers. As a result of challenging dramatic ideas, perhaps Pascalus began to engage in theological inquiries of the sort that would erupt some twenty years later in Tournai during that infamous performance of *Elijah and Jezebel*.[29] In that sense, Pascalus bequeaths not so much the fear that theater will erupt into heresy (although that is definitely part of it). Rather, his legacy is the fear that any theatrical eruption of reality reveals the fantastically transitory, arbitrary, and precarious nature of social institutions in whose utter stability one normally needs to believe: law, politics, and religion.[30] By his apocryphal death, Pascalus exemplifies Baudrillard's contention that the primary danger of simulation is that it tends to make the law itself seem like make-believe (*SW,* 177). Even when justice triumphs, it doesn't really win—and even when it *does* win, it might owe its Pyrrhic victory to theater.

If Pascalus was truly hanged, then he eradicated in one fell swoop the prothespian claim made by Fred Belton much later, in 1880: "Ah, ye who think the actor's life is passed in idleness and dissipation, hear this truthful confession, and blush that you should ever malign a profession that in the heavy criminal calendar is unknown. *No actor yet was ever hanged! What other profession, trade, or even creed can say this?*"[31] Alas, he spoke too soon—and Jacob Larwood knew it, boldly proclaiming that "there are one or two examples of actors who have fully *deserved* hanging, and there is at least one instance of a comedian who, in this respect, obtained his deserts" (*TA,* 215).[32] The just deserts of Pascalus are also those of theater: both have made it impossible to distinguish between the false drama of the stage and the far more dangerous but supposedly much more verifiable dramas of politics, law, and religion.[33] Pascalus incarnates the permanent and potentially mortal effects of any act of impersonation along with something else that was just as dangerous. Unlike "Despair," who ostensibly died by his own hand, Pascalus had help. If he had verifiably become a reformer, then he had help from the Catholic Church, which ensured the deadly dénouement of his heretical life.

The dénouement for "Despair" was just as deadly. Its message was not: "Beware the theater because it will kill you!" It was: "Beware the theater because it will make you kill *yourself.*" In a city where theater had become ensnared in theological polemic about what was real and what was symbolic, "Despair"'s last breath might well represent the dying gasp of an ecclesiastical community that found itself powerless to stop theater's power. What better way to kill it off than to suggest that theater (through the thespian incarnation of Despair) kills itself?

At first, "Despair" appears to be another method actor *avant la lettre.* The anonymous man has understood all too well the principles of internal motivation that would be developed by Stanislavski some four hundred years later. When it came to rendering something like a suicide on stage, Stanislavski urged that "what counts in the theatre is not the material of which Othello's dagger is made, be it steel or cardboard, but the inner feeling of the actor who can justify his suicide. What is important is how the actor, a human being, *would have acted* if the circumstances and conditions which surrounded Othello were real and the dagger with which he stabbed himself were metal."[34] With a poison as real as Pascalus's scaffold, Meaux's suicidal "Despair" proposes that an imaginary *he would have* became a historical *he did*. It is all the easier to imagine that "he did" when we review the suicide scenes of the Passion plays of Arnoul Gréban and Jean Michel.

Regardless of whether the character is played by a man or a woman, Jean Michel's Desesperance is an expert in nurturing sinful thoughts of self-murder. She is the Sweet Little Buttercup of the suicide business, touting an impressive stash of macabre merchandise, which, inconveniently for our story, includes everything *but* the poison that Meaux's "Despair" purportedly used:

> See here, all the tools of my trade:
> Am I not stocked with all the stuff
> That's suited cleverly enough
> To any canny, cagey guy
> Who's fixed it in his mind to die?
> See my best wares; and take your pick!
> I've daggers, knives, a nice ice-pick!
> I've matches, awls, sharp things galore;
> So take the best things in the store,
> Forged by the finest, you might note,
> And ready made to slit your throat.
>
> *Here Despair takes a dagger in hand and [she] shows it to Judas.*
>
> Take this and plunge it to the hilt
> Into your gut to ease your guilt.
>
> *Here [she] shows him a rope.*
>
> Or maybe hanging's what you hope.
> For sale right here, I've cords and rope.
> Strangle yourself! Take your best shot!
> Come on! Jump in! You pause a lot.
> Strike now while the iron is hot![35]

However, when Michel's Desesperance coaxes Judas to open his heart—not to the forgiveness of Christ, but to the oblivion of the despair she exemplifies—she encourages something that is as theologically problematic as it is scenically difficult:

Open your heart and place inside
Despair; then you won't hesitate.
Go hang yourself; do not abide!
I've saved this rope to seal your fate.[36]

An image from a fifteenth-century fresco displays not only Judas's open heart, the site of his despair, but his open *body* (fig. 8).

According to Jean–Claude Schmitt, "the password to medieval suicide was *desespoir*," a term that denoted "not a feeling nor a psychic state but a Vice."[37] Furthermore, Minois informs us that in theological writings from the fifth through the tenth centuries, "the joyful death of the martyr was contrasted to the death of the despairing sinner" whose despair was diabolically inspired (*HS*, 25).[38] "Killing oneself out of despair," he explains, "was considered the most culpable type of suicide," insofar as "persons afflicted with *desperatio* . . . believed their sins beyond all pardon; like Judas, they sinned against God by doubting his mercy, and they sinned against the Church by doubting its powers of intercession. Despair was among the gravest sins precisely because it contested the role of the Church in pardoning faults through absolution" (*HS*, 30).[39] A religious theater, meant to bring the word of God to his people, could not be permitted to denounce his ecclesiastical intermediaries while flaunting the sin of suicide in his face. Yet mystery plays had always done so.

When Arnoul Gréban's Despair emerges from the depths of Hell, even a repentant Judas doesn't stand a chance. She intimidates him into suicide with the warning that his sins are so unpardonable that he can never show his shameful face before a merciful Christ (who will nonetheless deny him mercy).[40] Meanwhile, in Jean Michel's version, Satan puts in a personal appearance to make sure that Judas's state of despair is such that he has abandoned all hope (23913–15). As a stage direction calls for Judas to place the rope around his neck, he responds in word and deed:

JUDAS attaches his rope.

It is my wish to hang, in spite
Of God's command, upon this site.
I'll suffocate by my own hand
And for eternity be damned,
Forgiveness never meant to be.
Myself, I'll fix the hanging-tree.[41]

In Meaux, it is as if an ecclesiastical wish for theater's death has become "Despair" 's sin of death, while at the same time the Church's death-wish for theater has

Figure 8. The Hanging of Judas. Fifteenth-century fresco, Notre-Dame des Fontaines, La Brigue.

become the actor's transgression. With distinctly Catholic sensibilities, the legend of Meaux conflates the Church's approval of a hanging-death for heretics, its *dis*approval of Judas's despair-motivated suicide, and "Despair"'s self-murder by poisoning.

At this point, several ambiguities arise, both in the Gospel narratives and in the legend of Meaux. While the theological symbolism of Judas's despair was clear, the actual mode of his death was not: his "presumed suicide soon became the archetype for a shameful, damnable death, not so much for the act itself as for the despair that prompted it. St. Matthew alone states that Judas hanged himself; the other evangelists say nothing about his death, and the Book of Acts reports that he died of a fall. . . . 'His body burst wide open, all his entrails spilling out'" (*HS*, 25).[42] As in the fresco portrayal (fig. 8), "medieval miniaturists reconciled the two accounts by depicting Judas hanged with his belly split open" (*HS*, 25). So too did medieval dramatists, as when Lynette Muir notes that the actor playing Judas in the Mons Passion play "has a bag of pig's entrails under his robe," prepared to respond to this stage direction: "Here dies Judas, with entrails rushing from his chest and his soul departs."[43]

On one hand, it makes sense that an actor playing Despair would contemplate suicide. Any "Despair" would have been well rehearsed in the hideous arguments in favor of self-murder from having recited them on stage. Despair is the one who does all the talking about suicide, and who "climbs up with [Judas] to help him while the devils wait below."[44]

On the other hand, Petit de Julleville, Carro, and Rochard all speak of a male character Desespoir, while the mystery plays cast a female Desesperance. If the theatrical productions of Meaux had really culminated in a suicide, it would be most unusual *not to know* whether the dead sinner was a man or a woman.[45] Even so, this is the precise detail our legend fails to supply: Did a "Desespoir" poison *him*self? Did a "Desesperance" kill *her*self? Or did a man playing a female Desesperance kill himself? Gustave Cohen resolves the problem by stating that "the man who played Lady Despair poisoned himself," but he adduces no proof beyond his general expertise in mystery plays.[46] And nobody comes forward to ask or to answer another question: Why poison?

Few metaphors are as well suited to the theater's long-censured risks as poison. Previously, theater had poisoned the mind of poor "Ajax," and even today poison appears as the dangerous lining of so many psychic clouds. For example, one of the standard admonitions of modern urban legends is that a large number of experiences related to pleasure, beauty, entertainment, or leisure contain a deadly germ that, once sprouted, endangers the persons involved. As Brunvand puts it, "the idea of some dangerous, potentially fatal, foreign element getting inside a human body is a common one in urban legends" (*CD*, 107).[47] There's the one about "The Poison Dress" with the ten-thousand-dollar price tag. The garment infects its extravagant purchaser because the dress's previous owner had buried her dead mother in the dress, only to retrieve it, steeped in formaldehyde, from the mortician after the funeral.[48] There is "The Poinsettia Myth," which warns that children will die after ingesting the cheery Christmas plant's poisonous leaves (which are, in reality, perfectly safe if not necessarily tasty).[49] There is the hideous tale of "The Spider Eggs in Bubble Yum," in which a child falls asleep while chewing the gum and later awakens with "a mouth full of spider eggs."[50] Most gruesome of all, there is the one about "The Accidental Cannibals," in which a family is said to have received "a package from relatives in the United States containing an unlabeled jar of blackish-brown powder, which they assumed was an instant drink of some sort. After the family had used up most of the powder making hot drinks, a letter arrived from the United States explaining that the jar had contained the ashes of their grandmother" (*BT*, 75). The anxiety that underpins these legends is one and the same: "Beware, lest pleasant façades reveal their poisonous influence too late." In Meaux, the façade is a theater that has been poisoned by poverty, heresy, and suicide.

Lest the reader fear that we have taken a powder from the Middle Ages, consider this. One needn't be a medievalist to see that Meaux's very old anxieties frequently resurface today in debates about the influence of the media.[51] The end of the last millennium saw distraught parents suing record companies, alleging that their teenage children had committed suicide after having listened repeatedly to sad or violent rock lyrics. Theoretically, the youths had turned to heavy metal to express themselves, to lift their troubled spirits, or even to revel in a dark beauty. Now, from the ashes of dead children, parents rise up to retaliate against musicians, artists, and deep-pocketed record companies by filing wrongful-death suits based on the age-old fear that some art forms are as hazardous as the theater of Meaux once was when it ostensibly prompted the suicide of "Despair." We can no more know for certain if "Despair"'s demise was real than we can seek answers from today's dead children. But what we *can* know is that just as Meaux's civil and ecclesiastical authorities held theater liable and sought to regulate, discipline, censor, and punish it, so too do modern authorities seek similar remedies.[52] Instead of yesterday's death-wish for theater, we have today's death-wish for music, film, and television—or, at a minimum, we have a wish to censor those art forms into nothingness. In Meaux, an ecclesiastical community sought the metaphorical death of theater. In the United States, a civil (or uncivil) community seeks the metaphorical death of the record industry.

Finally, let us fantasize for a moment that audiences at Meaux saw Jean Michel's or Arnoul Gréban's Passion plays.[53] Judas's farewell speech might well be construed as an *adieu* to theater. As he commends his soul to "all the devils large and small," his lexicon bears an eerie resemblance to all the scenic properties and devices that attended the typical staging of the Hell Mouth:

> Oh, highest tower of Despair,
> Walled round with many piteous tears
> And draped by screams that serve as biers,
> An endless wall does shroud you well:
> 'Twas fashioned in the forge of Hell.
> A bottomless abyss surrounds
> You with no limits and no bounds.
> The only comfort of your halls
> Is the eternal plaintive calls.
> Await me now, my hateful home.
> In you I'll dwell; I'll never roam.
> Await me, caverns hideous;
> For in your sulfurous abyss
> I'll die a thousand deaths in Hell.
> Await me, painful prison cell
> And furnace shooting out black fire,
> Where snake-infested ditches mire
> The senses. Muddy rivers flow.
> Such pain and grief, I now shall know;
> For I am plunging into you. . . .

Here Judas hangs himself with the devils below him.[54]

In the legend of Meaux, theater pays the price for "Despair" 's self-inflicted death in that the legend imagines Aristotelian catharsis taken to the extreme. Instead of purging and relieving pity, fear, and all such "violent disturbances of the soul," it offers ecclesiastics a way to suggest that theater *creates* those psychic disturbances in the first place.[55] If theater can create them, then Meaux's Catholic Church can hope to destroy them. It can attempt to do so with a triple purge of the violent emotions themselves, the persons afflicted with those emotions (in this case, Protestant heretics), and, in the ultimate *coup de théâtre,* the theater itself.

Our last casualty, Meaux's wooden theater, was certainly real enough to die. If we believe Carro and his sources, there really *was* a theater at Meaux, albeit one that was "a bit ephemeral . . . for it was only made of wood and covered with a canvas as in the circuses of antiquity."[56] "It was situated at the site where the *collège* is now located," says Carro, who goes on to cite Rochard: "It was hollow underneath so that experts might stay inside for the purpose of creating wonderful special effects. The performances lasted for two years, except during the winter. The first summer, the aforesaid theater was covered with cloth, even though it was quite large, but that didn't last long, and, indeed, it was torn apart by the wind—even though there were a great number of cords both above and below."[57] Did the theater blow away? or was it blown away by ecclesiastical rage?

If Meaux's wooden theater did not last long, neither did the evidence of its existence. Needless to say, one cannot combine a fact-finding mission with a trip to Euro-Disney by taking the RER to Meaux to look for the theater today. One of the first things Carro tells us is that "the theater was demolished and its land sold off."[58] Nonetheless, Mademoiselle Lebert was kind enough to give us directions in her "Théâtre à Meaux," which reveals a final irony. In the quintessential poetic justice for the Catholic Church, there sits atop the former site of Meaux's mortal theater a convent: "the theater was in the rue Poitevine, at the site where the *collège* was once located and where there is, at present, the convent of the Ursulines."[59] Meaux's theater imploded; its actors ceased to be actors, and its stage ceased to be a stage. The show could not go on. But Catholicism *could,* especially when it came to death by drama.

Death by Drama

We don't know the truth about the past but we can invent a fiction
as like it as may be.

—Plato, *Republic*

According to the legend, when Philip II made his triumphal entry into
Tournai in 1549, he was greeted by a painstakingly realistic performance
of the drama of Judith and Holofernes.[1] Frédéric Faber relates that producers Jean de Bury and Jean de Crehan had arranged a very special entertainment for the future monarch. A convicted heretic and murderer
was to assume the role of Holofernes long enough to be decapitated during the play by another convicted felon. The latter, having been pardoned,
would just as briefly assume the role of Judith, his executioner:

> Jean de Bury and Jean de Crehan, duly charged with decorating the
> streets, had imagined rendering in its purest form *[au naturel]* the bib-
> lical exploit of Judith. Consequently, for filling the role of Holofernes,
> a criminal had been chosen who had been condemned to have his flesh
> torn with red-hot pincers *[tenaillé]. This poor fellow, guilty of several
> murders and ensconced in heresy [convaincu d'hérésie],* had preferred de-
> capitation to the horrible torture to which he had been condemned,
> hoping, perhaps, that a young girl would have neither the force nor the
> courage to cut off his head. But the organizers, having had the same
> concern, had substituted for the real Judith *[la véritable Judith]* a
> young man who had been condemned to banishment and to whom a
> pardon was promised if he played his role well.[2]

The story goes that the two substitutions were accepted by the two unnamed men. Being an actor/executioner was apparently preferable to being banished, and death by decapitation during drama was preferable to
being skinned alive (something that the Eel of Melun might himself have

understood). "Judith" had only one condition to meet: to provide acting so good that it wasn't acting at all. But acting what—the biblical tale? the play that commemorated it? the crimes, punishments, and pardons of medieval criminals? or something else that Tournai wanted to say to, or about, the visiting Spaniard?

The fantastic narrative next shows Philip arriving just as the axe is falling. As real blood supposedly begins to flow, it prompts applause in some, indignation in others, and curiosity in the prince, who remains implacable as the body of "Holofernes" goes through its last spasms:

> In fact, as Philip approached the theater where the mystery play was being represented, the so-called Judith [la prétendue Judith] unsheathed a well-sharpened scimitar and, seizing the hair of Holofernes, who was pretending to be asleep, dealt him a single blow with so much skill and vigor that his head was separated from his body. At the [sight of] the streams of blood that spurted out from the neck of the victim, frenetic applause and cries of indignation rose up from amid the spectators. Only the young prince remained impassive, observing the convulsions of the decapitated man with curiosity and saying to his noble entourage: "nice blow" [bien frappé].[3]

If the suicide of Despair represented a Catholic hegemony's wish that theater kill itself, then the snuff drama of Tournai does it one better by placing in the hands of the Catholic Church a theatrical instrument of demise. "Beware the theater," it cautions, "because it will *execute* you." It also trumps the execution of Meaux's Pascalus, for it times its own decapitation of a heretic with an ongoing theatrical performance. The convicted heretic of our title piece lives theater, heresy, and execution simultaneously. He also dies from them.

This was not the near-deaths of two priests at Mctz. It was not the two fatalities caused by wayward cannonballs in those two fourteenth-century Paris-area plays. It was not the apocryphal demise of fetuses at the *Eumenides*, not the squealing Eel of Melun, not the on-stage deaths by more-or-less natural causes of Messieurs Palmer, Bond, or Jordans (*TA*, 198–200). It was no special effect produced by some blood-filled bladder designed to make Jacob Mousse's tortured Host bleed.[4] It was not Rey-Flaud's undocumented claim that the citizens of faraway Arles had once imported a professional executioner from Avignon to *play* one in their Passion play (although, presumably, not to execute anybody for real [*PDMA*, 153]).[5] Nor was Holofernes any Desdemona to Cavell's confused yokel. There was no confusion in Tournai as to whether or not the man (Holofernes *or* the actor) would rise again to play another day (*MWM*, 328). He would not—at least not bodily. His spirit lives on in a legend whose dénouement is shrouded in secrecy.

In a technique we have seen many times before, the final twist of the tale from Tournai is to transform the absence of evidence into a virtue.[6] Although "Judith" is granted some sort of amnesty, "he" vanishes anyway and takes his story along with him. Even as the executioner's disappearance guarantees the impossibility of confirming or denying the decapitation, the event is justified and authorized by another legend: the so-called Black Legend of Philip himself.[7] "Judith" is said to have become his special servant, coming across with sinister, unknown services that were probably "against nature": "The sang-froid of the prince in the face of this atrocity would serve to foretell the cruelty of his reign. It was even said that he took into his personal service the young man who had 'struck so well' and that he employed him in secret acts of iniquity."[8] Without enumerating all the off-color puns it was possible to make in Middle French about men penetrating, cutting, and striking with their "lances," let's just say that "Judith" 's secret "personal service" might have been conducted in Philip's royal chamber.[9]

If the tale from Tournai is true, it testifies to the presence of genuine Austinian speech acts on stage and to death as theater's ultimate performativity.[10] So, no matter how much we might like Richard Schechner's definition of theater as "restored behavior," the behavior of 1549 can never be "restored"—not unless another actor is killed on stage on another day.[11] To *restore* it would be to consent to what we would call today a snuff film. Tournai suggests, moreover, that even Foucault didn't go far enough when he said that "public torture and execution must be spectacular" (*DP*, 34)—although it was clearly that. For example, the *Justinian Digest* had long combined legal deterrence with dramatic catharsis when it established that "notorious brigands" were to be hanged "on a gallows in the places which they used to haunt, so that *by the spectacle others may be deterred from the same crimes,* and so that it may, when the penalty has been carried out, *bring comfort to the relatives and kin of those killed* in that place where the brigands committed their murders."[12] Elsewhere, Rey-Flaud reports (again, without documentation) on a medieval Brussels execution that was termed "the most beautiful ever seen," and on the purchase by the town council of Mons of a criminal from a neighboring town so that it might mount a spectacular drawing and quartering (*PDMA*, 152). Tournai is also the tale of the deliberate, legally sanctioned infliction of death by drama. It contradicts Augusto Boal's declaration that the stage supplies "harmless and pleasant discharge for the instincts that demand satisfaction and that can be tolerated much more easily in the fiction of the theater than in real life."[13] Instead, Tournai says that such violent instincts are tolerable, nonfictional, entertaining, and above all, *legal* in a way that is anything but harmless. Tournai is the story of the death penalty as entertainment. It shows that the only difference between murder and state execution is that the former is illegal while the latter is not.[14]

Long before contemporary debates raged about the existence of snuff films, long before the film *8MM* took the position that they exist, long before all three major television networks released radio tapes from Georgia's Death Row on 2 May 2001, and long before convicted Oklahoma City bomber Timothy McVeigh recommended that his execution be televised, Tournai's spectacle stood at the same phenomenological crossroads of life and death.[15] It tells us that if an early execution could be scripted like a theater piece, then a theater piece could be scripted like an execution. Tournai's *tour de force* is to equate the spectacle of a public execution with the public execution of a spectacle.

Nor can current efforts to bar large audiences from witnessing the death penalty in action efface its status as spectacle. If a tree falls in the woods and no one hears it, it still makes a noise. If a man is executed and no one sees it, he still dies. It doesn't matter how many spectators are watching or who they are: the Tournaisians of 1549 or the Oklahomans who experienced on 11 June 2001, in person or via closed-circuit television, the Justinian-like comforts of an eye for an eye, a tooth for a tooth of McVeigh. In that sense, it is surprising to read Wendy Lesser's comment about the unsuccessful 1991 lawsuit filed by San Francisco's KQED against Daniel Vasquez (warden of San Quentin) for the right to televise the execution of Robert Alton Harris: "to step over this line—the line between simulated or unplanned death and real, scheduled death—is to create a new kind of violence on TV."[16] There was nothing new about it. Medieval Europe had long ago invented snuff.

Nor would the message of any such execution be stable by any means.[17] Paul Zumthor considered Tournai to be a "desymbolized one-way pseudo-communication [in which] the actor takes on the latent violence of the people for whom he dies."[18] Bruce Wilshire noted of Christ's Passion in general that "the actor stands in vicariously and sacrificially for the audience in this confrontation with, and in some sense transcendence of, the myth of sacrifice itself" (*RPI*, 129).[19] As Tournai stages the legal sacrifice of a human life to theater, we see that there is little that is vicarious or pseudo-communicative about it. If the execution was indeed an act of pseudo-communication, then one of its more falsified aspects was that the two "actors" of its crowning moment did not really choose to communicate at all—even through the illusive communications of drama. For the criminal / executioner / Judith, a new chance at life was an offer he couldn't refuse; for the beheaded criminal / Holofernes, there was perhaps the long-shot hope of a narrow escape. At a minimum, the only real choice for "Holofernes" was *how* he would die and not *if* he would die: the very choice that many modern opponents of the death penalty find more barbaric than capital punishment itself.

Viewed in that light, "Holofernes" would have resembled rather closely the "actors" of Roman gladiatorial display who, according to David Marshall, "affect dying even as death really occurs . . . [and] become actors who die for the pleasure of their spectators, and what seems worse, who must perform their own deaths with broad, theatrical strokes."[20] At the same time, however, "Holofernes" hacks away at Wilshire's phenomenological argument that within the theatrical frame, the performer "cannot artistically perform his own death": "Since the application of the concept of 'performance' requires that the person's behavior as *persona* be bounded and controlled within his ongoing life as person, and since this is impossible in this case, the person can 'perform' his own death only in the most abysmal self-deception" (*RPI*, 268–69). Tournai says that he *can*. Hideous though his choice was, "Holofernes" chose beheading—which, for Wilshire, gave him enough of the "control" that he deems the prerequisite for art.[21] It says that "Holofernes" can choose to perform his own death without deception of himself or his audience. Indeed, it is the lack of deception that is abysmal—abysmal but theatrical.

Consider here Schechner's analysis of the scenic situation of Belle de Jour, a Manhattan sadomasochistic theater. In the early 1980s, audiences on West Nineteenth Street beheld such violent consensual acts as Belle driving a three-inch nail through a man's penis. This was "no Grand Guignol trick," assures Schechner: "Belle thrives on giving her audiences the real thing."[22] He then contrasts Belle's participants to the unwilling gladiatorial prey of ancient Rome:

> Where does this leave the bleeding gladiator or even the authentic sadomasochist at Belle's? Their conditions, theatrically speaking, are very different. The gladiator doesn't want to play. He is not playing. He is a spectacle for the spectators. He is one with the animals, brought in under guard to be used as entertainment. The spectators are "at play," but the gladiator is a slave given only the choice of death now or death later. But still, his own situation, which is not play, is presented within the play frame. (*BTA*, 301)

"Holofernes" stands theater on its head as he loses his own. He predicts that Kubiak will be right in a terrifyingly literal way to write that theater exhibits "real bodies living and dying in real time" (*ST*, 11). But he also says that Kubiak is wrong to say that theater "always seems to leave real violence behind because this is precisely theatre's function—to conceal violence even when (or especially when) it is seemingly exposing it in the violent spectacle" (*ST*, 160). There was nothing hidden about Tournai's mortal theater—unless, of course, it was its truth.

The legend of Tournai recounts the real performance of a pseudo-communica-tion based on a pseudo-choice during a pseudo-event whose apocryphal status is justified by apocryphal sources. With a genealogical complexity that is rivaled only by its vanishing evidence, Tournai poses two simple yet simply irresolvable ques-tions: did "snuff drama" exist? and, if so, where was the evidence?

We cannot verify Faber's vague reference to an "unedited manuscript belonging to the late Monsieur H. Delmotte, père," because that manuscript ostensibly was destroyed in a fire in May 1940.[23] Rey-Flaud's unattributed version of the snuff story doesn't clear things up (*PDMA*, 19). Nor does A. Delangre's redissemination in 1905 of Faber's own version of the story. Delangre cites Faber virtually verbatim and adds that "the official account of the memorable entry of the young prince is silent on the atrocity of which our community magistrates were accused, but a note in the manuscript substantiates that account."[24] That elusive manuscript note was presumably "published in the *Feuille de Tournai* of 23 July 1848," but the archival bounty hunter can only join the mildly exasperated Jesse Hurlbut in asking another question, which has yet to be answered: "Anyone happen to have *that* in your li-brary?"[25]

Initially, it seems just as difficult to prove or disprove the existence of Tournai's snuff drama as to prove or disprove the existence of a snuff film. Sociologists Eithne Johnson and Eric Schaefer recall, for instance, that "despite the mythic status of the snuff film, no agency, from the FBI to the Adult Film Association of America (AFAA), has been able to authenticate the existence of the genuine article." Simi-larly, John McConahay warrants that "there is little, if any, evidence that such films exist." When pressed for details, "those who claim that snuff films exist will admit that they have never seen one, but that they know someone who has."[26] That situa-tion so exasperated Andrea Dworkin during her testimony before Attorney Gen-eral Meese's Commission on Pornography in 1986 that she countered that there was "a great deal of evidence" but that it "would not hold up in the sphere of social policy as evidence. And I suppose until we can bring you a film, you will not believe that one exists."[27] "She is right," avers McConahay—in the same way that any cu-rious medievalist would be right to demand "Holofernes"'s head on a platter.[28] Our platter is perforce empty, but the theatrical table is real.

First of all, it behooves us to review the large number of features of the Tournai legend that are *not* open to question.

1. There is no doubt that the Judith play (or *a* Judith play) exists and that it calls for a decapitation scene. At least two short, fifteenth-century versions are extant: one in the vast cycle of the *Mystery of the Old Testament*, and another discovered in recent years by Alan Knight.[29] In the *Old Testament*, didascalia specify that Judith

"gets up and takes Holofernes's knife" and then *"cuts off his head."*[30] In *How Judith Killed Holofernes,* from Lille, she *"cuts off Holofernes's head"* and *"parts company with the army . . . carrying the head of Holofernes."*[31]

2. Philip really *did* go to Tournai. Two contemporaneous chroniclers, C. Calvete de Estrella and Vicente Alvarez, place the Catholic prince there during his crown-prince tour. Calvete gives a long account that parallels quite closely that of Pasquier de le Barre, the author of the *Journal d'un bourgeois de Tournai,* who was born in Tournai in the first quarter of the sixteenth century.[32] Alvarez, in contrast, devotes a scant twenty lines to the royal entry of 1549, pausing only long enough to convey that Philip left Lille on 7 August, stayed in Tournai for one day, and departed the fortified city for Douay on 9 August.[33]

3. Jehan de Crehan was a *real person,* and so, probably, was Jean de Bury as well. Moreau has uncovered the trace of the *juré,* Jean de Crehem,[34] while the nineteenth-century historian A.-G. Chotin attests to the supervisory role of *"jurés* Jean De Buri et Jean De Créhan" in the festivities of 1549.[35]

4. There really *were* plays performed in Philip's honor in Tournai in 1549. Pasquier de le Barre tells us that impressive theaters were built for that very occasion;[36] he lists in sumptuous detail a large variety of processions, visual tableaux, and performances depicting such characters as King David, Samson, Hercules, Jonas, and Esther.[37] Later, Chotin indicated that "all the streets were adorned" and that "everywhere there were theaters, *portiques,* and *arcs-de-triomphe*" because different neighborhoods were competing for a prize for the best decor.[38]

5. Tournai really *did* have a history of prosecuting and executing heretics—especially heretics who had something to do with the theater. For example, among the theatrical promoters of the plays of 1549 were Robert d'Alençon, Hercule Clément, and Jean Tallemant—Calvinists one and all. Each one was later convicted of heresy (*JBT,* 328).[39]

6. The region had a further history of proffering decapitation as a "kinder" alternative to more horrific modes of execution, such as being burned alive. On 26 October of that same year of 1549, the reformer Michel Destoubequin rejected the tradeoff. His mentor, John Calvin, eulogized him in these terms: "A young man, who has lived here among us, having been arrested in the city of Tournai, was condemned to have his head cut off if he recanted and to be burned alive if he persisted in his thinking. When they asked him what he wanted to do, he responded in a simple way: 'He who shall grant me the grace of dying patiently in his name shall also grant me the grace of enduring the flames.'"[40]

7. Although public executions normally accommodated the spectacular performance of public contrition by the condemned, exceptions could be made. Heretics

who were deemed too far gone in their thinking were denied that companion spectacle.[41] So too was "Holofernes" denied: not only because there is no such scene of repentance in the Judith play, but because, in one of the few things the story *does* say about him, he is too "ensconced" in heresy to have any real hope of eternal salvation.

8. There *was* real censorship of the theater in Tournai. Philip's father, Charles V, enacted legislation not three years after his son's visit that ensured preapproval of any plays staged in the region, and Philip himself issued an edict in 1560 that established regular censorship of the theater.[42] Their interventions would hint at a reaction to something that had offended them: something on the order of the complaint by town officials in neighboring Mons that the theater "brought about a disdain for things holy and for good princes."[43]

All that said, however, a bit of point/counterpoint quickly reveals an equal number of features of Tournai's death by drama that are very much open to question.

1. Even Faber appears skeptical when he introduces the story with this caveat: "if one subscribes to the teachings of a certain manuscript account . . ."[44]

2. Notwithstanding Pasquier's impressive list of the plays in Philip's honor, he never mentions a *Judith* play. Nor, for that matter, do the two Spanish chroniclers, a surprising omission in that Calvete de Estrella's account, like that of Pasquier, is almost forty pages long.

3. Pasquier gives a long list of the entrepreneurs of the 1549 performances: "Jehan Talleman, merchant, Robert d'Alenson, esquire, Hercules Clement, Paul Teureau and Pasquier de le Barre" (*JBT*, 328). Nowhere does he name Jehan de Crehan and Jean de Bury in that context.

4. Not a single extant, contemporaneous account alludes in any way to the infamous decapitation.[45] Therefore, much as modern critics are wont to make silences speak, it is difficult to fathom why *both* versions of Philip's visit—French and Spanish—would excise such a stunning event.

5. In spite of a host of seemingly authorizing details, there are moments of the story that just don't make sense. What could be more preposterous than the notion that the condemned man playing Holofernes would be so kind as to *pretend* to be asleep (*HTB*, 14)? Nor is there any Cavellian doubt here about which man Faber is pointing to (*MWM*, 328). It has to be *the condemned man* who is *pretending* to be asleep because, according to the biblical tale, Holofernes really *was* asleep.

6. Equally preposterous is the notion that, with so many neighborhoods presenting productions, Philip would just happen by the Judith play at the precise moment of the decapitation—or that a novice executioner would get a decapitation right the very first time. Beginner's luck?

7. The idea that Philip II could have watched the *coup de théâtre* poker-faced is more in line with the Black Legend than it is with reality.[46] In fact, Philip could barely make a move without giving rise to a new legend about his cruelty. On 1 April of that same tour, the citizens of Brussels had him listening to the music of an organ fashioned of some twenty live cats, who meowed in pain when their tails were pulled.[47]

8. The texts and stage directions of the extant Judith plays definitely call for Judith to cut off Holofernes's head. But one need not extrapolate from there that the decapitation was carried out with the extreme realism ascribed to Jean de Crehan, Jean de Bury, or to the narrator of *How Judith Killed Holofernes*, no less:

> By her hand, she cut off his head
> And then to Bethulia brought it—
> This head now from his body split.
> *You'll see all of this presently*
> If silent you will kindly be.[48]

In other words, despite Rainer Warning's elegant reference to Tournai's "ritual transmutation into a performative," there is nothing to demonstrate conclusively that this *was* a genuine performative.[49] Perhaps everything played out as in the Majorca *Judith*, which directs that *"Holofernes is to be sleeping in his bed; and there is to be made a head like his, so that it can be held and cut from a dummy body [una stàtua]."*[50] Additionally, the Passion plays of Mons and Valenciennes strongly imply that dummies were used during such decapitations. In the Valenciennes Passion play, Saint John the Baptist is executed on Day Twelve (the day of the miracle of the loaves and the fishes), "there was exhibited a marvelous special effect; for a false head was cut off from a live body, and a great abundance of blood came out."[51] Meanwhile, torturer Achopart of Mons almost sounds like Philip when he responds to a cleaved child: "There you go! In one blow, he's sliced in two: good job, huh?"[52]

In the end, the story seems both true and false, and neither true nor false. Yet we cannot leave it at that. It is one thing to fantasize a dead heretic. It is quite another thing to actually kill one in the context of a play, however well suited that play might be to the task.

1. Perhaps Pasquier de le Barre failed to mention the stupendous production supervised by Jean de Crehan and Jean de Bury because the former was no friend of his. When Pasquier ran for the position of procurator general on 15 January 1566, Jehan voted against him.[53] Perhaps he *did* mention it, but the record was simply lost, like the *Registre de cuir noir.*[54] Or perhaps there was no Judith play performed in 1549—and no decapitation.

2. Perhaps the truth lies somewhere in between, and neither a man nor a dummy was used on stage in 1549 but, instead, another *type* of living being. The *Acts of the Apostles* offers some help in this regard, for one of its nine decapitations states that "a false head is needed for the decapitation of Simon Magus . . . and Daru [the executioner] *must cut off the head of a sheep in his place.*"[55] It is not clear if the sheep is dead or alive.

3. Regardless of whether *Judith* was performed, the legend would have exemplified the theological discord surrounding her own apocryphal story at the same historical moment when the Catholic Philip marched into the "heresy-infected" city of Tournai.[56] As Solomon Zeitlin affirms, the acts of Judith and Holofernes are "fictitious and bear no resemblance to actual actions or events."[57] Indeed, by 1549, the entire Book of Judith had been deemed inauthentic by Protestant reformers, who had excluded her story from their Bibles, while the Catholic church retained it in the Douay Bible.[58]

4. Since Tournai was a contested site during the Reformation, having changed hands from England to France to Spain,[59] it is reasonable to surmise that not every Tournaisian would have been happy to welcome Philip. Given local traditions of civil disobedience, according to which citizens retained the right to disobey a monarch who had exercised "arbitrary and corrupt rule . . . until he had repaired his ways," a play might just do the trick.[60]

5. Just as the heroine of the Book of Judith resented the colonizing Holofernes, so too might the Tournaisians have resented Philip. When Judith asks God's help in foiling "a prince excellent and feared," she could easily have inflamed Tournai's Protestant fervor in much the same way that the original Judith had served to "inflame the Judaeans' patriotism" and "rally the true people of God," as she does in figure 9.[61] "Give me the courage and the heart," she says, "to break this tyrant's strength apart."[62] Still more to the point is her proclamation of victory over Holofernes in the *Old Testament* as she proudly displays his head to trumpet fanfare.[63] Judith even describes her role as a first-time executioner in language that spookily befits our snuff story: "Now look ye here! See that I'm no novice! / I deliver the head of Holofernes."[64] Perhaps the spectators of Tournai were imagining that the head on display was Philip's, whose execution would have been justice, not murder: "'Tis God's will; it is right and just / To kill who violates us all."[65]

6. As improbable as it sounds that a Protestant heretic would have been executed during a series of theatrical spectacles that had been organized by Protestant sympathizers, let us note the following. Even if one were to reckon that "Holofernes" was a martyr to the Reformist cause, he was not only a heretic but a murderer, and a murderer is far from the ideal poster child for martyrdom. The

Figure 9. Judith Decapitating Holofernes. Hartmann Schedel, *Liber chronicarum* (Nuremberg, 1493).

Catholic Philip is, of course, depicted as the inspiration for the spectacular decapitation of a heretic who has offended *his* religion, not the Reformist sensibilities of many Tournaisians.

    7. The snuff legend also links Philip's cruel justice to his deviant sexuality, a connection that had long been memorialized by the crazed processional lustiness of the ritual *charivari*.[66] Additionally, there was some evidence in nearby Metz that Catholic communities avenged perversity with perversity, as when a lurid punitive parade of 12 April 1513 flaunted a "young lad of approximately sixteen years of

age" being scourged for having molested a seven-year-old girl: "he was beaten more horribly than anyone had ever been beaten before, and in a manner that no one had ever seen before."[67] Meanwhile, the Franciscan brother Jean Vitrier had preached at the turn of the fifteenth century in Tournai's cathedral that it was "better to cut your child's throat than to place him in the nonreformed religion . . . better to take your daughter by the hand and walk her to the bordello than to place her in the nonreformed religion."[68] Either Philip was an innocent bystander who might never have *stood by* the decapitation at all, or, in a Reformist fantasy, he was a cold-blooded, imperialistic, murderer of questionable sexuality. He was a future monarch who liked capital executions as much as Caligula did—and who liked even better the private erotic services provided by an erstwhile executioner.[69]

8. Finally, as the snuff drama of Tournai weaves together the larger themes of reality vs. representation, Catholic vs. Protestant, and legal vs. illegal, it raises anew one of the eternal anxieties of art: that the representational uncertainty of violence creates an audience demand for violent reality, sexuality, and death itself. To comprehend such a credible threat, one need only substitute today's "cinema" or "media" for yesterday's "theater." Tertullian once worried that "these tragedies and comedies, bloody and lustful, impious and prodigal, teach outrage and lust," and he urged that theater audiences with "a mind for blood" substitute the "the blood of Christ."[70] In contemporary America, the feminist attorney Brenda Feingen Fasteau followed in the footsteps of Catherine MacKinnon by declaring of the 1976 movie *Snuff* that "we have to deal with the possibility that this film is going to create a demand for real snuff films and that real women are going to be murdered."[71] Supporters of the film were even redeposited into a kind of Garden of Eden reserved for anybody who would lust after death as art (and from which they would presumably be expelled): "the first *taste of the forbidden* would initiate an appetite with a terminal trajectory from bad to worst. Contact with the film could lead even to *confusion or disregard of the distinction between reality and representation.*"[72] Just as the procurator general of Paris and John Calvin feared in their different ways that the inability to distinguish realism from reality would lead to conduct unbecoming, so too do modern commentators from all walks of political life resurrect those age-old fears.[73]

So, what happened in Tournai? Thanks to the apocryphal staging of apocrypha, the tale establishes a fascinating relativism according to which the merely "incredible" seems "truer" than the flat-out preposterous. If it's "preposterous" to think that a heretic play-acted his own death, then it's only "incredible" to think that Philip II enjoyed seeing one put to death. All that need be logical is *somebody's* belief that Tournai's theatrical entrepreneurs, sympathetic to the Reformist cause, would have chosen the story of Judith in the first place—or that, in the afterlife of the legend, someone else picked that play because it suited such sensibilities so well.

By the same token, it may seem preposterous to think that Philip II fortuitously happened by to catch the crowning moment of a snuff drama in progress, which reenacted a biblical story that Catholics like himself believed to be *true*. But it's not incredible at all to think that the reformers who had organized the performance would have sought to *make history* by suggesting that it was they—and not the Catholics—who understood the distinction between real and apocryphal history, to say nothing of real and apocryphal performance. Even if the decapitation did *not* occur, it is still legitimate to think that, with the performance of 1549, the Protestants of Tournai were imagining that Judith's apocryphal story was not as real as *their* theater—and that Philip's violence was *more* real than all of it. The moral of the Protestant story would be something along these lines: Judith's justifiable homicide of Holofernes was the decision of a stage-master, not the word of God. And Philip's political power, along with that of Catholicism itself, was but a theatrical fiction. Tournai's Reformist theater could transform the fiction of Catholic power into the power of Protestant fiction.

On 4 March 1695, another Judith would grace the stage in a *Tragedy, based on the Holy Scriptures*. The author, the Abbé Boyer, asserted that theater's mission was to reshape the truth in the name of theology, a mission that playwrights of his day no longer grasped:

> Being accustomed to fashioning events that have no logic or verisimilitude, to giving great historical names to fabulous fictions, and, consequently, to confusing truth with lies, they dare not treat reasonably subjects that cannot be altered without a kind of sacrilege. They are ignorant of the talent of invention, or make poor use of it. They do not know that it involves embellishing the truth, not disfiguring it; enriching it, not dishonoring it.[74]

Be it Boyer's effort to extol the virtues of Catholicism or Tournai's attempt to do the same for Protestantism, one truth remains self-evident: Although Tournai looks to be the tale of a theater made more real by a legend, it is also the tale of a legend made more real by the theater. The legend of a snuffed-out life hangs on for dear life as two genres that specialize in make-believe—theater and the urban legend—make it all believable.

Whether Tournai constitutes a wish-fulfillment narrative of sixteenth-century observers who wished Philip dead, of contemporaneous Catholics who wished the same for heretics, or of otherwise-invested later historians and critics, the conclusion is unaltered. The Tournai decapitation endures as what Kubiak calls a *"true perjury"*: "the terror of theatre moves somewhere between the propositions of the axiom—what seems true is a lie—while deception itself seems to be the truth of what is seen."[75] We cannot determine definitively that the tale from Tournai is true—nor can we determine definitively that it is *untrue*. Even so, if we appear to be on the verge of concluding that a conclusion is impossible, we must think again.

From Roman gladiatorial display to the supposed snuff death in Tournai, there is a way in which the spectacle of theater has always been life-threatening—or, at least, in which audiences have been conditioned to *believe* that it is. There comes, however, a moment of truth, and it sends us hurtling back to the medieval future.

If it has seemed all along that I have been trying to transform the absence of evidence into a critical virtue, then consider this. Snuff films exist. I have seen one. But it wasn't called *Snuff, Mondo, Haven of Horror,* or *Faces of Death*.[76] It wasn't even called a snuff film. It was called investigative reporting.

The Moment of Truth

For the theater as for culture, it remains a question of naming and directing
shadows: and the theater, not confined to a fixed language and form, not only
destroys false shadows but prepares the way for a new generation of shadows,
around which assembles the true spectacle of life.

—Antonin Artaud, *Theater and Its Double*

"All I want to know," says Mrs. Christian of the apparent snuff film she
discovers in *8MM*, "is that this atrocity is false." As her character gives
voice to the desire and dread that have dogged modern ethicists and students of popular culture, something has been lost in the shuffle.

As we began and now end with snuff, it is worthwhile to recall with
Brunvand that "part of every legend is true" (*CD,* xii). We could just as
readily cite Tobin Siebers on the subject: "if life is an idea too difficult to
understand, all stories are parables. There is no story that is not true."[1] Or
we could look to Ambrose Bierce for this definition of mythology: "the
body of a primitive people's beliefs concerning its origin, early history, heroes, deities and so forth, as distinguished from the true accounts which it
invents later."[2] Or to Francis Greig for a reminder that half the lies circulating around the world are true.[3] Or to Plato himself for this cautionary
query: "Don't you understand . . . that we begin by telling children fables,
and the fable is, taken as a whole, false, but there is truth in it also?"[4]
"'True' and 'false,'" writes J. L. Austin, "are just general labels for a whole
dimension of different appraisals which have something or other to do
with the relation between what we say and the facts" (*PP,* 237–38).

We started from the premise that, independently of the truth-value of
our stories, what mattered was that their tellers believed them to be true.
But each chapter in this book has also shown us something else.

Beliefs do matter a great deal. As Stephen Knapp and Walter Benn

Michaels explain, "Having beliefs just *is* being committed to the truth of what one believes and the falsehood of what one doesn't believe."[5] In the end, however, it is insufficient to leave it at that by stating, as the bottom line, that the vast majority of our narrators held beliefs in the truth of what they said. It must also matter whether or not their beliefs were true.

If beliefs alone were important, then it wouldn't matter very much whether or not a gentleman in the audience ever fell in love with and married the girl playing Saint Catherine in Metz. It wouldn't matter that, having ditched an enamored widow in favor of a clergyman, Lyonard became a priest, or that an "Ajax" went mad, or that other unfortunate thespians expired on stage. We would never need to know for sure whether early spectators died at the *Eumenides*, or whether Jehan Hemont and Perrin Le Roux met their fiery ends from fourteenth-century special effects gone awry. Nor would we need to know whether two priests narrowly escaped death in a Passion play, or whether the Eel of Melun ever made a fool of himself for assuming that such things were possible. Truth would take a back seat to the fact that somebody at some time truly believed that Chaumont's stage devils took to the streets, or that a church was built in the Marais atop the razed home of a Jew, or that the quarry of Doué-la-Fontaine became a populist theater, or that Meaux's actors met the sad fates of their characters, or that a condemned heretic and murderer was executed during Tournai's snuff drama.

But it *does* matter. Austin puts the whole thing most compellingly: "What, finally, is the importance of all this about pretending . . . ? Truth is."[6]

Truth *has to* matter. It matters to anxious fliers who have every right to wonder, as they placidly sip cocktails at an airport bar, if they risk awakening from a drugged stupor in a hotel bathtub minus one kidney.[7] It matters to anxious academics on the road, who cling to their computers while going through airport security, lest they be victims of the "computer heist."[8] It matters to a global community upon whom the real terrors of airports were indelibly imprinted by the events of 11 September 2001. It mattered to Erving Goffman, who admonished that "all the world is *not* a stage": "Whether you organize a theater or an aircraft factory, you need to find places for cars to park and coats to be checked, and these had better be real places, which, incidentally, had better carry real insurance against theft."[9] And it surely mattered to Stanislavski's Grisha, who stated with some annoyance that "I don't see how there can be any question of truth in the theatre since everything about it is fictitious, beginning with the very plays of Shakespeare and ending with the papier mâché dagger with which Othello stabs himself." His colleague, Tortsov, tried to placate him with the assurance that Grisha had "a perfect right to call it [the dagger] an impostor," but he was adamant that "if you go beyond that, and brand all art as a lie, and all life in the theatre as unworthy of faith, then you will have to change your point of view" (*AP*, 128–29). I changed *my* point of view the first time I ever saw a snuff film.

How vividly I recall it. It was not *Snuff*. It was not a commercial for *Rescue 911*, tempting viewers with the guarantee that "in this dramatic story someone's life is on the line." It was not the Fox network's *Stunts Gone Bad*, or the network brass debating whether or not to televise the executions of Timothy McVeigh or Robert Alton Harris before him. Nor was it *Witness to the Execution*, a made-for-TV movie that dramatized analogous events.[10] It was not the best-selling video series, *Faces of Death*, whose producers pride themselves on providing only "natural" snuff.[11] It was not ABC's *20/20* or a plethora of sky-cams hoping to catch live on video real "hostage dramas," real murders, or real cases of police brutality.[12] It wasn't any one of innumerable disseminations of surveillance videos from nanny-cams or convenience stores, which have captured on tape abusive babysitters or armed robberies or murders.[13] It was not a distraught man on a Los Angeles freeway blowing his brains out on 6 May 1998, in full view of television audiences as the cameras rolled.[14] It was not the infamous telecast of the live suicide of R. Budd Dwyer, a Pennsylvania state treasurer who, under criminal investigation, swallowed his gun on the air on 22 January 1987 during a press conference.[15] It was not the curiously clairvoyant scene from the 1976 film *Network*, in which anchorman Howard Beale follows through on his threat to commit suicide on the air. It was not the sight of two outlaws throwing a man off a bridge in the Congo on 7 May 2001 and firing their automatic weapons at him (without so much as the usual television anchor's warning about graphic imagery).[16] It was not the hideous state's evidence against the serial killer Charles Ng, whose videotaped record of his atrocities found its way onto the local news in Kalamazoo, Michigan, where the parents of one of the murdered women saw "a terrified young woman moments before her murder. Bound to a chair, Brenda O'Connor was tormented by her captors as they threatened to rape and kill her."[17] Even the most diehard fans of Baudrillard can scarcely suggest that what matters most about these acts is whether or not we *believe* that the brutalized child in the nanny-cam footage is being beaten, that teenagers are murdered while minding the safe at a Seven-Eleven, that the man on the freeway died, that Budd Dwyer blew his brains out, or that Brenda O'Connor was tortured to death. Real death, rape, terror, beatings, shootings, and tortures have truly taken place.

The snuff film I saw wasn't even the notorious episode of *60 Minutes* that, on 22 November 1998, showed Dr. Jack Kevorkian euthanizing Thomas Youk in real time. Somehow, both liberal and conservative audiences cried foul at having been subjected to a snuff film. In the controversy surrounding the piece, Peter Jennings announced that "millions of people saw Dr. Kevorkian kill a man on television," while Tom Brokaw filed "Death by Doctor," referring to Youk's demise as Kevorkian's "latest death."[18] Denunciations by the *National Review* also came speedily as its editorial board interrogated the "judgment of *60 Minutes,* which made its snuff film from footage supplied by Kevorkian. . . . A venerable show has made itself an accomplice to a murderous farce."[19] William F. Buckley himself weighed in, asking of euthanasia the "toughest ethical question of the modern world": "Will we in the future need snuff films to certify to the bona fides of both parties?"[20] The only reason, it seems, that two fourteenth-century religious plays did *not* become murderous farces was that, unlike Youk, Jehan Hemont and Perrin le Roux did *not* want to die.[21] Nor did Brenda O'Connor. There is no getting around the fact that these deadly events must matter a great deal to the victims and to those who watch.

It might well be reassuring for today's moviegoers to tell themselves that the snuff scenes in *Interview with the Vampire* or *8MM* are clever or provocative or frightening, but fake. Any comfort quickly dissipates, though, when we are confronted with the painful reality of snuff by any other name.

Part of every legend is true.

I saw my first snuff film on 12 July 1981. It was another *60 Minutes* piece, reported by Morley Safer, entitled "Looking Out for Mrs. Berwid." Ostensibly, it was a meditation about the protections afforded to the criminally insane at the expense of their victims. Adam Berwid was an inmate at the Pilgrim State Psychiatric Hospital in New York's Nassau County. Although he had threatened on numerous occasions to kill his estranged wife, Eva, he had no difficulty obtaining a day pass to leave the grounds of the institution in order to purchase a new coat. Safer wondered: "While the appropriate institutions were looking to help the potential murderer, Adam Berwid, who was looking out for Mrs. Berwid, the potential victim?" Notwithstanding the legal imperative in Berwid's dossier that called explicitly for notification of Mrs. Berwid in the event that Mr. Berwid were ever released for any reason, no one called her. In the old "you are there" style, Safer intoned:

> Eva Berwid now has only hours to live. Shortly after breakfast, pass in hand, Adam Berwid walks off the hospital grounds. He boards a train and, within the hour, he is only blocks away from Eva Berwid's home. Instead of buying that overcoat, he goes to a sporting goods store and buys a hunting knife. It's now 4:00. . . . He came to the house. He came around the back and looked in the window and saw his wife and children. At the same moment, she saw him. As she dashed for the phone, he broke in. She did manage to dial 9-1-1, the police emergency number.[22]

The *60 Minutes* piece then featured the actual death rattle of Mrs. Berwid's 911 call and the macabre sounds of her final words at the very moment when they were being shrieked. Those words were barely recognizable as Adam Berwid stabbed his wife with a hunting knife while she pleaded plaintively with a dim-witted 911 operator that "he's killing me." The operator responded, "Stop screaming and tell me where you are. Where are you?"

Viewers could readily have concluded that they had just seen a snuff film. I did. There was no way to have been any closer to a murder than to have been there at the scene—or to have been that 911 operator—or to have been Mrs. Berwid, who would never live to tell her tale.

Part of every legend is true.

In 1981 there was no outcry, no shock, no outrage. I wrote a letter to *60 Minutes* to protest their brutal representation of brutality, and I received a response that the staff of the news magazine was sorry to have upset me. Some years later, people were very upset indeed by the relentless airing of Nicole Brown Simpson's terrified 911 call predicting potentially lethal abuse at her husband's hand. Such brutality was newsworthy, we were told, and hiding it would be detrimental to the pursuit of truth and justice. People were also very upset by the snuff death of Thomas Youk. It is not clear that Richard Schechner beheld the televised death of Eva Berwid, but he made this pertinent remark in 1985 about Belle de Jour's dominatrix performance at her S/M theater in New York: "if this seems strange, even obscene, it is not too different from what NBC presents each night on its local nightly news, the 'Six o'Clock Report,' on Channel 4 in New York."[23] From ancient Greece to Greenwich Village, part of every legend is true.

Schechner was right. One can turn on the TV any time and find a murder. It is thus difficult for us to follow the sage advice of Gustave Cohen, who scolded crabby critics to be more patient with the medieval theater: "Our ancestors were hardly more gullible than we are: they knew full well that Jerusalem lay at a distance of more than twenty-five centimeters from Damas, but they were happy to let themselves be seduced. We are a bit more difficult, the magic has spoiled us, that's all."[24] Nowadays, as *Fear Factor* and *The Amazing Race* attempt to rival *Survivor,* and as performance artists indulge in the most violent realities, there is little magic left to spoil us.[25] In 1993, at a San Francisco club called The Quake, a young, possibly underage woman had her nipples pierced publicly as she was stretched upon a cross while rock music blared against a backdrop of drug and alcohol abuse. Several hundred attendees of the rave were riveted to the spectacle that was taking place, and a witness relates that the star/victim then joined the audience to view the next performance: a man having his testicles pierced, a man who later disappeared without a trace.[26]

Part of every legend is true.

Postmodern theorists of the theater have gotten a lot of play out of the insight that theater's special contribution to culture is its uncanny power to make even real things seem theatrical—and to make hyperreality seem like theater.[27] The converse is also possible: that reality seems *more* real *because* of theater. The chicken or egg question—Is life theaterlike? or is theater lifelike?—is ultimately less important than the inescapable conclusion that life and theater each seem more real when permeated with the theatricality of the other.

As brutal, cruel, and dark an epoch as the Middle Ages has eternally been imagined to be, the modern world is not so different: we today also inhabit a culture of fear, some of us more than others. Whether or not theater releases those fears cathartically or nurtures and perpetuates their urgency, drama has long brought fear and trembling to life as urban legends have kept them going. The story that never dies is that of the pleasures and pains of living and dying. Theater keeps that story alive in real time, and lest it ever be forgotten, urban legends ensure its endurance, for better or for worse. So does truth.

Bruce Wilshire once asserted that "through the proxy of theatre's drama we discover actual and possible 'dramas' of everyday life in which we are tested and confirmed, both individually and collectively" (*RPI*, 240). That fantastic test has always been the dream work of drama and urban legends alike. It always will be. We can still hear Stanislavski's clarion call to his actors: "Now [your imagination] is wide awake. You find it easy not only to invent fictions but to live them, to feel their reality" (*AP*, 146). It is only when we cease to feel that the legends and their theater will die.

Part of every legend is true.

Original Documents in French and Latin

Introduction. Medieval Urban Legends?

Intro.1. *HMS*, 178.

Et n'allez pas croire à une fantaisie ou à une invention du narrateur fidèle qui nous a décrit ces merveilles; les costumes d'apparat du temps exigent autant de richesse, et il a pris soin de prévenir notre étonnement en ces termes, au début de sa fidèle relation:

Ne pensez pas, amyables lecteurs*
Que de la Monstre ici après déduite
Soit une fable, ou que les directeurs
Ayent voulu que vérité escrite.
Il est certain qu'elle a été réduite
De point en point, selon la veue d'oeil.
Et voudrois bien que selon le mien veuil
Dieu tout-puissant la voir vous eust permis:†
Lors vous diriez: L'auteur de ce Recueil
A plus laissé que davantage mys.

*Thiboust's original version contains only variants in punctuation: here, he places a comma after *lecteurs*.—JE.
†Thiboust has a semicolon after *permis*.—JE.

Intro.2. *Le Mystère de la Résurrection Angers (1456)*, ed. Servet, vol. 1, Day 1, 218–25.

Je proteste publiquement
Pour tous joueurs generaument
De cest mistere, et pour chacun,
Que ou cas qu'il seroit par aucun
Contre la foy riens dit ou fait,
Il soit reputé pour non fait.
Car nous n'entendons dire ou faire
Riens qui soit a la foy contraire . . .

Intro.3. *HMS*, 70.

Mais remettons les choses au point. Les conventions que nous raillons là-bas, nous les acceptons chez nous, tout n'est-il pas convention dans le théâtre? Vous vous rendez au spectacle et vous achetez au bureau le droit de pénétrer du regard tous les détours des appartements, tous les secrets des hommes qui vous confient mille choses personnelles où vous n'avez que faire; vous ne vous étonnez pas de voir des gens penser tout haut, ce qui est une habitude de maniaque; vous ne craignez pas de voir les flots du Rhin qui déborde se déverser sur vos chapeaux de soie et vos habits noirs, bien que la scène vous domine de plusieurs mètres. De grâce, soyons un peu moins sévères, et que celui qui ne s'est jamais laissé aller de bon coeur à l'enchantement de l'illusion théâtrale jette au passé la première pierre. Nos ancêtres n'étaient pas beaucoup plus crédules que nous, ils se doutaient bien que Jérusalem était séparé de Damas par plus de 25 centimètres, mais ils se laissaient volontiers séduire; nous sommes un peu plus difficiles, la féerie nous a gâtés, voilà tout.

Chapter 1. Lusting after Saints

1.1. *CPV,* ed. Bruneau, 2:394–95.

La vie de sainte Katherine de Sennes jouués en la court des Grant Prescheurs.—Item, en la dicte année, fut fait et jués en Mets le jeu de ma damme saincte Katherine de Senne, vraye religieuse de l'ordre des Jacopins. Et fut ce jeu fait en la court des Grant Proicheurs, parmy les trois feste de la Panthecouste. Et, pour le faire, en furent abatue les estaige qui estoient couvert tout en l'antours encontre la muraille, et qui couvroie les ancienne épitaffle et sépulture. Et le fist faire et juer damme Katherine Baudoche à ses frais et despans. Et gist ycelle damme au dit Grant Preschers, en la chaipelle qu'elle fist faire et fonder, qui est scituée en l'entrée d'icelle église et fondée on non de la dicte saincte Katherine. Et pourtait le parsonnaige de saincte Katherine une jonne fillette, aagée de environ XVIII ans, laquelle estoit fille à Dediet le Woirier; et fist merveilleusement bien son debvoir, au grés et plaisir d'ung chacun. Touteffois, avoit ladicte fille XXIIIᶜ vers de parsonnaige, mais néantmoins elle les sçavoit tout sus le doyt. Et parloit celle fille cy vivement et piteusement qu'elle provocquoit plusieurs gens à pleurer, et estoit agréable à toutte gens. Et, à l'occasion de ce, fut celle fille richement mariée à ung jantilz homme, soldoieurs de Mets, appellés Henry de la Tour, qui d'elle s'enamourait par le grant plasir qu'il y print.

1.2. *CVM,* ed. Huguenin, 360–61.

Item, en ladicte année, fut faict et jué en Mets le jeu de madame saincte Caitherine de Sienne, vraye religieuse de l'ordre des Jaicopins. Et fut ce jeu fait en la cour des grans Proischeurs, parmy les trois festes de la penthecoste. Et pour le faire, en furent abattus les estaiges qui estoient couverts tout à l'entour encontre la muraille et qui couvroient les anciennes epitaphes et sepultures. Et le fist faire et juer dame Caitherine Baudoiche, à ses frais et despens; et gist icelle dame ausdits grans Proischeurs, en la chapelle qu'elle fist faire et fonder, qui est située en l'entrée d'icelle eglise, et fondée au nom de ladicte saincte Caitherine. Et portoit le personnaige de Saincte Caitherine une jonne fillette, aigée de environ dix huit ans, laquelle estoit fille à Dediet le vairier, du Four du Cloistre, et fist merveilleusement bien son debvoir au gré et plaisir d'ung chescun. Touttesfois avoit ladite fille vingt trois cents vers de personnaige; mais neantmoins elle les sçavoit tous sur le doigt: et parla celle fille si vivement et piteusement qu'elle provocqua plusieurs gens à pleurer, et estoit agreable à toutes gens. Et à l'occasion de ce, fut celle fille richement mariée à ung gentil homme, soldoieur de Mets, appellé Henry de Latour, qui d'elle s'enamoura par le grant plaisir qu'il y print.

1.3. *CMJH*, 103.

Item, en ladite année [1448] fut fait le jeu de saincte Katherine de Sienne as Proichours permey les iii. festes de la Penthecouste et le fit faire dame Katherine Baudouche à ses frais et fist une jonne fille de environ xviii. ans saincte Katherine, qui merveilleusement fit bien son debvoir et ses personnaiges, et avoit xxiii. c. vers de personnaige; et pleust mont [mout] à beaucoup de gens, et en fuit marieé à ung soldiour appellé Hanry de la Tour qui d'elle s'en amourait pour le grant plaisir qu'il y print.

1.4. Épîtres familières de Jean Bouchet, Epistle 92. Cited by Petit de Julleville, "1535. Issoudun.—La Passion," in *LM*, 2:129–30.

Je vous supply que tous voz personnages
Vous assignez a gens selon leurs aages,
Et que n'usez tant d'habitz empruntez
(Fussent-ils d'or) qu'ilz ne soient adjustez
Commodement aux gens selon leurs roolles.
Il n'est pas beau que les docteurs d'escolles,
Pharisiens, et les gens de conseil
Ayent vestement a Pilate pareil,
Ne a Herode. . . .

Chapter 2. Queer Attractions

2.1. *CPV*, ed. Bruneau, 3:114.

Le jeu saincte Barbe jouués per personaige.—Item, en la devent dicte année [1485], le XXIIIIe jour de juillet, fut juez en Mets, en la place de Chambre, le jeux de la Vie et Passion ma damme saincte Barbe. Et durait trois jours; et fut le mieulx juez et le plus triumphamment que jamaix je vis, et au greys de touttes gens. Et furent sur eschauffault, en la place de Wiéseneuf, VIII jour devant; auquelle il firent tout le mistère sans pairler. Et puis, à ce jour devent dit, fut le jeux En Chambre. Or estoit pour lors demourant en Mets ung josne filz barbier, nommés Lyonairt, lequelle estoit ung très biaulx guerson, resamblant à une pucelle. Et estoit nascionez de Nostre Damme d'Ay en Allemaigne; mais il avoit loing tamps demourés en Mets, chieu maistre Hannès le barbier, au Quartaulz. Celluy Lyonart portait le personnaige de saincte Barbe; et le fist sy bien et sy honnorablement qu'il fist plorer encor VI mil parsonnes. Car il estoit biaulx jonne filz, comme dit est; et tenoit sy bonne faconde et manier, avec cy bonne myne et geste, luy et ses pucelle, qu'il estoient agréable à ung chacun, et n'estoit possible de mieulx faire. Et tellement fut en la graice d'ung chacun qu'ilz n'y avoit seigneur, clerc ne laiz, que ne désirait à avoir ledit guerson pour le nourir et gouverner; entre lesqueulx y avoit une riche weve, en Salnerie, qui le voulloit avoir pour son héritier. Toutesffois, entre les aultres, y olt ung noble seigneur d'Église, nommés maistre Chardely, chantre et chainoigne de la Grant Église de Mets, lequelle estoit ung homme saige, docte et scientificque personne, et à celluy fut le guerson donnés. Et incontinant le mist ledit Chardely aux milleur escollez de Mets; là où il proffita plus en ung ans que d'aulcuns en dix; car cest anffans avoit ung entendemant sur tous overs. Au bout de l'an le mist ledit Chardely aux estude à Paris, là où en brief tamps fut maistre és ars. Et, depuis l'ay veu régenter et tenir les escolle à l'église de Sainct Salvour à Mets; et, aprez, l'a veu estre chainnoinne de Nostre Damme d'Ars et pourter grant office.

2.2. *CVM,* ed. Huguenin, 473.

Le vingt quatriesme jour de jullet, fut jué à Mets, en la plaice en Chambre, le jeu de la vie et passion de madame saincte Barbe, qui dura trois jours, et fut le mieulx jué et le plus triumphamment que on vit de long temps, et au gré de touttes gens. Et furent faits eschauffauls en la plaice de Vezegnuef, huit jours devant, ausquelz ilz se representerent et firent tout le mistere sans parleir. Et puis, audit vingt quatriesme jour de jullet, fut fait le jeu devantdit en Chambre. Et y alloient les gens prendre leurs places, aux quaitre heures du matin: et debvoit on jouer, trois jours de suitte, assavoir, le diemanche, lundy et mairdy. Mais, le mairdy, il vint ung si horrible temps, environ deux heures apres midi, qu'il estoit quasi nuit, et fallut laisser le jouer; et ne peult on eschevir le jeu, pour les pluyes, que le diemanche apres.

Or estoit pour lors, demeurant en Mets, ung jonne fils bairbier, nommé Lyonard, qui estoit ung tres beaul filz et ressembloit une belle jonne fille, et estoit nationné de Nostre Dame d'Aix en Allemaigne; mais il avoit long temps demeuré à Mets, en l'hostel maistre Hannès, le bairbier, du Quartaul, qui fist le personnaige de saincte Barbe si preudemment et devotement que plusieurs personnes plouroient de compassion; car il tenoit si bonne faconde et maniere avec si bonne mine et geste avec ses pucelles, qu'il estoit à chescun agreable, et n'estoit possible de mieulx faire. Et tellement fut en la graice d'ung chescun, qu'il n'y avoit seigneur, clerc ne lay, qui ne desirast à avoir ledit gairson pour le nourir et gouverner; entre lesquelx y avoit une riche veufve en Salnerie qui le voulloit avoir pour son heritier. Touttesfois, entre les aultres, un seigneur chainoine de la grande eglise, nommé maistre Jehan Chardelly, qui aussy estoit chantre, homme de lettres et bien scientificque, le print en si grant amour qu'il luy fut delivré et le mist à l'escolle où il prouffita plus en ung an que aultres en dix: puis l'envoya à Paris, aux estudes, où en brief temps apres, fut fait et passé maistre ès arts: et depuis l'ay veu regent et maistre de l'escolle à St Salveur, et apres, l'ay veu estre chainoine de Nostre Dame d'Aix et porter grant office.

2.3. *CPV,* ed. Bruneau, 3:124.

La vie saincte Katherinne juée per personaiges.—Item, en cest année [1486], és trois feste de Pantecouste, fut juez en Mets et en la place de Chambre le mistère de la Vie et Passion de la glorieuse saincte Katherine du mont de Synay, et fille du roy d'Alixandrie. Duquel jeux porta le personnaige de la saincte Katherine le devant dit Lionart, qui l'an devant avoit estés la saincte Barbe; et fist merveilleusement bien son devoir. Mais, toutteffois, ce mistère ne fut pas desjay sy agréable au peuple ne à tous les auditeur que avoit estés celluy de saincte Barbe. Car le dit Lionairt avoit desjà ung peu mués sa vois. Et, avec ce, n'estoient pas les dict ne la rétoricque de son parsonnaige sy bien couchiez ne sy piteux.

2.4. de Vigneulles, *Gedenkbuch des Metzer Bürgers Philippe von Vigneulles aus den Jahren 1471–1522,* ed. Michelant, 14.

Or en ycelluy temps, l'on juoist le jeu saincte Katherine du mon de Sinay en chambre; duquel je avois esté requis pour en estre et se devoit juer ès festes de la Pentecouste, ledit an mil iiij.c et iiij.xx et vj [1486]. Et fut cellui jeu moult bien jué avec biaulx mysteres et fut la ste Katherine ung jonne filz barbier, natif de nostre-dame d'Ais en Allemaigne; lequel l'an devant avoit desjay esté la ste Bairbe au jeu ste Bairbe, et fist par trois jours sy bien son personnaige, qu'il n'estoit possible de mieulx faire. En cellui temps je resamblois tant bien à cellui gairson que l'on m'ait prins xvij fois pour lui, et pour ce me amoit fort ledit gairson et voulloit tousjours que je fusse l'une de ses demoiselles à cellui jeu; mais je avois le cuer aultre part et avois deliberé que en ces jour, je m'en yrois avec mon compaignon, et que secrètement nous partiriens de Metz comme dit est.

Chapter 3. Of Madness and Method Acting

3.1. Jean Gerson, *De distinctione revelationum,* in *Oeuvres complètes,* ed. Glorieux, 3:44.

Morbos affert incurabiles ex laesione cerebri et rationis perturbatione, quo fit ut per maniam aut furiam vel caeteras passiones melancolicas sic profundantur et intime radicantur phantasmata interius reservata in cerebro, quod esse reputantur verae res extrinsecus apparentes, et audire se putat homo, videre vel tangere quod nullo modo sensu exteriori percipitur.

Chapter 4. Two Priests and the Hand of God

4.1. *CPV,* ed. Bruneau, 2:245–46.

La Passion par parsonaige juée en Chainge.—Item, l'an dessus dit, on moix de juillet [1437], fut jués en Mets le jeux de la Passion Nostre Seigneur Jhésu Crist, en la place en Change. Et fut fait le paircques d'ugne très noble fasson: car il estoit de IX sciège de hault, ensi comme degrez, tout à l'antour; et par derrier estoient grand sciège et longne pour les seigneurs et pour les dames. Et pourtoit le parsonnaige de Dieu ung prebstre appellés seigneur Nicolle, de Neufchastel en Loherenne, lequelle alors estoit curé de Sainct Victour de Metz. Et fut cestui curé en grand dangier de sa vie, et cuidait morir, luy estant en l'airbre de la croix: car le cuer luy faillit, tellement qu'il fut estés mort, s'il ne fut estés secorus; et couvint que ung aultre prebstre fut mis en son lieu pour parfaire le parsonnaige de Dieu. Et estoit celluy prebstre alors l'ung des bouriaulx et tirant dudit jeux. Maix, néantmoi[n]s, on donnist son parsonnaige à ung aultre, et parfist celluy du crucifiement pour ce jour. Et, le lendemains, ledit curey de Sainct Victour fut revenus à luy, et parfist la résurrection; et fist très haultement son parsonnaige. Et durait celluy misterre par quatre jours.

En celluy jeux, y olt encor ung aultre prebstre, qui ce appelloit seigneur Jehan de Nissey, qui estoit chappellain de Mairange, lequelle pourtoit le parsonnaige de Judas; mais, pour ce qu'il pandit tropt longuement, il fut pareillement transis et causy mort, car le cuer luy faillit; parquoy il fut bien hastivement despandus, et en* fut pourtés en aulcuns lieu prochain pour le frotter de vin aigre et aultre chose pour le reconforter.

La bouche de l'anfer d'ycelluy jeux estoit très bien faicte, car, par ung engiens, elle ce ouvroit et recleoit seulle, quant les diables y voulloient antrer ou issir; et avoit celle hurre deux gros yeulx d'assier qui reluisoient à merveille.

D'icelluy jeux estoit maistre et portoit l'original ung clerc des Sept de la guerre de Mets, appellés Forcelle.

Et y avoit pour celluy tampts moult de noble seigneurs et de damme estrangiers et privée† en la cité de Mets. Premier, y estoit seigneur Conraird Baier, alors évesque de Mets, le conte de Vauldémont, seigneur Baudouuin de Fléville, abbé de Gouxe, la contesse de Sallebruche, et le conseillé de Bar et de Loherenne, monsseigneur Hue d'Autelz et ces deux frères, Le Brun de Salz, Charles de Servoille, Henry de la Tour, et plusieurs aultres seigneur et dammez d'Allemaigne et d'aultre païs, dont je n'en sçay les noms. Et, pour ce, fut ordonnés de mestre par tout la cité, de nuit, des lanternes aux fenestre et de la clartés aux huis, tout ledit jeux durant.

La vengence de la mort de Nostre Seigneur jués par parsonaige. —Item, le XVIIe jour de septembre ensuiant, fut fait le jeu de la vangeance Nostre Seigneur Jhésu Crist,‡ on propre paircque et on meisme lieu que la Passion avoit estés faicte. Et fut la cité de Jhérusalemz très biens et subtillement ouvrée et faictes, et le port de Jaffet ou Jopan,§ dedans ledit parcquez. Onquel jeux Jehan Matheu, le plaidieur, fut et pourtait le personnaige de Vaspasiens, et le curé de Sainct Victour, qui avoit esté Dieu à la Passion, fut Titus. Et durait ce mistère environ quaitre jour.

*en deleted from *CVM*, 200.—JE.
†Huguenin gives *et princes* (*CVM*, 200).—JE.
‡Huguenin adds *et destruction de Jherusalem* (*CVM*, 201).—JE.
§*au joxant* (*CVM*, 201).—JE.

4.2. *HTF,* 1745 ed., 2:253–56.

La plus célèbre [représentation de la *Passion*] fut celle que Conrard Bayer Evêque de Mets fit exécuter auprès de cette Ville en 1437. & où il invita la Noblesse de la Lorraine, du Palatinat du Rhein, & des Provinces circonvoisines. Un Auteur, qui se dit Curé de S. Euchaire Paroisse de la Ville de Metz, nous en rapporte les particularités dans sa Chronique, intitulée, Histoire de Metz véritable.*

L'An MCCCCXXXVII. [1437] le troisième Juillet, (dit cet Auteur) fut fait le Jeu de la Passion Nostre-Seigneur, en la Plaine de Veximiel; & fut fait le Parc d'une très-noble façon, car il estoit de neuf siéges, de hault ency comme degrès. Tout autour & parderriere estoient grans siéges & longes pour les Seigneurs & Dames: Et fut Dieu un Sire appellé Seigneur Nicolle Don Neufchastel en Lorraine, lequel estoit Curé de sainct Victour de Metz, lequel fut presque mort en la Croix, s'il n'avoit esté secouru, & convint que un autre Prestre fut mis en la Croix pour parfaire le personnage dou Crucifiement pour ce jour, & le lendemain ledict Curé de sainct Victour, parfit la Résurrection, & fit très-haultement son personnage, & dura ledit Jeu. Et un autre Prestre, qui s'appelloit Messire Jean de Nicey, qui estoit Chapelain de Métrange, fut Judas, lequel fut presque mort en pendant, car le cueur lui faillit, & fut bien hativement despendu, & porté en voye. Et estoit la bouche d'Enfer très-bien faite, car elle ouvroit & clooit quant les Diables y vouloient entrer & issir, & avoit deux gros eulx d'acier, & fut un Clerc des sept de la guerre de Metz, appellé Fourcelle, Maître dudict Jeu, & pourtour† de l'Original, & y avoit pour ledict temps moult de Seigneurs, & de Dames Estrangeres en ladicte Cité de Metz, dont les noms s'ensuivent ci-après: [here follows a list with some variation of the same cast of characters as found in app. 4.1, above].

*Ce passage se trouve écrit à la main à la tête de l'Exemplaire du Mystère de la Passion, Edition de Vérard, fol. 1490. *Bibl. du Roy.*
†Ordinairement le Maître du Jeu étoit porteur de l'Original de la Pièce qu'on représentoit, c'est-à-dire, qu'il souffloit les Acteurs: on appelloit aussi celui qui remplissoit cet emploi, Protocole. . . .

4.3. *CMJH,* 285.

Le jour de la sainte Croix, ondit mois de Septembre [1513], fuit faite une porcession [*sic*] generalle à Nostre Dame as Champs, et fuit commandé par Messeigneurs les administratours de l'eveschié de Mets que tous presbtres de Mets y fuissent, sus peine de perdre ung marke d'argent; et donnont lesdits seigneurs xl. jours de perdons à tous ceulx qu'à ladite procession yroient, per quoy il y heut ung grant monde de gens.

4.4. *CPV,* ed. Bruneau, 4:154. (Compare to *CVM,* ed. Huguenin, 687.)

Item, en ce meisme temps [1513], le mairdi des feste de Panthecouste, fut une procession génералle ordonnées de messeigneurs les aministrateur de l'Église, avec messeigneurs de Justice. En laquelle procession furent donnés XL jours de pardon à tous ceulx et celles que dévotement yroient à la dicte procession. Et fut l'une des [plus] belle que l'on eust veu de loing temps: car tout les prebstres de Mets, josnes et vieulx, y furent commendés sur ung marc d'argent, c'il n'estoient tant impotent qu'il ne puissant aller. Et fut faicte en ung jour des Quatre Temps, que l'on jûnoit. La dicte procession pertist de la Grant Église et s'en aillait à Saint Vincent oultre Mezelle, et dellà à Nostre Damme des Carmes; puis retournairent à la dicte Grant Église, à laquelle fut dicte la grant messe moult triumphamment.

4.5. *HTB,* 4.

Ils simulaient la mise en croix. On le dépouillait de tous ses vêtements, et on l'étendait sur l'instrument du supplice, sur lequel on lui clouait les mains et les pieds. On avait même poussé l'imitation jusqu'à simuler le sang qui aurait dû en couler, et cela à l'aide de petites vessies pleines de liquide rouge attachées aux membres et par lesquelles on fixait le supplicié à la croix.

S'il faut en croire les manuscrits qui rapportent ce fait, cette cérémonie produisait un immense effet sur la multitude.*

*Mme Clément, née Hémery, *Histoire des fêtes civiles et religieuses, usages anciens et modernes de la Belgique méridionale.* Avesnes, C. Vireux, 1846, p. 344–45.

4.6. Clément-Hémery, *Histoire des fêtes civiles et religieuses,* 344–45.

Voici le texte des manuscrits qui citent cette coutume:

C'est l'église des Augustins qui sert, pour ainsi dire, de salle de théâtre à ce spectacle tragi-comique. On y voit au pied de l'autel un vaste échafaud sur lequel esté levée une croix très-haute. De côté et d'autre sont dressées des espèces de loges pour les dames, les gens de qualité, et pour les premiers de la ville; le reste de l'église ne suffit pas pour contenir la foule incroyable de peuple qui se presse de toutes parts pour accourir à cette scène. Une procession se fait au son lugubre de plusieurs instruments. On y voit d'abord marcher les confrères, dit *de la Miséricorde,* le visage masqué, les pieds nus, et en habits de la confrairie; viennent ensuite des prisonniers traînant à leurs pieds de gros boulets de canon, qui y sont attachés avec des chaînes de fer; arrivent enfin des religieux Augustins travestis en Juifs, et au milieu d'eux le représentant du Sauveur, garotté, couronnée d'épines, revêtu d'une robe de pourpre. Après l'avoir ainsi promené en procession dans toute la ville, les religieux, travestis en bourreaux, armés de clous, de marteaux et des autres instruments de la Passion, le conduisent au lieu du supplice, le font monter sur l'échafaud, et y montent avec lui. Aussitôt, ils le dépouillent jusqu'à la chemise, tirent ses habits au sort, et l'étendent enfin sur la croix, où ils lui attachent les pieds et les mains avec des courroies qui recouvrent de petites vessies pleines de sang; lesquelles percées par les clous, font croire aux assistants qu'on a rééllement cloué les pieds et les mains du crucifié. A cette vue, tout le peuple se sent les entrailles émues; et, se retraçant l'image du Sauveur, il laisse couler ses larmes. Quelques-uns des plus dévôts se laissent tellement emporter à leur douleur, qu'ils se frappent rudement la poitrine, et se la meurtrissent à force de coups.

4.7. "Accounting," *LCR*, ed. Cohen, 475 (original emphasis).

A Maistre Jehan de Neelle, bacheler en theologie et religieux du couvent de St Franchois de ceste ville de Mons, le xxiie jour dudit mois d'apvril, en recompense de ce qu'il avoit esté requis et par lui emprins *la parchon du personnaige de Dieu audit Mistere de Passion* etc., en quoy faisant il avoit occupét son temps pour aprendre sadicte parchon en delaissant son praticque de preschier et autrement etc., et de laquelle dicte parchon il avoit, pour certaine cause, esté deportét, et icelle remise en la main de Jehan le Francque, a esté payéz à ladicte ordonnance: xii l.

4.8. André de la Vigne, "Procès verbal," cited by Petit de Julleville, "1496. Seurre.—Saint Martin," in *LM*, 2:70–71.

Puis après commença a parler Luciffer, pendant le quel parlement celuy qui jouoit le personnaige de Sathan ainsi qu'il volut sortir de son secret par dessoubz terre, le feu se prist a son habit autour des fesses, tellement qu'il fut fort bruslé; mais il fut si soudaynement secouru, devestu et rabillé, que sans faire semblant de rien, vint jouer son personnaige; puis se retira en sa maison. De ceste chose furent moult fort espoventez les dits joueurs; car ils pensoyent que puisque au commencement incontinent les assailloit, que la fin s'en ensuivroit. Toutefois moyennant l'ayde de mondit seigneur Saint Martin, qui pris la conduite de la matiere en ses mains, les choses allerent trop mieulx cent foys que l'on ne pensoit. Après ces choses le pere, la mere Saint Martin avecques leurs gens marcherent oudit parc, et firent ung commancement si tres veyf que tout le monde tant les joueurs que les assistans furent moult esbahis et defait. En abolissant la cremeur devant dicte, les dits joueurs prindrent une telle hardiesse et audasse en eulx, qu'onques lyon en sa tayniere ne meurtrier en un boys ne furent jamais plus fiers ne mieulx assurez qu'ils estoient quand ils jouoient.

On commença ceste matinée entre sept et huit heurcs du matin, et finist on entre unze et douze. Pour le commencement de l'après disnée qui fut a une heure, le Sathan revint jouer son personnage et pour son excuse dit a Luciffer:

Malle mort te puisse avorter,
Paillart, fils de putain cognu,
Pour a mal faire t'enorter,
Je me suis tout brulé le cul.

Et puis parfist son parsonnage pour celle clause et les autres joueurs ensuivant chascun selon son office.

4.9. *AD*, 2:506.

Les anciens avoient des machines de toute espèce pour leurs Pieces de Théâtre. Les unes qui ne descendoient point jusqu'en bas, & qui ne faisoient que traverser le Théâtre; d'autres dans lesquelles les Dieux descendoient jusques sur la Scène, & d'autres enfin qui servoient à élever ou à soutenir en l'air les personnes qui sembloient voler. Comme les dernieres étoient toutes semblables à celles de nos vols, elles étoient sujettes aux mêmes accidens. Car nous voyons dans Suétone, qu'un Acteur qui jouoit le rôle d'Icare, & dont la machine eut malheureusement le même sort, alla tomber près de l'endroit où étoit placé Néron, & couvrit de sang ceux qui étoient autour de lui.

Chapter 5. Dying to Play

5.1. Arch. Nat. JJ 116, no. 254, cited by Thomas, "Le Théâtre à Paris et aux environs," 609–11.

Avril 1380. Lettres de rémission accordées par Charles V à Guillaume Langlois, cause involontaire d'un accident mortel survenu pendant une représentation de la Passion à *Paris, le 27 mars 1380.*

Charles, etc. Savoir faisons a touz presens et avenir a nous avoir esté exposé de la partie de Guillaume Langlois que comme, le mardi apres Pasques darr. passé, es jeux qui furent faiz et ordenez en l'onneur et remembrance de la Passion nostre Seigneur Jhesu Crit [*sic*] en nostre bonne ville de Paris par aucuns des bourgois et autres bonnes genz d'icelle, le dit exposant eust esté requis, prié et ordené de ceulx qui es diz jeux faisoient les personnages des figures des ennemis et deables de estre aux diz jeux pour getter des canons, quant temps seroit, afin que leurs personnages fussent mieulx faiz, si comme es diz jeux on a acoustumé a faire par chascun an a Paris, et lors avint que avec ledit exposant vint et s'embati illec amiablement Jehan Hemont, varlet d'estuves, pour lui cuidier aidier a jouer et faire getter des diz canons quant lieu et temps seroit, comme autreffoiz on a accoustumé a faire, et il soit ainsi que ilz ordenerent et mistrent a point iceulx canons pour getter et faire bruit sur l'appointement et arroy du cruxifiement que on a acoustumé a faire en iceulx jeux en remenbrance de la mort et passion de nostre seigneur Jhesu Crit [*sic*], et pour ce que illec ou lesdiz exposant et Jehan Hemon estoient fu mise une broche chaude et boutee en un canon estant ou dit lieu, la cheville d'icellui canon par force de feu s'en issy et sailli plus tost et autrement que cuidoient et pensoient yceulx exposant et Hemon par tele maniere que ledit Hemon d'icelle cheville fu feru et attaint d'aventure en l'une de ses jambes, et aussi fu ledit Guillaume par la force du feu qui en yssi embrasé et brulé parmi le visage et fu grant doubte et en aventure d'estre mort où affolé de touz poins; apres lesqueles choses ainsi avenues ledit Hemon, qui estoit bon et vray ami d'icellui exposant et qui ne vouloit que pour la bleceure qu'il avoit ainsi de la cheville dudit canon il fust aucunement dommagé ne poursuy pour luy ne a sa requeste pour lors ne ou temps avenir, ledit Jehan Hemon estant en bon et sain propos, de sa propre et bonne volenté, senz aucune induccion, quitta et clama quitte entierement, bonnement et absoluement pour lui et pour ses hoirs ou aians de lui cause ledit exposant dudit fait ainsi avenu et de tout ce qui pour raison d'icellui ou temps avenir s'en pourroit ensuir, en disant et confessant qu'ilz ayoient esté et estoient bons amis ensemble, si comme plus a plain est contenu en certaines bonnes lettres de quittance passees par .ij. notaires le tiers jour de ce present moys d'avril et seellees du seel de nostre chastellet de Paris, et pour ce que depuis ledit fait, ainsi que le .xxvij. jour ou environ de ce present moys, ledit Jehan Hemon est alé de vie a trespassement, ledit exposant, nonobstans les choses et la quittance dessus dite sur ce faite, comme dit est, de doubte que il ne soit pour occasion de ce ores ou autreffoiz poursuiz, grevez ou travailliez en corps ou en biens, supplie par nous lui estre sur ce gracieusement et piteablement pourveu. Nous adecertes inclinans a sa supplicacion, considerans les choses dessus dites et attendu que les jeux qu'il faisoit estoient en significacion et exemple de bien et que ledit suppliant est de bonne vie, renommee et honneste conversacion, audit suppliant ou cas dessus dit ledit fait ainsi avenu avons remis, quittié et pardonné . . . sauf le droit de partie, se aucun estoit, se aucun l'en vouloit poursuir civilement tant seulement. Si donnons en mandement au prevost de Paris. . . .

Donné a Paris l'an de grace mil ccc et iiii^{xx} au mois d'avril et le XVIIe de nostre regne. Es requestes de l'ostel.

N. GAIGNART. ROONY.

5.2. Arch. Nat., JJ 125, no. 17, cited by Thomas, "Le Théâtre à Paris et aux environs," 611.

1384. Lettres de rémissions accordées par Charles VI à Fremin Severin, cause involontaire d'un accident mortel survenu pendant une répétition de Théophile *à Aunay-lès-Bondy, le 19 juin 1384.*

Charles, etc. Savoir faisons a touz presens et avenir de la partie des amis charnelz de Fremin Severin, demeurant a Aunay pres de Livry nous avoir esté signifié que comme les habitans de la dite ville d'Aunay et du pays d'environ eussent entrepris que le dimenche apres la nativité saint Jehan Baptiste ilz feroient uns jeux ou commemoracion du miracle qui a la requeste de la Virge Marie fust fait a Theophile, ou quel jeu avoit un personnage de un qui devoit getter d'un canon, et il soit avenu que le dimenche devant la dite feste saint Jehan derr. passé lesdiz habitans fussent en l'eglise de la dicte ville d'Aunay pour recorder leurs personnages, ledit Fremin qui devoit jouer du dit canon eust emplie de papier seulement la bouete du dit canon senz ce que fer ne boys y eust, et au temps qu'il devoit lachier ledit canon icellui Fremin eust dit aus gens que la estoient "Traiez vous arriere; vous n'avez que faire de estre si prez pour touz perilz," néentmoins feu Perrin Le Roux se mist d'aventure au devant dudit canon quant vint a lachier et si que en lachant ledit canon le papier qui en la boite d'icellui canon estoit le frappa en l'eul, lequel feu Perrin Leroux est alé de vie a trespassement le vendredi apres ensuivant, pour laquelle chose nous ont supplié lesdiz amis que considéré que ledit Fremin a tousjours esté de bonne fame et renommee . . . nous lui vueillons faire nostre grace, mesmement que ledit feu Perrin a dit qu'il estoit en coulpe dudit coup et non pas le dit Fremin. Nous, considerans les choses dessus dictes, audit Fremin Severin au cas dessus dit avons quitté et remis . . . le fait dessus dit . . . satisfaction faite a partie. Si donnons en mandement au prevost de Paris. . . .

Donné a Paris l'an de grace mil ccc iiii^{xx} et quatre, et de nostre regne le quart. Es requestes de l'ostel.

J. CLERICI. T. D ESTOU[TEVI]LE.

5.3. *AD,* 2:491.

Dans la Tragédie des *Euménides* d'Eschyle, Oreste, au premier Acte, paroissoit entouré de Furies endormies par Apollon. Elles avoient un habit noir & ensanglanté. D'une main un flambeau qui jettoit une lueur pâle & tremblante, de l'autre un fouet de serpens. Leur tête étoit couverte de couleuvres furieuses; leur visage étoit si horrible, si blême & si effrayant, qu'au moment où elles se réveillèrent, & où elles commencèrent à marcher tumultueusement sur le Théâtre, des femmes enceintes accouchèrent d'effroy; des enfants moururent de peur.

5.4. Gosselin, *Recherches sur les origines et l'histoire du théâtre à Rouen avant Pierre Corneille,* 62.

Il était rare que ces assemblées si nombreuses ne donnassent pas lieu à quelque tumulte ou à quelque scène dramatique, on n'en revenait guère sans avoir été témoin ou acteur dans une bataille "à sang et plaies"; les coups de poing étaient plus rares que les coups de dague, d'espée et de bâtons, après lesquels il fallait bien venir s'expliquer devant la justice et lui raconter ces incidents imprévus, mais toujours assurés, du jeu d'un mystère. C'est ce qui eut lieu pour celui-ci: la guerre commença de la part des deux frère[s] de Rupière, seigneurs du lieu, contre un sieur Legrand; on se battit avec un tel acharnement que le jeu du mystère en fut interrompu et que, par suite, les de Rupière furent amenés prisonniers au château de Rouen.*

*Arrêt du Parlement (Tournelle), 20 novembre et 23 mars 1516.

5.5. 12 August 1486, Archives d'Angers, BB 4, fol. 29, cited by Port, *Inventaire analytique*, 349–50.

Item, que durant lesd. jeuz, de chacun des deux coustez de la ville n'y aura que ung portal ouvert, et encores n'y aura que la planche et le guychet, mais toutes voyes pour le jour seront baillées les clefs au cognoistable, qui pourra faire ouverture, s'il voit que besoign en soit, jusques à neuf heures.

Item, que à la garde de chascun desd. portaulx y aura xx hommes par jour, chascun en son tour, bien armez.

Item, que les xxv hommes, qui autres fois ont esté gaigées de la ville, seront mis surs et en bon habillement de guerre, accompaigneront M. le gouverneur et yront par la ville avecques l'un ou l'autre sur ce commis, pour obvier aux inconvéniens des crocheteurs et autres mauvaises gens, pour la seureté et garde de toute la ville et des habitans.

Item, que chacune nuyt le guet et arrière-guet seront renforcez, et en chacun portal y aura ung guet.

Item, sera enjoinct aux hostelliers de la ville et des faubourgs qu'ilz se prennent bien garde quelx gens arrivent à leurs maisons, et n'en reçoyvent aucuns de Broychessac [Brissac] ne d'ailleurs, où il y a peste. . . .

Item, sera publié à son de trompe inhibition et deffense faicte à tous de porter bastons invasibles ne deffensables par la ville, fors seullement ceulx qui sont ordonnez pour la garde d'icelle, sur paine de prinson et d'amende arbitraire.

Item, et sur pareilles peines, que chacun face sillence et obbéisse à ceulx qui sont ordonnez estre au jeu pour faire lad. sillence.

Item, et pour mieulx commancer et avoir sillence, si l'on voit qu'il soit expédiant, sera dicte une messe ou jeu sur ung autel honnestement droissé.

Item, que durant led. Mistère, les chaignes de lad. ville et le portau de Boisnet seront fermez, et les clefs baillées à M. le maire.

5.6. Mons, *Conseil du samedi 26 juin 1501*, cited by Gustave Cohen in *LCR*, 590–91 (original emphasis).

Item, parlét de gaits, durant le *Mistere de la Passion*, tant as portes comme en le Maison de la Ville et se doit avoir ii hommes du gait au resteau et que le gait se face de nuit as dites portes. Conclut de faire le gait as portes de viii hommes et que les portiers avecq ceulx du gait soient au destre de leurs barieres et de savoir quelz gens entrent en la ville, aussi que le gait se face en la Maison de la Ville et que les hostelains raportent chacune nuit les noms de leurs hostes au gait de le Maison de la Ville et que on doit tendre les kaisnes aprochant le Marchiét, afin que on ne puist carier sur le Marchiét.

Item, parlét du *Parcq* qui semble trop petit et se on feroit hours au deffallant du *Parc* allans jusques as maisons. *Conclut de faire ung Hourt depuis le deffallant du Parcq jusques as maisons en gardant les entrées des maisons et de garder l'entrée de le Maison de le Ville ample, sans la renclore en le closure du Parcq.**

*D'après cette importante mention, il semble que face à la scène qui s'allonge entre la Maison dite de la Seuwe et l'actuelle maison Franeau on ait dressé en arrière du *parc* ou parterre, assez près des maisons alignées sur l'Hôtel de Ville des *hourts* ou estrades destinées aux spectateurs. Ces *hourts* n'étaient pas de telle hauteur que les chanoinesses de Sainte Waudru ne pussent suivre la pièce du premier ou du deuxième étage de l'hôtel de leur greffier Joachim Riotte "Au grand Godet."

Chapter 6. The Eel of Melun

6.1. *LM*, 2:144n.

Nous n'osons rappeler ailleurs qu'en note une légende bien connue, mais vague et peu authentique. Un habitant de Melun, nommé Languille, jouait dans un mystère le rôle de saint Barthélemy. Au moment du supplice il se mit à crier, avant que l'acteur qui faisait le bourrreau [*sic*] l'eût touché. De là le proverbe: "Il est comme Languille de Melun, qui crie avant qu'on l'écorche." Voy. le Roux de Lincy, *le Livre des proverbes*, 2e éd. t. II, p. 49.

6.2. Le Roux de Lincy, *Le Livre des proverbes français*, 2:49–50.

L'ANGUILLE de Melun. Il fait comme L'Anguille de Melun, il crie avant qu'on l'escorche.
"Il y avoit à Melun-sur-Seine près Paris un jeune homme nommé L'Anguille, lequel, en une comédie qui se jouoit publiquement, représentoit le personnage de saint Barthélemy. Comme celuy qui faisoit l'exécuteur le voulut approcher, le couteau à la main, feignant de l'escorcher, se prit à crier avant qu'il le touchast, ce qui donna sujet de rire à toute l'assemblée et commencement à ce proverbe, qui depuis s'est appliqué à ceux qui craignent le mal avant qu'il arrive." (FLEURY DE BELLINGEN, *Etym. des Prov. franç., p. 140*).
Cette origine est la plus répandue, mais rien ne prouve qu'elle soit vraie. Dans les Adages françois, qui datent de la fin du XIVe siècle, on lit:
Il est des anguilles de Melun, il crie avant qu'on l'escorche.

6.3. Fleury de Bellingen, *L'Étymologie ou explication des proverbes françois*, 140.

Il fait comme les Anguiles de Melun, il crie devant qu'on l'escorche.

SIMPLE. Et l'Anguile de Melun n'oubliez pas de l'escorcher.
Cos. Je la tiens par la queuë: Dans Melun, qui est une Ville de la Province de Brie, située sur la Rivière de Seine à neuf ou dix lieuës au dessus de Paris, il y avoit un jeune homme nommé l'Anguile, lequel en une Commedie qui se jouoït publiquement, representoit le Personnage de Sainct Barthelemy: Comme l'executeur le voulut approcher, le cousteau à la main, pour faire semblant de l'escorcher, il se prit à crier, auparavant qu'il le touchat, ce qui donna sujet de rire à toute l'assemblée, & commencement à ce Proverbe, *il fait comme les Anguiles de Melun, il crie devant qu'on l'escorche.*

6.4. Edouard Fournier, ed., *Harangue de Turlupin,* in *Variétés historiques et littéraires de la Bibliothèque Elzévirienne,* 6:53–54 (original emphasis).

Je suis Turlupin, fils de Jacques Bonhomme, non de celui qui crioit antan comme les anguilles de Melun et se plaignoit à tort.*

*L'origine du dicton: *Il crie comme l'anguille de Melun, avant qu'on ne l'écorche,* n'est pas bien certaine; seulement, l'on n'en est plus à croire qu'il s'agit d'un nommé Languille, natif de Melun, etc. Je vous fais grâce de l'histoire. Ce qu'il y a de plus probable, c'est qu'il ne faut voir là qu'une allusion au *cri* des marchandes de poissons, vendant toute fraîches, avant de les écorcher, les anguilles si renommées de Melun. *Anguille de Melun, avant qu'on ne l'écorche!* crioient-elles de leur plus forte voix; et il n'en fallut pas davantage pour que le peuple imaginât son dicton. Le *cri* dont je viens de parler se retrouve presque textuellement dans: *le Coq à l'asne et chanson sur ce qui s'est passé en France puis la mort de Henry de Valois, etc.,* 1590, in-8:

> . . . . On oit crier
> Les *anguilles de Melun,*
> Suivant le dire commun,
> *Sans qu'on parle d'escorchier.*

6.5. Antoine Oudin, *Curiositez françoises* (1640), 13–14.

Anguille de haye, *sorte de couleuvre.*
A bon pescheur eschappe l'Anguille. i. *un habile homme peut perdre une occasion.*
Il y a Anguille sous roche. i. *quelque danger ou mal caché dessous.*
Escorcher l'Anguille par la queüe .i. *faire une chose à rebours. Et entreprendre une chose difficile.*
Rompre l'Anguille au genoüil .i. *entreprendre un affaire fascheux & qui ne peut reüssir*
Il ressemble les Anguilles de Melun, il crie devant qu'on l'escorche .i. *il se plaint devant que d'avoir souffert le dommage.* vulg.

6.6. Georges Duval, *Languille de Melun, Vaudeville-Poissard en un acte,* pp. 12–13.

LANGUILLE
Pour l'intelligence de l'explication de çà, il faut que vous sachiez que nous avons à Melun, rue de la Savaterie, zun spectacle distingué zau possible d'amateurs de société bourgeoise, où c'qu'on entre *gratis,* moyennant qu'on paie à la porte une menuiserie pour les frais, que je suis moi, zun des premiers et des plus calés sujets de ce spectacle. . . .
Air: *Toujours debout.*

> Nous possédons dans notre ville
> Un jeune auteur assez fertile,
> Qui composa dernièrement
> Une espèce de tragédie,
> Dont la scène était en Turquie.
> Un homme trouvé nuitamment
> Dedans le sérail du sultan,
> Se défendait avec courage;
> Etait pris, et suivant l'usage,
> Condamné tout incontinent

A certain supplice piquant.
Or de ce misérable drôle,
On m'avait confié le rôle;
J'en était même assez content,
Je joue, et tout allait bien, quand
Avec une effroyable broche,
Un grand soldat de moi s'approche;
La peur me saisit aussitôt,
Je me mets à crier bien haut,
Brisant la corde qui m'attache,
Du poteau, zeste, je m'arrache;
Et si je n'avais détalé,
J'étais un garçon empalé.

JAVOTTE

Queu dommage c'aurait été pour un jeune homme si ben planté.

LANGUILLE

Je ne perd pas de temps: de loin je distingue les mats du coche de Montereau, qui courait hardiment un quart de lieue à l'heure. Je fais un paquet de mes hardes les plus indispensables, et je galope après à toute bride, poursuivi par une trentaine de petits vauriens qui criaient: arrêtez donc Languille de Melun, qui crie avant. . . . [original ellipsis].

Air: *Tarare Pompon.*

Près de toi quelle ardeur,
Malgré moi, me transporte;
Qui fait donc de la sorte
Ici, battre mon coeur.
Oui trop aimable fille,
D'un amour peu commun,
Tu fais griller Languille
    De M'lun.

Chapter 7. The Devil Who Wasn't There

7.1. *CPV,* ed. Bruneau, 3:114–15. (Compare to *CVM,* ed. Huguenin, 473.)

Ung enffans nés ayant la moitiet forme de diable.—Or avint que, en ce meisme tamps, fut juez ung jeux à Bar le Duc, auquelle estoient aulcuns hommes pourtant le parsonnaige de dyablez. Et, entre eulx, en y olt ung que en son habit voult avoir la compaignie de sa femme. Et elle le différoit, et demandoit qu'il volloit faire; et il luy respondit: "Je veult," dit il, "faire le dyable." Et, quoy que sa femme se sceût deffandre, force luy fut de obéyr. Cy avint qu'elle fut grosse et portait son tairme. Maix il avint qu'elle enfanta et délivra de ung corps* qui estoit, dès le fault[†] en aval, forme d'homme, et, dès le fault en amont, forme de dyable. De laquelle chose on en fut moult esbahis. Et ne l'oisairent baptiser jusques ad ce que l'on aroit estés à Romme pour sçavoir que l'on en feroit.

*Huguenin says *ung enffant* (*CVM*, 473).—JE.

†*Faux du corps*, partie où le corps s'amincit, au-dessous de la poitrine et au-dessus des hanches.

7.2. Petit de Julleville, "Vers 1500. Chaumont.—Saint-Jean- Baptiste," in *LM*, 2:81–82 (original emphasis).

A toute époque, les plus goûtés parmi les acteurs du Pardon paraissent avoir été les *Diables*. On a conservé* les statuts en vers français d'une association ou confrérie dont les membres étaient chargés de remplir à Chaumont ces rôles. Dans le mystère, ils avaient mission de torturer l'âme d'Hérode. Pendant trois mois avant les jeux, depuis le dimanche des Rameaux† jusqu'à la Saint-Jean, ils avaient le privilège de parcourir costumés la ville et les campagnes environnantes pour faire l'annonce de la fête: des *Sarrasins* qui faisaient partie du cortège d'Hérode se joignaient à eux. Ces promenades amenèrent d'étranges abus: diables et sarrasins, nombreux comme une armée, commencèrent à piller, au profit de la fête de la Saint-Jean, les villages et les marchés. Leurs exactions les firent redouter et haïr, et contribuèrent beaucoup à la suppression des mystères. La dernière représentation eut lieu en 1663. Quant au Pardon proprement dit et aux fêtes religieuses dont il était l'occasion, on les célébrait encore dans la première moitié de notre siècle.

Un dicton champenois confirme la mauvaise réputation des diables de Chaumont. On disait plaisamment: "S'il plaît à Dieu, à la Vierge, à Saint-Jean, je serai diable et paierai mes dettes."

*Voy *Revue des sociétés savantes*, 5ᵉ série, t. I, p. 12.

†Ils prenaient même une part tumultueuse à la procession de ce jour et s'efforçaient d'empêcher le célébrant (qui figurait Jésus) de franchir la porte du Barle (qui figurait Jérusalem).

7.3. Gosselin, *Recherches sur les origines*, 62–63 (original emphasis).

En 1539, à deux lieues d'Avranches, une représentation plus solennelle [qu'avant] avait lieu dans la paroisse de Tirepied, on y jouait *"la vie et mystère de madame sainte Barbe"*; lequel jeu, commencé le dimanche 10 août, devait se continuer pendant quatre dimanches consécutifs; les acteurs étaient nombreux (de 40 à 50); mais, cette fois encore, le jeu du mystère devait être troublé et tourner au tragique: un sieur Jacques de Vaulevrier, qui avait été volé dans une hôtellerie tenue à Avranches par la veuve de Montléon et ses fils, avait obtenu contre ceux-ci, au Parlement de Normandie, un arrêt de prise de corps; depuis le 23 mai, escorté du sergent Dufeu, il avait maintes fois essayé d'exécuter cet arrêt, mais toujours les Montléon lui échappaient. Apprenant qu'ils avaient chacun un rôle dans le mystère, dont le jeu devait commencer à Tirepied le 10 août, de Vaulevrier s'y rendit avec le sergent Dufeu. Mais le moment était mal choisi, les Montléon devinant le motif de la présence de Vaulevrier et du sergent Dufeu, le firent connaître à leurs compagnons du mystère et tous "embastonnés d'épées et courtes dagues, ayant bastons de guerre, harquebuttes et harquebouses, portant grandes barbes, ayant tabours de suisse," firent une telle reception à de Vaulevrier, que celui-ci décampa promptement sans même oser regarder derrière lui. Il ne renonça pas cependant à exécuter son arrêt, et le dimanche suivant, 17 août, toujours escorté du sergent Dufeu, il revint à Tirepied, à une heure plus avancée. "Il s'était dit que pendant qu'on serait occupé à jouer, il pourrait plus facilement prendre et saisir les Montléon"; mais il avait compté sans le *Diable,* qui était le propre cousin des Montléon! ce cousin, nommé Hamel, était aussi méchant qu'un démon, et comme il était le chef et l'organisateur du jeu, il avait choisi le rôle qui convenait le mieux à sa nature, celui du diable. Montléon lui ayant signalé la présence de son ennemi, Hamel interrompit le jeu du mystère, fit appel à tous les acteurs, et se mettant à leur tête dans ses habits de diable, se rua contre Vaulevrier et son malheureux sergent qui ne songèrent plus qu'à décamper au plus vite et à "reprendre le chemin de s'en retourner sans *attendre la fin du jeu.*" Cependant Hamel et sa troupe "tous armés d'arquebuses chargées, le *feu* en la corde," les poursuivirent longtemps; Hamel, que ses habits de diable empêchaient de courir, les lacéra, et armé d'une épée à deux mains, ne renonça à la poursuite que lorsque les fuyards eurent mis entre eux et lui la rivière de Sées, après quoi les vainqueurs, retournant à Tirepied, reprirent la continuation du jeu si malheureusement interrompu. Tout n'était pas dit cependant, le mystère eut une cinquiéme journée devant le Parlement; Montléon y fut condamné au fouet et au bannissement, Hamel à des dommages-intérêts et à des amendes qui atteignirent le chiffre de 750 liv. t. et l'on renvoya instruire contre les autres complices.*

*Arrêts du Parlement (Tournelle) 16 décembre 1639 et 16 octobre 1640.

7.4. *CMJH*, 268–69, 346.

[1512]. Item, le xe. jour d'Octobre, ung dimanche fuit jué ung jeu sus Saint Illaire, de ii. gens estant en mariage. Après qu'ils eurent vesqus certain temps en mariage, heurent aiccord ensemble de vivre chaistement le demeurant de leur mariaige. Or avint que le marit volt avoir compagnie à sa femme, laquelle de son povoir y resistoit pour le voeu qu'ils avoient faict. Toutefois faullit qu'il fût. La femme courroucée dit que le diable y heust part, et que se elle concepvoit ung enffant que à diable fuit il et qu'elle ly donnoit; dont elle fuit mal avisée, car à celle heure elle conceut ung filz, de quoy elle en maldit l'heure plus de cent mil fois, car ce devint ung si bel enffant et si saige que point on en sceust trower; de quoy le père en avoit si grant joie que tout son reconffort estoit ondit enffant, et toutes fois que la mère le veoit, fondoit en larmes, de quoy le père s'en esmervilloit, et plusseurs fois ly en demandoit la cause, et aussy faisoit l'enffant, quant il commença à devenir grant, ce que jamaix ne leur voulut dire, tant que une fois que l'enffant, qui jay avoit environ xiii. ans d'aige, très instamment l'en prioit, laquelle ly dit qu'elle l'avoit donné à sa conception à diable et comment le diable l'infestoit et demandoit et ly disoit que dedans ces xv. ans il prenroit et emporteroit. Le pouvre enffant, bien estonné et esbahi, dit qu'il y porveroit et qu'il s'en iroit à Romme, se recommandant à la benoite Vierge Marie, laquelle moult humblement saluoit tous les jours. Or pour abrégier l'histoire, à bout des xv. ans, iii. diables le vinrent prenre: Sathan, Astarot et Leviatan et l'emportirent en enfer. Ce veant, la Vierge Marie priait Dieu Nostre Signour, son enffant, qu'il ly voulsist rendre cest enffant que les diables en avoient porté, qui estoit son bon ami. Nostre Signour permist et ly donnait congié de l'aller prendre tout dedans enffer, acompaignié de sainct Michiel, de sainct Gabriel et Raphael, qui fuit une chose bien belle à veoir, et de la joie que le père et la mère heurent de veoir leur enffant et d'estre quitte du diable, car il leur racontait tout ensy que la chose estoit avenue et des grants et horribles torments d'enfer qu'il avoit veus; et fuit ledit jeux aussy bien jué qu'on en vit point de longtemps.*

*Ce Mystère, qui fait partie du Recueil des Miracles de Notre-Dame, par personnages, a été publié à Tubingue, en 1865, par Ch. Adelbert von Keller, professeur à l'Université, sous le titre suivant: "Un miracle de Nostre Dame, d'un enfant qui fu donné au diable, quant il fut engendré." Il est tiré du ms. 819, f. fr. Bibl. Imp. à Paris.

7.5. *CPV*, ed. Bruneau, 4:136–37 (original emphasis). (Compare to *CVM*, ed. Huguenin, 679–80.)

Ung homme avoir le colz rompus par sa malle fortune.—Item, en celle meisme année [1512], avindrent encor plusieurs aultre besoingne et diverse adventure. Entre lesquelle, on moix d'octobre, ung pouvre homme qui pourtoit vendre l'estrain parmy la cité, ne n'avoit aultre mestiés, par quoy l'on le appelloit comunement *Blan Trains*, cellui, ung jour, ce trouva au cabaret chiez ung demourant derrier Sainct Gergonne, nommé l'*Oste c'il Dure*. Et là ce mist à juer a cairte en l'encontre d'ung aultres; car de juer estoit grant costumier. Et, en juant qu'il faisoient, ce esmeut courous entre eulx, comme bien souvant il avient. Et tellement monta le huttin que celluy Blan Train, en sa fureur, jura Dieu et ces sainct que jamaix plus à luy ne jueroit a cartes ne à aultre jeux; et, encor plus fort, dit qu'il ce donnoit au diable, et que le diable luy turdist le col se jamaix plus avec luy juoit. Et quant il olt ce dit par plusieurs fois, et qu'il ce olrent assés demenés et huttinés l'ung encontre l'aultre, firent paix et acort ensemble, et fut tout leur huttin appaisantés. Et dès incontinant racomensairent à juer de plus biaulx; et sambloit que jamaix n'en deussent pertir. Mais, pour Dieu, entendés le miraicle que alors évidentement ce moustra: car celluy Blan Train, qui ainsy avoit jurés et requis le dyable de son ayde, comme ce on luy eust donné d'une massue par dessus la teste, cheut à terre; et, en cheant, se print à braire et à crier, disant à haulte vois: "Ha! le diable m'enporte! le diable m'enporte!" Et, en disant ces mot, perdit la moitiet de luy, et olt la teste tornée ce que devant derrier; et, en tenant diverse grimaiche, demorait en cest estat, tellement que l'on cuidoit qu'il fût mort; ne jamaix ne polt plus pairfaitement perler.

7.6. *CMJH*, 270.

Item, ondit mois d'Octobre [1512] ung pouvre homme porteur d'estrain, aussy s'appelloit il Blancstrain, accoustumé de juer souvent as cartes, estoit en l'hostel d'ung cabaret appellé l'hoste Sidure. En juant as cartes, dit que à diable fuit il et que le diable ly tordit le col, s'il juoit jamais as cartes avec celluy avec qui il juoit; et en l'heure il recommençait à juer à ly, et tout incontinent cheut à terre en criant: *Le diable m'emporte, le diable m'emporte,* perdit la moitié de son corps et heust la teste tournée, sens devant dairier et demourait en tel estat tant qu'il fuit mort.

7.7. Marot, *Oeuvres de Clement Marot*, ed. Guiffrey, 2:523–24n.

Semble que soions enragés,
Car nous sommes tous enchaynés
De cordes & de chesnes de fer.
Semble que soions arrivés,
Et illec expres admenés
Pour iouer ung grant Lucifer.*

*Lucifer tenait un rôle important dans les anciens mystères (voy. *Mistere de la Passion*, imprimé en février 1512 par Michel Le Noir, & joué à Paris, à Poitiers & à Angers jusqu'en 1539). Lorsque le roi des enfers apparaissait sur les tréteaux des confrères de la Passion, entouré de son cortège infernal, c'était toujours une explosion de bruit de chaînes, de pleurs & de grincements de dents, premier trait de ressemblance avec ce qui devait se passer dans les ténèbres de la prison. Les pieux entrepreneurs de ces représentations théâtrales s'ingéniaient, du reste, à donner un aspect terrifiant à leurs exhibitions diaboliques. Les moyens, à la vérité, étaient des plus primitifs; mais l'effet n'en était pas moins grand. Rabelais nous a conservé quelques détails sur cette mise en scène, qui réussissait toujours à impressionner vivement l'imagination populaire. . . .

Ce qui complète enfin ce rapprochement, c'est un petit tableau que nous empruntons à l'introduction du drame d'*Adam,* publié par M. Luzarche. Avec quelques légères retouches, on en ferait une scène copiée sur nature; nous nous bornons à transcrire mot pour mot: "Satan paraît au milieu d'une troupe de démons, dont trois ou quatre portent des fers & des chaînes qu'ils attachent au cou d'Adam & d'Eve. Les uns les poussent, d'autres les attirent vers l'enfer; un autre groupe de diables en occupe l'entrée & fait un vacarme horrible en s'entretenant de la chute des deux malheureux pécheurs; on se les montre d'abord, puis on les saisit & on les précipite dans le gouffre."

7.8. *Adam. Représentation de la chute du premier homme,* ed. Luzarche, 12.

Alors viendra le diable accompagné de trois ou quatre diables semblables à lui, portant dans leurs mains des chaînes et des liens de fer, qu'ils mettront au cou d'Adam et d'Eve. Quelques-uns les pousseront et d'autres les tireront vers l'enfer; mais d'autres diables près de l'enfer viendront au devant des arrivants, et ils feront une grande joie de leur perdition, et chacun des autres diables les montrera, et ils les recevront et les jetteront en enfer, et ils en feront sortir une grande fumée, et ils vociféreront en se réjouissant dans l'enfer, et ils choqueront leurs chaudières et chaudrons pour être entendus au dehors, et après un petit intervalle, les diables sortiront courant par les *places* (c'est-à-dire hors de la scène parmi les spectateurs), mais d'autres resteront dans l'enfer.

7.9. *[Adam.] Ordo repraesentationis Adae,* ed. Bevington, in *Medieval Drama,* 105.

Tunc veniet diabolus et tres vel quattuor diaboli cum eo, deferentes in manibus catenas et vinctos ferreos, quos ponent in colla Adae et Evae. Et quidam eos impellent, alii eos trahant, ad infernum; alii vero diaboli erunt juxta infernum obviam venientibus, et magnum tripudium inter se facient de eorum perditione; et singuli alii diaboli illos venientes monstrabunt, et eos suscipient et in infernum mittent. Et in eo facient fumum magnum exurgere, et vociferabuntur inter se in inferno gaudentes, et collident caldaria et lebetes suos, ut exterius audiantur. Et facta aliquantula mora, exibunt diaboli discurrentes per plateas; quidam vero remanebunt in inferno.

7.10. Oudin, *Curiositez françoises,* 164–65.

le Diable n'est pas tousiours à une porte. i. *le mal-heur ne poursuit pas tousiours une personne.*

en Diable, tant que tous les diables .i. *bien fort.*

en Diable & demy; comme trente mille diables, *idem.* . . .

*faire [his asterisk] le Diable à quatre .i. *faire bien du bruit, ou du renversement. vulg.* . . . . .

le Diable s'en pende, *on se sert de ces mots, lors qu'on a regret à quelque chose, ou que quelque mal est arrivé.* . . .

Diablerie .i. meschantes actions.

7.11. *SBD,* chap. 10, "De l'incredulité," 76.

Incredulité, infidelité et mescreance, est moins sentir et croire, ou aultrement qu'il ne convient de l'infinie bonté, misericorde, sagesse et puissance de Dieu. Laquelle du tout ne se poeut fier en Dieu, mais en chose incertaine cherche aultres moiens pour avoir ayde et secours. Pleine de inconstance crainct où il n'y a point de matiere de paour, se fie où il n'y a point de seureté, sans aulcun certain propos ne arrest, mais muable comme la lune, subjecte à toute tromperie et deception. Car là où n'est la lumiere de foy, la clarté de la parolle de Dieu, là regnent les princes de tenebres, là sont les trebuchementz et tombementz en la fosse: pour le bon chemin, on prend le maulvais; pour la volunté de Dieu, le songe des hommes; pour les choses qui sont agreables à Dieu et à ses sainctes ordonnances, ce qui est en abhomination et est doctrine diabolique. Car tout ce [qui] vient de ceste incredulité, et tout ce que faict celluy qui n'ha foy, ne poeut estre que peché, quelque belle couleur qu'il ayt de saincteté de bonne oeuvre.

Chapter 8. The Laughter of the Children

8.1. Roy, *Le Mystère de la Passion en France du XIVe au XVIe siècle*, 315n.

Le témoignage peu connu et peu suspect du pieux L. Vivès vaut pour la France, comme pour l'étranger; le voici.—Saint Augustin, *De la Cité de Dieu*, illustrée des Comm. de Jean Loys Vivès de Valence (édit. de Gentian Hervet, 1584) livre VIII, chap. xxvii, p. 254. *Scandale grand de representer la passion de nostre Seigneur par personnages. . . .*

C'est maintenant la coustume, au temps qu'on célèbre la sainte feste de Jésus-Christ, qui a délivré le genre humain par sa mort, d'exhiber au peuple des jeux qui ne diffèrent presque rien de ces vieux jeux scéniques des païens. Et quand je ne dirais autre chose, quiconques orra dire qu'on fait des jeux en une chose fort sérieuse, il estimera que c'est une chose assez laide et deshonneste. Là on se rit de Judas, qui se vante des choses les plus ineptes du monde, cependant qu'il trahit Jésus-Christ: là les disciples s'enfuyent les gensdarmes, les poursuyvans, non pas sans une grande risée des joueurs, et des spectateurs. Là S. Pierre coupe l'oreille à Malchus: le peuple habillé de noir luy applaudissant, comme si la captivité de Jésus-Christ estoit ainsi vangée. Et un peu après luy qui avait combattu si vaillamment, estant espouventé à la demande d'une simple chambrière, renie son maistre, la multitude se riant de la chambrière qui luy demande, et sifflant Sainct Pierre qui le nie. Entre tant de gens qui jouent, entre tant de risées, tant de folies, il n'y a que Jésus-Christ seul qui soit sérieux, et qui tienne aucune sévérité; et là où il s'efforce d'esmouvoir les passions de douleur et de tristesse, je ne scay comment il refroidit, non pas seulement là, mais aussi aux choses sacrées et saintes, avec une grande meschanceté et impiété, non pas tant de ceux qui regardent ou qui jouent, comme de ceux qui font faire ces choses. Nous parlerons par aventure de ceci en un lieu plus commode.

8.2. Procureur général, cited by Sainte-Beuve, in *TPF.* 193–95 (original emphasis).

Ces gens non lettrez ni entenduz en telles affaires, de condition infame, comme un menuisier, un sergent à verge, un tapissier, un vendeur de poisson, qui ont fait jouer *les Actes des Apostres,* et qui, ajoutant, pour les allonger, plusieurs choses apocryphes, et entremettant à la fin ou au commencement du jeu farces lascives et momeries, ont fait durer leur jeu l'espace de six à sept mois, d'où sont advenues et adviennent cessation de service divin, refroidissement de charitez et d'aumones, adultères et fornications infinies, scandales, dérisions et mocqueries. . . .

Tant que lesdicts jeux ont duré, le commun peuple dès huit à neuf heures du matin, ès jours de festes, délaissoit sa messe paroissiale, sermons et vespres, pour aller ès dictz jeux garder sa place, et y estre jusqu'à cinq heures du soir: ont césse les prédications, car n'eussent eu les prédicateurs qui les eussent escoutez. Et retournant desdicts jeux se mocquoyent hautement et publicquement par les rues desdictz jeux des joueurs, contrefaisant quelque langage impropre qu'ils avoyent oï desdictz jeux ou autre chose mal faite, criant par dérision que *le Sainct- Esprit n'avoit point voulu descendre,* et autres mocqueries. Et le plus souvent les prestres des paroisses, pour avoir leur passe-temps d'aller ès dictz jeux, ont délaissé dire vespres, ou les ont dictes tout seuls dès l'heure de midy, heure non accoustumée; et mesme les chantres ou chapelains de la saincte chapelle de ce palais, tant que lesdictz jeux ont duré, ont dict vespres les jours de feste à l'heure de midy, et encore les disoyent en poste et à la légère pour aller ès dictz jeux. . . .

Tant les entrepreneurs que les joueurs sont gens ignares, artisans mécaniques, ne sachant ni A ni B, qui oncques ne furent instruicts ni exercez en théâtres et lieux publics à faire tels actes, et davantage n'ont langue diserte, ni langage propre, ni les accens de prononciation décente, ni aulcune intelligence de ce qu'il dient; tellement que le plus souvent advient que d'un mot ils en font trois; font point ou pause au milieu d'une proposition, sens ou oraison imparfaite; font d'un interrogant un admirant, ou autre geste, prolation ou accent contraires à ce qu'il dient, dont souvent advient dérision et clameur publicque dedans le théâtre même, tellement qu'au lieu de tourner à édification leur jeu tourne à scandale et dérision. . . .

Il y a plusieurs choses au *Vieil Testament* qu'il n'est expédient de déclarer au peuple, comme gens ignorans et imbécilles qui pourroyent prendre occasion de judaïsme à faute d'intelligence.

8.3. *HTF,* 2:228–29.

Un Dimanche matin Pont-Alais eut l'impudence de faire battre le tabourin* dans le Carrefour qui est proche de l'Eglise de saint Eustache, pour annoncer une Pièce nouvelle qu'il devoit donner le même jour. Le Curé qui faisoit alors le Prône, interrompu par le bruit qu'il entendoit, & voyant ses Auditeurs sortir en foule de l'Eglise pour aller entendre Pont-Alais, descendit de sa Chaire, se rendit dans le Carrefour, & s'approchant de Pont-Alais: Qui vous a fait si hardi, lui dit-il, de tabouriner pendant que je prêche? Et qui vous a fait si hardi de prêcher pendant que je tabourine? reprit insolemment Pont-Alais. Cette réponse fit juger au Curé qu'il ne lui convenoit pas de pousser plus loin la conversation, mais il porta ses plaintes au Magistrat, qui fit mettre Pont-Alais en prison. Et ce ne fut qu'au bout de six mois que ce dernier obtint sa liberté, & la permission de continuer ses Jeux.

*Avant que l'on fut dans l'usage d'afficher le titre des Pièces au coin des rües, on faisoit battre le Tabourin par les Carrefours de la Ville, & lorsqu'un certain nombre de gens s'étoit assemblé, un Acteur, qui accompagnoit le Joueur de Tabourin, faisoit l'éloge de la Piece, & invitoit le Public à la venir voir.

8.4. Bonaventure des Periers, *Nouvelles récréations et joyeux devis suivis du Cymbalum mundi,* ed. Lacour, 2:156–58.

Or est il que maistre Jehan du Pontalais, qui avoit à jouer ceste aprésdisnée là quelque chose de bon, et qui congnoissoit assez ce prescheur pour tel qu'il estoit, faisoit ses monstres par la ville, et par fortune luy falloit passer par devant l'eglise où estoit ce prescheur. Maistre Jehan du Pontalais, selon sa coustume, fit sonner son tabourin au carrefour, qui estoit tout vis à vis de l'eglise, et le faisoit sonner bien fort et longuement tout exprés pour faire taire ce prescheur, afin que le monde vint à ses jeux. Mais c'estoit bien au rebours, car tant plus il faisoit de bruit, et plus le prescheur crioit hault; et se battoyent Pontalais et luy, ou luy et Pontalais, pour ne faillir pas, à qui auroit le dernier. Le prescheur se mit en colere, et va dire tout hault par une auctorité de predicant: "Qu'on aille faire taire ce tabourin." Mais pour cela personne n'y alloit, sinon que, qu'il sortoit du monde, c'estoit pour aller voir maistre Jehan du Pontalais, qui faisoit tousjours battre plus fort son tabourin.

Quand le prescheur veid qu'il ne se taisoit point et que personne ne luy en venoit rendre responce: "Vrayement, dit il, j'iray moymesmes." Et descend de la chayre en disant: "Que personne ne bouge; je reviendray à ceste heure." Quand il fut au carrefour, tout eschauffée, il va dire à Pontalais: "Hé! qui vous fait si hardy de jouer du tabourin tandis que je presche?" Pontalais le regarde et luy dit: "Hé! qui vous fait si hardy de prescher tandis que je joue du tabourin?" Alors le prescheur, plus fasché que devant, print le cousteau de son famulus qui estoit auprés de luy, et fit une grand'balaffre à ce tabourin avec ce cousteau; et s'en retournoit à l'église pour achever son sermon. Pontalais print son tabourin et courut aprés ce prescheur, et l'en va coiffer comme d'un chapeau d'Albanois, le luy affublant du costé qu'il estoit rompu. Et lors le prescheur, tout en l'estat qu'il estoit, vouloit remonter en chayre, pour remonstrer l'injure qui luy avoit esté faicte, et comment la parole de Die estoit vilipendée. Mais le monde rioit si fort, le voyant avec ce tabourin sus la teste, qu'il ne sceust meshuy avoir audience, et fut contrainct de se retirer et de s'en taire, car il luy fut remonstré que ce n'estoit pas le fait d'un sage homme de se prendre à un fol.

8.5. Vinchant, *Annales de la province et comté du Hainaut*, 5:267–69.

Or, voicy comme le menu peuple abusoit de la prospérité et richesse. Il employoit tout le temps qu'il pouvoit avoir à jeux et banquets; on faisoit les dédicasses des paroisses, non pas avec dévotion, mais avec pompe, vanité, convives et festins durant huit jours, avec les amys qui y venoient bien de vingt lieues long; et après disner, au lieu d'aller à vespres et au sermon, on passoit le temps à voir des jeux, comédies ou farceries. On ne se contentoit pas que les confrères des archiers et arbalestriers avoient leur feste et récréations ordinaires sans dissolution et excès, ains avec grands despens et superflus, on instituoit jours de combat ou courses avec les villes voisines pour gagner le prix, et faisoit-on des réthoriques: ainsy appelloit-on les comédies, farces, ou fables qu'on exhiboit en rithmes vulgaires sur eschaffaut au grand contentement et affluence du peuple. En ces réthoriques se commettoient des grands abus. Et d'autant qu'on y discouroit en présence du menu peuple, ignorant et indiscret (et souventeffois par manière de risée et mocquerie), des points de la religion et affaires d'estat des princes et république, ce qui apportoit un mespris des choses saintes et des bons princes. . . .

Quant aux réthoriques, comédies et farces, elles estoient en ce temps fréquentées en la ville de Mons, de sorte que les manans d'une rue souloient provoquer ceux d'autres pour emporter le prix. Et d'autant que ceux de la rue des Rattes, qui se nommoient de Notre-Dame, emportoient le plus souvent le dessus, ladite rue changea lors de nom et fut appellée la rue Notre-Dame, comme encore elle s'appelle telle présentement. A cest effet fut posée l'image de la Vierge par lesdits réthoriciens d'icelle rue; mais à cause que lesdites réthoriques et comédies incitoient la jeunesse, fils et filles, à méchanceté et impudicité, outre ce qu'en icelles se mesloient quelques hérésies, les principaux bourgeois d'icelle ville défendoient à leurs enfants de se trouver à telles réthoriques, mesme d'user de langue françoise en leurs bénédictions et actions de grâce quand ils prenoient leurs repas, à cause que ces réthoriciens, et après eux les hérétiques occultes, en usoient en leurs banquets.

8.6. Petit de Julleville, "1452. Beauvais.—Saint Pierre," in *LM*, 2:22–23.

Le 29 mai 1452, l'on commença de jouer le mystère de saint Pierre à Beauvais. Comme les échafauds avaient été dressés sur une place appartenant au chapitre de Saint-Pierre, avant le commencement des jeux, à huit heures du matin, les chanoines firent faire une proclamation pour

> faire deffense a ceux qui sont et seront en la-ditte place . . . durant tous les jours, temps et espace de iceux jeux et mystere de monseigneur saint Pierre et ce qui s'en depend, qu'ils ne facent trouble, noise, desbats ne chose qui puist ou doibt empescher les joueurs et ne monter sur les hours et eschaffaux estant en ladite terre et justice de mesdits sieurs du chapitre, sans permission et licence de ceulx a qui il appartient, sur peine d'amende et pugnition telle que raison donnera.*

> *Biblioth. nat., mss., collection de Picardie, t. 158, f° 82, v°.

8.7. *LM*, 1:410.

Mais il y a dans chaque homme, chez les plus raffinés et chez les plus grossiers, comme une source latente d'émotions pathétiques, qui a besoin de s'épancher au dehors; pour décharger le coeur qu'elle gonfle et qu'elle oppresse. Le théâtre tragique excelle à satisfaire ce besoin, à soulager doucement cet appesantissement de l'âme; il y réussit par une pitié douce, et par une terreur d'imagination, qui n'ont rien de l'amertume et de la violence d'une terreur et d'une pitié réelles. La soif d'émotion est satisfaite; et l'âme n'est point déchirée. Ainsi les passions, comme dit Aristote, sont "purgées et purifiées," c'est-à-dire satisfaites sans souffrance, et amorties sans explosion violente.

Tels étaient, croyons-nous, les sentiments complexes et divers qui remplissaient l'âme des spectateurs au moyen âge, durant la représentation des mystères. Ils riaient des plaisanteries grossières des bourreaux, des mendiants, des valets; ils pleuraient en voyant le Sauveur des hommes en butte à tant d'outrages et à de si cruelles tortures. Ils riaient et ils pleuraient dans la même heure, tour à tour, et presque en même temps comme font les enfants.

8.8. Marot, *Oeuvres de Clement Marot*, ed. Guiffrey, 4:326–27, ll. 38–48.

> O vous, humains Parisiens,
> De le pleurer pour recompense
> Impossible est: car quand on pense
> A ce qu'il souloit faire, & dire,
> On ne se peult tenir de rire.
> Que dy je? on ne le pleure point?
> Si faict on: & voici le poinct:
> On en rit si fort en maints lieux
> Que les larmes viennent aux yeulx:
> Ainsi, en riant, on le pleure:
> Et en pleurant on rit à l'heure.

8.9. *HMS*, 49–50.

Cette trop grande liberté laissée au public aboutissait à des excès, à des folies et à d'insolentes audaces (surtout à propos du drame des pasteurs), que souvent des ordres sévères durent tenter de réprimer. Mais comment réprimer aussi les sentiments violents de cette foule, également excessive dans le rire et dans les larmes, car lorsque le soldat, en tuant les Innocents, s'écrie:

Enfant, apprends à mourir,

le public s'amuse de cette féroce plaisanterie, comme plus tard il s'amusera des hideuses farces des bourreaux et des "tyrans." Mais aussitôt qu'il voit Rachel, la mère éplorée, se précipiter en sanglotant sur le corps de son enfant mort, alors tous les coeurs simples gémissent, et ce sang versé les trouble d'une impression physique. La douleur de cette mère, tombant sur les cadavres des innocentes victimes, agite de sanglots les mères qui sont dans l'assistance.

Dans ce passage rapide du rire aux larmes, nous entrevoyons toute l'âme du premier moyen âge. Comme des enfants, il rient d'un long et gros rire épais, pour la moindre chose, pour un bâton levé, pour un âne qui parle, un juif qui remue la tête et frappe du pied; et ils pleurent, se pâment avec la même facilité.

Il en était ainsi de ces rudes guerriers de l'épopée qui, si leur corps était bardé de fer, avaient une âme enfantine et faible, et s'évanouissaient comme des femmes.

Ames mal faites pour les luttes morales, mais merveilleusement aptes à toutes les joies et à toutes les douleurs, que venaient éveiller en elles ces premiers drames, simples, naïfs et rudes.

Chapter 9. Burnt Theatrical Offerings

9.1. Boussu, *Histoire de la Ville de Mons*, 95.

[1321]. Philippes Roi de France ayant chassé les Juifs de son Royaume, quelques-uns vinrent s'établir à Mons. Le Comte voulut bien les souffrir dans la basse Ville; on leur désigna un endroit le long de la riviere, qui retint le nom de la ruë des Juifs: ils s'y logerent sous condition qu'ils appelleroient dans leur Synagogue quatre Chrétiens pour y être témoins de leurs actions: l'on nommoit ces quatre personnes les Croisez, à cause d'une croix qu'ils portoient sur l'épaule; ils tiroient certain gage des Juifs reglé pars les Echevins.

9.2. *JBP*, ed. Tuety, re-ed. Beaune, 417–18.

Item, fut faite une des plus piteuses et la plus dévote procession qu'un eût oncques vue à Paris, car l'évêque de Paris et celui de Beauvais, et deux abbés portèrent le corps Notre Seigneur de Saint-Jean-en-Grève sur leurs épaules, et de là allèrent aux Billettes quérir à grande révérence le canivet de quoi le faux Juif avait dépiqué la chair Notre Seigneur, et de là furent portés avec la sainte croix et autres reliques sans nombre à Sainte-Catherine-du-Val-des-Écoliers; et y avait devant plus de 500 torches allumées, et de peuple bien 9 ou 10 000 personnes, sans ceux de l'église; et avait après ces saintes reliques tout le mystère du Juif qui était en une charrette lié, où il avait épines, comme si on le menait ardoir, et après venait la justice, et sa femme et ses enfants; et parmi [les rues (y) avaient deux échafauds de très piteux mystères, et furent] les rues parées comme à la Saint-Sauveur. Et fut fait cette procession, pour ce qu'on avait bonne espérance d'avoir paix entre le roi de France de d'Angleterre, et fut le 15e jour de mai, au vendredi, l'an 1444.

9.3. *CMJH*, 233.

1503. Item, le ix.e jour de Décembre fut mise on pillory une jonne fille; et à ii. heures on la monit bruler devant le Pont, pour tant qu'elle avoit esté grousse d'enffant et en enffantant print son enffant et le gettait en ung puix en la maixon de Clément d'Oultre Seille, à Porsailly; et servoit en la maixon dudit Clément ladite fille.

9.4. Hillairet, *Connaissance du Vieux Paris*, 56 (original emphasis).

Emplacement du couvent des *Carmes-Billettes*, édifié sur l'endroit où fut jadis la maison du juif Jonathas.

En 1290, une pauvre femme ne put, dit-on, retirer ses habits qu'elle avait mis en gage, qu'à la condition d'apporter à Jonathas l'hostie qu'elle recevrait à la communion. Une fois celle-ci reçue à l'église Saint-Merri, le jour de Pâques, la pauvre femme courut la remettre au juif. Jonathas la prit et la perça de plusieurs coups de canif; aussitôt il en coula un sang abondant. Jonathas la jeta alors dans une chaudière remplie d'eau bouillante, celle-ci devint aussitôt rouge comme du sang alors que l'hostie s'élevait au-dessus d'elle. Le quartier fut ameuté; Jonathas fut arrêté et condamné à être brûlé vif. Ses biens et sa maison furent confisqués au profit de Philippe-le-Bel, et on construisit sur l'emplacement de celle-ci une chapelle expiatoire, appelée *la chapelle du Miracle* que l'exhaussement de la rue a enterrée et fait disparaître vers 1410.

9.5. *HVP*, ed. Lobineau, vol. 2, bk. 16, p. 833.

L'évesque de Paris, celui de Beauvais, & deux abbez, portérent le S. sacrement sur leurs espaules, depuis l'église de S. Jean en Greve / jusqu'aux Billettes, où l'on prit le saint canif /,* & la procession alla à Ste Catherine du Val des escoliers. Le luminaire estoit de plus de cinq cent torches, qui précedoient les saintes reliques, que l'on y porta en grand nombre. On compta à la suite de la procession neuf à dix mille personnes, sans les ecclesiastiques. Après les saintes reliques paroissoit *le mystère du Juif,* c'est-à-dire une representation dramatique de tout ce qui s'estoit passé dans le XIII. siecle, lorsque l'on mena au supplice le Juif sacrilege dont nous avons parlé dans son lieu.

*This bracketed phrase is omitted by the brothers Parfaict in *HTF,* 2:331n.—JE.

9.6. *HVP*, ed. Lobineau, vol. 1, bk. 9, pp. 458–60.

An. 1290. LXIV. *Histoire de la Sainte Hostie prophanée par un Juif. Et convent de Billettes.*

Au commencement du pontificat de Simon Matiphas arriva dans la ruë des Jardins le miracle de l'Eucharistie devenu depuis si celebre. Une femme avoit engagé pour trente soûs, c'est-a-dire pour environ un demi-marc d'argent, ses plus beaux habits à un Juif usurier. Vers la feste de Pasques de l'an 1290. cette femme alla redemander ses habits au Juif & le pria de les lui prester pour ce jour-là seulement, qui cette année tomboit au 2. d'Avril. Le Juif lui dit que si elle vouloit lui rapporter le pain de l'Eucharistie que les Chrestiens appellent leur Dieu, il lui rendroit ses habits pour toujours & sans argent. La femme s'y engagea, & le jour de Pasque venu, elle se presenta à la communion dans l'église de S. Merri sa paroisse. Elle receut la sainte hostie, prit soin de la conserver en entier, & la livra au Juif. Celui-ci la recevant, "Je sçaurai bien-tost," dit-il, "si c'est-là le corps de J. C. comme les Chrestiens le publient." En mesme-tems il met l'hostie sur un coffre, & la perce de plusieurs coups de canif. On assure que le sang en sortit aussi-tost en abondance, comme d'un corps vivant. Le Juif d'abord surpris, appelle sa femme & ses enfans, qui furent frappez d'étonnement à ce spectacle. Mais le Juif, au lieu de cesser, enfonça un clou, à coups de marteau, dans la sainte hostie, qui continua de verser du sang. La femme, toute effrayée, voulut arrester son mari; mais lui, de rage, prend l'hostie & la jette dans le feu. L'acte dressé à ce sujet assure que l'hostie en sortit sans estre endommagée, & se mit à voltiger par la chambre. Le Juif essaya de la précipiter dans le lieu le plus infect de la maison, & la jetta enfin dans une chaudiere d'eau bouillante. On dit que l'eau en fut rougie, que l'hostie en sortit entiere, & que la femme vit dessus la representation de J. C. attaché à la croix. Penetrée de tant de prodiges elle se retira dans un cabinet écarté pour n'estre plus spectatrice des fureurs de son mari. Dans le mesme tems on sonna la grande messe aux religieux de Ste Croix de la Bretonnerie qui estoient dans le voisinage. Le fils du Juif estoit sur la rue des Jardins à la porte de la maison de son pere, & demanda aux passans où ils alloient. "Nous allons," dirent-ils, "à l'église, adorer Dieu." "C'est en vain," dit l'enfant, "car mon pere lui a donné tant de coups, qu'il l'a tué. La plupart méprisérent le discours de l'enfant; mais une femme, plus curieuse, entra dans la maison sous prétexte de demander du feu. Elle vit l'hostie, & la receut dans sa robe, d'où elle la fit passer dans un vase qu'elle avoit dans les mains, & la porta sur le champ au curé de S. Jean en Gréve, à qui elle fit le recit de tout ce qui s'estoit passé. L'évesque Simon fut informé de tout par le curé, & fit arrester le Juif & toute sa famille. Il fut interrogé par l'évesque, & ne nia pas le fait. L'évesque l'exhorta vivement à renoncer à son erreur; mais le Juif endurci la soustint avec opiniastreté. L'évesque le livra au bras seculier, & le malheureux fut condamné à estre bruslé vif. Comme on l'approchoit de la pile de bois destinée à son supplice, il s'écria: "Ah! que n'ai-je un livre qui est à la maison! le feu ne pourroit agir sur moy." Le juge envoya querir le livre, on l'attacha au cou du Juif, & lui & son livre furent bien-tost consumez par les flâmes. La femme & les enfans se convertirent & receurent le batesme, & l'évesque leur donna la confirmation. Telle est l'histoire de la sainte hostie que l'on conserve encore aujourd'hui dans l'église de S. Jean en Gréve, où elle est portée en procession tous les ans, le jour de l'octave du S. Sacrement. Ce miracle fit bruit dans les pays étrangers, & Jean Villani [d. 1348] auteur du tems, le rapporte dans son histoire de Florence. Un bourgeois de Paris, nommé Rainier Flaming bastit au mesme lieu où la chose estoit arrivée, une chapelle qui fut appellée, *la chapelle des Miracles*, en 1294. On la donna ensuite aux freres hospitaliers de la Charité N.D. de Châlon-sur-Marne, à la demande de Louis de Joinville, pour y fonder un monastere; & cinq ans après Philippe le bel acheta une maison voisine qu'il leur donna pour aggrandir le lieu de leur demeure. Les freres de la Charité N. D. celebroient autrefois la memoire du miracle par une procession qu'ils faisoient le Dimanche de la *Quasimodo.* Mais, pour un plus grand détail de ces choses, il faut sçavoir premierement que Rainier Flaming, dans le dessein de bastir une chapelle dans ce lieu *où les Juifs avoient percé la Sainte Eucharistie d'un cousteau, & l'avoient jettée dans une chaudiere d'eau bouillante convertie miraculeusement en sang,* s'adressa au pape Boniface VIII. pour en avoir la permission. Le pape, par sa bulle du 17. Juillet 1295. manda à l'évesque de Paris d'accorder à Flaming ce qu'il souhaitoit, si le lieu lui appartenoit, ou après qu'il l'auroit acquis, s'il ne lui appartenoit pas, & de conserver le patronage de la chapelle à lui & à ses successeurs. . . . La reine Clemence de Hongrie seconde femme de Louis X. legua par son testament du 5. Octobre 1328. au couvent de Paris, *où Dieu fut bouliz,* la somme de dix livres parisis. . . . Ce monastere portoit le nom de prieuré, & les religieux faisoient profession de la regle de S. Augustin. Ils portoient aussi le nom de Billettes, qui estoit peut-estre celui de la maison du Juif, & avoient dix-sept maisons de leur ordre en France. . . . Ils [les Carmes reformez] ont conservé la feste solemnelle de la *Quasimodo* establie par leurs predecesseurs en memoire du miracle de la sainte Hostie, & montrent encore le canif dont le Juif s'estoit servi pour son crime, avec le vase de bois dans lequel l'hostie fut portée au curé de S. Jean.

9.7. de Vigneulles, *Gedenkbuch,* ed. Michelant, 244–45.

Le lundi devant, première feste de pentecouste, fut jué en chambre le jeu de la ste hostie, laquelle ste hostie est à ste Marie de Paris, et fut un mystère fort biaulx et les secrets moult bien faits; / car premierement y avoit comment une weve femme de Paris avoit vendu à ung juif celle ste hostie et lui livrait le jour de paicques et / * le traistre juif voulant aprower, s'il estoit dieu, print la dite ste hostie et la mist sus une tauble et fraipait d'ung coustiaulx parmi; alors par ung secret, qui estoit fait, sortit grand abondance de sang et sailloit en hault parmi la dite hostie, comme se ce fut ung enfant, qui pissait, et en fut le juif tout gaisté et dessaigné et faisoit moult bien son personnaige. Aprez, non content de ce, il ruait la dite hostie au feu et par ung engien elle se levait du feu et se ataichait contre le contrefeu de la cheminée et le traistre la perçait de rechief d'une daigue et par ung aultre engien et secret elle jectait de rechief sang abondamment. Puis ce fait, il la reprint et l'ataichait avec deux cloz contre une estaiche et la vint fraipper d'ung espieu et la dite hostie jectait arrière sang abondamment et jusques tout enmey le paircque trinçoit [*sic*] le sancq et en fut le lieu tout ensanglanté. Et alors comme enraigié print l'hostie et la ruait en une chaudière d'yawe boullant et elle se elevait en l'air et montait en une nueé et devint ung petit enfant en montant à mont et se faisoit tout ceci par engiens et secrets, et s'y fist encor ledit jour plusieurs choses, que je laisse; car la femme, qui l'avoit vendue, fut prinse à la cité de Senlis et brulée pource, que depuis elle avoit murtri ung sien enfant. . . .

Le lundemain, qui fut le mairdi, fut jué au meisme lieu ung miraicle de st Nicollays du Bair. . . .

Le lundemain, qui fut le mercredi, devoit estre encor jué ung jeu et chose mourale; mais pour la pourcession, qui se fist, et aussy pour la june on ne juait point pour le dit jour jusques au dimanche aprez, qui fut le dimanche réaulx, et aussy le mercredi, il plut et tonnait très bien et fut celle pluye moult bonne pour les biens de terre. Et fut ce mistère et chose mourale jué le dimanche au dit lieu en chambre et estoit le jeu de la faulse langue, laquelle ne scet dire bien de soy, ne d'aultrui; parquoy aprez plusieurs mistères et choses faictes, son ame fut pendue par la langue à plus hault de l'enfer et les dyaubles luy firent plusieurs tourmens en jectant feu et grele par tout son corps. Et duraient ces tourmens moult longuement, qu'elle estoit toute en feu et en flammes et ne bruloit point et remuoit celle airme les bras par engiens et estoit une chose bien ingenieusement faicte; et je le sçay à vray, car je, Philippe, estois l'ung des gouverneurs et recuillois l'airgent, qui se levait ez trois jours sus les hors et eschauffaults, et montait la somme environ à xxxiij francs et y avoit Andrieu, mon filz, v personnaiges ès dits trois jours.

*Petit de Julleville omits this phrase from "1513. Metz.—La Sainte Hostie. Saint Nicolas de Bari," in *LM,* 2:103.—JE.

9.8. *Mistere de la Sainte Hostie,* Bib. Nat., Rés. Yf 2915, fols. 24v–r.

Et outre plus mes bonnes gens
Si ne soyez pas negligens
Qui devant voz yeux avez veu
Le beau miracle: non pas jeu.

S'il vous plaist, vous le retiendrez.
Et de bon cueur le servirez
En maintenant la confrairie:

Laquelle est bien auctorisée
Au propre lieu ou ce fut faict.
S'il plaist au doux pere parfaict. . . .

Amen. *La condamnation du faux juif comme il fut ars et bruslé dehors Paris au marché aux pourceaux.*

9.9. *CMJH*, 294–95 (original emphasis). (Compare to *CPV,* ed. Bruneau, 4:189–90.)

1515. En ladite année et on dit caresme, ung frère de l'Observance, appellé frère Ollivier, proichoit le caresme à Sainct Pierre, et proichoit très bien à gré du peuple. Le jour du grant Venredi, il proichit la Passion en la grant esglize où il fit ceu que jamais on n'avoit veu, car il monstrit une hostie sacrée et fit crier le peuple *miséricorde,* en monstrant ladite hostie. Et puis quant Pilaite volt donner la sentence, commençoit à crier de toutte sa puissance: *à la mort, à la mort,* et en criant ensy, la trompette de la Cité commencit à sonner pareillement: *à la mort, à la mort.* Et quant Nostre Seigneur fuit mort en la croix, il monstroit ung crucifix, en faisant encor crier *miséricorde,* et crioient les gens à haulte voix. Le jour de Paisque, il proichit encor en la grant esglize, et à l'heure qu'il fit dire l'*Ave Maria,* les chantres de l'esglize sur les petites orgues commencèrent à chanter moult mélodieusemen *Regina;* et à la fin du sermon les grosses orgues commencèrent à juer bien longuement, tant que les gens furent hors.

Chapter 10. Theater's Living Dead

10.1. Jean Chonet, *Compte de sa composition,* in *Mystère des Trois Doms,* ed. Giraud, 591–92 (my emphasis).

Au nom et loange de Dieu, soit notoire et magnifest pour le temps advenir, comme l'an de grace courant mil et sincq cens et neuf et le vintz et septiesme de may, qui fust le premier jour de Pendecostes, et subsequammant les aultres jours aprés, par deliberacion preallablement feicte, tant entre messieurs de chapitre et aultres habitués de l'esglise Sainct Barnard, que messieurs les consulz, conseilhiers, manantz et habitans de la ville de Romans, comme sceront pluseurs cy aprés nommés, fust joyée et magnifestée la vie et saincte ystoire des gloriculx martirs, amys de Dieu, sainct Severin, Exupere et Felicien, vulgarement appellés Troys Domps, repousans en ladicte esglise Sainct Barnard. *Lesquielx par avant nous demonstrarent estre noz intercesseurs et amys envers Dieu le Createur;* d'aultant que l'année de la grant secheresse, que fust l'an mille sincq cens et quatre, *avoir yceulx requis et pourté en procession generale,* soubdeinemant nous donnarent pluye, et ce le xv jour de juing, auquel jour ou landemein fust preché le beau miracle en la place, en tant qu'il fust dist leur saincte vie estre magnifestée dans sincq années aprés. Et *despuys regnant aulcune peste en ceste ville,* l'an mil V^c et sept, fust instituée confrarie, tant a l'onneur dudict monsieur saint Barnard que dedicts corps sainctz et aultres respousans en ladicte esglise, *et faict requeste a yceulx, cessast incontinant ladicte peste,* estant au moys d'oust fort asognée. Pour quoy ayant ad ce consideracion et inclinacion de devocion fervante, et non sans cause, *tant par le voloir de Dieu que pour leurs evidans miracles cotidiens,* fust mys sus ledict mistere et ordonné, et choisis les personages pour le joier, estant le livre permierement bien acoustré cellon la matiere subjecte; et y avoit de personages environ cent, ainsi comme cy aprés sceront denommez, et joié par les gens samblablement escriptz au pié d'iceulx; *sans la translacion, que ne ce peult joier, a cause du principal mistere qu'estoit moult grant.* Et lequel affere, a l'yde de monsieur le chanoine Pré de

Grenoble, fatiste, et de maistre Françoys Tevenot, poinctre de ceste ville, faysant les feinctes et conduisant ycelles, en sourtirent tous a honneur et grandissime loange. . . . Et en oultre furent feictes de moult belles et singulieres feinctes, dignes de memoire, que sceroient tropt longues a reciter, comme plus a plein sont notées audict livre an marge. . . . Considerant aussi la noblesse et belle compagnie que la estoit, et pour les bons pieurs tant hommes que femmes de toutes estimes; non obstant qu'il plouvoit chescune nuytée et matinée jusques a l'heure qu'on debvoit entrer, a laquelle survenoit le beau temps jusques a la fin, et ce tous les troys jours, qu'estoit a tous chouse miraculeuse et pour tieulle tenue. *Et en la fin dudict mistere furent retournées les chasses desdicts corps sainct et chief a ladicte esglise en procession generale, que la avoient estez durant ledict mistere,* avesquez gros chierges, en chantant: *Te Deum laudamus.*

10.2. Jean Bouchet, Epistle 91, cited by Petit de Julleville, "1535. Issoudun.—La Passion," in *LM*, 2:128–29.

> De toutes part, par un tressainct vouloir
> Qu'avons conceu, entreprendre et vouloir
> Jouer, monstrer, equiper et sus mettre
> Du Christ occis la tragedie en mettre,
> Qui est pour seur conclud et ordonné,
> Car ce bon Christ, cest an, nous a donné
> Tant de ses biens et par cy fait espandre
> Qu'il faut pour luy la pluspart en despendre. . . .
> Par quoy comme eulx appliquons nostre estude
> A eviter vice d'ingratitude.

10.3. *SBD*, chap. 27, "De l'adoration et service des sainctz," 168–70.

Le service, adoration et prieres faictes aux sainctz, et à tous aultres qui sont hors de ce monde, est une chose faicte sans foy, contre la parolle de Dieu. En quoy Dieu est deshonoré, en tant que son honneur est donné à la creature. Et faict on deshonneur aux sainctz, pource que contre ce qu'ilz ont faict, dit et enseigné, on ha recours à eulx. Car ilz ne veulent qu'on ayt fiance en eulx, mais en Dieu. Et ont defendu, selon la parolle de Dieu, toutes images qu'on faict pour honorer, et faire aulcune inclination devant icelles, toutes ces offrandes, chandelles, voeuz neufvaines et toutes ces manieres de faire, dequoy le monde est de present tout plein, ce que nostre Seigneur n'a point commandé, mais l'a defendu, tellement qu'il veult que ceulx qui ont trouvé ces choses soient mauldictz, voire mesmes quant seroient anges du ciel. . . .

Et ceulx qui disent que les sainctz sont noz intercesseurs, advocatz et moyenneurs entre Dieu et nous, le chemin, la vie et l'esperance, ilz blasphement, faisans oultrage aux sainctz et deshonneur à notre Seigneur Jesus. Lequel seul est nostre mediateur, qui intercede pour nous envers le Pere, nostre advocat, qui parle pour nous, le seul chemin, la vie et verité, et nul aultre.

10.4. Guillaume le Doyen, *Annales et chroniques du païs de Laval,* 133–34.

> Par lieux fust joué mysteres,
> Et mesmement en Avenieres
> Le mystere Monsieur St Blaise

A volée, où fust chascun aise
Pour l'espace de quatre jours
Ou Monsieur en vit tout le cours.
Mais durant le jeu, sans que huche,
Descendit une Coqueluche
Du pais d'amont juc à ce val,
Qui nous fist souffrir moult de mal;
Et prenoit en la teste et rains
Tant que par terre en jecta maints
Et des tirans joue le quart
Combien que du mal eu ma part.

10.5. *Mystère des Trois Doms*, ed. Giraud, "Introduction," vii–ix.

En 1787, les *Affiches du Dauphiné* en donnèrent une courte analyse,* reproduite la même année dans le *Journal de Paris*[†] et empruntée à ce dernier par l'*Esprit des journaux*.[‡] L'auteur de cet article est un romanais, qui s'est caché sous le voile de l'anonyme:[§]

. . . Il n'est pas possible, dans cette pièce, d'assigner le lieu principal de la scène, car il varie sans cesse; et la durée de l'action n'est pas renfermée entre deux soleils, car des émissaires entreprennent et terminent de longs voyages pendant le cours de la pièce. La scène, ensanglantée par le martyre des trois Doms, tantôt est à Rome, tantôt à Vienne, tantôt à Lyon, d'autres fois dans les Alpes; et cependant le théâtre représente sans cesse l'enfer et le paradis, l'Europe, l'Asie et l'Afrique, qui sont cantonnées dans trois tours. On y personnifie des êtres métaphysiques, par exemple: la *dame Silence* fait presque tous les frais du prologue; *Soulas humain*, *Grâce divine* et *Confort divin* donnent du secours aux héros de la pièce et de l'ennui à ceux qui la lisent. L'enfer vomit des diables, impatientants par leurs propos orduriers. Ces diables n'ont que des sottises à dire à la déesse Proserpine, qui, par un mélange singulier de la fable et de la religion révélée, vient aussi figurer sur le théâtre. . . .

L'auteur a flétri, dans cette pièce, la mémoire de *Getta*, du meurtre de *Papinien*, qui lui survécut, et tandis que tous les historiens s'accordent à dire que la mort de l'un et de l'autre fut le crime de *Caracalla*. Mais cette licence est supportable sous le rapport que l'on n'a jamais exigé, dans les pièces de théâtre, que l'histoire soit aussi fidelement suivie que dans *Rodrigue*. . . .

Les reliques des saints martyrs étaient aussi portées sur les théâtres de ces représentations. Il y a même sur leur translation une pièce en un acte, qui n'a pas été jouée. . . .

Cette pièce . . . fut suivie d'une procession générale et terminée par un *Te Deum*. Il est à présumer, sans doute, que nos bons aïeux croyoient sanctifier leurs plaisirs, en faisant servir la religion à tous leurs divertissements. Leur naïveté, en cela, mérite plutôt des éloges que du blâme.

*N° 12, du 20 juillet, XIVe année, p. 51.
†Année 1787, n° 264, p. 1143.
‡Decembre 1787, t. XII, p. 231–3.
§"Analyse d'un manuscrit peu connu et très-curieux, qui existe à Romans en Dauphiné, fait par M. *** de la même ville." Nous ne croyons pas à la sincérité de la rectification insérée dans le n° 13 des *Affiches* (p. 56^b), touchant l'origine de cet article.

10.6. Archives Communales de la Ville de Valence, ser. BB, 3, fols. 1r, 3r, 4r, 114, cited in *Mystère des trois doms*, ed. Giraud, 856.

Deliberaciones facte in domo civitatis, die tercia mensis julii, anno Domini M° quingentesimo. . . .

Et primo, quia instat tempus dierum sanctissime Penthecostes, quibus speratur, Deo dante, quod hystoria et misterium martirii gloriosorum trium martirum sanctorum Felicis, Fortunati et Achilei publice demonstrabitur in platea Clericorum hujus civitatis, fuit deliberatum quod requirantur domini de ecclesia ut dignentur, pro majori reverencia et honore debitis dictis tribus sanctis martiribus, facere deferri super loco fercium reliquiarum eorumdem, et quod ibi singulis diebus trium dierum Penthecostes per unum ex deputatis martiribus publice ante incoacionem misterii celebretur una missa, et quod non pulsentur vespere donec finito misterio cujuslibet diei; et ad hoc faciendum fuerunt commissi . . . qui super premissis requestam facere habeant.

10.7. *Mystère des Trois Doms*, ed. Giraud.

> TIERCE [Le tiers Chanoyne]
> Vecy propremant la teneur
> Du thumbeau ou gist Severin;
> Exupere y est, suis seur,
> Et Felicien le begnyn. (10412–15)

> PASCASE
> La chasse n'est pas trob pesante;
> S'il vous plaist, vous la pourterés . . .
> A Saint Romans presenterés
> La garde de ce relicquiere:
> Par ainssi Dieu contanterés . . . (10461–67)

> TIERCE
> Une chasse vous a donnée,
> Qu'on apporte tout maintenant,
> Laquelle veult que honnorée
> Soyt ycy continuellemant.
> Troys corps sains y font tenemant,
> De noveau pour luy relevés;
> Pour quoy apprestés vistemant
> Le lieu ou ilz soyent venerés. (10503–10)

10.8. *Mystère des Trois Doms*, ed Giraud, ci–cii.

Hélas! un jour vint où cette pieuse habitude de porter triomphalement en procession les reliques des trois saints dut mettre au coeur des Romanais un regret amer. Le 23 janvier 1524, fête de saint Barnard, la procession accoutumée eut lieu. Quatre jeunes gens portaient la triple châsse (*triarchum*)* qui renfermait les restes des martyrs. Tout à coup, dans la rue Saunerie, entre les maisons du chanoine François Odde et de noble Guillaume Tardivon, disent les livres capitulaires† qui n'oublient aucun détail, les jeunes gens, non par malice, mais à bout de forces, laissent tomber à terre leur précieux fardeau, qui se brise en deux parties. Les reliques de la châsse du milieu sont répandues sur le sol, au grand scandale du clergé et de tout le peuple, et il s'en dégage comme un nuage de poussière. On recueille en toute hâte ces saints débris et on les rapporte à l'église de Saint-Barnard. Le mardi suivant, 2 janvier,[‡] on se dirige processionellement vers le lieu du désastre. Les quatre jeunes gens tiennent chacun à la main, pour réparer leur faute involontaire, un cierge de quatre livres. Enfin le jeudi, 24 mars on dépose ce qu'il reste des reliques des trois *doms* derrière le grand autel de l'église collégiale, sous la châsse de saint Barnard.

*Faut-il la reconnaître dans cet article de l'inventaire du trésor de l'église de St-Barnard à la fin du XIIIᵉ siècle: "Tria vasa cristallina . . . ; in omnibus hiis continentur reliquie" (*Cartulaire*, f⁰ 185 v⁰; Giraud, *Essai*, 2ᵉ p., t. II, p. 110 *bis*)?

†P. 817–8.

‡Le ms. porte certainement par erreur "vigesima secunda januarii."

10.9. "Analyse d'un manuscrit . . . faite par M. M***," *Journal de Paris* 264 (21 September 1787): 1144.

Il semble que ce mélange du sacré & du profane le plus odieux & le plus indécent auroit dû corrompre les moeurs publiques & la foi; & il est bien singulier que l'on en tolérât la représentation; car la moralité d'une pièce de cette nature est sans doute bien difficile à saisir & à démêler. Il est vraisemblable que dans ce tems-là les impressions du mal étoient moins dangereuses; ces spectacles aujourd'hui seroient regardés, avec raison, comme très scandaleux.

Chapter 11. The Mysterious Quarry

11.1. *MAA*, 27–28.

Près du village de Doué (Maine-et-Loire) existait une carrière, qui fut aménagée en forme d'amphitéâtre [*sic*] au xvᵉ ou au début du xviᵉ siècle; on y donna des représentations de mystères, auxquelles Rabelais fait allusion au chapitre III du Tiers Livre et au chapitre XIII du Quart Livre. A la fin du xviᵉ siècle, elles avaient cessé, lorsque l'amphitéâtre fut exploré par un ami de Juste-Lipse. Celui-ci, le prenant pour une ruine romaine, lui fit place à la fin de son traité *De amphitheatris;* il y publia à l'appui de sa description deux curieux dessins datés de 1584, et termina par l'anecdote suivante, qui provient, elle aussi, de son ami: "On raconte qu'en 1539 ce grand roi François Iᵉʳ permit à des acteurs des environs qui jouaient les *Actes des Apôtres,* de se servir de cet amphithéâtre. Ils le nettoyèrent, l'ornèrent et il y vint une foule de spectateurs. Cette représentation qui dura trente jours, rapporta aux paysans un profit considérable. Aussi demandèrent-ils au roi d'interdire à l'avenir l'extraction des pierres à moins de trente perches de ce lieu. Car, par suite de nombreuses excavations, la ruine, si l'on n'avait pris cette mesure, n'eût pas tardé."

Cette tradition est-elle exacte? Ou bien est-ce une légende formée d'après les représentations de la *Passion* à Saumur et à Angers et celle des *Actes* à Bourges? Les détails sont précis et inspirent confiance; mais, bien que l'histoire de cet amphithéâtre ait été étudiée à fond et que l'on ait exploré les archives du Maine-et-Loire, on n'a retrouvé aucune autre mention de cet événement.*

*Au XVIᵉ siecle, on voyait sur la scène six ouvertures rondes par où les acteurs se rendaient aux deux salles souterraines de droite, et une ouverture centrale où était fiché un mât; un vélum était soutenu par les cordes qui étaient attachées au mât. M. Le Moy, le savant historien de l'Anjou, m'ap-prend que cet amphithéâtre a été restauré en 1924 et que des comédiens en tournée y donnent des représentations. Cf. H. Clouzot. *Le théâtre populaire de Doué en Anjou (Revue d'art dramatique,* 1902), et surtout Ol. Couffon, *L'amphithéâtre de Douces,* Laval (Extrait du *Bulletin de Mayenne-Sciences,* 1912 et 1913); cet ouvrage contient de nombreuses vues datant des quatres derniers siècles; elles sont éditées aussi, a Doué, par la maison Ogeard.

11.2. Justus Lipsius, *De amphitheatro liber* (Antwerp: Plantin, 1585), chap. 6, pp. 30–31.

Narrant regem vel heroëm potius, verè magnum Franciscum, anno domini [1539] circumforaneis quibusdam histrionibus, qui Apostolorum acta repraesentabant, permisisse hunc Amphitheatri locum ad spectacula ea edenda. Illos purgasse, ornasse, & magnum populum contraxisse. ex quo conventu, qui dies triginta perseveravit, multum atque uberem quaestum ad paganos redisse. Eâ re motos, impetrasse à rege, Nequis in posterum illic lapidem excîdisse vellet, propius ab eo Amphitheatro perticas xxxvi. Crebris enim effossionibus, absque eo interdicto fuisset, interitus iam imminebat huic loco. Tantum scivi, tantum audivi. Siquid aliter est: mendacium ego fortasse dixi, at non sum mentitus.

11.3. Chassanée, *Catalogus gloriae mundi,* p. 577 (original emphasis).

Nos autem Hedui, anno Domini 1516. excellens & magnificum amphitheatrum, in campo S. Lazari, qui est in medio civitatis nostrae construximus, & erat è ligno quadrato, artificio solemni fabrefactum, impensis Ecclesiae & civium, nec in Gallia fuit simile. Ducentenarias enim cellulas cum quadraginta in superiori parte habuit: parietibus è ligno intermediis divisas, & tabulatis coopertas, quae loca erant viris Ecclesiasticis, Nobilibus, Senatoribus, Equitibus, & Gentilibus, civium patritiis. In cavea vero, seu inferiori parte, erant gradus & sedilia ita disposita, ut altiora in ambitu semper excrescerent, ubi plebs promiscue sedebat, quae habuit & velaria lintea, quibus substantes seu subsidentés adumbrabantur, ne à pluvia offenderentur. Etiam ludentes in medio Caveae, seu Theatralis Scenae, iisdem tantum tegebantur, quos fossa aquis vallata, & aliis obstaculis, à plebeiis discriminabat. In eo amphitheatro octoginta millia hominum non gravate collocari poterant, & quia indicta fuerant spectacula finitimis, spectatores propre infiniti affuerunt, quae spectacula fuerunt excellentissima, causa divi Lazari, patroni Heduorum, facta, ubi vita eiusdem dignis versibus non ad Pompam, sed ad divinae maiestatis laudem, & beati Lazari, vehementissimè & gratis, quatuor diebus, recitata fuit. Unde à Deo datum est, ut nulla exsibilatio, nulla plebis consternatio, aut derisiorè quid gestum fuerit, & licet nocte plueret, tota die tamen, nulla aëris serenitas maior, iisdem diebus visa fuit, de quo aliquid iam supra tetigi *in 60. consid. & in praced. par. in 52. consid.*

11.4. *MAA,* 78–79.

Signalons enfin une magnifique représentation, mentionnée par Chaumeau et qui a dû avoir lieu vers 1515, puisque l'historien berrichon qui vivait encore en 1560, y avait assisté: Louis XII, dit-il, résidait souvent à Bourges, et

"il s'accorda avec les bourgeois de Bourges que l'histoire de la *Passion* fut jouée à Bourges en telle pompe et solennité, par l'espace de plusieurs jours, au lieu du théâtre, appellé fosse des Arenes, qui contenoit tous les jours vingt cinq ou trente mille personnes que j'ose bien affermer n'avoir jamais veu telle sumptuosité en habitz, richesses, grace de joueurs, et grandeur de la chose enrichie, et de fainctes admirables."*

*Histoire de Berry, 1556, p. 156.

11.5. Vinchant, *Annales de la province et comté du Hainaut,* 5:267. (See also above, app. 8.5.)

Quand il advenoit que les pasteurs ou autres théologiens en leurs prosnes ou prédications réfutoient et blasmoient leurs erreurs et abus, on disoit d'eux communément qu'ils estoient les Scribes et Pharisiens qui empeschoient la populace d'aller au Christ et de s'approcher de luy. Bref, durant les guerres entre l'empereur et le roy de France, les marchands des Pays-Bas, qui traffiquoient ès pays voisins, où il y avoit des hérétiques, apportoient d'Allemagne le luthéranisme, le calvinisme de France, et de Wesphale et Frise-Orientale l'anabaptisme, et ont à la parfin incité tellement les pauvres gens à estre hérétiques, par dons et autres moyens, qu'aucuns d'eux ne leur bailloient point d'ouvrage, sinon à condition qu'ils iroient aux presches des ministres huguenots.

Ce discours est véritable, car j'ay ouy gens anciens et dignes de foy dire d'avoir vu la plus-part des choses susdites se pratiquer en la ville de Mons durant leur jeunesse.

Chapter 12. Seeing Is Believing

12.1. *HV,* 395–97.

Ces niaisieries là, & ces folles despenses eussent esté aucunement tolerables, si l'honneur de Dieu n'y eust point esté interessé, voire mais le Diable, dont les intentions ne visent qu'à iouer des tragedies honteuses à Dieu, & lamentables aux hommes: pretendoit par ces fadaises d'ouvrir la porte aux sacrileges de Luther, & de Calvin, lardant ces comedies, & spectacles d'entre-ieux, & farces profanes: qui mettoient au rabais la dignité des choses sacrées, & des Ministres de l'Eglise. . . .

Aux festes de la Pentecoste de l'an M. D. XLVII. [1547] les principaux bourgeois de la ville representerent sur le Theatre en la maison du Duc d'Arschot (où est à present la cour de derriere de la maison de l'Aucteur),* la Vie, mort, & Passion de Nostre Seigneur, en vingtcinc iournées; en chacune desquelles l'on fit paroistre[†] des choses estranges, & pleines d'admiration. Les secrets du Paradis, & de l'Enfer estoient tout à faict prodigieux, & capables d'estre pris par la populace pour enchantemens. Car l'on voyoit la Verité, les Anges, & divers autres personnages descendre de bien haut, tantost visiblement, autrefois comme invisibles, puis paroistre tout à coup; de l'Enfer Lucifer s'eslevoit, sans qu'on vist comment, porté sur un Dragon. La Verge de Moyse, de seche, & stérile, iettoit à coup des fleurs, & des fruicts; les ames de Herodes, & de Iudas estoient emportées en l'air par les Diables; les Diables chassés des corps, les hydropiques & autres malades gueris, le tout d'une façon admirable. Icy Iesus Christ estoit eslevé du Diable, qui rampoit le long d'une muraille plus de quarante pieds de haut: là il se rendoit invisible: ailleurs il se transfiguroit sur la montaigne de Thabor. On y vit l'eau changée en vin, mais[‡] si mysterieusement, qu'on ne le pouvoit croire: & plus de cent personnes de l'auditoire voulurent gouster de ce vin; les cinc pains, et les deux poissons y furent semblablement multipliés, & distribués à plus de mille personnes: nonobstant quoy il y en eut douze corbeilles de reste. Le figuier maudit par nostre Seigneur parut seche,[§] & les fueilles flestries en un instant. L'eclypse, le terre tremble, le brisement des pierres, & les autres miracles advenus à la mort de Nostre Sauveur furent representés avec des nouveaux miracles. La foule y fut si grande, pour l'abord des estrangers, qui y vindrent de France, de Flandre, & d'ailleurs: que la recepte monta iusques à la somme de quattre mille six cens & quattre-vingts livres: combien que les spectateurs ne payassent qu'un liart, ou six deniers chacun. Les vers furent du depuis imprimés à Paris, sans le nom des Aucteurs.**

*Petit de Julleville omits this parenthetical remark (*LM*, 2:155).—JE.
†*On* vit *paraître* (*LM*, 2:155).—JE.
‡Petit de Julleville has *mais* (*LM*, 2:156).—JE.
§*séché* (*LM*, 2:156).—JE.
***sous le nom des Aucteurs* (*LM*, 156).—JE.

12.2. Jean Bouchet, Epistle 90, cited by Petit de Julleville, "1534. Poitiers. La Passion," in *LM*, 2:125 (my emphasis).

> J'ay veu jouer ces mysteres trois foys
> Dont suis content, veu mes ans, toutesfois
> Desire fort, disant mes patenostres
> De veoir jouer les Actes des Apostres,
> Parce que c'est la prosecution
> Du fruict tant doulx de celle passion
> De Jesu Christ, voire la forme et guise
> Comme a esté plantée saincte Eglise.
> Il est tout vray que les voy par escript
> Et oy prescher; *plus content est l'esprit*
> *De veoir qu'ouyr; la chose qu'on voit vifve,*
> *Icelle oyant, est plus apprehensive.*

12.3. *SBD*, chap. 27, "De l'adoration et service des sainctz," 170–72.

Les miracles et aultres choses qui sont advenues ne nous doibvent mouvoir aulcunement, pour nous tirer hors de la parolle de Dieu et prendre aultre foy et creance que selon la parolle de Dieu. . . . Nostre bon maistre Jesus nous a assez adverty des miracles qui debvoient estre faictz au temps de l'Antechrist; lequel a tout changé et destruict, tellement qu'il n'est rien demouré pur sur la terre. Et cecy debvoit venir par faulx prophetes, faulx instructeurs et docteurs de mensonges; qui au lieu de edifier par verité, ont destruict par mensonges en faulx signes et miracles pour la seduction de ceulx qui n'ont creu la verité. Car qui bien y regarderoit, on ne trouveroit aulcun vray miracle, mais toute tromperie et de deception pour attraper argent. Et Dieu, pour les siens, affin qu'ilz reviennent et retournent à la lumiere de verité, et pour la condemnation des infideles qui ne veulent regarder que "par avarice le service des sainctz et toute telle seduction a esté introduicte et les miracles controuvez et faictz," n'a-il pas demonstré et revelé en plusieurs lieux la faulseté des miracles et des inventeurs d'iceulx? En quoy nous congnoissons le jugement de Dieu et sa vengeance sur les idolatres. Lesquelz advertyz de telles tromperies veulent neantmoins perseverer en leurs iniquitez, sans soy retourner au vray Dieu.

12.4. *HP*, 139–40 (original emphasis).

Le dimanche 26 novembre 1559, on joue une farce qui mettait en scène un *badin* et *ung qui représentoit le monde. Au beau milieu de cette pièce, le monde demandoit au badin de quel estat qu'il demandoit à estre pour mieulx vivre au monde . . . ; l'estat de prestise luy fust mis en avant, le badin demandoit si on ne ouvroit point estant prebstre et après que le monde eust respondu que non, le badin disoit qu'il voulloit doncq estre prebtre et que estant prebtre aroit bon temps et hanteroit les filles, le jeu.* . . . Les deux dimanches suivants, l'*histoire d'Helie et Jesabel* fut représentée. Ce fut l'occasion de nouvelles attaques. L'auteur avait mis dans la bouche du prophète la tirade suivante: *Vous avez délaissié le Dieu vif pour adorer le dieu Bal et voz idolles qui n'ont aulcunes vertuz pour garir maladies qu'il soit. Vous faictes des dieux de bois de pierre, de plaestre, de arain et images. Ils ont des oelz et ne voyent goutte et aultres membres dont ne se peullent ayder. Vous allumés des chandelles contre le commandement de Dieu, lequel veult estre adoré seul.* L'acteur ayant répété plusieurs fois les mots *estre adoré seul,* un spectateur s'écria *Vela qui touche,* tandis que d'autres se mettaient à discuter des *hérésies* déclarant, par exemple, *qu'il n'y avoit purgatoire et que on estoit bien en ung purgatire en ce monde et que on povoit bien mengier chair en tout temps moyennant que on n'en fist des excès* et ajoutant que *si on faisoit l'office en l'église en franchois, lez gens y iroient plus volentiers.** Ainsi le théâtre a donné l'occasion aux protestants tournaisiens d'exposer publiquement et sans grands dangers certaines de leurs idées et de les faire adopter par une partie de leur concitoyens.

**Idem.* Déposition des Tournaisiens Antonine Playart et Sébastien Plouquet. [A.G.R., *Etat et Audience,* no. 1712/3, Acte du 14 decembre 1559 (139n).]

12.5. *JBT,* ed. Moreau, 311–13.

Et quant iceulx theologiens luy demanderent qu'il sentoit du Sainct Sacrement de l'autel, de la messe, de la consecration, de l'adoration de la saincte ostie, du purgatoire, de la veneration des saincts, du liberal arbitre, des bonnes oeuvres, de la justification, des ymaiges, du baptesme, des voeuz, de la confession auriculaire, de la virginité de la vierge Marie.

A ces demandes il respondit que le vray corps et sang de Christ estoit là receu non de bouce, ains d'esprit par foy et que la substance du pain et vin n'estoit en riens chambgée. Mais, quant, selon l'institution de Christ, la cene est distribuée à l'assemblée des chrestiens en langue vulgaire adfin que tous en entendent l'usaige et le fruict, lors le pain et le vin sont vrayement consacréz asscavoir par les parolles de Christ, car ce grondement duquel les prebtres usent envers le pain et le vin est mieulx seant aux sorciers et enchanteurs que aux crestiens.

La messe papalle (disoit il) ne s'acorde en riens avecq la cene du seigneur, mais est un service controuvé par les hommes au deshonneur et oultraige de Christ. L'adoration du pain consacré est vraye ydolatrie, car là la creature est adorée au lieu du createur. Il ne sçait et ne cerche aultre purgatoire que le sang de Christ, lequel ne nous pardonne seullement la coulpe, ains aussy la peine deue à noz pechéz. Partant les messes et aultres prieres pour les morts sont choses perdues et blasphematoires pour ce qu'elles sont instituées sans la parolle de Dieu. . . .

Il est fort dangereulx pour l'idolatrie de laisser les imaiges aux temples. . . .

Chascun doit confesser ses pechéz à Dieu et reclamer sa mercy; s'il advient aussy que la conscience ayt quelque scrupule, il fault demander conseil au ministre de l'Eglise pour recevoir consolation. Au regard de la confession auriculaire, elle n'est fondée en l'Escripture et n'est possible de s'en acquiter, mais est une gehenne des consciences merveilleusement dangereuse.

Chapter 13. The Suicide of Despair

13.1. *HM,* 210–13.

Faisons ici une observation à propos des tristes spectacles que cette histoire nous a présentés, et qu'elle nous offrira encore. Si l'histoire, l'histoire vraie, est en général très-mal édifiante, il faut remarquer que le bien est peu bruyant et peu empressé de se faire valoir. Le mal au contraire frappe beaucoup plus les yeux et les esprits, ses effets sont retentissants: il occupe l'attention publique et par conséquent prend plus de place dans le souvenir des peuples, et dans les pages des écrivains.

Tandis qu'on donnait à la population de Meaux ces spectacles si cruellement lugubres, elle s'en préparait de plus propres à réjouir et les yeux et l'esprit. Elle se construisait, avant qu'il y en eût à Paris, un théâtre pour des représentations dramatiques. Théâtre un peu éphémère, car il n'était qu'en bois, et couvert de toile comme un cirque de l'antiquité, mais dont la description conservée par Rochard, ne laisse pas que de donner une idée assez considérable. Il était situé où est maintenant le collége:

> "Il était creux par-dessous, par le moyen de quoi se faisaient de belles machines y ayant gens expérimentés pour cet effet. Les réprésentations durèrent deux années excepté les hivers. Le premier été, ledit théâtre était couvert de toile, quoiqu'il fût grand, mais cela ne dura guère en ce qu'elle fut rompue du vent non obstant qu'il y eût grande quantité de cordes par-dessus et par-dessous. Le circuit dudit théâtre était haut et fait par degrés de planches, et au haut il y avait des loges tout autour fermant à clef, lesquelles étaient louées à des habitants de Meaux."

Ce n'étaient pas des acteurs de profession qui donnaient des représentations sur ce théâtre, mais bien des gens de la ville qui y jouaient des *Mystères* tant de l'ancien que du nouveau Testament. Les représentations n'en étaient pas moins très-suivies, le chroniqueur ajoute que c'était quelque chose de beau et de bon à voir, et que cela attira à Meaux grand nombre de peuple de toutes parts. La première représentation eut lieu le 1er mai 1547. Nous ferons deux remarques au sujet de ce théâtre: c'est que le goût du spectacle n'était pas alors nouveau à Meaux; ensuite que les pièces étaient soumises à la censure, car dès vingt ans avant, en 1527, l'évêque Briçonnet avait défendu ces représentations dans son diocèse, à moins que les pièces n'eussent été auparavant examinées par lui ou par ses grands vicaires.

Après deux années de représentations et malgré leur succès, le théâtre fut démoli et le terrain vendu; l'on ne voit pas que les jeux de la scène aient été repris de longtemps à Meaux. Peut-être la fin misérable de plusieurs des gens qui y avaient pris part en fut-elle la cause, fin qui dans le récit du chroniqueur semble un peu tourner à la légende. Suivant ce récit, en effet, ceux qui avaient fait les personnages de diables moururent fort pauvres, celui qui avait joué le rôle de Satan, un nommé Pascalus, auquel le sobriquet de *Diable* était resté, fut pendu, et celui qui avait représenté le *Désespoir* s'empoisonna lui-même.

Sans trop vouloir dépoétiser la légende, on pourrait remarquer que ceux qui avaient fait les démons étaient de pauvres diables auxquels la passion scénique avait fait prendre en désaffection leur métier ordinaire, ainsi que l'auteur l'insinue lui-même; et quant à Pascalus, nous le verrons plus tard jouant, au sèrieux, dans les troubles religieux et civils un rôle dangereux,* qui pouvait bien, comme cela arriva en effet, le conduire au gibet, abstraction faite de ses antécédents diaboliques.

*Petit de Julleville has rendered this as "un rôle *plus* dangereux" (*LM*, 2:144).—JE.

13.2. Mémoires manuscrits sur la ville de Meaux par Rochard, cited by Lebert, "Le Théâtre à Meaux," xix.

L'an 1547 fut représenté audit Meaux, par personnages, plusieurs misteres, tant du vieux que du nouveau Testament. La première représentation en fut faite le premier jour de may;

c'estoit quelque chose de beau et de bon à voir; cela attira audit Meaux grand nombre de peuple de toute part. Le théâtre estoit dans la rue Poitevine, au lieu ou a esté le colege et ou est de présent le couvent des religieuses Ursulines, lequel théâtre estoit creux par dessous, par le moyen de quoy se fesoient de belles machines, y ayant gens experimentez pour cet effet. Les dites réprésentations durèrent deux années, excepté les hivers. Le premier esté, ledit théâtre estoit couvert de toile, quoyqu'il fut grand, mais cela ne dura guère en ce qu'elle fut rompue du vent, nonobstant qu'il y eut grande quantité de cordes par dessus et par dessous. Le circuit dudit théâtre estoit haut et fait par degré de planches, et au haut il y avait des loges tout autour fermantes a clefs, lesquelles estoient louées à des habitants dudit Meaux. Il se trouva auxdittes représentations des habitants dudit Meaux qui fesoient fort bien leurs personnages et estoient tellement affectionnés qu'ils préféroient ces exercices à leurs ouvrages ordinaires; dont plusieurs en devinrent gueux. Et ce que l'on a remarqué de plus singulier, c'est que ceux qui fesoient les personnages de diables moururent fort pauvres; celui qui joua Satan fut depuis pendu et celuy qui représentoit le désespoir s'empoisonna luy-même.

13.3. Petit de Julleville, "1507. Châlons-sur-Marne.—La Passion," in *LM*, 2:91.

La *Passion* fut jouée à Châlons-sur-Marne, en 1507. Une délibération du conseil de ville datée du lundi 3 mai de cette année* fournit sur cette représentation des détails curieux:

> Item a esté fete requeste par cellui qui joue le personnage de Lucifer qui est povre, que aucuns de messieurs qui ne jouent le veuillent aider a acoustrer. . . .
>
> Messieurs les abbez, bailly de Chaalons et plusieurs gens de bien dudit Chaalons qui ne jouent point se sont offert et ont promis d'acoustrer a leurs despens cellui qui joue le personnage de Lucifer pour ce qu'il est pouuvre et bon joueur.

*Communication due à l'obligeance de M. Pelicier, archiviste de la Marne.

13.4. Jean Michel, *Le Mystère de la Passion (Angers 1486)*, ed. Jodogne.

DESESPERANCE
Oeuvre ton cueur et metz dedens
de[se]sperance et tu n'as garde;
abrege ta vie et te pends:
vecy ung las que je te garde. . . . (23797–800)

Or tien, regarde mes atours.
Suis je pas pourveue d'oultis
bien ingenÿeux et soubtilz,
s'ung homme est cautelleux et fin,
pour le mectre bientost a fin?
Choisy sur moy [tous] les plus beaux!
Vecy dagues, vecy cousteaux,
forcettes, poinçons, allumelles;
advise, choisy les plus belles
et celle de meilleure forge
pour te coupper a cop la gorge.

Ycy prent Des[es]perance une dague en sa main et la monstre a Judas.

Tien cestuy cy, frappe en ta pance
et luy fourres jusques au manche.

Ycy luy monstre ung cordeau.

Ou, si tu aymes mieulx te pendre,
vecy las et cordes a vendre
pour se estrangler tout a ung cop.
Que actens tu? Tu demeures trop;
bas le fer tandis qu'il est chault. . . . (23821–38)

JUDAS
Je te requiers que tu me pendes.

DESESPERANCE
A celle fin que trop n'atendes,
ce las ycy me chergeras
et, pour acquicter tes amendes,
toy mesmes propre te pendras.

JUDAS
Je le vueil, mais tu m'ayderas
pour me despecher plus en haste. . . . (23846–52)

DESESPERANCE
Monte sus et je t'aideray.

JUDAS
A ce seur ycy me pendray
de mes propres mains par le coul,
mais avant nouray mon licoul
et y feray ung las courant.

DESESPERANCE
Monte hault, pense au demourant;
j'ayderay a porter le fais.

Ycy monte Judas au hault d'un arbre foullu de branches de seur et Desesperance monte avec luy pour luy aider et les dyables demeurent au bas. . . . (23857–64)

SATHAN
Il souffist.
Tu renonces a ton pardon
et a tout espoir?

JUDAS *atache sa corde*
Se fais mon
et me vueil, en despit de Dieu,
pendre et estrangler en ce lieu,
moy mesmes, de mes propres mains,
et estre dampné pour le mains,
sans espoir de misericorde.
Moy mesme atacheray la corde,

despitant la digne bonté.
    O grefve ponderosité *Pause*
de raige que mon cueur deporte,
il fault que desormais te porte
en eternelle desplaisance!
Haulte tour de Desesperance,
bastillee de pleurs piteux,
couverte de crys despiteux
et enclose de mur pardurable,
faicte et forgee du grand dyable,
environnee de puis parfons,
d'abismes sans rive ne fons,
dont les salles pour tout solas
sont pleines de immortelz helas,
actens moy, redoubté manoir,
et me fais dedens toy manoir,
actens moy, tres orrible gouffre,
car, sans fin, en l'eternel souffre,
languiray de mort rigoreuse.
Actens moy, chartre doloreuse,
fourneau de feu noir ardant,
fosse de serpens habandont,
riviere de puant bourbier,
a mon gref deul et destourbier,
par dedans toy, plunger m'en voys.
Mais, au partir, a haulte voix,
dyables, dyables petis et grans,
corps et ame vous recommans;
au dyable soye je commandé.

Ycy se pend Judas et les dyables sont desoubz luy (23913–50)

13.5. Arnoul Gréban, *Le Mystère de la Passion,* ed. Jodogne.

JUDAS

Desesperance, beste horrible,
te semble mon cas si terrible
qu'il me tient le cueur a mercy?

DESESPERANCE

Il est de legier entendible
qu'a ton pechié est impossible
de jamais acquerir mercy.

JUDAS

Helas, mon maistre est tant begnin
et a pardonner tant enclin:
se j'aloye mercy prïer,
le me pardonrroit il?

DESESPERANCE
Nennin,
car qui sert de couvert venin,
la mort le suit pour son loyer.

JUDAS
Jamés ne l'oÿs sermonner
fors de pardonner, pardonner:
c'est signe qu'il ayme le don. . . .
Las, vrayëment l'ay je trahy
et a son mand desobëy;
mais pitié est an sa commande.

DESESPERANCE
Mais tu es de luy tant haÿ
que de t'oser veoir devant luy,
oncques ne fut honte plus grande. . . . (21763–86)
Riens n'y vault le braire
n'a mercy retraire:
va t'en brief, ta mort portraire,
de ton bon gré vouluntaire
faire et taire;
il te fault passer ce pas. . . . (21875–80)

JUDAS
Puisque desesperer me fault
et priver de toute esperance
et que le don d'espoir me fault,
je n'ay plus mestier d'asseurance.
Abrege moy, Desesperance:
il est temps qu'a ma mort entendes. . . . (21899–904).
Deables horribles et deffais,
tourbe villaine et interdicte,
orde compaignie maudite
en enffer pardurablement,
je ne fais autre testament
sinon qu'en l'eternelle flame,
vous habandonne corps et ame.
A vous me rens, a vous me donne,
a vous m'oblige et habandonne
sans jamais espoir d'eschapper (21927–36).

Chapter 14. Death by Drama

14.1. *HTB*, 14–15 (original emphasis).

Après l'abdication de son père, le roi Philippe II fit, en cette même année 1549, son entrée solennelle à Tournai. La ville se surpassa pour recevoir dignement ce prince. Dans les registres de la ville, se trouve une longue description de tout ce qui décorait les rues: arcs-de-triomphe, fontaines, théâtres, etc.

On représenta des mystères sur ces théâtres, et si l'on s'en rapporte à une certaine relation manuscrite, on y donna celui de Judith et Holopherne, avec un réalisme qui n'a pas encore été atteint dans les temps modernes, où cependant l'on se pique d'être à l'apogée dans l'espèce. Voici cette relation:

> Jean de Bury et Jean de Crehan, jurés chargés de la décoration des rues, avaient imaginé de *rendre au naturel* l'exploit biblique de Judith; en conséquence, on avait choisi un criminel condamné à être tenaillé pour remplir le rôle d'Holopherne; ce malheureux, coupable de plusieurs assassinats et convaincu d'hérésie, avait préféré la décapitation à l'horrible supplice auquel il était condamné, espérant peut-être qu'une jeune fille n'aurait ni la force, ni le courage de lui couper la tête; mais les jurés ayant eu la même appréhension, avaient substitué à la véritable Judith un jeune garçon condamné au bannissement et auquel on promit sa grâce, s'il jouait bien son rôle. En effet, lorsque Philippe s'approcha du théâtre où l'on représentait le mystère, la prétendue Judith dégaina un cimeterre bien affilé, et, saisissant les cheveux d'Holopherne qui feignait de dormir, lui appliqua un seul coup, avec tant d'adresse et de vigueur que la tête fut séparée du corps. Aux flots de sang qui s'élancèrent du col du supplicié, des applaudissements frénétiques et des cris d'indignation s'élevèrent du milieu des spectateurs, le jeune prince resta seul impassible, regardant avec curiosité les convulsions du décapité et disant aux seigneurs qui l'accompagnaient: *bien frappé.* Ce sang froid du prince, devant cette horreur, pouvait faire présager les cruautés qui signalèrent son règne. On dit même qu'il attacha à sa personne, le jeune homme qui avait si bien frappé, et qu'il l'employa à des actes secrets d'iniquité.*

Toutefois, si un acte aussi barbare avait pu se produire en plein public et devant même le roi, celui-ci ne se montra pas toujours aussi tolérant. En 1552, les consaux reçurent l'ordre du souverain de ne plus permettre dorénavant "aucun jeu" sans avoir fait examiner par l'official, ou juge ecclésiastique, délégué par l'évêque, quelle était la composition du répertoire des comédiens qui voulaient obtenir licence de jouer en ville.[†]

Les magistrats tinrent cependant peu compte de cette invitation.

*Manuscrit inédit de feu M. H. Delmotte, père.
[†]*Bullet. de la Soc. Hist. de Tournai.*

14.2. *HTF,* 13:403n.

Ce qui peut encore les rebuter davantage, (ajoute l'Auteur) c'est qu'étant accoutumés à forger des évenemens qui n'ont ni suite ni vraisemblance, à donner de grands noms historiques aux fictions fabuleuses, & à confondre ainsi la vérité & le mensonge, ils n'osent avec raison traiter des sujets qu'on ne peut altérer sans une espece de sacrilége. Ils ignorent le talent d'inventer, ou en font un mauvais usage. Ils ne sçavent pas qu'il consiste à parer la vérité, non à la défigurer; à l'enrichir, non à la deshonnorer, & et qu'enfin le secours des Episodes doit soutenir les sujets, & non pas les étouffer.

N O T E S

Prologue

1. *Vanishing Hitchhiker* (hereafter *VH*), xi–xii; see also Brunvand, "Urban Legends," 572. Brunvand's eight books on urban legends are culled largely from his syndicated newspaper column. The *Smithsonian* article was Wolkomir, "If Those Cobras Don't Get You, the Alligators Will," a profile of Brunvand himself.

2. For a résumé of these legends, see *VH*, 90–101; also Brunvand, *Baby Train* (hereafter *BT*), 255; and Dickson and Goulden, *There are Alligators*, 1–3.

3. See also Brunvand, *Choking Doberman* (hereafter *CD*), 118–27. A variation on the mouse in the Coke bottle is the severed digits in the soup can (*VH*, 81–84).

4. See, however, the image of a deep-fried chicken head allegedly served by McDonalds in "News Quiz," *Time*, 11 December 2000

5. Brunvand, *Mexican Pet* (hereafter *MP*), 21–23. For a poetic meditation on a similar subject, see Charles Baudelaire, "Le Joujou du Pauvre," *Spleen de Paris*, in *Oeuvres complètes*, ed. Pichois, 1:304–5.

6. For the medieval period, "French theater" denotes the art form of at least two countries, France and Belgium.

7. PERFORM is an electronic discussion group devoted to all medieval performance genres. Founded in May 1992 by Clifford Flanigan and Jesse Hurlbut, it now boasts over four hundred subscribers.

8. Hurlbut, posting to PERFORM, 31 January 1995. I too fell for it, recirculating the tale as fact in my *Rhetoric and the Origins of Medieval Drama* (hereafter *ROMD*), 103.

9. As told by Faber, *Histoire du théâtre en Belgique* (hereafter *HTB*), 14–15; see below, chapter 14.

10. *Pour une dramaturgie* (hereafter *PDMA*), 19.

11. I *did* write it up in "Medieval Snuff Drama."

12. "Simulacra and Simulations," in *Selected Writings* (hereafter *SW*), trans. Poster, 178.

13. *Writing of History* (hereafter *WH*), 47.

14. Burke, *Philosophy of Literary Form*, 119.

15. *Role Playing and Identity* (hereafter *RPI*), 258.

16. *Stages of Terror* (hereafter *ST*), 162.

17. On the Baudrillardian mystification of death, see Butterfield, "Ethical Value and Negative Aesthetics"; and also Ariès, *Western Attitudes toward Death*.

18. On the philology of *histoire*, see Le Goff, *History and Memory*, 101–3. This philological complexity makes France an especially rich site for exploring our questions.

19. See below, chap. 14, for the full account. The subject was dramatized in 1999 in the film *8MM* (see Roeper, *Urban Legends*, 145–47). On snuff films, see, for example, Johnson and Schae-

fer, "Soft Core/Hard Gore"; McConahay, "Pornography"; Schechner, "News, Sex, and Performance Theory," chap. 7 of *Between Theater and Anthropology* (hereafter *BTA*); Landess, "Snuff Film"; and Kerekes and Slater, *Killing for Culture.*

20. For compelling analyses of this phenomenon, see Diehl, *Staging Reform* (hereafter *SR*) and Kobialka, *This Is My Body* (hereafter *TMB*), discussed below. On the debate about sources, see Breisach, *Historiography*, 161.

21. See "The Baby-sitter and the Man Upstairs," *VH*, 53–57; or "The Hippie Baby-sitter" (*VH*, 65–69). In the latter, years before the film *The Hand That Rocks the Cradle*, a babysitter puts her charge in the microwave. Contemporary France now regales itself with mostly *American* urban legends in Campion-Vincent and Renard, *Légendes urbaines.*

22. "C'est aux Spectacles qu'une Nation se fait le mieux connoître, & découvre son esprit sans y songer" (Clément, *Anecdotes dramatiques* [hereafter *AD*], iii). On this topos, see also Kruger, *National Stage*, chap. 1.

23. *Medieval Popular Culture* (hereafter *MPC*), xix. Spiegel makes a similar point in *Romancing the Past*, 10.

24. See editor Gérard Moreau's footnote (xvi) in *Journal d'un bourgeois de Tournai* (hereafter *JBT*).

25. See especially Moreau, *Histoire du protestantisme* (hereafter *HP*); and Parker, *Dutch Revolt.*

26. See *JBT*, 333–59; and Cloquet, *Tournai et Tournaisis*, 33.

27. On the Judith plays, see below, chapter 14, n. 29.

28. See *HTB*, 15n; and Hurlbut, posting to PERFORM, 3 February 1995.

29. On the FOAF, see, for example, *VH*, xi. At the SNOPES website or "FOAF Newsletter," one finds that the Internet is a burgeoning site for the dissemination, investigation, and interpretation of urban legends.

30. I refer to her book of the same title, and to her magnificent *Return of Martin Guerre.*

31. We shall see in the introduction that this is a question of "performativity," as understood by J. L. Austin in *How to Do Things with Words* (hereafter *HDTW*); and *Philosophical Papers* (hereafter *PP*), chap. 10.

32. Goffman, *Frame Analysis* (hereafter *FA*), 15.

33. Coldewey makes a similar point in "Thrice-Told Tales," 25.

34. On the ideology of the anecdote, see Gallagher and Greenblatt, *Practicing New Historicism*, chap. 2; and the earlier work of Taylor, "The Anecdote"; and Thompson, "Unfinished Business."

35. Greenblatt, *Shakespearean Negotiations*, 1.

36. Wilkinson, "Choice of Fictions," 80, which appeared in a special issue of *PMLA* devoted entirely to "The Status of Evidence."

37. Schmitt, *Holy Greyhound*, 234; also cited in *MPC*, xvii. See also Bristol, "Theater and Popular Culture."

38. *HYL*, 204. Greig retells urban legends in short story form. He too is waiting to have his name filled in: the dust jacket informs us that "Francis Greig is the pseudonym of an English poet and critic who, in this his first book of prose, wishes to remain anonymous."

39. *There Are Alligators*, 134; reprised at greater length in *Myth-Informed*, 149–58.

40. As Boureau shows in his exquisitely researched *Lord's First Night*, a contemporary culture immersed in claims of sexual harassment may find it more politically expedient, for example, to believe in something like the *droit de cuissage* (introduction). Or a medieval culture may believe in the seemingly indisputable "reality" of the myth of Pope Joan (Boureau, *Myth of Pope Joan*). See also Nora on the mythic origins of "chauvinism," "From *Lieux de mémoire*," xxi.

41. Brunvand, *Too Good to Be True* (hereafter *TGT*), 451. Indeed, Campion-Vincent and Renard curiously claim that "everything is a symbol in these stories" ("tout est symbole dans ces histoires"), *Légendes urbaines*, 340.

42. See act 2, scene 2 of any edition of Shakespeare's *Hamlet*.

43. Each makes the point in a different way, States in *Great Reckonings in Little Rooms* (hereafter *GR*), chap. 1; and Wilshire *RPI*, prol. and chap. 1.

44. Propp, *Theory and History of Folklore*, 6; his emphasis.

45. See, for example, Aarne, *Types of the Folktale;* and Briggs, *Dictionary of British Folk-Tales.* For an accessible introduction to the folklorist's methods, the generalist will enjoy Dundes, *Folklore Matters;* and Dundes, ed., *Study of Folklore;* or Flahault, *Interprétation des contes.* Specific approaches to the interplay between medieval literature and folklore include Walter, "Myth and Text in the Middle Ages"; and Mandel and Rosenberg, eds., *Medieval Literature and Folklore Studies.*

46. I refer to the remarkable storytelling abilities of Davis, *Return of Martin Guerre;* Boureau, *Lord's First Night* and *Myth of Pope Joan;* and Le Roy Ladurie, *Beggar and the Professor* and *Carnival in Romans.*

47. *Question and Answer*, 7.

48. Davis, *Fiction in the Archives*, 3–4.

49. See especially "Symbolic Function and Imitation," in *Essential Piaget*, ed. Gruber and Vonèche, 661–62. For anthropological and ethnographic approaches to performance, see Carlson, *Performance*, chap. 2 and conclusion; and Schechner, *Performance Theory*, chaps. 1 and 4. On human beings as natural performers, see, for example, Turner, *Dramas, Fields, and Metaphors*, 123; and Walton, *Mimesis as Make-Believe.*

50. The dark side of intellectual fun is a leitmotif of Bronner's *Piled Higher and Deeper*, chap. 4.

51. See Isidore of Seville (c. 570–636), *Etymologiarum*, ed. Lindsay, book 18.41. See also both Plato and Tertullian (c. A.D. 160–225) on the corrupting nature of the theater: *Republic*, ed. and trans. Shorey, 605; *De spectaculis*, ed. and trans. Glover, chap. 17. For an introduction, see Barish, *Anti-theatrical Prejudice*, chaps. 1–3; and for the debates surrounding the NEA and NEH, see Steiner, *Scandal of Pleasure*, introd.

52. *Tragédie religieuse en France* (hereafter *TRF*), ix.

53. Even *Medievalism and the Modernist Temper*, ed. Bloch and Nichols, contains barely a trace of drama, except in Seth Lerer's superb "Making Mimesis." See elsewhere Solterer, "Waking of Medieval Theatricality."

54. Dickson and Goulden attribute this statement to "a wizard whose name is lost to recorded history" (*There Are Alligators*, 129). See also Joynes, *Medieval Ghost Stories.*

55. Larwood, *Theatrical Anecdotes* (hereafter *TA*), 76.

56. "Ne voulant riens mesler, quant aux presentes observations, de bruict et rumeur populaire, nous sommes efforcéz de recouvrer la verité des choses, tant par escript que par le recit de ceulx qui ont esté presens ou qui ont heu charge aux affaires" (*JBT*, 4).

57. This is the situation, for example, in chapters 10, 12, and 14.

58. Although I resurrected my college Russian in order to consult Constantin Stanislavski in the original, I do not include Russian materials in the appendix. Instead, I cite from Elizabeth Hapgood's accessible yet controversial translations. On her abridgments, emendations, and other editorial liberties, see Gray, "From Russia to America," 154–55; and Benedetti, *Stanislavski*, 315–18.

59. My guiding principle is twofold: (1) Our legends doubtless originated in oral tradition, but even when transcription errors have occurred, they owe their postmedieval survival more to printed sources than to manuscripts. (2) I believe that curious readers who wish to "verify" a story

are more likely to consult a book than a manuscript. (As it is, the books are often inaccessible enough.) Again, I cite them "as is," with errors in spelling, grammar, etc.

60. In our first story, for example, Petit de Julleville cites from Jean François Huguenin's edition of the *Chroniques de Metz* (*CVM;* chapter 1, note 1, below). The superior edition by Charles Bruneau (*Chronique de Philippe de Vigneulles, CPV*), would not be available until almost fifty years after *Les Mystères* appeared. I therefore cite from Bruneau, but give the relevant page numbers in Huguenin—as, for the most part, does Bruneau himself.

Introduction: Medieval Urban Legends?

1. I document each story in the appropriate chapter. For the Old French text of the epigraph to this chapter, see the bilingual edition by David Bevington, *Medieval Drama,* p. 119, vv. 883–90.

2. For enlightening introductions to this topic in medieval culture, see especially Greetham, "Facts, Truefacts, Factoids"; Postlewait, "Writing History Today," 84–85; Spiegel, *Romancing the Past;* Otter, *Inventiones;* Morse, *Truth and Convention,* especially 92–124; Koopmans, *Théâtre des exclus,* 33–35; or more generally, Lamarque, *Truth, Fiction, and Literature;* White, *Metahistory;* and Riffaterre, *Fictional Truth.*

3. Also Campion-Vincent and Renard, *Légendes urbaines,* 342.

4. Petit de Julleville confined his work *Les Mystères* (hereafter *LM*), to religious drama, which is our focus as well. The reception of comic genres has yet to be archived on the same scale.

5. "Et appert bien que par devotion / Avez joué, sans ostentation" (Jean Bouchet, Epistle 90; cited by Petit de Julleville, "1534. Poitiers—La Passion," in *LM,* 2:124.

6. "Hommes graves qui savoient si bien *feindre,* par signes et gestes, les personnages qu'il représentoient, que la pluspart des assistants *jugeoient la chose être vraie et non feinte*" (Chaumeau, cited by Thiboust, *Relation de l'ordre de la triomphante et magnifique monstre,* 10–11 (my emphasis); and later by Petit de Julleville, *LM,* 2:133. See also on this passage Elliott, "Medieval Acting," 241; and Hashim, "Notes toward a Reconstruction."

7. Here I have taken a liberty with chronology, the better to underscore post hoc the believability of the events of the preceding chapters and ad hoc those that follow. Interestingly, the issue of liability is more prominent today in film and television, as in the suits against Oliver Stone's *Natural Born Killers* and MTV's *Beavis and Butthead.*

8. The pervasive devil refuses to be contained by a single chapter, so he shall also prowl other pages of this book.

9. See especially *SR,* 105–6.

10. I don't mean to oversimplify or homogenize complex theological positions any more than theater pieces would have done (see below, chaps. 10 and 12). On the reenactive functions of the Mass and medieval drama, see O. B. Hardison's *Christian Rite and Christian Drama* (hereafter *CRCD*), Essay 2; and *ROMD,* 51–54.

11. *Essai de poétique médiévale,* 447.

12. *Theatre Semiotics,* xviii (my emphasis). See also Spiegel's claim that "texts both mirror *and* generate social realities, are constituted by *and* constitute social and discursive formations" (*Romancing the Past,* 10 [original emphasis]).

13. I refer to Jordan, *Invention of Sodomy;* and to a *60 Minutes* piece aired in 1999 in which a disillusioned young man sued the San Francisco Jesuits for their having created a climate of sexual harassment. He lost.

14. *Staging Real Things* (hereafter *SRT*), 21. Pywell does not say *when* the performance of *The Hunchback* took place: only that it was "many years" before his book was published in 1994.

15. The special problem of medieval theatrical violence is the subject of my *Medieval Theater of Cruelty* (hereafter *MTOC*). For exciting work on this vast topic, see especially Haidu, *Subject of*

Violence; Barker, *Culture of Violence;* and the superb essays compiled by Redmond, *Violence in Drama.*

16. *Great Cat Massacre* (hereafter *GCM*), 15.

17. See, e.g, Denis Diderot's "Paradoxe du comédien"; *RPI,* chaps. 8 and 18; *GR,* 184; and Schechner on New York's Squat performance group in *BTA,* 302–9.

18. Richard Dorson also coined the term *fakelore* when critiquing popularized "treasuries" of urban legends (*American Folklore and the Historian,* chap. 1); see also *GCM,* 16; and Siebers, *Morals and Stories,* chaps. 2, 4, and 13.

19. *Republic,* ed. and trans. Paul Shorey, 382a (my emphasis).

20. *Poetics,* ed. and trans. W. Hamilton Fyfe, 1451b, 1461b.

21. *Devil's Dictionary,* 148.

22. Stanislavski (1863–1938), *An Actor Prepares* (hereafter *AP*), 128. Any actor alive is familiar with method acting, as disseminated in the English language trilogy of *An Actor Prepares, Creating a Role,* and *Building a Character.* I have removed the translator's italics, which do not appear in the Russian text.

23. The first quotation is anonymous, and appears in *HYL,* ix. The second, attributed to B. S. Johnson, is the epigraph to Tallis, *In Defence of Realism,* chap. 2.

24. *Chroniques de la ville de Metz (CVM),* 473; also app. 2.2. Also cited by Petit de Julleville, "1485. Metz.—Sainte Barbe," in *LM,* 2:48. This phrase does *not* appear in the *Chronique de Philippe de Vigneulles (CPV),* 3:114; app. 2.1.

25. *CVM,* 473.

26. *Mystère des Trois Doms,* ed. Giraud, 592 ("Compte de sa composition"); app. 10.1.

27. Chaumeau, *Histoire du Berry* (1566), 156; also cited by Thiboust, *Relation de l'ordre,* 10–11; and by Lebègue, *Mystère des actes des apôtres* (hereafter *MAA*), 78–79. See app. 11.4.

28. Chaumeau, cited by Lebègue, *MAA,* 78–79; app. 11.4.

29. See *JBP,* 417–18; app. 9.2; and *HTF,* 2:331n. From 1745 to 1749, the brothers Parfaict published fifteen of their intended eighteen volumes (which were to take the reader to the year 1752). I cite from the eighteenth-century edition because vol. 2 did not survive the Burt Franklin reprint very well: pp. 267–98 are missing, and many other pages are misnumbered. (Our quotation, for example, appears in a note on p. 365 of the reprint.) As it happens, the brothers Parfaict were not exactly paragons of scholarly care. One of the kinder assessments is by W. L. Wiley, who notes that their "dating of performances is often open to question but [their] criticism is sometimes quite astute" (*Early Public Theatre,* 41).

30. "Item, en ladite année [1437] fut faite en Metz le Jeus de la Passion, le iiie jour de Jullet, honorablement per iiii. jours" (*Chronique de Metz de Jacomin Husson, 1200–1525* [hereafter *CMJH*], ed. Michelant, 66).

31. *MAA,* 27; see app. 11.1.

32. Thiboust, *Relation de l'ordre,* 16; also excerpted by Cohen in *Histoire de la mise en scène* (hereafter *HMS*), 178, 226–29; app. Intro.1; and by Petit de Julleville in *LM,* 1:377.

33. *HMS,* 178; app. Intro.1.

34. See *CMJH,* 277–78, for the gluttonous parish priest who, in 1513, steals geese from his impoverished neighbors at Easter, assaults the honest citizen who tries to stop him, and ultimately has his own goose cooked when his house catches fire because he can't wait for a clean chimney. See also Davis on letters of remission that read like *fabliaux, Fiction in the Archives,* 1–2.

35. See *VH,* 9, 14; or Dickson and Goulden, *There Are Alligators,* 130–31. Indeed, Jacomin mentions "some 48 stables and homes" that burned in the fire above (*CMJH,* 277–78).

36. I make this point in "Medieval Snuff Drama," 177–80.

37. *TGT,* 450.

38. See *CBA*, 85–86; also *VH*, xi; and *Study of American Folklore* (hereafter *SAF*), 91.

39. See above, note 27.

40. For the beginning of this genealogy, see Gatton, "There Must Be Blood," 83; discussed below in chap. 9.

41. I could scarcely avoid footnoting Grafton's *Footnote: A Curious History*, 235, 233.

42. The Tournai decapitation circulated in similar privileged circles. See my "Medieval Snuff Drama," 198–99.

43. We have a good example of this in chapter 6. Also, J. M. B. Clément actually *disguises* his main source (which may be L. P. de Bachaumont, *Mémoires historiques*) in *AD*, i.

44. "L'obscurité à laquelle ces Pieces furent condamnées, par le bon-goût & la politesse, les anéantit tellement aux yeux du Public, qu'il n'en resta que des notions très vagues; qui bientôt devinrent fausses," *HTF*, 1:xvii.

45. See, e.g., Dickson and Goulden on a "true" haunted car, *There Are Alligators*, 133–34. See also below, chap. 5.

46. See Eco, *Open Work*, 106–13.

47. Both NBC and ABC aired the story on 24 May 1999. It is discussed below, chap. 4.

48. See below, chaps. 8 and 13.

49. "Pour les bonnes gens inciter / A bonnes euvres non pas *faintes*" (*Cycle de mystères des premiers martyrs*, ed. Runnalls, 37–38). See Luke Wilson on "promissory performances" of the English Renaissance stage, *Theaters of Intention*, chap. 4.

50. *Mystère de la Résurrection Angers (1456)*, ed. Servet, vol. 1, Day 1, 218–25; app. Intro.2.

51. Theater may thus be "performative," a speech act in the Austinian sense, including his further precisions about illocutionary and perlocutionary acts. See *HDTW*, Lectures 1 and 9; and Worthen, "Drama, Performativity, and Performance."

52. Brunvand draws on the work of folklorist Linda Dégh, e.g., "What Is a Belief Legend?" He also closes *TGT* with six legends that really *are* true.

53. For alterity, see especially Warning, "On the Alterity of Medieval Religious Drama"; and Jauss, "The Alterity and Modernity of Medieval Literature." I question the alterity of medieval drama in the introduction of *MTOC*.

54. App. Intro.3. See Petit de Julleville's comments in *LM*, 1:375; and also Jubinal, ed., *Mystères inédits*, xlii–xliii. Compare also with Bertolt Brecht on tolerable "incorrectness," "Short Organum for the Theatre," in *Brecht on Theatre*, 182.

55. For an excellent assessment of the visual perception of religious truth from Eusebius through the Reformation, see Miles, *Image as Insight*.

56. *Must We Mean What We Say?* (hereafter *MWM*), 327–29 (original emphasis).

57. News, KCOY, Channel 12.

58. Theiner, "Medieval English Literature," 240.

Chapter 1. Lusting after Saints

1. *CPV*, ed. Bruneau, 2:394–95; app. 1.1. Bruneau's conservative edition *(CPV)* is based on MS. M in Philippe's own hand and hosts all the author's "spelling fantasies" (xxiii). On the numerous manuscripts of Philippe's memoirs and Bruneau's editing principles, see xx–xxiv. Compare also to *CVM*, ed. Huguenin, 360–61; app. 1.2. Huguenin's is the version cited—without page numbers—by Petit de Julleville, "1468. Metz.—Sainte Catherine de Sienne," in *LM*, 2:32. The 1838 Huguenin edition *(CVM)* is a composite based on the manuscript chronicles of Philippe de Vigneulles, Jean Aubrion, and others (see his preface, v–vii). (That is why his edition contains the bracketed phrase "of Four du Cloistre" while Bruneau's does not.) To many, Huguenin was "almost unusable" due to such methodological shortcomings as his inability to

"read sixteenth-century writing" (Bruneau, xxii). Nevertheless, Petit de Julleville relied widely on his work, which predates Bruneau's by almost a century. As I explained above in the prologue, I will not normally include both Huguenin's and Bruneau's versions, but I make an exception in this first entry so that the reader can assess the kind of variants at issue. Note, e.g., Bruneau's imperfect verb tenses (*parloit, provocquoit, s'enamourait*) as contrasted to Huguenin's *passé simple*.

2. See *There are Alligators*, 130–31; see also *VH*, 14.

3. Graham Runnalls in *Mystères français imprimés* (hereafter *MFI*) lists no extant medieval *Mystère de Sainte Catherine*.

4. For women on the medieval stage, see Petit de Julleville, *LM*, 2:32; also editor Bibolet's comments in *Mystère de la Passion de Troyes*, 1:xxii–xxiii.

5. See especially Elliot, *Spiritual Marriage*.

6. See the *Farce du Cuvier*, in *Théâtre français*, ed. Fournier, 192–98.

7. *Quinze joyes du mariage*, ed. Rychner, "Premiere joye," 6–13.

8. See especially Stephen Wright's superb "Joseph as Mother."

9. "Li nostre sont verai martirs, / Dieu les ressoice en sa compaigne" (*Guerre de Metz en 1324*, stanza 247). See also *CVM*, 39–51; and for saintly martyrdom in general, Brown, *Cult of the Saints*, chap. 4.

10. "Invitent populum circumstantem adorandum infantem," in Bevington, ed., *Medieval Drama*, p. 58; also discussed by William Tydeman in *Theatre in the Middle Ages* (hereafter *TMA*), 223.

11. "Medieval Acting," 243.

12. See *CMJH*, 103; app. 1.3.

13. *CPV,* 2:394; also *CVM*, 361; apps. 1.1, 1.2. Compare to Jacomin Husson, *CMJH*, 103; app. 1.3.

14. "On remarquera d'abord que la pièce fut jouée dans un monastère, ce qui était assez rare, depuis qu'on jouait en français. . . . Ce fut une dame pieuse qui fit tous les frais de la représentation" (*LM*, 2:32).

15. See *CMJH*, 61–62; and below, note 23. It is unclear whether this was the play of Saint Catherine of Alexandria (or Mount Sinai) or Saint Catherine of Siena. For the former, see Cazelles, *Lady as Saint*, 113–37; and for the medieval play devoted to her, see apps. 2.3, 2.4.

16. In *Curiositez françoises*, Antoine Oudin (1595–1653) defines the expression as "not knowing what to do" ("il ne sçait à quel Saint se voüer. i. *il ne sçait ce qu'il doit faire*" [495 (original emphasis)]).

17. "*Elle est promise à une autre personne, elle a de l'inclination pour un autre*" (*Curiositez françoises*, 495 [original emphasis]).

18. This discrepancy is probably due to an editorial misreading of *ii score* for *iii score*. Petit de Julleville also references Jacomin's version (*LM*, 2:32) but does not cite it. Meanwhile, Gustave Cohen, following Petit de Julleville, also refers to a *1468* performance (*HMS*, 206).

19. Catherine [Benincasa] of Siena (c. 1347–80) is well known in our time thanks to Rudolph Bell's fascinating (if controversial) *Holy Anorexia*, chap. 2. For her life (as reconstructed by her own writings and by such texts as Raymond of Capua's *Life of Saint Catherine*), see Bynum, *Holy Feast and Holy Fast* (hereafter *HF*), 165–80; also Bynum, *Fragmentation and Redemption* (hereafter *FR*); *Butler's Lives of the Saints* (hereafter *BLS*), 2:192–98; and Berrigan, "Tuscan Visionary."

20. *CPV,* 2:245; app. 4.1. Also *CVM*, 200.

21. See *CVM*, 192–93, 140, 163–64.

22. *There Are Alligators*, 129.

23. Lynette Muir thinks that she is a furrier's daughter; *Medieval European Stage* (hereafter

MES), ed. Tydeman, 347. In other theatrical records, we find a *Jehan* Dedier on the stage, but he is a notary, not a glazier. Philippe de Vigneulles tells us, for example, that this "noctaire de la court de Mets" played Saint Catherine on 16–18 June 1435 (*CPV,* 2:236). Jacomin Husson says that the performance on the Place en Change started on 15 June 1434, with Dedier acting alongside another man from the legal profession, "Jehan Matheu the lawyer" (*CMJH,* 61–62). Jacomin is also cited with numerous orthographic variations by the brothers Parfaict, in *HTF,* 2:316; and by Petit de Julleville, who places the performance in 1433 (*LM,* 2:11). The brothers Parfaict despaired of viewing the text of the play, although they did pick up the trace of a "Life of Saint Catherine of Mount Sinai in verse, published in Paris by Allain Lotrian with no date" (*HTF,* 2:316n). For Jehan Matheu's appearance in 1437, see app. 4.1.

24. *CPV,* 2:394; app. 1.1; compare to *CVM,* 361; app. 1.2.

25. For the words and music, see *Medieval Lyric,* ed. Switten and Chickering, 1:165–66.

26. See, e.g., *Miracle de la nonne qui laissa son abbaye,* ed. Wilkins.

27. "Pour l'honneur de Dieu, en mémoire de sa passion, pour le bon exemple des chrétiens" (cited by Petit de Julleville, "1434. Draguignan.—La Passion," in *LM,* 2:12).

28. "*Attento quod erit maximum exemplum honorque et utilitas et commodum ville . . .*" (cited by Petit de Julleville, "1453. Montélimar.—Sainte Catherine," in *LM,* 2:24 [original emphasis]). See also *TRF,* 4. Again, it is unclear which Saint Catherine is honored.

29. On Saint Genesius, see *BLS,* 3:398–400; and Jean Rotrou (1609–50), *Le Véritable Saint Genest, Tragédie,* ed. Dubois. As George Steiner shows in *Death of Tragedy,* however, a saint's martyrdom was no *tragedy* given the promise of a compensating Heaven. On "going through the motions" leading to the real thing, see also Pascal's *Pensées,* in *Oeuvres,* ed. Lafuma, p. 551, fr. 418-233.

30. See, e.g., Tertullian, *De spectaculis,* chap. 17.

31. I cite from Bell (*Holy Anorexia,* 42), who draws largely from Raymond of Capua. Catherine reportedly had her first vision at the age of six and by age twelve was vowing never to marry (*BLS,* 192–93). Hagiography is not our focus, but see Monika Otter on its pretensions to veracity, in *Inventiones,* 40. I am not saying that saint's lives were untrue: to medieval Christians they *were* true. But their veracity required a leap of faith.

32. Unless, of course, "Catherine" really *was* on stage in both 1448 *and* 1468—which, as suggested above, seems doubtful.

33. *CPV,* 2:394; *CVM,* 361; apps. 1.1, 1.2. The cloister probably had some kind of semipermanent structure for outdoor devotional practices.

34. "Il fallut bouleverser la cour du couvent pour disposer un théâtre." This story bears out scholarly contentions that, following in the tenth-century tradition of Hrotswitha, cloistered nuns led rich theatrical lives. See, e.g., Wilson, ed., *Plays of Hrotsvit of Gandersheim,* xxv–xvii; and Wilson, "The Saxon Canoness"; Antonia Pulci (1452–1501), *Florentine Drama,* ed. and trans. Cook; Schulenburg, "Female Sanctity"; and Weaver, "Convent Wall."

35. Psychoanalysis of Henry is beyond both my purview and my skill, but one thinks of Carol Clover on the cinematic spectacle of female suffering in *Men, Women, and Chainsaws,* chap. 1.

36. *Etymologiarum,* bk. 18, "De ludis circensibus" (chap. 27), and "De circo" (chap. 28).

37. Bouchet, Epistle 92 (cited by Petit de Julleville, "1535. Issoudun.—La Passion," in *LM,* 2:128–30); app. 1.4. For a later period, see Elliott, *Playing God,* 27. We shall see in chapter 7 that "type-casting" the Devil was problematic.

38. See also Berrigan, "Tuscan Visionary," 252–55.

39. See also *HF,* 169; and Bell, *Holy Anorexia,* 28.

40. See also *FR,* 172–73; and *HF,* 168.

41. See also Bell, *Holy Anorexia,* 25.

42. Bynum further notes that Catherine's "chief and repeated miracles were cures of illness (the chief miracle performed by all saints, of course) and miraculous feedings or food multiplications" (*HF,* 170). Compare to the theatrical version of the miracle of the loaves and the fishes in chapter 12, below.

43. Cited by Berrigan, "Tuscan Visionary," 259.

44. "Medieval Acting," 243. Although Elliott does not give the full citation, he is referring to Gilder's *Enter the Actress,* 83–84.

45. *Enter the Actress,* 84.

Chapter 2. Queer Attractions

1. I make this argument in "Emotion Memory." For the French text of the epigraph to this chapter, see Cousin d'Avalon, *Comédiana* (1801), 18, which diverges from Chetwood's 1749 account of Mrs. Woffington (*History of the Stage,* 252).

2. There are many versions of Barbara's Life. The brothers Parfaict cite and discuss extensively a five-day play of some 25,000 verses, 371 folios, and 97 characters, which they date to approximately 1480 (*HTF,* 2:5–70, 501); along with a version in "two little days," which they date to 1534 and consider vastly inferior (*HTF,* 2:9n; excerpted in 3:36–41). J. M. B. Clément records a later "Sainte Barbe, *Tragédie d'un anonyme,* 1534" (*AD,* 2:151). For the printed history of the two-day version, see *MFI,* 155–58; see also a 512-verse poem of her life in Cazelles, *Lady as Saint,* 102–12.

3. In Mons, for example, Mary Magdalen was played by a man (see *Livre de conduite du Régisseur* [hereafter *LCR*], ed. Cohen, 525). For helpful approaches to the historical interrelations of theater and transvestism, see Zeitlin, "Playing the Other"; Case, "Classic Drag"; Rackin, "Androgyny, Mimesis"; Levine, *Men in Women's Clothing,* introduction and chap. 1; Sponsler, *Drama and Resistance,* chap. 2; Jardine, "Boy Actors, Female Roles"; Orgel, *Impersonations;* and Carlson, *Performance,* chap. 7. See above, chap. 1, note 23.

4. *CPV,* 3:114; app. 2.1; compare to *CVM,* 473; app. 2.2. I reproduce both versions because of the interesting variants: e.g., *CVM* doesn't quantify the weepers and describes Lyonard playing "prudently and piously" rather than "honorably." That version is discussed by Cohen, in *HMS,* 206, 232; it is cited by Petit de Julleville with numerous minor variants (punctuation, orthography, and so on), "1485. Metz.—Sainte Barbe," in *LM,* 2:48. I follow Petit de Julleville's understanding of Lyonard's *métier* as barber's apprentice (*LM,* 2:52). Compare also Lyonard to Stephen Hammerton, "a most noted and beautiful woman-actor" cited by Larwood (*TA,* 36).

5. *CVM,* 473; app. 2.2. This information does not appear in *CPV.*

6. *CPV,* 3:114; app. 2.1; *CVM,* 473; app. 2.2.

7. See Jean-Claude Schmitt, *Raison des gestes;* Bremmer and Roodenburg, eds., *Cultural History of Gesture;* and Enders, "Of Miming and Signing." Barry Unsworth brilliantly captures the art of gesture in his novel *Morality Play.*

8. *CPV,* 3:114; app. 2.1; *CVM,* 473; app. 2.2.

9. "Dum et omnibus habetur percognitum, qualiter ego minime habeo, unde me pascere vel vestire debeam, ideo petii pietati vestrae, et mihi decrevit voluntas, ut me in vestrum mondoburdum tradere vel commendare debere" (in Riché and Tate, eds., *Textes et documents,* 282–83).

10. This scenario is complicated by Lynette Muir's belief (in a work in progress) that plays in Metz were also performed in German. For the moment, our story dispenses with the need to know, by emphasizing what Quintilian called in the first century of our era the universal language of gesture *(communis sermo).* See *Institutio oratoria* (hereafter *IO*), XI.3.87; and Ward, "Quintilian and the Rhetorical Revolution of the Middle Ages."

11. "Conclut de faire le gait as portes de viii hommes et que les portiers avecq ceulx du gait

soient au destre de leurs barieres et de savoir quelz gens entrent en la ville, aussi que le gait se face en la Maison de la Ville et que les hostelains raportent chacune nuit les noms de leurs hostes" (meeting of 26 June 1501, cited by Gustave Cohen, in *LCR*, 590; see also the meeting of 19 June 1501, in *LCR*, 589).

12. See app. 1.4 (Jean Bouchet on type-casting).

13. The connections between queer theory and theater are too vast to be elaborated adequately here, but see the suggestive work of Case, "Toward a Butch-Femme Aesthetic"; and Harris, "Toward a Lesbian Theory of Performance."

14. See *CPV*, 3:124; app. 2.3; also *CVM*, 476–77.

15. "A ces mots Marcian commande à ses Bourreaux d'attacher Barbe à un Pilier, & de la fouetter de toutes leurs forces" (excerpts from the five-day *Barbara*, in *HTF*, 2:40). Given the three-day duration of the Metz play of 1486, we cannot tell which version was performed: an abbreviated five-day play, an amplified two-day play, or some other version that has not survived (see above, note 2).

16. *HTF*, 2:40; for a psychoanalytic perspective, see Spector, ed., *On Freud's "A Child Is Being Beaten."* According to Suetonius, Caligula enjoyed watching torture and decapitations while he was "lunching or revelling" ("Caligula," in *Lives of the Caesars* [hereafter *LC*], 1:bk. 4, 32. Also, John Callahan recalls that in the Grand Guignol (1897–1962) a sort of latter-day Barbara was "bound, gagged and whipped; then the tips of her breasts were clipped off with hedge shears and her eyes were scooped out with a soupspoon and a jackknife" ("Outdone by Reality," 80; cited in "Ultimate in Theatre Violence," 170).

17. Marcian commands: "Gardez que jamais ne mengez, / Tant que vous aurez, comme fors, / Tranché ses mammelles du corps" (*HTF*, 2:47); and "Barbe, je te condamne & juge . . . / D'estre parmy Nychomédye, / Nue du pie jusques au chef / Desmonstrée sans nul couvert chef; / Sans chemise, & sans vestement: / Et non pas par cy seullement, / Mais par la terre universelle / De ton Pere . . ." (*HTF*, 2:48).

18. See *HTF*, 2:54.

19. "Ces larmes réhabilitent un peu les épisodes que les lecteurs modernes jugent répugnants." For a similar assessment of medieval tears, see Clément-Hémery, *Histoire des fêtes civiles et religieuses*, 345 (discussed below, chap. 4).

20. *CVM*, 473; app. 2.2. *CPV* refers to "Master Chardely . . . who was a wise man and a learned and highly educated person" (*CPV*, 3:114); see app. 2.1.

21. See *HTF*, 2:51.

22. "Truant, mengue un petit, / S'il te semble bon au vergueust / Mes membres sont sus & jus / Roustiz, & sans plus de débat, / Fay les mectre dedans ung plat" (*HTF*, 2:45–46). These meanings of *membres* are attested in Godefroy's multivolume *Dictionnaire de l'ancien français*. The Littré dictionary lists the contemporary sexual connotations of the *membre* but gives no date for their earliest attribution. Barbara's language here sounds a lot like what the Serpent says to Eve in the *Jeu d'Adam* (Bevington, ed., *Medieval Drama*, p. 93).

23. For Henry, see apps. 1.1, 1.2.

24. Jacques Lacan would call this "veiling." See, e.g., "Signification of the Phallus," in *Ecrits*, trans. Sheridan, 285–91; compare to Freud, *Introductory Lectures*, ed. and trans. Strachey, Lecture 10. For an introduction to violence, spectacle, and male homoeroticism, see Goldberg, *Sodometries*, chap. 4.

25. *CVM*, 473; app. 2.2.

26. Compare the vow of Guibert de Nogent's mother that he "shall never become a clerk, nor any more suffer so much to get an education" (*Self and Society*, ed. Benton, 50).

27. *CPV*, 3:114; app. 2.1; *CVM*, 473; app. 2.2.

28. See *TA*, 230–31 (cited above, chap. 1).

29. Colonialism lies beyond the scope of this book, but see, e.g., Said, *Culture and Imperialism;* and Dougherty on its own legends, *Poetics of Colonization*, 41.

30. *CPV,* 3:114; app. 2.1; *CVM*, 473; app. 2.2.

31. "Et le xxiiiiᵉ jour de Jullet fut jué le jeu de Ste. Barbe en grand triomphe, en Chambre et moult bien jué" (*CMJH*, 139).

32. See above, note 10.

33. On the psycho-political move that defines queer behavior as "other," see, e.g., Sedgwick, *Epistemology of the Closet*, 18–22, 57–63.

34. The fear of things foreign is a theme of such urban legends as the Mexican pet (a rat) or the imported carousel horses infested with snakes (*MP*, 21–23; and *CBA*, 37–39).

35. *CPV,* 3:124; app. 2.3. Compare to *CVM*, 476, in which the bracketed phrase appears (but which is similar enough not to warrant reproduction). Pentecost is normally celebrated in May or June (fifty days after Easter). Petit de Julleville also paraphrases this text with variations in "1486. Metz.—Sainte Catherine du Mont Sinaï," in *LM*, 2:52–53.

36. *Gedenkbuch des Metzer Bürgers Philippe von Vigneulles aus den Jahren 1471–1522*, ed. Michelant, 14; app. 2.4. This text is also cited with variations by Petit de Julleville, in *LM*, 2:53.

37. While law students like the Basochiens retained close ties to the theater, that was not necessarily the case for theology students. See Harvey, *Theatre of the Basoche;* Fabre, *Études historiques;* and *ROMD*, chap. 3.

38. *CPV,* 3:124; app. 2.3. Compare to *CVM*, 476–77, which reads: "les personnaiges et la rethoricque ne le langaige n'estoient point si bien aornez *en doulceur et devoltion* comme ceulx du jeu et mistere de saincte Barbe" (my emphasis). Petit de Julleville omits the italicized phrase, in *LM*, 2:53. See also Larwood on the "curious, unequal sound of a boy who attains the age of puberty" (*TA*, 35).

39. See especially Carruthers, *Book of Memory*, introduction; Yates, *The Art of Memory;* and Coleman, *Ancient and Medieval Memories*. See also Quintilian's statement that "a liar should have a good memory" (*IO*, IV.2.91).

40. *Gedenkbuch*, 14; app. 2.4; also *LM*, 2:53. Philippe was back on stage in 1512 at the ripe old age of forty-one, this time playing a man in *Esther:* "Et durait deux jours et furent les secrets bien faits; de quoy je Phelippe de Vigneulles en fus l'ung des maistres et sy juais le personnaige de Egeus, prevost et gairdien des dames" (*Gedenkbuch*, 222). Also Petit de Julleville, "1512. Metz.—Esther. L'Enfant donné au diable," in *LM*, 2:102. Jacomin Husson includes the date (19 September) in a more detailed account (*CMJH*, 268).

41. See above, note 3.

42. See app. 1.1. If that performance occurred in 1448, Philippe hadn't even been born yet.

43. *Gedenkbuch*, 14; app. 2.4.

44. The whole point of my *ROMD* was to show that training in rhetorical delivery was training in theatricality.

45. Again, the date (1448 or 1468) depends on whose account we accept: Jacomin's or Philippe's. See chap. 1, note 18, above.

46. Trans. Cazelles, *Lady as Saint*, p. 125, ll. 1000–1006; see also *De Sainte Katherine*, 771–816; *BLS* 4:420–21; and *HF,* 81. The queen, who takes pity on Catherine, is likewise condemned to "be taken / And that her breasts / Be pierced and pressed / Between iron prongs, forcefully, / And that they be squeezed, / Then pulled off" (Cazelles, *Lady as Saint*, p. 128, ll. 1582–87).

47. Compare to Cazelles, *Lady as Saint*, 126–27.

48. Ibid., p. 124, ll. 995–96.

49. See *De spectaculis*, chap. 17; and *IO*, 1.10.31. In "Delivering Delivery" I explore the slip-

page of gender and genre in rhetoric and theater. Bruce Holsinger does so for music and pedagogy in *Music, Body, and Desire,* chap. 6.

50. For an introduction to the topic, see, e.g., Jordan, *Invention of Sodomy.*

51. "Short Organum," in *Brecht on Theatre,* 182.

52. Normally, this is a performative that does not reach fruition. See *HTDW,* 13–24; and Gould, "Unhappy Performative."

Chapter 3. Of Madness and Method Acting

1. "Saltatio," 83 (my emphasis). See also Nagler, *Sourcebook of Theatrical History,* 28–34. For Lucian, drama is inseparable from dance, music, pedagogy, song, and religion.

2. "Saltatio," 82.

3. We return in chapters 4 and 5 to the legends and realities of death on stage, but for a sampling, see *TA,* 198–200.

4. On this curse, see *Arden Shakespeare,* ed. Proudfoot, Thompson, and Kastan, 771; also Carroll, ed., *Macbeth,* 152.

5. I heard this one day on *Entertainment Tonight.*

6. Brunvand asserts that disseminators of urban legends are sophisticated, white, upper-middle-class "folk" (*VH,* xi).

7. I saw this happen. Arthur Janov's *Primal Scream* was on bookshelves everywhere, and she had a copy. In this game, players drew cards that invited deep, personal, and above all truthful revelations. Votes were then cast as to whether the performance was "right on" or a "cop-out." The winner was someone who never (or hardly ever) copped out—or who lied well enough to fool everybody.

8. Sarah Siddons (1755–1831) was the leading tragedienne of the late eighteenth century. See *Everyman Book of Theatrical Anecdotes* (hereafter *EBTA*), 55–58. David Graver has argued for a more complex understanding of the actor's incarnation of self and other, positing at least seven roles in "The Actor's Bodies."

9. Nor, for that matter, can I when I refer to "Ajax" or when I referred to "Catherine" in chapter 1. We do not know the actors' names. Compare Cavell's point with any ordinary conversation about movies. When speaking of *Ghost,* does one say that *Demi Moore* or *Molly* finally believes that *Sam Wheat* or *Patrick Swayze* is a ghost?

10. Eventually, of course, "poor Odysseus" of Trojan war fame *did* die: he just didn't die in *that way.*

11. "Que toutes gens ayans parsonnages du dit mistere s'assemblassent . . . chacun acoustré selon son parsonnage. . . . Et est assavoir qu'ilz estoient si grand train que quand Dieu et ses anges sortirent du dit lieu chevaulchant après les autres, les diables étoient desja oultre la tour de la prison" ("Procès verbal," cited by Petit de Julleville, "1496. Seurre.—Saint Martin," in *LM,* 2:69). Fournier also abridges this long excerpt (67–73) in *Théâtre français,* 172–74. Compare also to Thiboust, *Relation de l'ordre,* 20–23.

12. See my introduction, note 22, above.

13. See his aptly titled *Method or Madness?*

14. The bread and butter of folklore, oral history, civilization, and cultural history, memory is a huge piece of this critical puzzle; see Stanislavski on "Emotion Memory," in *AP,* chap. 9. In a sense, recent debates about the authenticity of "repressed memories" continue that age-old discussion.

15. *Poetics,* 1461b.

16. Although my actor friends tell me that many of Stanislavski's early students went mad, none has shown me anything like a reliable source. Instead, they cite Stanislavski's revisions and even repudiations of his techniques.

17. I will not use clinical definitions of *insanity, madness,* or *psychosis.* Instead, I confine myself to the common knowledge cited by most circulators of urban legends. Derek Davis, however, offers a psychiatric assessment of theater in *Scenes of Madness.*

18. *De distinctione,* in *Oeuvres complètes,* ed. Glorieux, 3:44; app. 3.1; translated by Boland, "Concept of *Discretio Spirituum,*" 90; my emphasis. On this text, see Sullivan, *Interrogation,* 33–35.

19. On drama's "pathology," see Boal, *Theater of the Oppressed,* 23.

20. Larwood cites this passage in *TA,* 66, as does Edwards in *Stanislavsky Heritage,* 294. The main argument of my *ROMD* is that, in theory and practice, legal rhetoric constitutes a rich body of theatrical knowledge. Legal themes also inform our chapters 5, 8, 9, 11, 13, and 14.

21. "Vultus/Accensus, gestus turbatus; et interiorem/Exterior sequitur motus, pariterque moventur/Alter et alter homo. Personam si geris ejus,/Quid recitator ages? Veros imitare furores" (*Poetria nova,* ed. and trans. Gallo, ll. 2049–53).

22. *TA,* 240 (original emphasis). See also Percy Fitzgerald on her hot tears, *Book of Theatrical Anecdotes,* 27.

23. Schechner, "Introduction: Exit Thirties," 17.

24. See, e.g., "The Hook," in which a maniac with a hook on one arm instead of a hand escapes from the "state insane asylum" and terrorizes a young couple who are necking in their car (*TGT,* 94–95). Insanity is also the catalyst for the plot of the film *Urban Legend,* which revolves around a deranged coed's vengeance.

25. "Saltatio," 83.

26. *Republic,* 606c.

27. "Saltatio," 83 (my emphasis). On safe distance, see "Saltatio," 71; and Aristotle, *Poetics* 1448b. The concept has been called into question by Geoff Pywell in *SRT;* Worthen, *Modern Drama,* especially 138–39; and Rogoff, *Theatre Is Not Safe.*

28. "Saltatio," 83.

29. They provide the antithesis of what Erving Goffman calls the audience's "onlooker" role in which they "give themselves over" to drama's "unreal world": "the onlooking aspect of the audience activity is not something that is a staged or simulated replica of a real thing, as is the action onstage" (*FA,* 130).

30. Contrast this story to the Eel of Melun of our chapter 6, who panics at a *perceived* crisis, not a *real* one.

31. "Saltatio," 84 (my emphasis).

32. *Othello* seems to precipitate both comic and serious phenomenological crises. See Larwood's lighthearted tale of the yokel "Peggy," who steps onto the stage as the Moor is saying "There comes the lady" (*TA,* 45–46).

33. Richmond is the Earl of Richmond of *Richard III,* the future Henry VII.

34. Mr. Taylor, cited by Larwood, in *TA,* 214. See also Goffman on sympathetic vs. unsympathetic audience laughter (*FA,* 130–31).

35. "Au fond, tous ou presque, nous portons en nous ce petit grain de sable, qui peut, du jour au lendemain, arrêter net le mécanisme de la raison" (*Théâtre de la mort,* 20–21).

36. Cited by Joseph Chaikin in *Presence of the Actor,* 32.

37. On "Mrs. Susannah Mountfort" (c. 1667–1703), see *EBTA,* 17–18.

38. See app. 1.4.

39. Richard Ryan (1796–1849), *Dramatic Table Talk* (hereafter *DTT*), 1:142–44 (original emphasis). This is probably a reference to Act 5, Scenes 4–5 of Racine's play, in which Orestes loses his reason.

40. *Sartre on Theater,* trans. Jellinek, 243. Sartre is speaking of his adaptation of Alexandre Dumas's *Kean.* See also *TA,* 21; and Woods, "Actors' Biography," 245.

41. Larwood says it was unforgettable "less than ten years ago," or in the 1870s, but even modern English Romanticists seem to have forgotten all about it.

42. See, e.g., *Zaïre*, ed. Jacobs. Mr. Bond has not earned a place in *EBTA*, but Richard Ryan mentions him in *DTT*, 1:144, where he incorrectly calls the play *Zara*. See also *TA*, 198–200, which includes Molière's apocryphal onstage death during the *Malade imaginaire* of 1673 (later proven to be false).

43. In a chronological mixup, Larwood even has Palmer dying twice: in both 1793 and 1798!

44. See Schechner on "restored behavior," in *BTA*, chap. 2.

Chapter 4. Two Priests and the Hand of God

1. See *LM*, 2:12. For French versions of our epigraph, see Pierre Bayle, "Poquelin," in *Selections from Bayle's Dictionary*, ed. Beller and Lee Jr., 186; and *TA*, 14.

2. *CPV*, 2:245–46; app. 4.1. Despite numerous minor orthographic variations, Huguenin's edition follows this account quite closely (compare to *CVM*, 200). Petit de Julleville also cites Huguenin (adding *further* minor variants) in "1437. Metz.—La Passion. La Vengeance de J.-C.," in *LM*, 2:12–13. The brothers Parfaict state much less dramatically that Nicolas "would have died on the cross had he not been rescued" (*HTF*, 2:253–54; app. 4.2). They also refer us to a handwritten passage on fol. 1490 of the Vérard edition of the *Passion* (*HTF*, 254n; app. 4.2). See also *HMS*, 197; Jubinal, ed., *Mystères inédits*, 1:xliii; and Muir, *Nicholas and the Devils*, a children's version of the tale.

3. Compare also Stephen Knapp and Walter Benn Michaels on "true belief," in "Against Theory," 26, 28.

4. See app. 4.3; and the versions in *CPV*, 4:154; app. 4.4. Compare also to *CVM*, 687. This is the same procession that precedes the *Mistere de la Sainte Hostie* (below, chap. 9). Petit de Julleville documents a similar "obligatory loan" in Romans in 1509 (*LM*, 2:96; also below, chap. 10). On the processional context of medieval drama, see Kipling, *Enter the King*; Campbell, "Cathedral Chapter and Town Council"; Knight, *Aspects of Genre*, chap. 6; Muir, *Biblical Drama*, chaps. 1–3; Axton, *European Drama*, chaps. 1–3; Kolve, *Play Called Corpus Christi*, chaps. 2–3; Rubin, *Corpus Christi*, 235–71; and Cohen, *Crossroads of Justice*, 198–201.

5. We can assume from the sheer physical force necessary that it was probably one or more male rescuers.

6. Cited by Meredith and Tailby, eds., *Staging of Religious Drama*, 109, also 101–16; Gatton, "There Must Be Blood"; *LM*, 1:chaps. 10–11; Sponsler, *Drama and Resistance*, chap. 6; *TMA*, chap. 6; and Côté, "Réalisations matérielles."

7. "Un bonet de fe[r]/sul cap, e pueis/des spongos sus/aquel bonet de fe[r]/totas plenas de /vermelo ho de sanc/e pueis metri-li la/falsa paruqua/susa la spongos" (*Quaderno di segreti*, ed. Vitale-Brovarone, ll. 7–15). On this text, see Butterworth, *Theatre of Fire*, 33–36.

8. *HTB*, 4 (my emphasis); app. 4.5. For other such reenactments, see *HMS*, 149n; and Elliott, *Playing God*, chap. 2.

9. Clément-Hémery, *Histoire des fêtes civiles* (1846), 345; app. 4.6. Faber prefaces his account with the caveat, "if we are to believe the manuscripts which related this incident." He likely never saw them because Clément-Hémery never cites them.

10. See *HTB*, 4; app. 4.5. Hurlbut electronically posted his comment to PERFORM (3 February 1995). Compare to the Filipino crucifixion discussed above in my introduction; and to *LM*, 1:374–75; and Gatton, "There Must Be Blood," 77.

11. See *MWM*, 328–29; cited above, in my introduction. I reserve the larger discussion of the interplay between theatrical ontology and the *ars moriendi* for a future book called "Back to the Medieval Future: Theater, Death, and Critical Intentions."

12. Compare also to Pywell's account of the assault at RATT that *required* audience intervention (*SRT,* 21).

13. Wilshire disputes Goffman's "nominalism" and binarism in *RPI,* 274–81.

14. See Goffman's classic treatment of "breaking frame," "flooding," and "downkeying" (*FA,* chap. 10); plus his comments on "interception" (*FA,* 125–27). See also Alan Read on intervention, *Theatre & Everyday Life,* 125–28.

15. *CPV,* 2:245; app. 4.1; also *CVM,* 200. Indeed, he returns as Titus in the *Vengeance* of 17 September 1437 (*CPV,* 2:246; app. 4.1). For the latter, see also *LM,* 2:13–14 (with minor orthographic variation); *HTF,* 254n, 316n (with inconsistencies in the date); and Jacomin Husson, who says that the performance began on 15 September but mentions no actors by name (*CMJH,* 66).

16. Cited above, chap. 1, note 10; see *TMA,* 223.

17. Cited by Petit de Julleville, "1452. Beauvais.—Saint Pierre," in *LM,* 2:23; app. 8.6.

18. "Quoique les bourreaux ne fissent que le semblant des tortures qu'ils infligeaient au personnage divin, *ce simulacre de passion* devait être épuisant. . . . D'autres rôles n'étaient pas moins fatigants [*sic*] ou même dangereux, par l'imprudence des machinistes, déjà très hardis, encore peu habiles" (*LM,* 1:375 [my emphasis]).

19. See, e.g., Elliott, *Playing God; TMB; SR; CRCD;* O'Connell, *Idolatrous Eye;* and Prosser, *Drama and Religion.*

20. *Question and Answer,* 5–6.

21. See Mark 27.46; or, e.g., the *Passion du Palatinus:* "*Hoc est: Deus meus, quare me dereliquisti?*" (*Jeux et sapience,* ed. Pauphilet, 247).

22. *Le cuer* in Old French denotes not only the bodily organ, but one's faith, will, thoughts, sincerity, and courage.

23. Cited by Cohen, in *LCR,* 475; app. 4.7. Mons is 183 miles from Metz.

24. This is the main premise of the provocative doctoral thesis of Dominguez, "Le Corps dans les mystères"; and, in a different way, of *TMB.*

25. "Par quoy pourrez avoir tres grant honneur / En vostre jeu. Dieu vous y doint bonheur. / C'est luy tout seul duquel tout bien procede; / Sans son secours homme n'est qui n'excede" (Épîtres familières de Jean Bouchet, Epistle 91; cited by Petit de Julleville, "1535. Issoudun.—La Passion," in *LM,* 2:130).

26. "Leur moyen habituel est de remplacer au moment de l'exécution, l'acteur par sa 'feinte', c'est-à-dire, son image feinte ou un simple mannequin destiné à le représenter" (*HMS,* 149).

27. *TMA,* 177; my emphasis. See also, on "risk management" in early English drama, Beckwith, *Signifying God;* and Evans, "When a Body Meets a Body."

28. *CPV,* 2:245; app. 4.1. Huguenin (*CVM,* 200) along with Petit de Julleville who follows him, refer to Jehan de *Missey,* as do most others who cite this text. The brothers Parfaict cite a less dramatic version that makes no mention of smelling salts (*HTF,* 2:254–55; app. 4.2). See also Cohen on stage hangings, in *HMS,* 239.

29. *CPV,* 2:245; app. 4.1.

30. Ibid.

31. For medieval vs. modern responses to violence, see, e.g., Haidu, *Subject of Violence,* introduction; and *MTOC,* 11–14.

32. One detail that is less "minor" to the theater historian is the function of the *maître du jeu,* a certain Forcelle who "carried the script" (*CPV,* 2:245; app. 4.1). Petit de Julleville believes that he *directed* the play (*LM,* 2:13), while the brothers Parfaict and Michelant feel that he merely served as prompter (*HTF,* 2:255n; app. 4.2; *CMJH,* 326n). Jacomin Husson also picked up the trace of "Fourelle" twenty-five years earlier on 14 September 1412, where he exercised the same

function in the *Play of Saint John the Baptist*, also on the Place en Change (*CMJH*, 45). Petit de Julleville believes that that play was performed in 1409 (*LM*, 2:8–9).

33. See Petit de Julleville, "1547. Valenciennes—La Passion," in *LM*, 2:155–56; also Meredith and Tailby, *Staging*, 105, 107.

34. "Procès verbal"; cited by Petit de Julleville, "1496. Seurre.—Saint Martin," in *LM*, 2:70–71; app. 4.8; also cited above, chap. 3, note 11. This story is discussed by Jubinal, ed., *Mystères inédits*, 1:xlvii (his long excerpt runs xliii–xlviii); *HMS*, 240; Meredith and Tailby, *Staging*, 261; and Butterworth, *Theatre of Fire*, 26. Butterworth also discusses the tragic incendiary night of the Wild Men, whose costumes were ignited by a hapless torchbearer in 1393 (chap. 2); as does Wickham, *History of the Theatre*, 85. For a fascinating contemporary perspective, see Read on "Combustion: Fire and Safety," chap. 8 of *Theatre & Everyday Life*.

35. "Procès verbal"; cited by Petit de Julleville, "1496. Seurre.—Saint Martin," in *LM*, 2:71; app. 4.8. "Et l'on répara l'incident par un couplet qui, s'il n'a pas le mérite de la distinction, a, au moins, celui de l'à-propos" (HMS, 240).

36. The same premise undergirds the innumerable urban legends that warn that "something icky is *in* us, or *on* us" (*CD*, 104; original emphasis). For a sampling, see *CD*, chap. 4; and *MP*, chap. 4.

37. "Nous ignorons malheureusement l'impression produite sur le public par la passion et la mort du Sauveur" (*TRF*, 6).

38. For those edifying intentions, see above, chap. 1, notes 27 and 28.

39. We return to this cornerstone of antitheatrical polemic in chapters 8, 9, and 12.

40. *Mystère de la Passion*, ed. Jodogne, 23987–24010. For Judas's suicide, see apps. 13.4 and 13.5.

41. "*Icy despend Desesperance Judas*" (*Mystère de la Passion*, ed. Jodogne, after verse 24018).

42. Hawkins, *Annals of the French Stage* (hereafter *AFS*), 1:14–15; my emphasis.

43. *AD*, 2:506; app. 4.9.

44. Again, see Brunvand's own caveat about printed sources in *CBA*, 85–86; or *VH*, xi.

45. HBO television special, *You Are All Diseased*.

46. ABC *World News Tonight*, 24 May 1999. I argue in "Medieval Death" that only intent (to kill or to watch) distinguishes this event from a snuff film.

47. NBC *Nightly News*, 24 May 1999.

48. Review of Francis Barker's *Culture of Violence*, 527.

49. I mean no false binary but rather Greenblatt's "spillage" or slippage (*Shakespearean Negotiations*, chap. 3).

50. I invoke the legendary Thespis, who ostensibly fathered drama in 6 B.C. when he used the mask of a historical figure during the Dionysian liturgy (see, e.g., Nicoll, *World Drama*, 26). Hardison posited a similar slippage between the Mass and liturgical drama (*CRCD*, Essay II); as did Petit de Julleville between expiatory processions and profane spectacle (*LM*, 2:80); as did I between forensics and medieval drama (*ROMD*, chap. 1).

51. We know of no medieval "rain checks." For these "rain-outs," see *CVM*, 473; app. 2.2; and, on the *Saint Laurent* of 1488, *CPV*, 3:131; *CVM*, 482; *LM*, 2:55. Jacomin places the latter play in 1466 (*CMJH*, 143).

52. Here lies buried another stunning document in Cohen's *Études d'histoire du théâtre*, chap. 10. Cohen transcribes the entire letter of remission issued to Jehan Martin on 13 August 1395, which forgives him for having failed to police his ward. Muir recently noticed it too, in *MES*, ed. Tydeman, 286. Notwithstanding its horrific content, Cohen is interested only in what the document tells us about the timing for setting up theatrical scaffolding (174–78). See app. 5.5, for legislation in Angers monitoring the presence of strangers.

53. *Method or Madness*, 90; original emphasis.

Chapter 5. Dying to Play

1. See Thomas, "Théâtre à Paris et aux environs." I reproduce both texts in their entirety in apps. 5.1 and 5.2. See also *MES*, 285.

2. I refer especially to Baudrillard's "Symbolic Exchange and Death," *SW,* chap. 5.

3. I mean here no lit-crit version of "if theater were outlawed, only outlaws would have theater." Nor am I suggesting that theater *should* be regulated or censored. But, since theater *can* involve real risks, one must address those responsibly (just as it is responsible to warn epileptic patrons about the theatrical use of seizure-inducing strobe lights).

4. See Blau, *The Audience,* 165, for this well-turned phrase summarizing Scarry's thesis in *Body in Pain,* 51–56.

5. Brook, *Empty Space,* 17.

6. Arch. Nat. JJ 116, no. 254, cited by Thomas, "Théâtre à Paris," 609–10; app. 5.1.

7. Thomas, "Théâtre à Paris," 610; app. 5.1 (my emphasis). For readability, I have broken up the interminable sentences of medieval legalese into *slightly* more manageable semantic units. Compare this to the stories of the devil's combustible *derrière* and the Wildmen of chapter 4.

8. See also *HDTW,* 16–17.

9. In addition to Gould, "Unhappy Performative," see *PP,* chap. 6; Williams, *Moral Luck;* and Statman, ed., *Moral Luck.*

10. See *FA,* 129–36; discussed above, chap. 4.

11. "Ethical Value and Negative Aesthetics," 70 (my emphasis).

12. See Rey-Flaud on this point, in *PDMA,* 11–12; Rey-Flaud, *Cercle magique.*

13. This is the larger topic of the essays in *Medieval Practices of Space,* ed. Hanawalt and Kobialka.

14. On the *temenos,* or "sacred spot cut off and hedged in from the 'ordinary' world," see Huizinga, *Homo Ludens,* 77. On the large-scale tendency of medieval society to "play itself out," see Le Goff, *Medieval Civilization,* 360–61; and *PDMA,* 75–79. On medieval theatrical space, see Konigson, *Espace théâtral médiéval;* Southern, *Medieval Theatre in the Round;* Mullaney, *Place of the Stage;* Carlson, *Places of Performances,* chap. 1; Read, *Theatre & Everyday Life,* chap. 4.

15. *Conseil du samedi 26 juin 1501,* cited by Gustave Cohen, in *LCR,* 591; see app. 5.6.

16. We return to specific legislation about public safety at the theater in chapters 8 and 11.

17. *Habits of Renaissance Thought,* 11. See also Cohen, *Drama of a Nation,* 65–73.

18. However, in an operation that is all too familiar today, he was *not* protected from future *civil* claims against him. I discuss the legal ramifications of Guillaume's intent in "Medieval Death," but suffice it to say that they problematize intentionality in much the same way that Umberto Eco does in his insightful "Interpreting Drama." See also Natalie Davis's superb analysis of such letters in *Fiction in the Archives.*

19. Cited by Thomas, "Théâtre à Paris," 610; app. 5.1.

20. Thomas, "Théâtre à Paris," 610–11; app. 5.1.

21. We return to this point in chapter 13 and in the epilogue.

22. The distortion of questions of intentionality in theater studies is the larger subject of my work in progress, "Back to the Medieval Future."

23. *Corpus Christi,* 265.

24. Isidore of Seville didn't see much difference between the theater and the circus in *Etymologiarum,* bk. 18, chaps. 27 and 28; see above, chap. 1.

25. *Devil's Dictionary,* 17. Bierce was familiar with a great deal of medieval esoterica, especially Baring-Gould's *Curious Myths of the Middle Ages* (*Devil's Dictionary,* 201).

26. Arch. nat. JJ 125, no. 17, cited by Thomas, "Théâtre à Paris," 611; app. 5.2. Théophile's is

the story of a corrupt but eventually repentant priest who sells his soul to the Devil for a larger prebend. The Virgin Mary comes to his rescue.

27. The text says that they were *in the church (en l'eglise)*, but this seems an unrealistic location for a cannon. The phrase could mean, e.g., "in the courtyard of the church."

28. Cited by Thomas, "Théâtre à Paris," 611; app. 5.2.

29. Here, the typically redundant French syntax gives new meaning to the standard expression, "the *late* Perrin": "lequel *feu Perrin Leroux* est alé de vie a trespassement." Either it means the overdetermined "the late Perrin died," or it should be "*from which blast [duquel* feu], Perrin passed away."

30. See apps. 4.1, 4.2.

31. She does this literally in Rutebeuf's thirteenth-century *Miracle de Théophile*, ed. Pauphilet, when she retrieves Théophile's contract with the Devil (pp. 155–56); see also Gregg, *Devils, Women, and Jews*, 217–18.

32. Cited by Thomas, "Théâtre à Paris," 611; app. 5.2.

33. Ibid. On the ontological status of the rehearsal, see *FA*, 126n; Kirby, *Formalist Theatre*, x–xi; and *RPI*, 99. See also Victor Turner's classic "Liminal to Liminoid," in *From Ritual to Theatre*, 20–60; and Flanigan, "Liminality, Carnival."

34. Even so, such medieval liminality might have been consonant with "living with the dead." See Geary, *Living with the Dead*; and Ariès, *Western Attitudes toward Death*.

35. See Nagler, *Source Book*, 5, who identifies his source only as "an ancient biography."

36. Ibid., 4. "On rapporte qu'à la représentation des Euménides d'Eschyle, vers l'an 460 avant Jésus-Christ, l'entrée des terribles déesses provoqua une véritable panique dans l'assemblée. Des femmes avortèrent, des enfants moururent, plusieurs spectateurs furent frappés de folie" (*Théâtre de la mort*, 13).

37. *AD*, 2:491; app. 5.3.

38. For a sampling of such on-stage violence, see Blau, *Audience*, 165–67; *BTA*, chap. 7; and *SRT*, chap. 1.

39. Johnson and Schaefer, "Soft Core," 46–47; Will, "Naïve Hopes and Real Decadence," C7, cited by Johnson and Schaefer, "Soft Core," 53 (my emphasis). Like Lucian ("Saltatio," 83), Will considers this to be a matter of social class. See also Kerekes and Slater, *Killing for Culture*, chap. 1.

40. Cited by Johnson and Schaefer, "Soft Core," 53.

41. For Hart's death, see above, chap. 4.

42. On this incident, see *TMA*, 223–24.

43. *Histriomastix*, p. 556r. The Garland edition of this text contains several anomalies, among them, two pages bearing the number 556.

44. Arrêt de Parlement (Tournelle), 20 novembre et 23 mars 1516, cited by Gosselin, *Recherches sur les origines*, 62; app. 5.4. See also Richard Axton on battle-play, in *European Drama*, chap. 2; and E. K. Chambers on folk drama, in *Mediaeval Stage*, 1:chaps. 6–9.

45. See *DTT*, 3:42–43. But Ryan engages in some fuzzy math, reporting that in addition to those "fifteen respectable persons," twenty others suffered "fractured limbs and other severe injuries, of which several did not long survive."

46. Goffman, e.g., considers all such disruptions from the soccer field to the orchestra to the theater to the boardroom in *FA*, 359–66.

47. "Pour sûreté de la ville et de la chose publique et pendant les jours que l'on représentera le mystère de la Passion, les portes de la ville soient gardées par quatre hommes au lieu de deux, et que les portes de la Madeleine et de Comporté soient fermées"; Boutiot, *Recherches sur le théâtre à Troyes*, 428; also cited by Petit de Julleville, "1483. Troyes.—La Passion," in *LM*, 2:44.

48. Archives d'Angers, BB 4, fol. 29, cited by Port, *Inventaire analytique*, 349; app. 5.5. Also cited by Jodogne in his edition of Jean Michel's *Mystère de la Passion*, xl–xli. For an excellent summary of this legislation, see Jodogne's edition, xli; see also Canetti, *Crowds and Power*.

49. Archives d'Angers, BB 4, fol. 29, cited by Port, *Inventaire analytique*, 349; app. 5.5. The Town Council of Mons enacted strikingly similar legislation on 19 June 1501 for one of their own Passion plays. See *Conseil du samedi 26 juin 1501*, cited by Gustave Cohen, in *LCR*, 591; app. 5.6.

50. Archives d'Angers, BB 4, fol. 29, cited by Port, *Inventaire analytique*, 350; app. 5.5; Jean Michel, *Mystère de la Passion*, ed. Jodogne, xli. See also *ROMD*, 98–99, for a similar edict of 1548 indicting Parisian students for bellicose behavior; and Pentzell, "Medieval Theatre in the Streets."

51. Archives d'Angers, BB 4, fol. 29, cited by Port, *Inventaire analytique*, 349; app. 5.5; Jean Michel, *Mystère de la Passion*, ed. Jodogne, xli.

52. One hardly dares mention the turn-of-the-millennium American craze for the voyeuristic television show *Survivor*, which has spawned a number of copy-cat programs exalting risk-taking (e.g., *Fear Factor* and *Amazing Race*). See also Goodman, "TV Shows Make Fantasy the Nation's Reality."

53. "Sur la scène, avec un *incroyable* réalisme, le Christ ou les martyrs sont bafoués, giflés, battus, torturés de mille manières" (*TRF*, 6 [my emphasis]).

54. *National Television Violence Study, 1994–95*, 3 (my emphasis).

Chapter 6. The Eel of Melun

1. "1547. Meaux.—L'Ancien Testament, La Passion," in *LM*, 2:144n; app. 6.1. Meaux's theater is the subject of our chapter 13.

2. *L'Anguille*, from the Latin *anguilla*, means "The Eel."

3. The cultural specificity of proverbial wisdom is notoriously difficult to translate. See Hamlet's famous line (Act 3, Scene 2) to Claudius after the staging of the deadly serious murder of Gonzago (*Arden Shakespeare*, l. 268). The Eel of Melun is by no means the first medieval theatrical subject to find his way into the French language. Consider "Revenons à nos moutons" from Scene 8 of the fifteenth-century *Farce de Maître Pathelin* (e.g., in Tissier, ed., *Recueil de farces*, vol. 7).

4. *LM*, 2:144n; app. 6.1. Unfortunately, the polyvalent meaning of the Eel's *cry* is somewhat lost in translation. In addition to denoting "a cry, scream, or shriek," *cry* was also the term employed for various proclamations, including pre-theatrical announcements. *Skinning (écorcher)* still refers today to what unscrupulous merchants do to their clients. (Americans prefer the more sheepish *fleecing*.) Meanwhile, David E. Kelley created a penny-pinching hospital administrator nicknamed "The Eel" for the 1990s TV drama, *Chicago Hope*.

5. He thus resists Grafton's contention that "a hundred years ago, most historians would have made a simple distinction: the text persuades, the notes prove" (*Footnote*, 15).

6. Le Roux de Lincy, *Livre des proverbes*, 2:49; app. 6.2. He does mention, however, that "in the *Adages françois*, which date from the end of the fourteenth century, we read: 'He is like the eels of Melun: he screams before you skin him.'" This suggests that Monsieur Eel's performance could have been as early as the fourteenth century (and thus contemporaneous with the deaths of Jehan Hemont and Perrin Le Roux of our chapter 5).

7. Even in Melun, a city sympathetic to the Albigensian heresy in its early years (1498–1504), citizens would probably not have mocked the martyrdom of saints, although "heretics" would come to question their veneration. See Renaudet, *Préréforme et Humanisme*, 351; and, on the worship of saints, app. 10.3.

8. Fleury de Bellingen, *Etymologie*, 140; app. 6.3. This text takes the form of a dialogue between Cosme and Simplician. Compare to app. 6.2.

9. *Livre des proverbes,* 2:49; app. 6.2.

10. For medieval notions of tragedy, see Kelly, *Ideas and Forms of Tragedy.*

11. This is the title of chap. 11 of his *Carnival and Theater.*

12. Compare, e.g., to my introduction, note 5; Lyonard's changing voice in app. 2.3; and Jean Bouchet's critique of the poor special effects of the Passion play in Poitiers (July 1534), Epistle 90, cited by Petit de Julleville, *LM,* 2:124.

13. "De vostre lance, qui forte est, / Ou costé destre le poignez, / Et gardez que ne vous *feignez;* / Mais bien en parfont le plaiez" (*Mystère de la Passion Nostre Seigneur du manuscrit 1131 de la Bibliothèque Sainte-Geneviève,* ed. Runnalls, ll. 3013–16).

14. "Je pry Mahon qu'il soit pendus / Qui de bien ferir se *faindra*" (*Geu Saint Denis,* ed. Seubert, ll. 629–30; my emphasis). This play is part of the same *Cycle de Mystères des Premiers Martyrs* cited above, introduction, note 49.

15. "Je te voy faindre"; "tout cecy n'est qu'esbat" (*LCR,* pp. 291–92 [it is more efficient to cite Cohen's edition by page number]). In my translation, I play deliberately on *Just Gaming* by Lyotard and Thebaud.

16. "En toy je croy sans *faintisce*" (*Mystère de la Passion à Amboise,* ed. Runnalls, 639).

17. This painful topic is the subject of our chapter 9.

18. "Seigneurs, pensés vous ad cela? / Avéz vous admiration / d'une meschante fiction? / Croyés vous que, pour verité, / Lazare soit resuscité? / Nenny, nenny, c'est fantasie, / c'est ung corps par nigromencie / qui par quelque diable se duyt!" (*Mystère de la Passion,* ed. Jodogne, ll. 14007–14).

19. According to the *Golden Legend,* Bartholomew had earlier promised the pagan king that he would "show him his god bound in chains" (*GL,* 111).

20. For examples, see Gatton, "There Must Be Blood," especially 82.

21. In *PDMA,* 153, he provides not a shred of evidence.

22. *LM,* 1:375; cited above, chap. 4, note 18.

23. *TA,* 259; cited above, chap. 3.

24. *Theater and Its Double,* trans. Richards, 25.

25. Rabelais, *Complete Works,* trans. Frame, 1016.

26. *Eel Capture, Culture, Processing and Marketing,* 155 (my emphasis). The salt method also kills the eel's "slipperiness" since it reduces the production of slime. These gory details didn't stop an anonymous reader from adding the following witticisms on a torn scrap of graph paper inserted inside the copy of the book that I consulted: "So one eel says to the other. . . . Elver, I hardly knew her!" and "What did the two larvae say to their parents after their baseball tryouts? — We feel they leptocephalus out because we weren't big enough." The connection with the author's final entry, "Spice Girls Rule," is rather more obscure.

27. Ibid., 153–54; my emphasis.

28. "M. Fournier, qui cite ces vers, pense que le proverbe tire son origine des cris habituels aux marchands" (*Livre des proverbes,* 2:50; app. 6.2).

29. Fournier, *Harangue de Turlupin le Soufreteux,* in *Variétés historiques et littéraires,* 6:53n; app. 6.4. Le Roux de Lincy refers us to the wrong volume and page of this text.

30. Ibid., 6:53n–54n; app. 6.4,(original emphasis).

31. *Synopsis of Biological Data on the Eel,* 50. My "research" for this book included inquiring of some thirty French fishmongers if they had ever heard an eel scream. I had fun asking, and I bought a lot of fish, but the answer was a unanimous no. Not a single merchant had ever heard of the Eel of Melun.

32. Ibid., 50.

33. *Eels: A Biological Study,* trans. Roquerbe, 1–3.

34. "Qui tient l'anguille par la cue il ne l'a mie" (Le Roux de Lincy, *Livre des proverbes*, 1:144–45).

35. See Briggs, *Dictionary of British Folk-Tales*, 2:185. This tale, which emphasizes the priest's surplice and stole, bears a passing resemblance to the *fabliau* "Estula" (discussed below in chapter 8 in connection with a rabbit-stealing priest). Compare to Jacomin Husson's goose-stealing priest (above, introduction, note 34); and to "The Eel Filled with Sand," no. 1804 in Aarne's *Types of the Folktale*, 496.

36. *Écorcher l'anguille par la queue* (literally, "to skin an eel by the tail") means to set about something the wrong way or from the wrong end. See Oudin, *Curiositez françoises*, 13, cited below, app. 6.5; *Dictionnaire de l'Académie Française* (1694); and Maloux, *Dictionnaire des proverbes*, 349.

37. *Eel Capture*, 155.

38. Rabelais, *Complete Works*, trans. Frame, 109. Readers of Rabelais will recall that this ridiculous war amounts to a food fight involving the market price of bread. Given the accessibility of Rabelais in many languages, I reproduce only select French passages.

39. *Gargantua*, chap. 47; *Complete Works*, trans. Frame, 109. The French reads: "Bren, bren! dist Picrochole; vous semblez les anguillez de Melun: vous criez davant qu'on vous escorche" (*Oeuvres complètes*, ed. Demerson, 180). Le Roux de Lincy cites this passage in *Livre des proverbes*, 2:49. In his index entry for eels of Melun, Frame notes: "strange result of the cry of the Melun eel-hawkers; Melun eels before they are skinned" (982).

40. *Pantagruel*, chap. 21; *Complete Works*, trans. Frame, 656. "Autres escorchoient les anguilles par la queuë, et ne crioient lesdictes anguilles avant que d'estre escorchées, comme font celles de Melun. Autres de néant faisoient choses grandes, et grandes choses faisoient à néant retourner" (*Oeuvres complètes*, ed. Demerson, 843).

41. "Le jeu de mots tient encore dans l'ambiguïté du sujet: on ne sait pas si ce sont ces poissonniers improvisés qui 'crient' les anguilles, ou si ce sont ces poissons qui poussent des cris" (*Oeuvres complètes*, ed. Demerson, 843n).

42. "On dit aussi, 'il ressemble a l'anguille de Melun, il crie avant qu'on l'escorche' pour dire qu'il se plaint d'un mal qui n'est point encore arrivé."

43. Today we would say: "to smell a rat."

44. *Curiositez françoises*, 13–14; app. 6.5. Le Roux de Lincy cites most of these and adds a few others in *Livre des proverbes*, 1:144–45.

45. Fournier, *Variétés*, 6:54n; app. 6.4; also cited with very minor variations by Le Roux de Lincy, *Livre des proverbes*, 2:50.

46. *Languille de Melun*, 12; app. 6.6. See also Larwood on another morbid Duval moment (*TA*, 314).

47. Ibid., 12; app. 6.6. In my translation, I have sacrificed literalism for poetic (or fishy) flavor, as it were.

48. Ibid., 12–13 (original ellipsis).

49. Compare, e.g., their *deliberate* effort to harm him physically with the comical but *unintentional* infliction of emotional distress by British audiences on the bald-pated Mr. Whitfield (*TA*, 214) or on Mr. Layfield of "green-eyed *lobster*" fame (*TA*, 107), discussed above, chap. 3.

50. *Languille de Melun*, 13; app. 6.6.

51. "On pense bien que ces substitutions exigeaient une grande habileté technique, pour ne pas trop désillusionner le spectateur, chez qui une fiction découverte aurait empêché l'émotion cherchée" (*HMS*, 149 [my emphasis]).

52. *Surprising Effects of Sympathy*, 24 (my emphasis). The comic response to mystery plays remains inadequately theorized, as I suggest in *MTOC*, 233–34.

Chapter 7. The Devil Who Wasn't There

1. *CPV,* 3:114–15 (my emphasis); app. 7.1. Compare also to *CVM,* 473, which refers to "the body" as a "child."

2. Jeffrey Burton Russell had enough material for five books: *The Devil, Mephistopheles, Prince of Darkness, Satan,* and *Lucifer* (see especially chaps. 4 and 9). Russell shows that the many different names of demons amount to a single evil (*Lucifer,* 64–67, 248–50). See also Gregg, *Devils, Women, and Jews,* chap. 2; and, for medieval English drama, Cox, "Devil and Society"; and Cox, *Devil and the Sacred.*

3. "La foule était groupée sur la place publique, et les *démons,* c'est-à-dire les personnages chargés de ce rôle infernal, parcouraient à plusieurs reprises les rangs des spectateurs, y jetant une gaieté mêlée d'effroi" (*Théâtre en France* [hereafter *TEF*], 3). His struggle to distinguish actors from demons predicts Cavell's point about pointing (*MWM,* 328; see above, chap. 3).

4. Cited by Petit de Julleville, "Vers 1500. Chaumont.—Saint-Jean-Baptiste," in *LM,* 2:82; app. 7.2. A papal bull of 8 February 1475 authorized these parades when the Feast of Saint John the Baptist (24 June) fell on a Sunday. See the *lettres patentes* in Jolibois, *Diablerie de Chaumont,* 142–48; also Koopmans, *Théâtre des exclus,* 161–66; Bristol, *Carnival and Theater,* chap. 9; and Miri Rubin on the "inherent destabilising element" of processional ritual (*Corpus Christi,* 265).

5. *LM,* 2:82; app. 7.2. I have found no other mention of this particular proverb; but see an English proverbial equivalent in which "devilling" means plagiarism (*TA,* 9–10).

6. Gosselin, *Recherches sur les origines,* 62; app. 7.3. He cites the *arrêts du Parlement* (16 December 1639 and 16 October 1640), recorded a century *after* the original incident. Petit de Julleville paraphrases Gosselin in "1539. Tirepied (Manche).—Sainte Barbe," in *LM,* 2:137–38. His own account is lackluster by comparison and omits many of the scintillating details.

7. Gosselin, *Recherches sur les origines,* 62–63; app. 7.3.

8. Ibid., 63; app. 7.3.

9. Again, see *FA,* chap. 10.

10. Gosselin, *Recherches sur les origines,* 63; app. 7.3.

11. Compare to apps. 5.1, 5.2.

12. "L'affaire se dénoua devant le Parlement" (*LM,* 2:138). Compare to the seventeenth-century reversal of legal fortune of the English actor Mathew Coppinger, who moved from on-stage judge to real-life thief (*TA,* 215–16).

13. Gosselin, *Recherches sur les origines,* 63; app. 7.3.

14. This is my argument in both *ROMD* and *MTOC.*

15. *SW,* 177 (original emphasis).

16. *CMJH,* 268–69; app. 7.4; also discussed by Petit de Julleville, "1512. Metz.—Esther. L'Enfant donné au Diable," in *LM,* 2:102. In *CVM,* we read only that there was played on that same day "a beautiful mystery play about one of the miracles of Our Lady" (677); and in *CPV,* nothing at all. For a description of this play and its manuscript sources, see *LM,* 2:226–31; and Penn, "Staging of the 'Miracles de Nostre Dame.'" The disturbing subject of marital rape lies beyond the scope of this book.

17. *CMJH,* 268–69; app. 7.4. She does not make the trip in the extant play texts (*LM,* 2:102).

18. *CMJH,* 269; app. 7.4.

19. See, e.g., "The Cardplayers and the Devil," in Briggs, *Dictionary,* 1:69; and Aarne, *Types of the Folktale,* 274–79, especially no. 813C, where the Devil says, "*May the Devil Skin me* if this is not true"—whereupon the Devil does. The spectacle of card-playing is a favorite theme of theater phenomenology; *FA,* 124–27; and Kirby, *Formalist Theatre,* x–xv. See also Isidore of Seville's grouping of theater, gambling, and dice games in *Etymologiarum,* bk. 18 (discussed in my *ROMD,* 77–89).

20. *CPV,* 4:136; app. 7.5; also *CVM,* 679. Blanctrain's name is a pun on his low social standing and his trade of carrying straw for sale. *Trainer* is to carry a burden, while *train* could refer to a beast of burden, a life style, a prosecution, or mistreatment. Legally, *blancs* referred to the "blank spaces" of what we call today the "boilerplate" contract that he unwittingly ratifies with the Devil.

21. *CPV,* 4:136; app. 7.5; also *CVM,* 679–80. Jacomin Husson's version is less dramatic (*CMJH,* 270; app. 7.6).

22. *CPV,* 4:137; app. 7.5. Bruneau notes that Philippe has corrected an earlier version that had Blanctrain additionally unable to eat or drink (137n). See also *CVM,* 680. As a teenager, I saw with my own eyes the dummy used in the *Exorcist,* which was prominently displayed for Halloween in the home of its creator, Dick Smith. Of special interest is the adverb *parfaictement,* which denotes both perfection and legal completion *(parfaire).*

23. I.e., actors tend not to display their backs to the audience, even when logic would dictate that they do so.

24. *Devil and the Sacred,* 125.

25. Prynne (1600–1669), *Histriomastix,* fol. 556r (original emphasis). The Garland edition has two different pages bearing the number 556. See also Bakeless, *Tragicall History of Christopher Marlowe,* 1:299–300; and Cox, *Devil and the Sacred,* 125.

26. *Gentleman's Magazine,* 2nd ser., 34:234 S 1850; cited by Bakeless, *Tragicall History,* 300 (original emphasis); and by Sinden in *EBTA,* 3. Vautrollier, recalls Bakeless, was a sixteenth-century Huguenot refugee who had presses in both London and Edinburgh (300n).

27. *Histriomastix,* fol. 556r. The "lost manuscript note" bears a striking similarity to our snuff story as told by Delangre, *Théâtre et l'art dramatique,* 6–7 (below, chap. 14).

28. Compare to the Furies of the *Eumenides* (app. 5.3). On the physical "look" of the Devil in early drama, see Russell, *Lucifer,* 67–80; and *AFS,* 1:15.

29. Ryan thinks that Bencraft *may have been* the actor in the prank, but he's not sure (*DTT,* 3:191). He gives no dates for the performance, but we do find a John Rich (1692?–1761), the "theatrical manager" and famous "pantomime performer" (*EBTA,* 22).

30. Dickson and Goulden, *There Are Alligators,* 129.

31. Literally, he could not be *found (non inventus);* nor, in the minds of many, was he "made up" *(inventus).*

32. See, e.g., *IO,* XI.3.62; and *AP,* 129–30.

33. "Tenebres des pauvres presionniers de la Conciergerie du Palais," in Marot, *Oeuvres,* ed. Guiffrey, 2:523, ll. 55–60; app. 7.7. The double-entendre of *enchainer* as "to bring about or occasion" and to "be chained" is lost in translation. Marot *was* detained at the Conciergerie between 1527 and 1536 (*TRF,* 14).

34. "Cette petite scène n'est point de pure imagination. Elle a été certainement prise sur nature" (2:523n).

35. Marot, *Oeuvres,* ed. Guiffrey, 523n; app. 7.7.

36. Ibid., 524n; app. 7.7. Compare to *Adam,* ed. Luzarche, 12; app. 7.8.

37. *[Adam.] Ordo repraesentationis Adae,* ed. and trans. Bevington, p. 105 after v. 590 (my emphasis); app. 7.9.

38. One assumes a learned milieu because the stage directions are in Latin. I'm not disputing the extrapolations that led Hardison to posit the liturgical origins of medieval drama (*CRCD,* Essay 6), but one can only extrapolate so far. Compare, e.g., the extrapolations about the *Eumenides* (app. 5.3).

39. "Interea demones discurrant *per plateas,* gestum facientes competentem"; "tunc recedat diabolus, et ibit ad alios demones, et faciet discursum *per plateam*" (*[Adam.] Ordo repraesentationis Adae,* ed. and trans. Bevington, 85, 89; my emphasis).

40. Marot, *Oeuvres*, ed. Guiffrey, 523n–24n. The learned Rabelais was the master of ambiguity. See Gray, "Ambiguity and Point of View."

41. See the full story in *Pantagruel* (1532), in Rabelais, *Complete Works*, trans. Frame, 465–67; *Oeuvres*, ed. Demerson, chap. 13, pp. 618–19.

42. These vestments recall *Estula*, in *Recueil général et complet des fabliaux*, ed. Montaiglon and Raynaud, 4:90. Compare, e.g., to the Cordeliers' actual lending practices in Romans in 1509 (*LM*, 2:96) and to the regulations cited by Faber (*HTB*, 12) regarding clerical involvement in Passion plays vs. "farces, mummeries, and dissolute plays" (Rabelais, *Complete Works*, trans. Frame, 465).

43. *Tiers Livre*, in Rabelais, *Complete Works*, trans. Frame, 267–70; *Oeuvres*, ed. Demerson, 384–85.

44. On poetic justice in urban legends, see *CD*, xii–xiii; *TGT*, chap. 3; also Nussbaum, *Poetic Justice;* Weisberg, *Poethics;* and Green, on "Folklaw," in *Crisis of Truth*, chap. 3.

45. *Pantagruel*, in Rabelais, *Complete Works*, trans. Frame, 466. Given the horrific 1998 dragging death of James Byrd, killed by white supremacists in Jasper, Texas, it is doubtful that this particular "gag" would hold up.

46. *Pantagruel*, in Rabelais, *Complete Works*, trans. Frame, 465–66 (my emphasis).

47. "Nous n'oserions assûrer que l'aventure . . . soit bien certaine" (*HTF*, 2:262).

48. "Rappelons ici l'anecdote célèbre, mais peu fondée. . . . Rien ne prouve que cette ancedote soit fausse; rien n'en confirme l'exactitude" (*LM*, 1:381).

49. "Tintamarre *effroyable* de chaudières et de casseroles" (*Mystère d'Adam*, ed. Chamard, 93 [my emphasis]).

50. Oudin, *Curiositez françoises*, 164–65; app. 7.10; see also *TRF*, 14; *LCR*, 343n; and Burrow, "'Young Saint, Old Devil.'"

51. *TMA*, 223–24; cited above in chap. 5.

52. *Malleus maleficarum* (1486), trans. Kors and Peters, in *Witchcraft in Europe*, 152. Compare with app. 3.1.

53. See *Malleus*, trans. Kors and Peters, in *Witchcraft in Europe*, 146–47. I include the Latin texts and discuss their mnemonic dimensions in "Violence, Silence."

54. *Malleus*, trans. Kors and Peters, in *Witchcraft in Europe*, 147.

55. Foxe, *Acts and Monuments*, 1:528, 5:409; also cited and discussed by Diehl, in *SR*, 100, 105.

56. *Passion*, 14007–14; cited above, chap. 6, note 18.

57. Farel, *Sommaire et brève déclaration* (hereafter *SBD*), ed. Hofer, chap. 10, p. 76; app. 7.11. Stephen Ozment discusses this work at length in *Reformation in the Cities* (hereafter *RIC*), 67–74. For readability, I have dropped the numerous brackets of Hofer's very careful edition.

Chapter 8. The Laughter of the Children

1. *AFS*, 1:15. Hawkins seems to paraphrase the proverbial expression, *tirer le Diable par la queue*, glossed by Oudin as "to work hard to earn one's living" (*Curiositez francoises*, 164). See also Russell on Saint Dunstan, *Lucifer*, 72–73.

2. See *DTT*, 2:25; also 3:117–19.

3. In *Recueil de farces françaises inédites*, ed. Cohen, 317–26; see especially ll. 209–17.

4. I've seen this routine on HBO: I just can't say when!

5. Nouvelle 13, *Grand Parangon*, ed. Mabille, 63–64.

6. In Cohen, *Recueil de farces*, 57–66. Or the two works share a source.

7. *A C. Mery Talys* in *Shakespeare Jest-Books*, ed. Hazlitt, 14–17; compare to the Oesterley edition, 7–11. See Coldewey's superb "Thrice-Told Tales," especially 24–29. Eamon Duffy mentions "John Adoyne" in *Stripping of the Altars*, 17.

8. *A C. Mery Talys*, 17 (original emphasis). See Coldewey, "Thrice-Told Tales," 25.

9. *Pantagruel*, in *Complete Works*, trans. Frame, 465–67; *Oeuvres*, ed. Demerson, 616–18.

10. *A. C. Mery Talys*, 17; "Thrice-Told Tales," 28 (original emphasis). See also Cox, *Devil and the Sacred*, chap. 3; Aarne, *Types of the Folktale*, no. 813, "The Dishonest Priest."

11. See Howard Bloch on the "ill-fitting coat of the fabliaux," *Scandal of the Fabliaux*, chap. 1; and for the goose-craving priest, *CMJH*, 277–78; above, introduction, note 34.

12. "Address to Young Men on Reading Greek Literature," 358.

13. "Ac deinde . . . pro risu astantium et concurrentium turpes gesticulationes sui corporis faciendo, et verba impudicissima ac scurrilia proferendo" (*Epistola et xiv. conclusiones facultatis theologiae Parisiensis;* cited and translated by Chambers, *Mediaeval Stage*, 1:294). See Eco, *Name of the Rose*, 471–79; and Olson on ethics, "Plays as Play," 213.

14. "Unde à Deo datum est, ut nulla exsibilatio, nulla plebis consternatio, aut derisiorè quid gestum fuerit" (*Catalogus gloriae mundi*, 577; my translation); also discussed by Petit de Julleville, *LM*, 1:404–5.

15. "Magis risum & clamorem causabat quam deuocionem" (Johnston and Rogerson, eds., *York*, 1:47–48, 2:732); discussed by Evans, "When a Body," 199. See also Bristol, *Carnival*, chap. 11.

16. Vives (b. 1492), *Scandale grand de représenter la passion de nostre Seigneur par personnages;* cited by Roy, *Mystère*, 315 (my emphasis); app. 8.1. Roy deems this text "barely known but barely suspect," given the piety of its author.

17. Procurator general (more or less the equivalent of the attorney general), cited by Sainte-Beuve in *Tableau historique et critique de la poésie française* (hereafter *TPF*), 193; app. 8.2. For a stage direction calling for the Holy Spirit to "come down," see Petit de Julleville, "1536. Bourges.—Les Actes des Apôtres," in *LM*, 2:131–32. For Quintilian, see *IO*, VI.2.35.

18. See *Rabelais and His World*, introduction and chap. 1; and Nichols, *Rire et théâtralité*.

19. See Foucault, *Discipline and Punish* (hereafter *DP*), 46–69.

20. Howard Harvey, e.g., believes that the *enfants sans souci* were a subsidiary of the Basochiens, the legal apprentices famous for both real and theatrical litigation in the fourteenth and fifteenth centuries; *Theatre of the Basoche*, 24–27.

21. According to Bernard Faivre, "Jean de l'Espine, called Pontalais or Songe-Creux, was a *farceur* who attained great celebrity between 1510 and 1540" (*Théâtre en France*, 1:67–68). For his story, see also *TPF*, 193.

22. *HTF*, 2:228–29; app. 8.3.

23. He had believed himself to be sufficiently covered by his authorization from a civil judge (*Archives de la Seine- Inférieure*, Registre de l'officialité [1462]); cited by Gosselin, *Recherches*, 19; and also by Petit de Julleville, "1462. Bouafles.—Les Miracles de Notre-Dame," in *LM*, 2:29.

24. I do not use the term *plagiarism* lightly, although it is often inappropriate to medieval conceptions of literary creation. Hawkins's first sentence, e.g., is none other than the Parfaicts' footnote in *HTF*, 2:228n; see app. 8.3. Clément also reproduces their version essentially verbatim (*AD*, 3:402–3).

25. *Nouvelles récréations*, ed. Lacour, 157; app. 8.4.

26. Ibid., 157–58; app. 8.4.

27. *In theatro ecclesiae* is the phrase employed by Honorius Augustodunensis in his famous description of the drama of the Mass; *Gemma animae* (c. 1100) in Bevington, *Medieval Drama*, 9.

28. Cited by Sainte-Beuve, *TPF*, 193; app. 8.2. See also Hallays-Dabot, *Histoire de la censure*, 14–16.

29. *TPF*, 193–94; app. 8.2.

30. "Sans farsses ne empeschemens des sermons ne vespres"; "sans pouvoir jouer aucunes

farses villaines et deshonnestes" (cited by Lebègue, in *MAA*, 30–31). Compare with the procurator general on "farces lascives et momeries" (app. 8.2).

31. Vinchant, *Annales de la province et comté du Hainaut*, 5:267; app. 8.5; also cited by Faber with several errors and variants (*HTB*, 12).

32. *VH*, 81–90, 53–57; *CBA*, 37–40; *CD*, 194–99.

33. The brothers Parfaict trace such objections back to an edict of 789 that suppressed the obscene plays of *farceurs*, dancers, and magicians (*HTF*, 1: 2). We discuss heresy in chapters 11 and 12, below.

34. Cited by Sainte-Beuve, in *TPF*, 193; app. 8.2. Compare also with Vives, *Scandale grand*, cited by Roy, *Mystère*, 315; app. 8.1; and Farel on laughter, *SBD*, chap. 19, 118–20.

35. Vinchant, *Annales du Hainaut*, 5:267; app. 8.5.

36. *TA*, 214; cited above, chap. 3.

37. Cited by Petit de Julleville, "1452. Beauvais.—Saint Pierre," in *LM*, 2:23; app. 8.6.

38. Archives d'Angers, BB 4, fol. 29; cited by Port, *Inventaire analytique*, 350; and also in Jean Michel, *Mystère de la Passion*, ed. Jodogne, xl. For the French, see app. 5.5.

39. "Surtout pour préparer les spectateurs au recueillement salutaire de leurs âmes . . . et de la ville" (Jodogne, ed., Jean Michel, *Mystère de la Passion*, xli).

40. "Ouvrez vos yeulx et regardez,/devotes gens qui actendez/A oÿr chose salutaire./Vueillez vous pour vo salut taire/par une amoureuse scilence" (Gréban, *Passion*, ed. Jodogne, 1–5). Another such plea appears below, chap. 14, note 48.

41. *Republic*, 606c; *Laws*, 700e–701. By *mousike*, Plato connotes theater, music, philosophy, singing, dancing, pantomime, rhetoric, social exchange, and pedagogy. He plays explicitly on the dual meaning of *nomos* as "law" and "chant" *(neume); also Laws*, 655d–e, 800.

42. Compare to Alan Knight, "Beyond Misrule."

43. See *Laws*, 655d–e.

44. *Laws*, 659d, 700c–d (my emphasis). On the medieval rule of the rod, see Ong, *Rhetoric, Romance, and Technology*, chaps. 5 and 6; and Holsinger's brilliant reading of its connection to music, *Music, Body, and Desire*, chap. 6. Also, Julius Goebel recalls that ninth-century Frankish bishops were empowered to flog men into accepting Christ; *Felony and Misdemeanor*, 170–71.

45. *Pantagruel*, in *Complete Works*, trans. Frame, 466; see above, chap. 7.

46. "Il faut transporter un public prêt à toutes les plaisanteries, disposé à saisir au vol le moindre sujet de ridicule, dans une atmosphère de douleur, de mystère et de mort, et l'y maintenir de force. Ce n'est pas si facile qu'on pense" (*Théâtre de la mort*, 16).

47. "Et se fut conclut que on n'entre oudit *Parcq* qu'il ne soit ix heures du matin et qu'il n'y entre nuls enffans qu'il n'ait x ans d'eaige, nulles anchiennes gens débilles, ne nulles femmes enchaintes" (Mons, Meeting of the Town Council of 26 June 1501; cited by Cohen, *LCR*, 591; original emphasis).

48. See, e.g., Nagler, *Source Book*, 5; above, chap. 5.

49. Vinchant, *Annales*, 5:269; app. 8.5; also cited by Faber, *HTB*, 12.

50. Consider director Steven Spielberg's suggestion to *Dateline NBC* (21 July 1998) that children under age fifteen were too young for the realistic *Saving Private Ryan;* or the public outrage at the abuse of child actors. See also Mullaney, *Place of the Stage*, 92–93; and Steiner, *Scandal*, introduction and chap. 1.

51. A stage direction of the Valenciennes Passion play of 1547, e.g., called for blood to be "seen issuing from infants' bodies" ("Item a loccision des inocens on voyoit le sang sortir de leurs corps"); *Mistére par personnaiges . . .* , Rothschild I.7.3, fol. 147r; also cited by Konigson, *Représentation d'un mystère de la Passion à Valenciennes en 1547* (hereafter *MPV*), 80; also discussed by Gatton, "There Must Be Blood," 82.

52. See Steiner, *Death of Tragedy;* Kerr, *Tragedy and Comedy;* and Percy Fitzgerald's amusing tale of "Rustics at Play," *Book of Theatrical Anecdotes,* 19.

53. "Une preuve convainquante que le Mystere de la Passion n'est pas vulgairement connu, c'est que bien des gens disent la Comédie de la Passion; titre que ce Poëme n'a jamais reçu que des ignorans, & des impies" (*HTF,* 1:xvi, note). The genre is thus known both "commonly" and "in a common way" *(connu vulgairement).*

54. *LM,* 1:410 (my emphasis); app. 8.7.

55. On this topos, see Bloch, "New Philology and Old French," 43–46; and, Saint Paul's "child" who sees "through a glass darkly," 1 Cor. 13.11–12.

56. "Ils étaient de médiocres psychologues. Ils savaient définir les vertus cardinales et les péchés mortels, mais ils ignoraient le processus d'un sentiment et ses formes complexes" (*TRF,* 22).

57. *Oeuvres de Clement Marot,* ed. Guiffrey, 4:326; ll. 43–48; app. 8.8; also in *HTF,* 2:245–47.

58. "Ils lui feroient grand'peur, s'il ne lui faisoient point de mal. . . . La mule effrayée jetta le Cavalier par terre, & gagna le Couvent au plus vite; le pauvre Sacristain demeura pour les gages sur le champ de bataille, *demi-mort* de peur & tout brisé de sa chûte" (*AD,* 2:567–58 [my emphasis]). Compare to *Pantagruel,* in *Complete Works,* trans. Frame, 465–67; discussed above, chap. 7.

59. *HMS,* 49–50; app. 8.9. Compare, e.g., to Lebègue on redemptive tears (*TRF,* 6; discussed above, chap. 2).

60. Homan, "Mixed Feelings," 94.

61. See *TA,* 214; discussed above, chap. 3.

62. On the "bewildering array of churches and sects" that would later come to be known as Protestants (Huguenots, Calvinists, Anabaptists, Lutherans, Anglicans, Hutterites, Mennonites, Amish), see especially Ozment, *Protestants,* ix.

63. Cited by Sainte-Beuve, *TPF,* 195; app. 8.2; and discussed by Elliot, "Medieval Acting," 245–46. See also Fabre-Vassas, *Singular Beast* (hereafter *SB*), 150.

64. "En induisant pour chose pie / Judaïque cérémonie" (Fournier, ed., *Théâtre français,* 420). The character Texte even uses the verb *to judaicize* (421).

65. "Le bateleur s'enfarinant la joue, / De l'Evangile au théâtre se joue, / Comme un Juif ou Païen" (cited by Lebègue, *TRF,* 372).

66. *Scandale grand,* cited by Roy, *Mystère,* 315; app. 8.1.

67. Cited and discussed by Ozment, *RIC,* 69–70. See *SBD,* chap. 19, 118–20, chap. 28.

68. See, e.g, Hallays-Dabot, *Histoire de la censure,* chap. 1; Maugras, *Comédiens hors la loi;* Gardiner, *Mysteries' End,* chap. 6; Dutton, "Censorship"; Elliott, *Playing God,* chap. 1; and Holquist, "Corrupt Originals."

Chapter 9. Burnt Theatrical Offerings

1. "Cette confrérie exista sans nul doute, et c'est peut-être pour elle et sur ses ordres, ou à ses frais, que fut composé et representé le mystère de la sainte Hostie" (*LM,* 2:576). We return shortly to Felibien's five-volume *Histoire de la ville de Paris* (1725; hereafter *HVP*). It was completed by Lobineau upon the former's death. See also Rubin's beautiful reconstruction of the Paris legend in *Gentile Tales* (hereafter *GT*), 40–46.

2. In his edition, Bevington remarks that it dates from "the late fifteenth century, not long after the year (1461) in which the miracle is supposed to have taken place" (*Medieval Drama,* 756). See, e.g, Spector, "Time, Space and Identity"; Spector, "Anti-Semitism and the English Mystery Plays"; Dox, "Medieval Drama as Documentation"; Clark and Sponsler, "Othered Bodies"; and Paxson, "Structure of Anachronism."

3. The *Sainte Hostie* (hereafter *SH*) is a play of 1,590 verses and 26 characters, which has yet

to be edited. It survives in two undated, sixteenth-century Parisian editions and a reissue in Aix of 1817 (*LM*, 2:574; also *MFI*, 160–61). I cite from one of the sixteenth-century editions, Bibliothèque Nationale, Réserve Yf 2915. I thank Alan Knight for sharing with me his personal copy of the microfilm.

4. I analyze the equation of Jews to pigs in "Homicidal Pigs"; as does Claudine Fabre-Vassas, in *SB*, especially chaps. 4–7.

5. "Affin qu'il en soit mention/Et mesmement dedans Paris/Qu'en l'hostel du maudict juif/Soit fondé un monastere" (*SH*, fol. 30v). For clarity, I have added punctuation, accents, or apostrophes; substituted *j* for *i;* and resolved the occasional abbreviation. Rubin states that the nickname "des Billettes" derives from the "badge in the shape of a lozenge *(billette)* which the brethren wore on their habits" (*GT*, 44).

6. A more detailed plot summary appears in *LM*, 2:574–76.

7. The "myth of ritual murder" refers, of course to the superstition that Jews kill Christian children. See especially Po-chia Hsia, *Myth of Ritual Murder* (hereafter *MRM*); and Michael Goodich on medieval children as victims, *Violence and Miracle*, chap. 5. Murder "by proxy" seems appropriate to the "mauvaise femme"; her child's fate may be traced to Jacob's polluting influence. I am deliberately suggesting a connection with the notorious Munchausen syndrome by proxy, in which mothers allegedly induce illness in their children in order to seek attention. David Allison and Mark Roberts argue that the syndrome is a kind of urban legend with medieval antecedents (*Disordered Mother*, 7, and foreword by Thomas M. Ryan, Esq., xxii).

8. "From *Lieux de mémoire,*" xv; also Clark, *Literary France*, prologue and chap. 1. On 5 October 1328 the church—by then a convent—received a bequest to the place "where God was boiled" (*HVP*, 1:bk. 9, 459; app. 9.6).

9. For Clark and Sponsler, "the memory of these events was inscribed in the very landscape of urban Paris" ("Othered Bodies," 77).

10. See Boussu, *Histoire de la Ville de Mons*, 95; app. 9.1.

11. "A l'occasion du sacrilege que quelques-uns de leur nation avoient commis à Bruxelles en poignardant les saintes Hosties, d'où il sortit un sang miraculeux que l'on conserve encore" (Boussu, *Histoire de la Ville de Mons*, 112). For another anti-Semitic legend preserved in a play, see Léopold Dupont on the *Miracle de Notre-Dame de Cambron* by Coppée (b. c. 1580), "Denis Coppée," 799.

12. On the "unbearable specter of cannibalism" that undergirds the myth of ritual murder, see *SB*, 5, 135–36, 148, 237–38; and Lestringant, *Une Sainte horreur*, chap. 3. Po-chia Hsia documents blood-stealing and bloodthirstiness but not blood-drinking per se in *MRM*, 30, 92.

13. In addition to *MRM* and *GT*, see Nirenberg, *Communities of Violence*, especially chap. 2; Kruger, "Spectral Jew," 19–32; Koopmans, *Théâtre des exclus*, 137–42; Sponsler, *Drama and Resistance*, chap. 6; and Gregg, *Devils, Women, and Jews*, 216–27.

14. Exemplary work includes Langer, *Holocaust and the Literary Imagination;* Langer, *Holocaust Testimonies;* Caruth, *Unclaimed Experience;* LaCapra, *Representing the Holocaust;* and Birnbaum, "Grégoire, Dreyfus, Drancy."

15. Scarry describes this ideological reversal of agent and victim (*Body in Pain*, 50–59); as does Rubin, *GT*, 44, 170–72. See also States and Cox on theater as community self-definition (*GR*, 157) or antidefinition ("Devil and Society," 409–10).

16. Nirenberg argues that contemporaneous chroniclers "celebrated the exile of the Jews but were unsure whether it had really occurred. Jews left France, but they were apparently never compelled by a royal edict of expulsion" (*Communities*, 67).

17. Here I amplify my argument in *MTOC* that the violence of remembering tends to excuse itself by suggesting that real violence happens only in performance (111–20).

18. *SH*, fol. 24v; app. 9.8.

19. *HVP*, 1:bk. 9, 459; app. 9.6. By this account, the pope granted permission only in 17 July 1295, or *after* the chapel had already been built. See also *GT*, 44.

20. *Parisian Journal*, trans. Shirley, 353. For the French, see *JBP*, 417–18; app. 9.2; also discussed by the brothers Parfaict, *HTF*, 2:331n; and *GT*, 161. The *bourgeois de Paris* also reports on an equally impressive procession of 3 June 1412, in which the faithful carried "the precious body of Our Lord which the false Jews boiled" (*Parisian Journal*, trans. Shirley, 63; *JBP*, 48). Clark and Sponsler cite both these records in "Othered Bodies," 77, and Shirley provides an excellent summary of the Paris legend, 93n. Compare both events to the Bourges procession that preceded the *Acts of the Apostles* in Bourges in 1536. It too featured Jews and Hosts (Thiboust, *Relation de l'ordre* e.g., 23–24).

21. *Gedenkbuch*, ed. Michelant, 244–45; app. 9.7.

22. "La première feste de la Pentecoste fut jué le Jeu en Chambre de la Sainte Hostie, et fuit ung bien biaulx miraicle et bien jué" (*CMJH*, 280; compare to *CVP*, 4:154).

23. *CMJH*, 322; app. 9.3. A more gruesome version (dated 1503) appears in *Gedenkbuch*, 144–45; *CPV*, 4:25–26; and *CVM*, 642. I explore it, with Munchausen by proxy, in "Dead Babies and Medieval Revisionist History," in progress.

24. *Connaissance du Vieux Paris* (1951), 56; app. 9.4; also discussed by Clark and Sponsler, "Othered Bodies," 77.

25. *Connaissance du Vieux Paris* (1951), 56; app. 9.4.

26. *HVP*, 2:bk. 16, 833; app. 9.5; also cited by the brothers Parfaict, *HTF*, 2:331n. Except for their reference to Book "XVL" (instead of XVI), they reproduce Felibien's text carefully (with the usual minor variants). I thus reproduce only Felibien's version, and indicate in appendix 9.5, their one omission.

27. *HVP*, 1:bk. 9, 458 (my emphasis). I include a long excerpt of this relatively inaccessible text in appendix 9.6.

28. Ibid., 458–59, 460; app. 9.6.

29. Ibid., 458 (my emphasis). See four such instances of dialogic speech in appendix 9.6. For the theatrical and iconographic dimensions of witnessing, see my *MTOC*, 185–92; and Miles, *Image as Insight*, chap. 3.

30. *CMJH*, 268–69; app. 7.4.

31. "Othered Bodies," 77. Colette Beaune believes that it was a *tableau vivant* in which an actor played the Jew; *JBP*, 418n.

32. *HVP*, 2:bk. 16, 833; app. 9.5; also cited by the brothers Parfaict, *HTF*, 2:331n.

33. *Parisian Journal*, trans. Shirley, 353; *JBP*, 417–18; app. 9.2.

34. *Connaissance du Vieux Paris*, 56; app. 9.4.

35. "Cy prent L'hostie et la cloue d'un clou en une coulonne et le sang en coule a terre" (fol. 10r); "Il le jette au feu et il ne se y veut pas tenir," "Le juif prent une lance et frappe L'Hostie contre la cheminee," "Icy prent un cousteau de cuysine: et hache l'hostie parmy la maison" (fol. 10v); "Icy apert un crucifix en la chaudiere contre la cheminee" (fols. 11v–12r). The kitchen knife is logical: the tortures occur where food is prepared in a kosher home. See *SB*, 132–33.

36. *HVP*, 1:bk. 9, 458 (my emphasis); app. 9.6. Compare these tortures to *SH*, fols. 10–12; the Croxton play, ed. Bevington, 70–73; and *GT*, 41.

37. *Gedenkbuch*, 244–45; app. 9.7. It is possible, of course, that some *other* version of the play, which has not survived, contained similar language. The *Sainte Hostie* was the first of three plays performed for the Pentecost holidays of 1513. Petit de Julleville summarizes them in "1513. Metz.—La Sainte Hostie. Saint Nicolas de Bari," in *LM*, 2:103–4. All three are documented in all editions of the *Chroniques de Metz*: see *CPV*, 4:154–55; *CVM*, 687; and *CMJH*, 280. Only the

Gedenkbuch contains the full details of the *Sainte Hostie*. On this passage, see Gatton, "There Must Be Blood," 83; *MTOC*, 194–95; and *SB*, 153, 157. Unfortunately, since Fabre-Vassas accesses the play through secondary sources, she commits some errors: e.g., *Léon* Petit de Julleville, Philippe de *Vigneules, Jonathan* for Jacob.

38. *HVP*, 1:bk. 9, 458 (my emphasis); app. 9.6. See also Rubin on the latrine connection, *GT*, 33.

39. *Gedenkbuch*, 244–45; app. 9.7. See also *SH*, fols. 9r–12v.

40. While there is no phonological or etymological relationship between *contre-feu* and *contre-foi*, Philippe appears to suggest one anyway (see my "Dramatic Memories," 214–15). *Contrefoi* as "incredulity" is attested as early as 1260. Furthermore, Jacob subjects the Host to an ordeal normally reserved for counterfeiters—boiling. Philippe de Beaumanoir, e.g., recommends that counterfeiters "must be hanged, and before that, boiled, and they have forfeited their possessions" (*Coutumes de Beauvaisis*, ed. Akehurst, sec. 835, p. 304). I thank Professor Akehurst for pointing this out to me.

41. *HVP*, 1:bk. 9, 458; app. 9.6.

42. See above, chap. 8, notes 63–67.

43. "On n'en scaura ja rien nullement/Et tu seras au moins paree/Sans payer mont ne *souldee*/N'esse pas grand gaigne en malheure" (*SH*, fol. 6r). The term *souldee* is of special interest in that it denotes not only "reward," "salary," or "profit," but is also part of the expression *aller querre soldes* (to go into service): precisely the fate of the Mauvaise Femme.

44. "Ains qu'il soit minuict/Celuy que mon pere a destruict/Luy en donra un bon payement" (*SH*, fol. 12v).

45. "Prenez y tous et toutes exemplaire. Il est payé de son salaire,/Ce faux juif de toutes pars./Luy et son livre sont ars/Fy de luy et de tous ses artz,/Il est payé de son salaire" (*SH*, fols. 30v–31r). The parallel between "burnt" *(ars)* and magic arts *(artz)* is lost in translation. Jacob is denounced as a practitioner of black magic (e.g., fols. 28v, 29v).

46. See, e.g., Petit de Julleville, "Vers 1500. Chaumont.—Saint Jean-Baptiste," in *LM*, 2:80–81: *entrepreneurs* sought permission to charge an entrance fee to defray the construction costs of their *Life of Saint John the Baptist*. In exchange, they offered prayers for the authorities' souls.

47. *Gedenkbuch*, 245; app. 9.7. Compare also to *CPV*, 4:155; and *CVM*, 687, where Huguenin does not identify Philippe as the speaker. On the substantial economic costs of medieval dramatic productions, see *LM*, 1:chap. 10; *HMS*, 67–104; and *TMA*, chap. 8.

48. Boussu, *Histoire de la Ville de Mons*, 95; app. 9.1.

49. *SH*, fols. 24r, 29r; app. 9.8.

50. *SH*, fol. 24v–r; app. 9.8.

51. *CMJH*, 294–95; app. 9.9. A more dramatic version still appears in *CPV*, 4:189–90, in which Philippe de Vigneulles describes props, scenery, and *coups de théâtre* in Oliver's *mistére*.

52. The term *holocaust* was known in medieval France in both latinate and vernacular forms (*holocaustum, holocauste*). See, e.g., Alan of Lille, *Art of Preaching*, in *Patrologia latina*, ed. Migne, 210:173–74; trans. Evans, *Art of Preaching*, 127.

53. *Book of Theatrical Anecdotes*, 17.

54. "Comme le titre de cet Ouvrage pourroit tromper des personnes mal instruites, il est bon de leur faire remarquer, qu'il n'a été composé que pour perpétuer la mémoire d'un Miracle authentique arrivé à Paris dans le treizième siècle, qui a occasionné la fondation de l'Eglise des Carmes Billettes de cette Ville" (*HTF*, 2:331–32n).

55. For the whole stage "drowned in blood," see *Gedenkbuch*, 244; app. 9.7; and Blau, *Blooded Thought*.

56. Haidu, *Subject of Violence*, 193–94. At the turn of the twenty-first century, the problem of censoring hate speech resurfaced in the debates about the racist remarks of baseball player John Rocker.

57. See *PDMA*, 152–53, 19.

58. "Violence and the Social Body," 77.

59. *Communities*, 17. I allude here to the subtitle of Scarry's *Body in Pain:* "The Making and Unmaking of the World."

60. See Roelker, *One King*, 201–5.

Chapter 10. Theater's Living Dead

1. Paul-Émile Giraud tracked down the manuscript and described it in detail in his edition of the *Mystère des trois doms joué à Romans en MDIX . . . avec le compte de sa composition, mise en scène et représentation* (1887), introduction, xi–xiv. In 1880 Petit de Julleville had reported it as lost ("1509. Romans.—Les Trois Doms," in *LM*, 2:95–96). Upon Giraud's death, Ulysse Chevalier completed the edition (*Trois Doms*, introduction, cxlvii–cxlviii). On Chanoine Pra, see *Trois Doms*, introduction, xxx–xxxii; and *LM*, 2:96–97.

2. *Trois Doms*, 591; app. 10.1.

3. Giraud published the *Accounting before* discovering the play-text. I will cite from his 1887 edition of the *Trois Doms*, which contains the play, the *Compte de sa composition* and an invaluable series of primary texts on the theater in Dauphiné. To avoid confusion, I refer to the relevant texts as follows: to Giraud's introduction as *Trois Doms*, introduction; to the actual dramatic text as *Trois Doms*, cited by verse numbers; and to the *Accounting* (cited by page number). See Giraud's summary of the *Accounting: Trois Doms*, introduction, xxvii–lxi.

4. "L'histoire de cette représentation est là tout entière avec des détails que nous ne possédons sur aucune autre" (*LM*, 2:96).

5. *LM*, 2:95 (my emphasis). We shall see below that he was quoting Giraud (*Trois Doms*, introduction, ix), and Giraud was quoting an article from the *Affiches du Dauphiné* of 1848.

6. On the theology of real presence, see *TMB;* Beckwith, *Signifying God;* and Brown, *Cult of the Saints*, chap. 5.

7. For an overview of divergent Catholic and Protestant views on these issues, see, e.g., *RIC*, chaps. 2 and 3, especially 143–44; Duffy, *Stripping of the Altars*, chaps. 5 and 11; and Le Goff, *Medieval Civilization*, 329–35. Miracles are the subject of our chapter 12. On theatricality and theology, see Rubin, *Corpus Christi; SR*, chap. 1; Beckwith, *Christ's Body;* Beckwith, *Signifying God; TMB;* Muir, *Biblical Drama*, 158–65; Dominguez, "Le Corps"; and *RPI*, 239–40.

8. Aulus Gellius, *Attic Nights*, trans. Rolfe, 2:bk. 6, chap. 5 (my emphasis). Larwood cites this apocryphal tale as fact (*TA*, 66).

9. "Opplevit omnia *non simulacris neque imitamentis*, sed luctu atque lamentis *veris* et spirantibus. Itaque cum agi fabula videretur, *dolor actus est*" (*Attic Nights*, 2.6.5 [my emphasis]). On this passage, see Ringer, *Electra and the Empty Urn*, 1–2; compare to Mrs. Montford (*TA*, 54–55); see above, chap. 3.

10. "Les habitants voulurent rendre grâces à Dieu de la cessation du fléau et en prévenir le retour par quelque oeuvre pie" (*LM*, 2:96).

11. Jean Bouchet, Epistle 91, cited by Petit de Julleville, "1535. Issoudun.—La Passion," in *LM*, 2:128–29; app. 10.2; see also app. 1.4.

12. See *Trois Doms*, introduction, xxvii.

13. *Accounting*, 591–92; app. 10.1. Compare to the processional spectacle that accompanied the *Sainte Hostie:* apps. 9.2 and 9.5. See above, chap. 4, note 4.

14. "De l'adoration et service des sainctz"; *SBD*, chap. 27, 168, 170; app. 10.3. Compare to

Calvin's *Institutes of the Christian Religion* of 1536 (published in French in 1541), 3.12, 3.20.20. See also Roelker, *One King, One Faith*, 202.

15. "Nous ne polrions mieulx honnorer les saincts qu'en ymitant leur foy et vertus . . . atendu que, de leur vivant, ilz ont reffusé tels honneurs; il ne convient doncques les invocquier pour intercesseurs attendu que cest honneur appertient à Christ" (*JBT*, 312). See app. 12.5. Compare to *SBD*, 168; app. 10.3.

16. *Protestants*, 25.

17. Again, the exception is *TMB*. See Rubin, *Corpus Christi; FR; Resurrection*, 104–8, 207–12; Brown, *Cult of the Saints;* Farmer, *Communities of Saint Martin*, 270–76; Noble and Head, *Soldiers of Christ*, 18–21; and for an earlier period, Raymond Van Dam, *Saints and Their Miracles*.

18. One recalls all those stories that ask if a true confession received by a false priest counts as "the real thing." See, e.g., Tentler, *Sin and Confession*, 103–30.

19. Le Doyen, *Annales et chroniques*, ed. Godbert, 133–34; app. 10.4; also cited (with minor orthographic variations) by Petit de Julleville, "1510. Laval.—Saint Blaise," in *LM*, 2:100. Medieval *coqueluche* is not the whooping cough but a highly contagious illness that caused pain, fever, and delirium as it attacked the head, stomach, and kidneys (Le Doyen, *Annales et chroniques*, ed. Godbert, 134n). Contrast this to Wilshire's statement that scenic "pestilence that 'kills' does not kill the beings performing or auditing" (*RPI*, 262).

20. Archives d'Angers, BB 4, fol. 29; cited by Port, *Inventaire analytique*, 349; app. 5.5; also in Jodogne, ed., *Jean Michel, Passion*, xli; and *LM*, 2:50.

21. On contagion, see Siraisi, *Medieval and Early Renaissance Medicine*, 128–30.

22. *Theater and Its Double*, trans. Richards, 23, 15.

23. Ibid., 27. We shall return in chapter 12, e.g., to the Reformist "infection" of Tournai (c. 1560). See *HP*, 139–40; and for Mons, Boussu, *Histoire de la Ville de Mons*, 193–94.

24. Le Roy Ladurie tells us, e.g., that Huguenots were in the minority in Romans as late as 1569; *Carnival at Romans*, 24–28. He also mentions the 1509 performance of the *Trois Doms* (25).

25. "Analyse d'un manuscrit peu connu et très-curieux, qui existe à Romans en Dauphiné, fait[e] par M. M*** de la même ville," cited by Giraud, *Trois Doms*, introduction, viii. Giraud published a long excerpt from the original article from the *Affiches du Dauphiné* (20 July 1787): 51; see app. 10.5. See also the version from the *Journal de Paris* 264 (21 September 1787): 1143–44; app. 10.9. Giraud explains this contorted genealogy in the *Composition, mise en scène* (1848), 30–31; and in *Trois Doms*, introduction, vii–ix.

26. *Trois Doms*, introduction, vii–viii; app. 10.5.

27. "['L'Analyse'] est rédigée dans l'esprit du temps, avec une intention très marquée de ridiculiser le drame du moyen âge" (*LM*, 2:95). Giraud cites Monsieur *** in *Trois Doms*, introduction, viii; app. 10.5; and "Analyse," *Journal de Paris*, 1144.

28. Again, see *Trois Doms*, introduction, vii–viii; app. 10.5; and *LM*, 2:95.

29. "Il ne nous paraît pas certain que les reliques des saints aient été réellement promenées sur la scène. A la vérité Romans possédait ces reliques: mais il semble plus probable qu'elles ne furent pas apportées au théâtre et qu'on fit seulement un simulacre de la translation" (*LM*, 2:96).

30. Petit de Julleville cites *A Rivallii de Allobrogibus libri novem. Viennae apud Girard* (1844), 363, in French translation (*LM*, 2:98); see also *Trois Doms*, introduction, lxxix.

31. "M. PETIT DE JULLEVILLE conjecture à tort 'que les reliques des saints ne furent pas apportées au théâtre'" (*Trois Doms*, introduction, p. c, note; refuting *LM*, 2:96).

32. "A la représentation du Mystère des saints Félix, Fortunat et Achillée (en 1500) les Valentinois prièrent le clergé d'apporter leur châsse sur la scène, 'pro majori reverentia et honore debitis dictis tribus sanctis martyribus'" (*Trois Doms*, introduction, pp. c–ci, note [my empha-

sis]). Giraud reproduces the Latin in *Trois Doms*, 856; as do I in appendix 10.6. A *triarchum* is a reliquary with three separate vessels for the remains of three saints.

33. *Affiches du Dauphiné*, quoted by Giraud, *Trois Doms*, introduction, ix; app. 10.5; and by Petit de Julleville, *LM*, 2:95. See Giraud's detailed summary of the *Translacion* (*Trois Doms*, introduction, lxxii–lxxiv); and the complete text, which appears as the final act of the *Trois Doms* (10018–11289). The bishop of Valence is even a character in the play.

34. *Translacion, Trois Doms*, 10507, 10461–67; app. 10.7. See also *Translacion*, 10404–567.

35. *Accounting*, 592 (my emphasis); app. 10.1; see also *LM*, 2:95.

36. *Accounting*, 592; app. 10.1. I believe that an imperfect translation as "safe and sound" might also capture the meaning (along the lines of the adverbial phrase "in a most holy manner"). One finds the expression "saine et entiere" in *Coment Judich tua Oloferne*, ed. Knight, v. 572. I thank Graham Runnalls, Alan Knight, William Kibler, Cynthia Skenazi, and Cynthia Brown for pondering this passage with me.

37. *Accounting*, 592; app. 10.1.

38. The *Accounting* records similar processions associated with the performances of 1504 and 1509 (592; app. 10.1).

39. "Les châsses des dits corps *saints et chefs*" (*Trois Doms*, introduction, c; my emphasis).

40. The linguistic difficulty here lies with resolving why the adjective for *aforesaid* is in the plural *(desdicts)*.

41. "Qu'ayés les troys Dons en memoyre" (10016).

42. *"Prennet le chief et le jouniet au corps"* (at v. 10001; original emphasis). On memory, dismembering, and re-membering, see my *MTOC*, 120–27.

43. *Trois Doms*, introduction, c.

44. See especially *Resurrection of the Body*, chap. 2.

45. *De laude sanctorum*, ed. Mulders, 69–93; trans. Hillgarth, *Conversion of Western Europe*, 22–27; and discussed by Bynum (*Resurrection*, 107).

46. On the *Summa theologica*, see Bynum, *Resurrection*, 263.

47. See *Trois Doms*, introduction, cii.

48. This scene recalls the celebrated legend of the vase of Soissons. When a reliquary was broken by a malevolent booty-hunter in Clovis's army, Clovis later took vengeance by splitting the knight in two with his sword. See Gregory of Tours, *History of the Franks*, trans. Brehaut, 37–38.

49. If the actual reliquary parallels the text of the *Trois Doms*, this would be Saint Séverin, who was laid to rest in a coffin *between* the other two saints (9984–88). Giraud also wonders whether this *triarchum* could be the same article inventoried in the thirteenth century as *tria vasa cristallina* belonging to the treasures of the Church of Saint Bernard (introduction, p. ci, note); app. 10.8.

50. *Trois Doms*, introduction, ci–cii; app. 10.8. Compare these odd tenses to app. 9.6,, on the *Sainte Hostie*.

51. *Trois Doms*, introduction, ci–cii; app. 10.8.

52. See *VH*, chap. 4; *TGT*, chap. 8; *CD*, chap. 4; and *MP*, chap. 4.

53. The closest we come are the vague allusions to cannibalism in host desecrations (see above, chap. 9, note 12).

54. *Affiches du Dauphine*, cited by Giraud, *Trois Doms*, introduction, viii–ix; app. 10.5; "Analyse," 1143–44; and *LM*, 2:95. See also Gustave Cohen's objection to this sort of objection, *HMS*, 70; app. Intro.3.

55. *Affiches du Dauphine*, cited by Giraud, *Trois Doms*, introduction, ix; app. 10.5.

56. Ibid., viii–ix; app. 10.5. See also "Analyse," 1144; and *LM*, 2:95.

57. *Affiches du Dauphine*, cited by Giraud, *Trois Doms*, introduction, ix; app. 10.5.

58. "Analyse," 1144; app. 10.9. See also Giraud on the survival of the legend of the Trois Doms, *Trois Doms*, introduction, cii–ciii.

59. See *SBD*, 172; app. 12.3.

60. See *DTT*, 3:117 and 2:25.

61. *Cost of Deception*, 11.

62. See *Cost of Deception*, 57–62, 28–31, 37–44.

63. Ibid., 11.

64. Ibid, chap. 4.

65. On this unholy alliance between Left and Right, see Steiner, *Scandal*, 60–61. I return to it in my work in progress, "Back to the Medieval Future."

Chapter 11. The Mysterious Quarry

1. See app. 7.3. Wilshire cites Chaikin, *Presence of the Actor*, 11 (*RPI*, 218).

2. "L'Oeuvre des trente ans de théâtre," 212–13; cited and discussed by Kruger, *National Stage*, 47–48. I provide my own translations, as hers contain a number of errors. See also Rolland's signature work, *Théâtre du peuple* (1913).

3. *MAA*, 27. See app. 11.1; for Rabelais, see below, note 19.

4. *MAA*, 27; app. 11.1. Bourges, e.g., is situated approximately 120 miles from Doué-la-Fontaine.

5. Ibid.; app. 11.1. Lebègue is translating from the Latin of Justus Lipsius, *De amphitheatro liber* (1585), 11:chap. 6, pp. 30–31; app. 11.2. We return shortly to some discrepancies in his translation. A *perche* is an early agrarian measurement of length equal to 1/100th of an *arpent* (an *arpent* being the approximate equivalent of 100 square meters).

6. Such an evolution would not have deterred Mel Brooks, who staged his Inquisition in a swimming pool in *History of the World*.

7. Today, there is nothing haphazard at all about the seating and its pleasant, grassy performance space.

8. On theater's public spaces, see Mullaney, *Place of the Stage*, chap. 1; and Carlson, *Places of Performance*, chap. 1.

9. See Nora, "From *Lieux de Mémoire*"; and Clark, *Literary France*, chap. 1. I am not calibrating the suffering of various "others" but pointing out that, like anti-Semitism, the fear of rising underclasses predates and postdates the Reformation.

10. On bourgeois and working-class participation in medieval theater, see *LM*, 1:chap. 10. The French tradition diverges from the English, influenced by guilds.

11. "Disant avec grant collère, chaleur et béhement, par plusieurs fois, qu'il ne permectroit les dis jeux, ains que s'ilz jouoient il les tireroit jus du théâtre et renverseroit ledit théâtre, priant que Dieu lui en donna la forche" (*Bulletin de la Société Historique de Tournai*, n. p.); cited by Faber, *HTB*, 15. I provide more extensive excerpts in "Of Protestantism."

12. "Découvrez les Arènes de Doué-la-Fontaine." One may contact the Tourism Office at Tourisme@ville-douelafontaine.fr. But don't expect a cyber-answer. They have yet to answer me.

13. "Situées dans le quartier de Douces, ce sont en réalité d'anciennes carrières à ciel ouvert, où des gradins furent aménagés au 15ᵉ· s.; des spectacles de théâtre et de musique, des expositions florales s'y déroulent. Au-dessous des gradins, de vastes souterrains furent longtemps habités: cuisines, salles communes" (*Châteaux de la Loire*, 107). But let the traveler beware! The site is protected by a portal, and closed between 1 November and 31 March. The Office of Tourism boasts that off-season visits may be arranged, but this is an urban legend.

14. *National Stage*, 53. She acknowledges her debt to Habermas, *Structural Transformation of the Public Sphere*, 141–235. Compare her innovative reading (47–54) to Plato, *Laws*, 700c–d; and de Lorde, *Théâtre de la mort*, 16; above, chap. 8.

15. Compare, e.g., to app. 5.5.

16. "On y enferma des prisonniers vendéens" (*Châteaux de la Loire*, 107).

17. "Aux origines incertaines, les Arènes pourraient dater de l'époque moyenâgeuse. Ses souterrains et les 1100 places de son amphithéâtre ont été taillés dans le falun. Ses caves ont successivement servi d'auberge, de prison et de dépôt d'armes" ("Doué-la-Fontaine: Cité des Roses et du Troglodytisme").

18. "Est et latomia supplicii genus ad verberandum aptum, inventum a Tarquinio Superbo ad poenam sceleratorum" (*Etymologiarum*, I, bk. 5, 27.23–24; my translation); see my *MTOC*, 43–44.

19. *Tiers Livre*, in *Complete Works*, trans. Frame, 269; *Oeuvres*, ed. Demerson, 384; and *Quart Livre*, in *Complete Works*, trans. Frame, 467; *Oeuvres*, ed. Demerson, 618.

20. *MAA*, 27; app. 11.1.

21. Ibid. It is unclear whether Lebègue attended the performances, since he thanks Monsieur Le Moy, "learned historian of Anjou," for the information (*MAA*, 28n).

22. *De amphitheatro liber*, 31 (my translation); app. 11.2. This is the final sentence of the book, which precedes an *Ad lectorem*.

23. *MAA*, 27. Compare apps. 11.1 and 11.2.

24. "Juge, en voyant ces ruines si amples, / Ce qu'a rongé le temps injurieux, / Puis qu'aux ouvriers les plus industrieux / Ces vieux fragmens encor servent d'exemples" (*Antiquitez de Rome*, Sonnet 27, 5–8). Du Bellay published this work in 1558, twenty-seven years before *De amphitheatro liber* appeared in 1585.

25. *De amphitheatro liber*, 30–31; app. 11.2. The precise Latin phrase is not without ambiguity: "ex quo conventu, qui dies triginta perseveravit, multum atque uberem quaestum ad paganos redisse." My skilled colleagues, Martin Camargo and Robert Morstein Marx, affirm that we can be reasonably certain that the figure of thirty days refers to the duration of the *performance* and not to the duration of the agreement *about* the performance.

26. See Petit de Julleville, "1536. Bourges.—Les Actes des Apôtres," in *LM*, 2:130–31, 1:376–78; *MAA*, 90–104; and Thiboust, *Relation*, 9.

27. *Chanson de Roland*, ed. Brault, Laisse 82, 2:1039–41.

28. *Catalogus gloriae mundi*, 577; app. 11.3. Petit de Julleville translates a long excerpt into French (*LM*, 1:405). Compare also the shape of this theater with Southern, *Medieval Theater in the Round*, chap. 4; and Schmitt, "Was There a Medieval Theatre in the Round?"

29. *Catalogus gloriae mundi*, 577 (my translation); app. 11.3.

30. Chaumeau, *Histoire de Berry*, 156; also cited by Lebègue, *MAA*, 78–79; app. 11.4. Lebègue dates this performance to c. 1515 "since the historian from Berry, who was still alive in 1560, had attended" (*MAA*, 78). Chaumeau's book was published in 1566, and Louis reigned from 1498 to 1515, so presumably Lebègue was trying to place the historian of Berry at the Bourges Passion play at an age advanced enough to retain such details.

31. For a sampling, see Harvey, *Theatre of the Basoche*, 228–30.

32. *MAA*, 27; app. 11.1.

33. *De amphitheatro liber*, 30–31 (my translation); app. 11.2.

34. Henry d'Outreman, *Histoire de la ville et comté de Valenciennes* (hereafter *HV*), 396–97; app. 12.1; see also *LM*, 2:156.

35. The cyclic *Apostles* is ascribed to the scholastic brotherly duo of Simon and Arnoul Gréban. For information on its textual transmission, see *MFI*, 117–19.

36. "Vous avez senti que le théâtre du peuple allait s'élever contre vous et vous vous hâtez de prendre les devants . . . afin d'offrir au peuple votre théâtre bourgeois, que vous baptisez [du] 'peuple'" ("L'Oeuvre des trente," 212–13); cited by Kruger, *National Stage*, 48.

37. Medieval French drama, e.g., was marked by tensions between the clergy and the popu-

lace, and between theology students and law students (especially the Basochiens). For an introduction to scholarship in this field, see my *ROMD*, 89–110.

38. *MAA*, 27; app. 11.1. A note in the reprint edition of *De amphitheatro liber* says that "the
plates are unsigned, and it is not known by whom they were drawn and engraved."

39. *MAA*, 27n; app. 11.1.

40. *Catalogus gloriae mundi*, 577 (my translation); app. 11.3; also *LM*, 1:405.

41. See Peters on the edict of the praetor, *Torture*, 30–31; Chambers on the *Benedictus levita*,
a "somewhat dubious collection" that may date from the reign of Louis the Pious (*Mediaeval
Stage*, 1:37–38); and for the injunction of 1548, *HTF*, 2:2–4. On the actor's role in society, see
Chambers, *Mediaeval Stage*, 1:58–69; and Dominguez, "Corps dans les mystères."

42. On the nineteenth-century retrofitting of socialism onto the Middle Ages, see Dakyns,
Middle Ages in French Literature; and for England, Chandler, *Dream of Order;* and Elliott, *Playing
God*, chaps. 2 and 3.

43. See Petit de Julleville, "1507. Châlons-sur-Marne.—La Passion," in *LM*, 2:91; app. 13.3.

44. See, e.g., Larwood on the silly country girl "Peggy" who interrupts Othello (*TA*, 45–46);
and Fitzgerald for silly gardeners and hecklers (*Book of Theatrical Anecdotes*, 19, 73).

45. I am not trying to oversimplify a complex social history that includes peasants' revolts and
chartes d'affranchissement.

46. If an actual quarry owner had indeed made such a generous donation, he would surely
have insisted on a written record—even if that record were later lost.

47. Nodier, quoted in translation by Frederick Brown, *Theater and Revolution*, 88, also 105–
17.

48. *Dramas, Fields, and Metaphors*, 123.

49. See *MAA*, 29; and *RIC*, 67.

50. Vinchant, *Annales*, 5:267; apps. 11.5 and 8.5. Compare also to Farel, app. 12.3.

51. Vinchant, *Annales*, 5:267; app. 11.5.

Chapter 12. Seeing Is Believing

1. On the *Mistére par personnaiges de la vie . . .* IESUS CHRIST, Bibliothèque Nationale, Rothschild I.7.3 (hereafter Valenciennes *Passion*), see "1547. Valenciennes—La Passion," in *LM*,
2:155.

2. See *MPV*, 64; also *LM*, 2:155; and *MFI*, 180. Konigson reconstructs a composite of the
1547 performance by drawing on five sources: the Rothschild headings to each day; the play text;
its didascalia; the twenty-five miniatures by Hubert Cailleau (c. 1526–90) of Rothschild I.7.3 (see
MPV, 61–64, 25–32 [on Cailleau]); and BN 12536, also illustrated by Cailleau.

3. "Item ung aultre biau secret au miracle des cincq pains dorge et deux poissons que iesus
multiplia sans voyr nulle apparence de sorte que on en dona a plus de mille persones des spectateurs et en fut recoeuilliet XII corbeilles plaines" (Rothschild I.7.3, *Mistére par personnaiges*, fol.
162r); also cited by Konigson, *MPV*, 103; and by Petit de Julleville, *LM*, 2:155. See Konigson's résumé of Day 12 (*MPV*, 103–8).

4. See *LM*, 2:155–56; and *MPV*, 23.

5. See *MPV*, 23. Henry Jr. was on born on 22 August 1546.

6. D'Outreman uses causative *faire* ("l'on *fit* paroistre"), while Petit de Julleville shifts agency
to the audience ("on *vit* paraître"). I include Petit de Julleville's variants in appendix 12.1, among
which this error: he quotes d'Outreman as saying that the play was "subsequently published in
Paris *under* the names of the authors [*sous* le nom des Aucteurs]" (*LM*, 2:156). D'Outreman says
it appeared "*without* the names of the authors [*sans* le nom des Aucteurs]" (*HV*, 397).

7. Compare to his mysterious appearances in chapter 7.

8. It is *Joseph's* staff that flowers (*MPV*, 23).

9. *HV,* part II, chap. 16, 396; app. 12.1.

10. "Item aussy aux noepces dArchitriclin ou leau quon versa dans les quenes deva[n]t tous fut muee en vin dont en burent plus de cent personnes des spectateurs et aultres beaux secretz furent veuz" (Rothschild I.7.3, fol. 99v); also cited by Konigson, *MPV,* 92; and by Petit de Julleville, *LM,* 2:155. Compare the New Testament account in John 2.

11. *HV,* 396; app. 12.1.

12. "Il y a en La compagnie/ung pety enfant josne et tendre/Lequel pour soubstenir sa vie/ a cincq pain[s] de orge quoy que on en die/Et deux poissons sambablement" (Rothschild I.7.3, fol. 168r); also cited by Konigson, *MPV,* 106. Compare to Jean Michel, *Passion,* ed. Jodogne, 10027–141; and Gréban, *Passion,* ed. Jodogne, 12802–13007.

13. "*Jésus:* En aves vous asses enfantz[?]/*Ensamble:* Ouy segneur" (Rothschild I.7.3, fol. 168r); and "*Andrieu:* douz corbelle nous avons/Emplis" (fol. 168v); also cited by Konigson, *MPV,* 106.

14. Compare to the *Jeu d'Adam* phenomenon, above, chap. 7.

15. Lucian, "Saltatio," 78; see also Nagler, *Sourcebook,* 31.

16. Gréban, *Passion,* ed. Jodogne, 1–5; cited above, chap. 8, note 40.

17. Epistle 90; cited by Petit de Julleville, "1534. Poitiers. La Passion," in *LM,* 2:125; app. 12.2. See also Davidson, "Anti-Visual Prejudice"; Runnalls, "Were They Listening or Watching?"; Duffy, *Stripping of the Altars,* 102–6; and Miles, *Image as Insight,* 100–112.

18. On the theatrical dimensions of transubstantiation, see *SR,* chap. 1; Beckwith, *Christ's Body,* 27–40; Beckwith, *Signifying God,* chap. 4; *TMB,* chap. 4; and Shuger, *Habits,* 10–13.

19. Archives d'Angers, BB 4, fol. 29; cited by Port, *Inventaire analytique,* 350; app. 5.5; also cited by Jodogne in his edition of Michel's *Passion,* xli.

20. "Cecy est mon corps en tout lieu/que desormais ainsi ferés;/le pain vous *transsubstancirés*/en moy, eternel et divin" (Michel, *Passion,* ed. Jodogne, 18862–65); "Car puissance sur luy nous donne/De *transsubstancïer* le pain/en luy mesmes et, pour certain,/chose n'est au monde plus digne!" (18898–901; my emphasis).

21. "A la reale verité,/il n'estoit pas resuscité/et n'estoit rien que enchanterie,/que fantosme, que resverie,/que ung corps faint, que une fiction/de ceste resurrection/du Lazare dont on fait feste" (14938–44). See also 14007–14, cited above, chap. 6, note 18.

22. For helpful historical synopses of this period, see Ozment, *Age of Reform;* and Roelker, *One King, One God.*

23. *SBD,* chap. 27, 170; app. 12.3.

24. Cited by Pasquier de le Barre, *JBT,* 311–12; app. 12.5. Pasquier reports at length on Brully's subversive preaching, interrogation, and execution (19 February 1545). Compare also to *SBD,* 224; and see Moreau's comparative analysis of Brully and Calvin, *HP,* 94–97.

25. See *DTT,* 3:189–91; cited above, chap. 7.

26. See app. 4.1. On auditory confusion, see app. 8.2; and Diehl on Calvin and Foxe, *SR,* 103–5. Gatton even suggests olfactory confusion, as when a fake body "full of bones and entrails" was roasted as Saint Barnabas ("There Must Be Blood," 87).

27. "Regectées et en ce non comprinses aucunes addicions particulieres que aucuns des joueurs d'iceluy mistere y cuiderent adjouster à leurs plaisances, pour ce qu'elles estoient impertinentes à la matiere" (cited by Lebègue, *MAA,* 7–8). See also Muir, "Apocryphal Writings"; and Cornagliotti, "Apocryphes et mystères."

28. Cited by Sainte-Beuve, *TPF,* 193; app. 8.2.

29. *HV,* 395; app. 12.1. For context, see Phillips, *Church and Culture,* chaps. 1 and 2.

30. See, e.g., *TRF,* 289–90.

31. Cited by Lebègue, *MAA*, 29–30; above, chap. 11.

32. "Car ce n'est nostre intention,/De mesler la Religion/Dans le sujet des choses feinctes,/Aussi jamais les lettres sainctes/Ne furent données de Dieu,/Pour en faire après quelque jeu" (cited by the brothers Parfaict, *HTF*, 3:229–30n; and by Lebègue, *TRF*, 290).

33. On this complex topic, see *TRF*, 58; *MAA*, 111; and *LM*, 2:80.

34. "Urban Legends," 572. For a clever assessment of this point, see Schwartz, "Teaching a Sacred Text," especially 188.

35. "Saltatio," 83; see above, chap. 3.

36. On the authenticity of on-stage miracles, see also the *Jeu de Saint Nicolas*, ed. Jeanroy, 106–11.

37. "Secret de la multiplication des pains et des poissons. Les paniers de nourriture doivent apparaître par les trappes. Les apôtres servent la foule *(et les spectateurs)*" (*MPV*, 106 [my emphasis]).

38. In the Valenciennes *Passion*, Jesus says: "Mes amis Chier/soies les Relief Recoeulons/quilz ne perissent En ches camps" (Rothschild I.7.3, fol. 168r); also *MPV*, 106.

39. Also Luke 9.13–17, Mark 6.30–43, Matt. 14.13–21.

40. See above, notes 3 and 10. While modern theater scholars readily imagine such copiousness, nothing in the props list indicates such quantities—especially given Jean Michel's reference to "quarter loaves" (see below, note 43).

41. *HV*, 396–97; app. 12.1. See Petit de Julleville's extensive excerpt from the financial accounting of the Valenciennes *Passion* (BN fr. 12536), *LM*, 2:152; also cited by Konigson, *MPV*, 21.

42. "Et cheux lesquels voloient monter sus ung hordement lequel on avoit faict audit lieu payointe XII deniers" (cited by Konigson, *MPV*, 21; and by Petit de Julleville, *LM*, 2:152).

43. "*Ycy s'assient six des apostres et departent le pain par quartiers a grand nombre. Et les autres six servent le peuple de pain et de pluseurs platz de poyssons*" (*Passion*, after 10124); "*Ycy menguent tout le peuple et tous les apostres . . .*" (after 10140). Gréban's stage directions simply say that the disciples "serve the people *[ilz servent le peuple]*" (after 12891).

44. Trans. Cazelles, *Lady as Saint*, 110, ll. 389–92; see also *HTF*, 2:49–51.

45. Greedy hoarders jump into the notoriously polluted East River to retrieve their ill-gotten gain; my local news once reported on one such armored truck (but I don't remember when).

46. *TA*, 230; discussed above, chap. 1.

47. *SBD*, 170–72; app. 12.3; compare to app. 10.3.

48. On humanistic relativism see Kristeller, *Renaissance Thought*, chap. 5; and Shuger, *Habits of Thought*.

49. See *HP*, 138–40. The year 1559 is the year of Grévin's *Trésorière* and Babinot's *Christiade* (above, chap. 8).

50. *HP*, 128, 139–40; and for similar terminology, see Boussu, *Histoire de la Ville de Mons*, 193–94.

51. *HP*, 139n, on the order from Marie of Hungary that "no performances would be permitted that had not first been reviewed by the magistrate of Tournai."

52. "Monseigneur le Vicaire de Tournai . . . dit que les joueurs de La Teste d'or jouent jeux diffamans gens d'église et de la justice" (cited by Moreau, *HP*, 139n).

53. *HP*, 140n; also *HTB*, 15.

54. See *TRF*, 58. Moreau notes that Tournai's Chambers of Rhetoric were influential in the spread of heresy (*HP*, 138–39). See also Hummelen, "Boundaries of the Rhetoricians' Stage"; Waite, "Vernacular Drama and Early Urban Reformation"; and Hüsken, "Politics and Drama."

55. For these transgressions, see apps. 8.1 and 8.2; and for physical violence, see app. 5.4.

56. *TRF*, 290; see also *HP*, 138–40; Miles, *Image as Insight*, 113–22; Beck, *Théâtre et propa-*

gande, introduction; Holl, *Das politische und religiose Tendenzdrama;* and Jonker, *Le Protestantisme et le théâtre.*

57. See *HP,* 139–40; app. 12.4. For the biblical story of Jezebel, see 1 and 2 Kings.

58. See *MWM,* 328–29; and also Burke, *Philosophy of Literary Form,* 155–57, 329–43.

59. Deposition of the Tournaisians Antoine Playart et Sébastien Plouquet, cited by Moreau, *HP,* 139–40; app. 12.4. I have replaced Moreau's italics with quotation marks. Compare to Farel's critique of lighting candles in honor of the saints (*SBD,* 168; app. 10.3).

60. Deposition of the Tournaisians Antoine Playart et Sébastien Plouquet, cited by Moreau, *HP,* 139–40; app. 12.4.

61. *JBT,* 311; app. 12.5. For the changes effected by reformers in all those areas, see *RIC,* 117–18, 24–31, 82–84.

62. *Institutes,* 1.11.1; see also *RIC,* 67; and *HP,* 90.

63. *Institutes,* 1.11.13. Farel and Brully preached against idolatry; *HP,* 70–71; *RIC,* 69; *JBT,* 313; app. 12.5.

64. Trans. Cazelles, *Lady as Saint,* 118, ll. 309–13.

65. *HTF,* 2:69–70.

66. *JBT,* 313; app. 12.5. See Moreau on Calvin, *Institutes,* 3.5 (*HP,* 96); Le Goff, *Birth of Purgatory;* and Bordier, *Jeu de la Passion,* 94–95.

67. "Nostre Seigneur n'a point donné de loy de jeusne ne de temps. Ains nous commande de vivre sobrement pour luy servir, ayder à nostre prochain, sans aulcune distinction des viandes" (*SBD,* 146).

68. "Quant le sainct peuple venoit à la table de nostre Seigneur, paravant on lisoit en langage que tous entendoient quelque portion de la saincte Escripture, en faisant oraisons entendues de tous, en grandz gemissementz. Et en la messe tout est dit en langage que le peuple n'entend point, en chantant et riant" (*SBD,* 120). See also *HP,* 140n.

69. Vinchant, *Annales,* 5:267; app. 8.5.

70. *JBT,* 311–12; app. 12.5.

71. See *TMA,* 223; discussed above, chap. 4.

72. App. 9.9. On the dialogic propensity of Renaissance preaching, see O'Malley, "Content and Rhetorical Forms"; Zink, *Prédication en langue romane;* Mazouer, "Prédication populaire"; Hindley, "Preaching and Plays"; Martin, *Métier du prédicateur;* and Manselli, *Religion populaire.*

73. Kirby, *Formalist Theatre,* 89.

74. See Carro, *Histoire de Meaux* (hereafter *HM*), 207; discussed below, chap. 13. Compare also to the *Play of Evil Tongue,* performed in Metz in 1513 with the *Sainte Hostie* (app. 9.7).

Chapter 13. The Suicide of Despair

1. *HM,* 211–13; app. 13.1. Carro asserts that the first performance took place on 1 May 1547 (*HM,* 212). Petit de Julleville also excerpts Carro in "1547. Meaux.—L'Ancien Testament, La Passion," in *LM,* 2:143–44.

2. Petit de Julleville interpolates his own voice at this point to say "says a historian of Meaux" (*LM,* 2:144).

3. *HM,* 212 (my emphasis); app. 13.1. It is logical to translate *Desespoir* (m.), as Despair poisons *him*self. But, in Michel and Gréban, *Deseperance* is gendered female (see discussion below; also apps. 13.4 and 13.5). See Paxson's sophisticated "Personification's Gender."

4. *IO,* VI.2.35; cited above, chap. 4.

5. "Saltatio," 19 (my emphasis).

6. *CD,* xii–xiii. See also Nussbaum, *Poetic Justice.*

7. Carro notes that Dr. Rochard "lived at the beginning of the eighteenth century [and] . . .

merely copied, abbreviated, and organized the manuscripts of L'Enfant and Janvier" (*HM*, v). L'Enfant, our most contemporaneous source, was a prosecutor living in Meaux at the end of the sixteenth century. He "left manuscript notes rather than memoirs," which are "extremely difficult to decipher" (*HM*, iii–iv). The *curé* Janvier was born in Meaux in 1618 and left six handwritten volumes (*HM*, iv).

8. The easiest access to Rochard is thus via Lebert, "Théâtre à Meaux," xviii–xix; app. 13.2.

9. My emphasis; app. 13.1.

10. See apps. 7.2, 7.3.

11. "Un pauvre diable. i. *un homme necessiteux ou mal-heureux*. Item, *de qui l'on doit avoir compassion*" (*Curiositez françoises*, 163 [original emphasis]).

12. "*On se sert de ces mots, lors qu'on a regret à quelque chose, ou que quelque mal est arrive*" (ibid., 165).

13. See *HM*, 204–10, also 517–20. Like Jacob's book in the *Sainte Hostie*, their books were burned as well.

14. See *DP*, chap. 2; and *ST*, 49.

15. What Carro sets up as an opposition—the "brutally lugubrious spectacles" of the execution of heretics vs. stage plays "more suited to pleasuring the eyes and spirit"—is really a logical continuation. See *HM*, 210–11; app. 13.1.

16. "[Roland] se tait, et ce silence est la chose la plus sublime de *La Chanson de Roland*" (*Légendes épiques*, 3:438–39). Alfred Foulet subsequently corrected him, arguing that there *was* no silence ("Is Roland Guilty?").

17. "Saltatio," 79.

18. Ibid., 83; and *Attic Nights*, 2.6.5 (above, chap. 4). On cathartic cures to mind and body, see "Saltatio," 79; and Boal, *Theatre of the Oppressed*, 28–29.

19. *History of Suicide* (hereafter *HS*), 68. See Minois's chap. 2 of *HS* on the hardening of early Christian positions against suicide; also the Protestant "diabolization of suicide," *HS*, chap. 4, especially 68–74. See also the case-studies in Schmitt, "Suicide au Moyen Age"; and Murray, *Suicide in the Middle Ages* (hereafter *SMA*), especially the French materials in 1:chaps. 9 and 10.

20. Pywell learned this secondhand from the RATT actress who had been assaulted during the show. See *SRT*, 24; above, introduction.

21. I reserve the intentionality of this case for my work in progress, "Back to the Medieval Future." See Murray's brilliant treatment of medieval intentionality in *SMA*, 2:chaps. 12 and 13. Sorry: no references yet to Howard Beale in *Network*, but stay tuned.

22. See Mollat, *Pauvres au moyen âge*, especially 303–28.

23. Rochard quoted by Lebert, "Théâtre à Meaux," xix. *Gueux* translates roughly as "bum," criminal connotations included.

24. "Les spectateurs enfin sont superstitieux et ils s'amusent à remarquer que les personnages, qui joueront les diables à Meaux en 1547, moururent fort pauvres" (*HMS*, 267).

25. Petit de Julleville, "1507. Châlons-sur-Marne.—La Passion," in *LM*, 2:91; app. 13.3. He thanks Messieurs Lhuillier and Lemaire (an archivist and an archaeologist) for their help with his entry on Meaux (2:143n)—but for what specifically is unclear.

26. On the Devil's special relationship with heresy, see Russell, *Prince of Darkness*, chaps. 5 and 11.

27. On the arbitrariness of medieval punishment, see, e.g., Cohen, *Crossroads of Justice*, chap. 11; Hanawalt, "Violent Death"; Roelker, *One King*, 144–49. Perhaps historians will succeed where I have not in picking up Pascalus's trace.

28. See *HM*, 212; app. 13.1; and *LM*, 2:143.

29. See *HP*, 139–40; app. 12.4.

30. Generally, see Greenblatt, *Shakespearean Negotiations,* chap. 1; and Dollimore, *Radical Tragedy,* chaps. 1 and 2.

31. Belton, *Random Recollections,* 113 (original emphasis).

32. He refers to Mathew Coppinger; above, chap. 7, note 12.

33. Given Anita Hill vs. Clarence Thomas or President Clinton vs. Paula Jones, it's unclear that these dramas are "verifiable."

34. *AP,* 129 (Hapgood's emphasis).

35. Michel, *Passion,* ed. Jodogne, 2382–38; app. 13.4. Compare with Gréban, 21881–98; app. 13.5. For other examples of Despair, see Fabre, *Études,* 245; and Murray *SMA,* 1:267–68, 366, who describes one of his cases as a "drama" (219).

36. Michel, *Passion,* ed. Jodogne, 23797–800; app. 13.4. For an introduction to this complex work, which is a revision of Gréban, see Accarie, *Théâtre sacré.* See also the hanging scene of the Mons *Passion,* ed. Cohen, in *LCR,* 302–6.

37. "Le maître-mot du suicide médiéval était 'désespoir.' . . . La *Desperatio* n'était ni un sentiment, ni un état psychique, mais un Vice" ("Suicide," 4); see also *SMA,* 2:chap. 11.

38. Catherine of Siena (above, chap. 1), notes Bynum, even justified her self-starvation this way: "since eating caused her torture, it was the sin of suicide for her to eat—a far worse homicide of the self than starving oneself, because it was homicide by greed" (*HF,* 169).

39. While Murray elegantly shows that the history of Judas is rife with anomalies (*SMA,* 2:324–25), Minois's assertion is indeed consistent with the vision we find in Gréban and Michel.

40. See Gréban, *Passion,* ed. Jodogne, 21753–54, 21763–880; and compare with Michel, *Passion,* ed. Jodogne, 23733–818. Paula Giuliano has translated the Third Day of Gréban's *Mystery of the Passion* (see 52–58), but I prefer to provide verse translations of Jean Michel, who has not been translated into modern French or English. Dominguez offers an excellent comparative analysis of these two suicide scenes in "Le Corps." See also Bordier, *Jeu de la Passion,* 325–49; Kelly, *Ideas and Forms,* 172–73; and Terwangue, *Le Personnage de Judas dans les mystères français.*

41. Michel, *Passion,* ed. Jodogne, 23915–21; app. 13.4. Compare to Gréban, 21941–67; and see Susan Snyder's well-written (if dated) discussion of Gréban in *Paradox of Despair,* 86–93.

42. Minois cites Acts 1.18. On the ambivalent medieval reception of the sins of Judas, see especially *SMA,* 2:356–68.

43. *Biblical Drama,* 132. See this variant stage direction in *LCR,* ed. Cohen, 306n: "*Ycy creve Judas par le ventre et les trippes saillent dehors, et l'ame sort.*" Muir also discusses Matt. 27.7 and Acts 1.18. See also *SMA,* 2:335–39.

44. Michel, *Passion,* ed. Jodogne, after 23864; app. 13.4.

45. Schmitt's study of fifty-four medieval suicides shows that men were three times more likely to commit suicide than women, and that 60 percent opted for hanging; "Suicide," 5. For more "absolute numbers," see *SMA,* 1:chap. 15.

46. "Celui qui jouait Déseperance s'empoisonna" (*HMS,* 267). Cohen cites L'Enfant, via a footnote in Rothschild's edition of the *Mistére du Viel Testament* (6:231); Rothschild reproduces L'Enfant's remarks as cited in an obscure article in the *Revue de Champagne et de Brie* of August 1882 (130).

47. The film *Alien* would also be a "Bosom-Serpent" legend; *CD,* 107–30.

48. See *TGT,* 196–97.

49. *MP,* 91–92.

50. *TGT,* 193–94.

51. J. D. Martinez, e.g., attributes a rampant lack of socialization to violence in the media, in "Fallacy of Contextual Analysis."

52. On this general principle, see *DP*, 46–69. See also Wendy Steiner on the "naive account of causality" by both the Right and Left, in *Scandal of Pleasure,* chap. 2.

53. Meaux is near Paris, where Passion plays were performed on numerous occasions. See *LM*, 2:175–85; and *MFI*, 138–48. Carro notes that Meaux's theater predates any such Parisian constructions (*HM*, 211; app. 13.1).

54. Michel, *Passion,* ed. Jodogne, 23927–46; app. 13.4. Compare to Gréban, *Passion,* ed. Jodogne, 21945–67; app. 13.5.

55. The phrase *vehementes animorum perturbationes* appears in a sixteenth-century Latin translation of *Poetics* 1449b. See *De poetica,* ed. Harles; and *Poetics of Aristotle,* ed. Margouliouth.

56. *HM*, 211; app. 13.1. Curiously, Petit de Julleville refers to a "permanent theater" (*LM*, 2:143).

57. *HM*, 211–12; app. 13.1.

58. *HM*, 212; app. 13.1.

59. "Théâtre à Meaux," xix; app. 13.2. Compare to *HM*, 211; app. 13.1; and *LM*, 2:143.

Chapter 14. Death by Drama

1. The Book of Judith is part of the Apocrypha, or the fourteen books of the Septaguint that appear in the Vulgate but were excluded from Protestant Bibles by many reformers. Eleven books were accepted by the Roman Catholic Church, however, and appear in the Douay Bible. See the introductory chapters by Morton Enslin (translator) and Solomon Zeitlin (editor), *Book of Judith;* and also the medieval *Judith,* ed. Griffith.

2. *HTB*, 14–15; app. 14.1.

3. Ibid. Compare to the audience reaction to "Ajax" (Lucian, "Saltatio," 83); above, chap. 3.

4. See app. 9.7.

5. See above, chap. 6.

6. We have seen likewise in chapters 9, 10, 11, and 13. See also Dickson and Goulden, *There Are Alligators,* 131–32.

7. On Philip's supposed implacability, see Gibson, ed., *Black Legend,* introduction and chap. 1; and Parker's revision of this aspect of it, *Philip II,* 20–23.

8. *HTB*, 14–15; app. 14.1.

9. Guillaume Coquillart makes this sort of pun in his *Plaidoyé d'entre la Simple et la Rusée,* e.g., ll. 97–99.

10. See *HDTW;* and *PP,* chap. 10.

11. See *BTA,* chap. 2.

12. My emphasis. "Famosos latrones in his locis, ubi grassati sunt, furca figendos compluribus placuit, ut et conspectu detereantur alii ab isdem facinoribus et solacio sit cognatis et adfinibus interemptorum eodem loco poena reddita, in quo latrones homicidia fecissent" (*Digest of Justinian,* ed. Mommsen and Krueger, trans. Watson, 48.19.28.15). On this text, see also Coleman, "Fatal Charades," 48–49.

13. *Theater of the Oppressed,* 29.

14. This is Lesser's position in *Pictures at an Execution,* 9. She critiques Joel Black's argument about the "artistry" of murder (*Aesthetics of Murder,* especially 5–17).

15. On the ontology of snuff films, see Johnson and Schaefer, "Soft Core," 40; and McConahay, "Pornography."

16. *Pictures,* 40; see especially chaps. 2 and 10.

17. With *DP*, see Cunningham, "Renaissance Execution"; and Mullaney, *Place of the Stage,* chap. 4.

18. "From Hi(story) to Poem," 238.

19. See also René Girard on the sacrificial crisis, *Violence and the Sacred*, chaps. 2 and 6.

20. *Surprising Effects of Sympathy*, 25; see also Kyle, *Spectacles of Death*, 34–37; and Black, *Aesthetics of Murder*, 2–5.

21. I return to questions of violence, intentionality, and the ontology of theater in my work in progress, "Back to the Medieval Future."

22. *BTA*, 298–99. See also Gordon, *Grand Guignol;* and Schneider, "Fading Horrors."

23. *HTB*, 15n; app. 14.1. This manuscript sounds suspiciously like the *Registre de cuir noir*, another version of Philip's Joyous Entry, which, reports Gérard Moreau, was destroyed in 1940 (*JBT*, 333n). He doesn't say how.

24. "Le compte-rendu officiel de la mémorable entrée du jeune prince reste muet sur l'atrocité dont on accuse nos magistrats communaux, mais une note manuscrite nous donne en substance la relation ci-rapportée" (*Théâtre et l'art dramatique à Tournai*, 6–7). His version contains the usual minor variants plus two major ones: Delangre deletes Philip's exclamation,"Well struck!" and never mentions the crimes for which the *malheureux* had been convicted.

25. See Delangre, *Théâtre*, 7n; Hurlbut, posting to PERFORM, 3 February 1995.

26. Johnson and Schaefer, "Soft Core," 40; McConahay, "Pornography," 63–64.

27. Dworkin, cited by McConahay, "Pornography," 64.

28. McConahay, "Pornography," 64. For a pictorial history of Judith, see Ciletti, "Patriarchal Ideology in the Renaissance Iconography of Judith."

29. See *Mistére du Viel Testament*, ed. Rothschild, 5:304–54; also edited separately by Runnalls as [Molinet, Jean?], *Mystère de Judith et Holofernés*. Knight discovered the 845-verse *Coment Judich tua Oloferne* in the Herzog August Bibliothek in Wolfenbüttel. It appears in Codex Guelf. 9 Blankenburgensis, which contains seventy-two plays from Lille. I thank him for sharing his edition in progress. Also, the brothers Parfaict state that Adrien d'Amboise, rector of the University of Paris in 1579, wrote *Holopherne, tragédie sacrée*, which was performed in 1580 (*HTF*, 3:427). Lebègue refers to Heyns's "tragédie sacrée" *Holoferne et Judith*, performed in Antwerp in 1582 (*TRF*, 153).

30. "ICY SE LIEVE ET PRENT LE COUSTEAU DE HOLOFERNÉS"; and "ICY LUY COUPE LE COL" (*Judith et Holofernés*, ed. Runnalls, after v. 2212 and 2228). Compare with the Rothschild edition, after 5:44068.

31. "*Ce temps pendant Judich coppe la teste a Olofernés, puis dist . . .*"; "*Judich se part de l'ost et emporte la teste de Olofernés et vi[e]nt a la porte, puis dit . . .*" (*Coment Judich tua Oloferne*, ed. Knight, after v. 678, 680).

32. See Calvete de Estrella, *El felicissimo viaje del muy poderoso principe Don Phelipe* (Antwerp, 1551), 1:408–42; compare to *JBT*, chap. 59. On Pasquier's life, see Moreau's introduction, *JBT*, ix–xxiii.

33. Alvarez, *Relacion del camino buen viage que hizo el principe de Espana Don Felipe* (Brussels, 1551); translated into French by Dovillée as *Relation du Beau Voyage* (86–87). One thus wonders what Delangre meant by the "official account" of Philip's visit (note 24, above): there are *several* accounts.

34. See *JBT*, xvi, note.

35. "Toutes [les rues] travaillèrent à l'envie sous les yeux des connétables et sous la direction des jurés Jean De Buri et Jean De Créhan" (Chotin, *Histoire de Tournai et du Tournésis*, 1:130).

36. *JBT*, 338, 346–47. Moreau notes that Tournai's Chambers of Rhetoric were instrumental in their construction (*HP*, 138–39).

37. *JBT*, 333–59. Compare with Calvete de Estrella, *Relacion del camino*, 1:414–23. Hoquet also gives a detailed summary in *Tournai et Tournaisis*, 33, but does not reveal his sources.

38. "Toutes les rues étaient parées. Partout s'élevaient des théâtres, des portiques, des arcs-

de-triomphe. Pour donner à la reception plus de pompe et de magnificence, des prix avaient été proposés par l'autorité communale aux rues qui étaleraient les plus riches décors, représenteraient les plus belles histoires et le mieux appropriées à la circonstance" (*Histoire de Tournai*, 1:130); see also *HTB*, 14; app. 14.1.

39. For those convictions, see *JBT*, 328n; *HP*, 139. Although Pasquier de le Barre was involved in the heretically inclined Chamber of Rhetoric, he "never became openly Protestant," but by 1549 he was "already sympathetic to the Reformation" (*HP*, 139). On Protestantism in Tournai, see Parker, *Dutch Revolt*, chap. 1; and, for a slightly later period (albeit with an error- riddled bibliography), Steen, *Chronicle of Conflict*.

40. "Un ieune homme, qui a yci habité avec nous, estant prins en la ville de Tournay, fut condamné à avoir la teste tranchée s'il se desdisoit, et à estre bruslé tout vif s'il persistoir *[sic]* en son propos. Quand on luy demanda qu'il vouloit faire, il respondit simplement: 'Celui qui me fera la grace de mourir patiement pour son nom, me fera bien la grace d'endurer le feu'" (*Opera Calvini*, 8:col. 407; cited by Moreau, *HP*, 117).

41. On the "script" of contrition, see, e.g., *HTB*, 3–4; Cohen, *Crossroads*, 189, 198–201; and Cohen, "To Die a Criminal," 289–300. Compare to the Meaux heretics whose tongues were cut out before their execution in 1546 (*HM*, 207; cited above, chap. 12).

42. See *HTB*, 15; app. 14.1; *HP*, 139n; *JBT*, xii, note; discussed above, chap. 12. See also vander Straeten, *Théâtre villageois en Flandre*, 60.

43. Vinchant, *Annales*, 5:267; app. 8.5.

44. *HTB*, 14; app. 14.1. Delangre deletes this phrase from *Art dramatique*, 6–7.

45. It didn't even make Walter Ravez's discussion of Tournai's early theater (*Folklore de Tournai*, 303–5).

46. Geoffrey Woodward finds that Philip II had "developed an iron self-control to mask his feelings in public" (*Philip II*, 6).

47. For the dates of the Brussels entry, see *JBT*, 331; and on this *Katzenmusik*, see *HTB*, 4–5. I discuss the latter in "Music of the Medieval Body in Pain."

48. "Mais depuis Judich se venga, / car de sa main le decola / et aporta en Bethulie / sa teste du corps departie, / conme vous verrez en presence, / s'il vous plaist a faire silence" (*Comment Judich*, ed. Knight, 57 62).

49. "On the Alterity," 285.

50. Cited in translation by Meredith and Tailby, *Staging*, 110.

51. "La XIIe Journee ou veu a este ung bancquet Magnificq Et Royal du jour natal d'Herode ou fut a la demande de la fille dherodias decapite jan baptiste ou se demonstra ung beau secret car a ung corps vif fut tranchiet une teste fainte dont sorty grande habundance de sang" (Valenciennes *Passion*, Rothschild I.7.3, fol. 162r; cited by Konigson, *MPV,* 103).

52. "Lors elle prend le cariot et met l'enffant fuitif dedens"; and "Le velà trenchié tout d'un cop / En deux pars: esse pas bien fait?" (*LCR*, 103–4); see also Gatton, "There Must Be Blood," 82.

53. See *JBT,* xvi, note.

54. Above, note 23.

55. My emphasis. "Une teste faincte pour une decollacion de Symon Magus, et fault que Daru descolle ung mouton au lieu de luy" (*Actes des Apôtres*, ed. Girardot, 22). See also Gatton, "There Must Be Blood," 87; and Sponsler, *Drama and Resistance*, chap. 6.

56. On this "infection," see *HP*, 140n. See also Callahan, "Ambiguity and Appropriation."

57. Introduction to *Book of Judith*, trans. Enslin, 1.

58. See above, note 1.

59. See Parker, *Dutch Revolt*, chap. 1; *HP*, 49–54.

60. See van Gelderen on the legal privileges of 1477 and the "Joyous Entry of Brabant," *Dutch Revolt*, xiv.

61. See Zeitlin, "Playing the Other," 1; and *Book of Judith*, trans. Enslin, 38.

62. "Donne moy constance et coraige,/que sa vertu mette en servaige" (*Coment Judich*, ed. Knight, 63, 365–66).

63. "ICY METTENT LA TESTE SUR LA PORTE, ET EST A NOTER QUE DES L'EURE QUE LA TESTE SERA MISE SUR LA PORTE, LES GENSDARMES SANS PARLER FERONT DE GRANS ADMIRACIONS" (*Judith*, ed. Runnalls, after v. 2282); and "ITEM IL FAULT QUE INCONTINENT QUE LA TESTE SERA MONSTREE QUE LA TROMPETTE SONNE" (after 2284).

64. "Regardez cy! Voyez se je suis novice!/D'Holofernés je vous livre le chef" (*Judith*, ed. Runnalls, 2277–78).

65. "Dieu le veult; aussi c'est raison/D'occire ung tel vïolateur" (*Judith*, ed. Runnalls, 2219–20).

66. See e.g., Rey-Flaud, *Charivari*, chaps. 12 and 15; and Bristol, *Carnival and Theater*, chap 10. Darnton also connects the *charivari* with *Katzenmusik* (*GCM*, 83).

67. "Le xii⁰. jour d'Abvril, ung mairdi, fuit battu ung jonne garson de environ xvi. ans et fuit battu le plus horriblement que jamais on en battit point, et d'une sorte qu'on n'avoit point veu" (*CMJH*, 277–78). See also McConahay on child pornography, "Pornography," 64.

68. "Il vaudrait mieux, avait dit le Franciscain, couper la gorge à son enfant que de le mettre en religion non réformée . . . il vaudrait mieux prendre sa fille par la main et la mener au bourdeau que de la mettre en religion non réformée" (cited by Renaudet, *Préréforme et Humanisme*, 297).

69. *LC*, 1:bk. 4, 32.

70. *De spectaculis*, chaps. 17 and 29; see also Isidore of Seville, *Etymologiarum*, bk. 18, chap. 59.

71. Fasteau, cited by Johnson and Schaefer, "Soft Core," 53, also 55–56. See MacKinnon's classic *Toward a Feminist Theory of the State*, especially chap. 11.

72. "Soft Core," 55 (my emphasis).

73. For Calvin's worries about such confusion, see *MAA*, 29 30; and for the procurator general, app. 8.2.

74. *Tragédie, tirée de l'Ecriture sainte* (cited by the brothers Parfaict, *HTF*, 13:403n); App. 14.2. As late as 1932, Jean Giraudoux published his own *Judith*.

75. See *ST*, 28, 64 (original emphasis).

76. These films are the subject of Kerekes and Slater, *Killing for Culture*, whose back cover even sports the warning, "Contains Adult Material."

Epilogue: The Moment of Truth

1. *Morals and Stories*, 210.

2. *Devil's Dictionary*, 227.

3. *Heads You Lose*, ix; cited above, introduction.

4. *Republic*, 377a.

5. "Against Theory," 26, 28 (original emphasis).

6. *PP*, 219. This statement only apparently contradicts the previous one, which applies to the declarative value of "Performative Utterances" instead of to "Pretending" per se.

7. See *BT*, 149–54. It was dramatized in the film *Urban Legend* and even inspired an episode of *Law and Order*.

8. Those with a taste for more urban legends of academia should consult Bronner, *Piled Higher and Deeper*.

9. *FA*, 1. At my own peril, I would point out that this was Alan D. Sokal's argument about gravity in his confession about his notorious hoax published as "A Physicist Experiments with Cultural Studies."

10. For the Harris execution, see Lesser, *Pictures*, chap. 2.

11. See Roeper, *Urban Legend*, 145–47; and Kerekes and Slater, *Killing for Culture*, 136–41.

12. Already on 25 September 1992, *20/20* featured video evidence of one neighbor murdering another; on 9 February 1996, it aired video surveillance footage that captured one man being stabbed to death and two others shot to death.

13. In a hideous piece of logic, the continued placement of a child at risk is the price to pay for collecting evidence.

14. This incident was reported by both Tom Brokaw and Peter Jennings, and is the subject of my "Medieval Death."

15. When Aaron Brown reported on the freeway suicide, he invoked the televised murder of Lee Harvey Oswald plus the Dwyer incident (ABC, *World News Tonight*, 6 May 1998). Brown did not give Dwyer's name, but Roeper did (*Urban Legends*, 146), as did Kerekes and Slater with pictures (*Killing for Culture*, 200–202).

16. This report was filed by Jim Wooten for ABC.

17. See Robins, "When Is the News Just Too 'Horrific?'" 53.

18. Both networks aired the story on 23 November. Youk, age fifty-two, had been suffering from Lou Gehrig's disease and had authorized Kevorkian to euthanize him.

19. "Dressed to Kill," 16.

20. "Killer Doc," 70.

21. See apps. 5.1 and 5.2. I explore other similarities and differences in my work in progress, "Back to the Medieval Future."

22. *60 Minutes* 13, no. 43; courtesy of Burrelle's Transcripts; see also my "Medieval Death."

23. *BTA*, 301; see above, chap. 14. See also Philo, *Seeing and Believing*, chap. 6.

24. *HMS*, 70; app. Intro.3.

25. On the self-conscious violence of modern performance art, see Blau, *Audience*, chap. 4; Garner, *Bodied Spaces*, chap. 5; *SRT*, introduction; and *BTA*, 298–99.

26. Chad Percival, a graduate student in my 1993 medieval drama seminar, states that he attended this event on 16 January 1993 while researching his paper for the course.

27. See especially Baudrillard, "Simulacra and Simulations," in *SW*, chap. 7; and *ST*, introduction.

WORKS CITED

This list is divided into several categories: (1) collections of theatrical anecdotes, folktales, legends, memoirs, proverbs, and dictionaries; (2) primary sources; and (3) secondary sources.

Collections of Theatrical Anecdotes, Folktales, Legends, Memoirs, Proverbs, Dictionaries

Aarne, A. *The Types of the Folktale: A Classification and Bibliography.* Trans. and enlarged by Stith Thompson. 2nd revision. Helsinki: Suomalainen Tiedeakatemia, 1961.

Bachaumont, L. P. de. *Mémoires historiques, littéraires et critiques de Bachaumont: depuis l'année 1762 jusques 1788; ou Choix d'ancedotes historiques, littéraires, critiques et dramatiques, de bon mots, d'Epigrammes, de Pièces . . .* Paris: L. Collin, 1808.

Baring-Gould, Sabine. *Curious Myths of the Middle Ages.* 1867. Rpt. New York: Oxford University Press, 1978.

Bayle, Pierre. *Selections from Bayle's Dictionary.* Ed. E. A. Beller and M. duP. Lee Jr. Princeton: Princeton University Press, 1952.

Bellingen, Fleury de. *L'Etymologie ou explication des proverbes françois, divisée en trois livres par chapitres en forme de dialogue.* La Haye: A. Vlacq, 1656.

Belton, Fred. *Random Recollections of an Old Actor.* London: Tinsley Brothers, 1880.

Bierce, Ambrose. *The Devil's Dictionary.* c. 1911. Cleveland: World Publishing, 1943.

Bonaventure des Periers. *Nouvelles récréations et joyeux devis suivis du Cymbalum mundi.* Ed. Louis Lacour. 2 vols. Paris: Libraire des Bibliophiles, 1874.

Briggs, Katharine M. *A Dictionary of British Folk-Tales in the English Language.* 2 vols. Bloomington: Indiana University Press, 1970.

Bronner, Simon J. *Piled Higher and Deeper: The Folklore of Campus Life.* Little Rock: August House, 1990.

Brunvand, Jan Harold. *The Baby Train and Other Lusty Urban Legends.* New York: W. W. Norton, 1993.

———. *The Choking Doberman and Other "New" Urban Legends.* New York: W. W. Norton, 1984.

———. *Curses! Broiled Again: The Hottest Urban Legends Going.* New York: W. W. Norton, 1989.

———. *The Mexican Pet: More "New" Urban Legends and Some Old Favorites.* New York: W. W. Norton, 1986.

———. *Too Good to Be True: The Colossal Book of Urban Legends.* New York: W. W. Norton, 1999.

———. *The Truth Never Stands in the Way of a Good Story!* Urbana: University of Illinois Press, 2000.

———. *The Vanishing Hitchhiker: American Urban Legends and Their Meanings.* New York: W. W. Norton, 1981.

Chetwood, W. R. *A General History of the Stage, From its Origin in Greece down to the Present Time*. London: W. Owen, 1749.

Clément, Jean Marie Bernard. *Anecdotes dramatiques*. Paris: Veuve Duchesne, 1775. Reprinted as *Anecdotes dramatiques [par] Joseph de la Porte [et] Jean-Marie Clément, Tomes 1 à 3*. Geneva: Slatkine, 1971.

Cousin d'Avalon. *Comédiana, ou Recueil choisi d'Anecdotes dramatiques, bons mots des comédiens, et réparties spirituelles, de bonhomie et du naïveté du parterre*. Paris: Marchand, 1801.

Dickson, Paul, and Joseph C. Goulden. *Myth-Informed: Legends, Credos, and Wrongheaded "Facts" We All Believe*. New York: G. P. Putnam's Sons, 1993.

———. *There Are Alligators in Our Sewers and Other American Credos*. New York: Delacorte, 1983.

Dictionary of 1000 French Proverbs, with English Equivalents. Ed. Peter Mertvago. New York: Hippocrene, 1996.

Dictionnaire des proverbes, sentences et maximes. Ed. Maurice Maloux. Paris: Larousse, 1960.

Dorson, Richard M. *American Folklore and the Historian*. Chicago: University of Chicago Press, 1971.

Fitzgerald, Percy. *The Book of Theatrical Anecdotes*. London: George Routledge and Sons, [1873].

Fournier, Édouard, ed. *Variétés historiques et littéraires; recueil de pièces volantes rares et curieuses en prose et en vers*. Bibliothèque Elzévirienne. 10 vols. Paris: P. Jannet, 1855–63.

Hawkins, Frederick. *Annals of the French Stage: From Its Origin to the Death of Racine*. 2 vols. London: Chapman and Hall, 1884.

Larwood, Jacob. [H. D. J. van Schevichaven]. *Theatrical Anecdotes or Fun and Curiosities of the Play, the Playhouse, and the Players*. London: Chatto and Windus, 1882.

Le Roux de Lincy, M. *Le Livre des proverbes français. Précédé de recherches historiques sur les proverbes français et leur emploi dans la littérature du moyen âge et de la Renaissance*. 2nd ed. 2 vols. Paris: Adolphe Delahaye, 1859.

Oudin, Antoine. [1595–1653]. *Curiositez françoises, pour supplement aux dictionnaires; ou, Recueil de plusieurs belles proprietez, avec une infinité de proverbes & Quolibets, pour l'explication de toutes sortes de Livres*. Paris: Antoine de Sommaville, 1640. Reprinted as *Curiositez françoises*. Geneva: Slatkine, 1971.

Roeper, Richard. *Urban Legends: The Truth behind All Those Deliciously Entertaining Myths That Are Absolutely, Positively, 100% Not True!* Franklin Lakes, N.J.: Career Press, 1999.

[Ryan, Richard]. *Dramatic Table Talk; or Scenes, Situations and Adventures, Serious and Comic, in Theatrical History and Biography*. 3 vols. London: J. Knight and H. Lacey, 1825.

Shakespeare's Jest Book: An Edition of A Hundred Mery Talys (1526). Ed. Hermann Oesterley; reedited by Leonard R. N. Ashley. 1866. Rpt. Gainesville, Fla.: Scholars' Facsimiles and Reprints, 1970.

Shakespeare Jest-Books. Ed. W. Carew Hazlitt. London: Willis and Sotheran, 1864.

Sinden, Donald, ed. *The Everyman Book of Theatrical Anecdotes*. London: J. M. Dent and Sons, 1987.

Troyes, Nicolas de. *Le grand parangon des nouvelles nouvelles composé par Nicolas de Troyes*. Ed. Emile Mabille. Paris: A. Franck, 1869.

Primary Sources

Adam. Représentation de la chute du premier homme. Imitation libre de la première partie du drame anglo-normand du XIIe siècle. Ed. Victor Luzarche. Paris: A. Wittersheim, 1855.

[Adam]. Le mystère d'Adam, drame religieux du XIIe siècle: Texte du manuscrit de Tours et traduction nouvelle. Trans. Henri Chamard. Paris: Armand Colin, 1925.

[Adam]. Ordo repraesentationis Adae. Ed. and trans. David Bevington. In Bevington, ed., *Medieval Drama,* 78–121.

[Alan of Lille]. Alanus de Insulis. *The Art of Preaching.* Trans. Gillian R. Evans. Cistercian Studies 23. Kalamazoo, Mich.: Cistercian Publications, 1981.

———. *Summa Magistri Alani Doctoris Universalis de arte praedictoria.* In *Opera omnia,* ed. J.-P. Migne, 110–98. *Patrologia Latina* 210. 1855. Rpt. Turnhout, Belgium: Brepols, 1976.

Alvarez, Vincente. *Relacion del camino buen viage que hizo el principe de Espana Don Felipe.* Brussels, 1551. Published in French by M. T. Dovillée as *Relation du Beau Voyage que fit aux Pays-Bas, en 1548, le prince Philippe d'Espagne, Notre Seigneur . . .* Brussels: Presses Académiques Européennes, 1964.

"Analyse d'un manuscrit peu connu & très curieux, qui existe à Romans en Dauphiné, faite par M. M***, de la même ville." *Journal de Paris* 264 (21 September 1787): 1143–44.

Aristotle. *De poetica liber Graece et Latine.* Ed. T. C. Harles. Leipzig: Siegfried Lebrecht Crusius, 1780.

———. *Poetics.* Ed. and trans. W. Hamilton Fyfe. In *Aristotle, Longinus, Demetrius.* Loeb Classical Library. 1927. Rpt. Cambridge, Mass.: Harvard University Press, 1946.

———. *The Poetics of Aristotle: Translated from Greek into English and from Arabic into Latin.* Ed. and trans. D. S. Margouliouth. London: Hodder and Stoughton, 1911.

Basil, St. "To Young Men on Reading Greek Literature." In *Readings from Classical Rhetoric,* ed. Patricia P. Matsen, Philip Rollinson, and Marion Sousa, 355–59. Carbondale: Southern Illinois University Press, 1990.

Baudelaire, Charles. *Oeuvres complètes.* Ed. Claude Pichois. Pléiade ed. 2 vols. Paris: Flammarion, 1975.

Beaumanoir, Philippe de. *Coutumes de Beauvaisis de Philippe de Beaumanoir.* Trans. F. R. P. Akehurst. Philadelphia: University of Pennsylvania Press, 1992.

Beck, Jonathan. *Théâtre et propagande aux débuts de la Réforme: Six pièces polémiques du Recueil La Vallière.* Geneva: Slatkine, 1986.

du Bellay, Joachim. *"Les Antiquitez de Rome" et "Les Regrets."* Geneva: Droz, 1960.

Bevington, David, ed. *The Medieval Drama.* Boston: Houghton-Mifflin, 1975.

The Book of Judith. Trans. Morton S. Enslin, ed. Solomon Zeitlin. Jewish Apocryphal Literature 7. Leiden: E. J. Brill, 1972.

Boussu, Gilles-Joseph. *Histoire de la Ville de Mons, ancienne et nouvelle; contenant tout ce qui s'est passé de plus curieux depuis son origine jusqu'à présent 1725.* Mons: Jean-Nicolas Varret, 1725.

Butler's Lives of the Saints. Ed. Herbert Thurston, S. J., and Donald Attwater. 4 vols. New York: P. J. Kenedy and Sons, 1956.

Calvete de Estrella, C. *El felicissimo viaje del muy poderoso principe Don Phelipe.* Antwerp, 1551.

Calvin, John. *Institutes of the Christian Religion.* Trans. Ford Lewis Battles, ed. John T. McNeill. 2 vols. Philadelphia: Westminster, 1960.

Cazelles, Brigitte, ed. *The Lady as Saint: A Collection of French Hagiographic Romances of the Thirteenth Century.* Philadelphia: University of Pennsylvania Press, 1991.

La Chanson de Roland: An Analytical Edition. Ed. Gerard J. Brault. 2 vols. University Park: Pennsylvania State University Press, 1978.

Chassanée, Bartholomew. [D. Bartholomaie Chassanai, Burgundi]. *Catalogus gloriae mundi.* Geneva, 1649.

Chaumeau, Jean. *Histoire de Berry.* 1556.

Chonet, Jean. *Composition, mise en scène et représentation du Mystère des trois doms [du chanoine Pra]; joué à Romans, les 27, 28 et 29 mai, aux fêtes de Pentecôte de l'an 1509; d'après un manuscrit du temps.* Ed. Paul-Emile Giraud. Lyon: Louis Perrin, 1848.

Chronique de Metz de Jacomin Husson, 1200–1525. Publié d'aprés le manuscrit autographe de Copenhague et celui de Paris. Ed. H. Michelant. Metz: Rousseau-Pallez, 1870.

Les Chroniques de la ville de Metz, recueillies, mises en ordre et publiées pour la première fois: Le Doyen de St Thiébault.—Jean Aubrion.—Philippe de Vigneulles.—Praillon.—Annales Messines, etc., 900–1552. Ed. Jean François Huguenin. Metz: S. Lamort, 1838.

Cohen, Gustave, ed. *Le Livre de conduite du Régisseur et Le Compte des dépenses pour le* Mystère de la Passion *joué à Mons en 1501.* Paris: Champion, 1925.

———. *Recueil de farces françaises inédites du XVe siècle.* Cambridge, Mass.: Mediaeval Academy of America, 1949.

Coment Judich tua Oloferne. Wolfenbüttel, Herzog August Bibliothek, Codex Guelf. 9 Blankenburgensis. [Edition in progress by Alan Knight].

Coquillart, Guillaume. *Plaidoyé d'entre la Simple et la Rusée.* In *Oeuvres,* ed. Michael J. Freeman. Geneva: Droz, 1975.

Le Cycle de mystères des premiers martyrs. Ed. Graham A. Runnalls. Geneva: Droz, 1976.

Dumas, Alexandre. *Kean: Cinq actes.* Adaptation by Jean-Paul Sartre. Paris: Gallimard, 1954.

Duval, Georges. *Languille de Melun, Vaudeville-Poissard en un acte.* Paris: Cavanagh, 1804.

Farce des Théologastres. In Fournier, ed., *Théâtre français,* 418–28.

Farel, Guillaume. *Sommaire et brève déclaration (1525).* Ed. Arthur-L. Hofer. Neuchâtel, Switzerland: Belle Rivière, 1980.

Felibien, Michel. *Histoire de la ville de Paris.* Reedited by Guy-Alexis Lobineau. 5 vols. Paris: G. Desprez et J. Desessartz, 1725.

Fouquet, Jean. *Le Livre d'heures d'Etienne Chevalier.* Ed. Germain Bazin. Paris: Somogy, 1990.

Fournier, Édouard, ed. *Le Théâtre français avant la Renaissance, 1450–1550: Mystères, moralités et farces.* 1872. Rpt. New York: Burt Franklin, 1965.

Foxe, John. *Actes and Monuments of John Foxe.* Ed. Stephen Reed Cattley. Introduction by George Townsend. 8 vols. London, 1837–41.

Gellius, Aulus. *The Attic Nights of Aulus Gellius.* Ed. and trans. John C. Rolfe. 3 vols. Loeb Classical Library. Cambridge, Mass.: Harvard University Press, 1927.

Geoffrey of Vinsauf. *Poetria Nova.* In *The Poetria Nova and Its Sources in Early Rhetorical Doctrine.* Trans. Ernest Gallo. The Hague: Mouton, 1971.

Gerson, Jean. *Oeuvres complètes.* Ed. Palémon Glorieux. 10 vols. Paris: Desclée, 1960–73.

Le Geu Saint Denis du Manuscrit 1131 de la Bibliothèque Sainte-Geneviève. Ed. Bernard James Seubert. Geneva: Droz, 1974.

Giraudoux, Jean. *Judith, Tragédie en 3 actes.* Paris: Grasset, 1932.

Gréban, Arnoul. *Le Mystère de la Passion.* Ed. Omer Jodogne. Brussels: Académie Royale, 1965.

———. *The Mystery of the Passion: The Third Day.* Trans. Paula Giuliano. Early European Drama Translation Series. Asheville, N.C.: Pegasus Press, 1996.

Gregory of Tours, Bishop. *History of the Franks.* Ed. and trans. Ernest Brehaut. New York: W. W. Norton, 1969.

Greig, Francis. *Heads You Lose: And Other Apocryphal Tales.* New York: Crown, 1982.

La Guerre de Metz en 1324: Poème du XIVe siècle. Ed. E. de Bouteiller. Paris: Firmin-Didot, 1875. Rpt. Amsterdam: Rodopi, 1970.

Guibert of Nogent. *Self and Society in Medieval France.* Trans. John F. Benton. Medieval Academy Reprints for Teaching 15. Toronto: University of Toronto Press, 1989.

Hrotsvit of Gandersheim. *Plays of Hrotsvit of Gandersheim.* Trans. Katharina Wilson. New York: Garland, 1989.

Isidore of Seville. *Isidori Hispalensis Episcopi Etymologiarum sive originum libri XX.* Ed. W. M. Lindsay. 2 vols. 1911. Rpt. London, 1962.

Le Jeu de Saint Nicolas. Ed. Alfred Jeanroy. Paris: Champion, 1925.

Jeux et sapience du Moyen Age. Ed. Albert Pauphilet. Pléiade ed. Paris: Gallimard, 1951.

Johnston, Alexandra, and Margaret Rogerson, eds. *York.* Records of Early English Drama 2. 2 vols. Toronto: University of Toronto Press, 1979.

Journal d'un bourgeois de Paris 1405–1449. Ed. A. Tuety. Paris, 1881. Reedited by Colette Beaune. Paris: Lettres Gothiques, 1990.

[Journal d'un bourgeois de Paris 1405–1449]. Trans. Janet Shirley. *A Parisian Journal 1405–1449.* Oxford: Clarendon Press, 1960.

Judith. Ed. Mark Griffith. Exeter Medieval English Texts and Studies. Exeter: University of Exeter Press, 1997.

Justus Lipsius. *De amphitheatris.* Antwerp: Plantin, 1585.

———. *De amphitheatro liber.* Ed. Theodore Besterman. Printed Sources of Western Art 10–11. Portland, Ore.: Collegium Graphicum, 1972.

Kors, Alan C., and Edward Peters, eds. *Witchcraft in Europe 1100–1700: A Documentary History.* 1972. Rpt. Philadelphia: University of Pennsylvania Press, 1986.

Le Doyen, Guillaume. *Annales et chroniques du païs de Laval depuis l'an 1480 jusqu'à l'année 1537.* Ed. H. Godbert, annotated by Louis la Beauluère. 1859. Rpt. Geneva: Slatkine, 1971.

Lucian of Samosata. "Saltatio." Ed. A. M. Harmon. In *Works,* vol. 5. Loeb Classical Library. 1936. Rpt. Cambridge, Mass.: Harvard University Press, 1972.

Marot, Clément. *Les Oeuvres de Clement Marot de Cahors en Quercy.* Ed. Georges Guiffrey. 5 vols. Paris: I. Claye, 1911. Rpt. Geneva: Slatkine, 1969.

The Medieval Lyric: Anthologies and Cassettes for Teaching. Ed. Margaret Switten and Howell Chickering. 4 vols. plus 5 audio cassettes. South Hadley, Mass.: Mount Holyoke College, 1988–99. Revised edition with 5 compact discs, 2001.

Meredith, Peter, and John E. Tailby, eds. *The Staging of Religious Drama in Europe in the Later Middle Ages: Texts and Documents in English Translation.* Early Drama, Art and Music 4. Kalamazoo, Mich.: Medieval Institute Publications, 1983.

Michel, Jean. *Le Mystère de la Passion (Angers 1486).* Ed. Omer Jodogne. Gembloux, Belgium: J. Duculot, 1959.

Le Miracle de la nonne qui laissa son abbaie. Ed. Nigel Wilkins. In *Two Miracles,* 13–53. Edinburgh: Scottish Academic Press, 1972.

Miracles de Nostre Dame par personnages. Ed. Gaston Paris and Ulysse Robert. Société des Anciens Textes Français 6. 8 vols. Paris: Firmin-Didot, 1876–93. Rpt. New York: Johnson Reprints, 1966.

Le Mistere de la Sainte Hostie. Paris, Bibliothèque Nationale, Réserve, Yf 2915.

Le Mistére du Viel Testament. Ed. James de Rothschild. 6 vols. 1878. Rpt. New York: Johnson Reprints, 1966.

Le Mistére par personnaiges de la vie . . . IESUS CHRIST en 25 iournées . . . lequel Mistére fut iouet en la ville de Vallenchiennes 1547 . . . Paris, Bibliothèque Nationale, Rothschild I.7.3.

[Molinet, Jean?]. *Le Mystère de Judith et Holofernés: Une édition critique de l'une des parties du "Mistere du Viel Testament."* Ed. Graham A. Runnalls. Geneva: Droz, 1995.

Montaiglon, A. de, and Gaston Raynaud. 6 vols. *Recueil général et complet des fabliaux des XIIIe et XIVe siècles.* 1872–90. Rpt. New York: Burt Franklin, n.d.

Moralités françaises. Ed. Werner Helmich. 3 vols. Geneva: Slatkine, 1980.

Le Mystère de la Passion à Amboise au moyen âge: Représentations théâtrales et texte. Ed. Graham A. Runnalls. Montreal: CERES, 1990.

Le Mystère de la Passion de Troyes. Ed. Jean-Claude Bibolet. 2 vols. Geneva: Droz, 1987.

Le Mystère de la Passion Nostre Seigneur du manuscrit 1131 de la Bibliothèque Sainte-Geneviève. Ed. Graham A. Runnalls. Geneva: Droz, 1974.

Le Mystère de la Résurrection Angers (1456). Ed. Pierre Servet. 2 vols. Geneva: Droz, 1993.

Le Mystère des actes des apôtres représenté à Bourges en avril 1536. Ed. Auguste-Théodore de Girardot. Paris: Librairie Archéologique Victor Didron, 1854.

Le Mystère des Trois Doms joué à Romans en MDIX . . . avec le compte de sa composition, mise en scène et représentation et des documents relatifs aux représentations théâtrales en Dauphiné du XIVe au XVIe siècle. Ed. Paul-Emile Giraud. Lyon: Auguste Brun, 1887.

Les Mystères de la Procession de Lille. Vol. 1. Ed. Alan E. Knight. Geneva: Droz, 2001.

Mystères inédits du XVe siècle. Ed. Achille Jubinal. 2 vols. Paris: Téchener, 1837.

Nagler, A. M., ed. *A Source Book in Theatrical History.* 1952. Rpt. New York: Dover, 1959.

National Television Violence Study, 1994–95: Executive Summary. University of California, Santa Barbara; University of North Carolina, Chapel Hill; University of Texas, Austin; University of Wisconsin, Madison. Studio City, Calif.: Mediascope, Inc., 1996.

Noble, Thomas F. X., and Thomas Head, eds. *Soldiers of Christ: Saints and Saints' Lives from Late Antiquity and the Early Middle Ages.* University Park: Pennsylvania State University Press, 1995.

Pascal, Blaise. *Oeuvres complètes.* Ed. Louis Lafuma. Paris: Seuil, 1963.

Pasquier de le Barre. *Le Journal d'un bourgeois de Tournai: Le second livre des chroniques de Pasquier de le Barre (1500–1565).* Ed. Gérard Moreau. Brussels: Palais des Académies, 1975.

La Passion de Palatinus. In *Jeux et sapience,* 211–78.

Plato. *Laws.* Ed. and trans. R. G. Bury. Loeb Classical Library. 2 vols. 1926. Rpt. Cambridge, Mass.: Harvard University Press, 1942.

———. *The Republic.* Ed. and trans. Paul Shorey. Loeb Classical Library. 2 vols. Cambridge, Mass.: Harvard University Press, 1935.

Port, Célestin. *Inventaire analytique des archives anciennes de la mairie d'Angers.* Paris: J. Dumoulin; Angers: Cosnier et Lachèse, 1861.

Prynne, William. *Histriomastix.* [1633]. New York: Garland, 1974.

Pulci, Antonia. *Florentine Drama for Convent and Festival: Seven Sacred Plays.* Trans. James Wyatt Cook. Chicago: University of Chicago Press, 1996.

Quintilian. *Institutio oratoria.* Ed. and trans. H. E. Butler. Loeb Classical Library. 4 vols. 1920. Rpt. Cambridge, Mass.: Harvard University Press, 1980.

Les .XV. joies de mariage. Ed. Jean Rychner. Geneva: Droz, 1967.

Rabelais, François. *Oeuvres complètes.* Ed. Guy Demerson. Paris: Seuil, 1973.

———. *The Complete Works of François Rabelais.* Trans. Donald Frame. Berkeley: University of California Press, 1991.

Riché, Pierre, and Georges Tate, eds. *Textes et documents d'histoire du moyen âge, Ve–Xe siècles.* Vol. 1. *Regards sur l'histoire.* Paris: SEDES, 1972.

Rotrou, Jean [1609–50]. *Le Véritable Saint Genest, Tragédie.* Ed. E. T. Dubois. Geneva: Droz, 1972.

Rutebeuf. *Le Miracle de Théophile.* In *Jeux et sapience,* 135–58.

De Sainte Katherine: An Anonymous Picard Version of the Life of St. Catherine of Alexandria. Ed. William MacBain. Fairfax, Va.: George Mason University Press, 1987.

Shakespeare, William. *The Arden Shakespeare Complete Works.* Ed. Richard Proudfoot, Ann Thompson, and David Scott Kastan. Walton-on-Thames, England: Nelson, 1998.

Suetonius. *The Lives of the Caesars.* In *Works,* ed. and trans. J. C. Rolfe. Loeb Classical Library. 2 vols. Cambridge, Mass.: Harvard University Press, 1914.

Tertullian. *De spectaculis.* Ed. and trans. T. R. Glover. Loeb Classical Library. 1931. Rpt. Cambridge, Mass.: Harvard University Press, 1977.

Thiboust, Jacques. *Relation de l'ordre de la triomphante et magnifique monstre du mystère des Actes des Apôtres par Arnoul et Simon Gréban. Ouvrage inédit de Jacques Thiboust, sieur de Quantilly, secrétaire du roi, élu en Berry . . . Le tout recueilli par Me* LABOUVRIE, NOTAIRE HONORAIRE. Bourges: Manceron, 1836. Rpt. Geneva: Slatkine, 1975.

Tissier, André, ed. *Recueil de Farces (1450–1550).* 12 vols. Geneva: Droz, 1986–96.

Tydeman, William, ed. *The Medieval European Stage, 500–1550.* Theatre in Europe: A Documentary History. Cambridge: Cambridge University Press, 2001.

Unsworth, Barry. *Morality Play.* New York: Nan A. Talese / Doubleday, 1995.

Victricius of Rouen. *De laude sanctorum.* Ed. Jacob Mulders. CCL 64. Turnhout: Brepols, 1985.

de Vigneulles, Philippe. *La Chronique de Philippe de Vigneulles.* Ed. Charles Bruneau. 4 vols. Metz: Société d'Histoire et d'Archéologie de la Lorraine, 1927–33.

———. *Gedenkbuch des Metzer Bürgers Philippe von Vigneulles aus den Jahren 1471–1522.* Ed. Heinrich Michelant. Stuttgart, 1852. Rpt. Amsterdam: Rodopi, 1968.

Vinchant, François. *Annales de la province et comté du Hainaut.* Vol. 5. Mons: Hoyois, 1852.

Vitale-Brovarone, Alessandro, ed. *Il quaderno di segreti d'un regista provenzale del Medioevo: Note per la messa in scena d'una Passione.* Alessandria: Orso, 1984.

Voltaire, François Marie Arouet de. *Zaïre.* Ed. Eva Jacobs. London: Hodder and Stoughton, 1975.

de Voragine, Jacobus. *The Golden Legend: Readings on the Saints.* Trans. William Granger Ryan. 2 vols. Princeton: Princeton University Press, 1993.

Secondary Sources

Accaric, Maurice. *Le Théâtre sacré de la fin du Moyen-Age: Étude sur le sens moral de la Passion de Jean Michel.* Geneva: Droz, 1979.

Allison, David B., and Mark S. Roberts. *Disordered Mother or Disordered Diagnosis? Munchausen by Proxy Syndrome.* Hillsdale, N.J.: Analytic Press, 1998.

L'Ancienne France. Le Théâtre—Mystères—Tragédie—Comédie—et la Musique—Instruments— Ballet—Opéra jusqu'en 1789. Paris: Firmin-Didot, 1887.

Ariès, Philippe. *Western Attitudes toward Death: From the Middle Ages to the Present.* Trans. Patricia M. Ranum. Baltimore: Johns Hopkins University Press, 1974.

Artaud, Antonin. *The Theater and Its Double.* Trans. Mary Caroline Richards. New York: Grove Weidenfeld, 1958.

Ashley, Kathleen M., ed. *Victor Turner and the Construction of Cultural Criticism: Between Literature and Anthropology.* Bloomington: Indiana University Press, 1990.

Austin, J. L. *How to Do Things with Words.* Edited by J. O. Urmson and Marina Sbisà. 2nd ed. Cambridge: Harvard University Press, 1978.

———. *Philosophical Papers.* Ed. J. O. Urmson and G. J. Warnock. 2nd ed. Oxford: Clarendon, 1970.

Axton, Richard. *European Drama of the Early Middle Ages.* London: Hutchinson, 1974.

Bakeless, John. *The Tragicall History of Christopher Marlowe.* Vol. 1. Cambridge, Mass.: Harvard University Press, 1942.

Bakhtin, Mikhail. *Rabelais and His World.* Trans. Hélène Iswolsky. 1965. Bloomington: Indiana University Press, 1984.

Barish, Jonas. *The Anti-Theatrical Prejudice.* Berkeley: University of California Press, 1981.

Barker, Francis. *The Culture of Violence: Essays on Tragedy and History.* Chicago: University of Chicago Press, 1993.

Baudrillard, Jean. *Selected Writings.* Ed. and trans. Mark Poster. Stanford: Stanford University Press, 1988.

Beckwith, Sarah. *Christ's Body.* London: Routledge, 1994.

————. *Signifying God: Social Relations and Symbolic Action in York's Play of Corpus Christi.* Chicago: University of Chicago Press, 2001.

Bédier, Joseph. *Les Légendes épiques: Recherches sur la formation des chansons de geste.* 4 vols. 3rd ed. Paris: Champion, 1929.

Bell, Rudolph M. *Holy Anorexia.* Chicago: University of Chicago Press, 1985.

Benedetti, Jean. *Stanislavski: A Biography.* New York: Routledge, 1990.

Berrigan, Joseph. "The Tuscan Visionary: Saint Catherine of Siena." In Wilson, ed., *Medieval Women Writers,* 52–68.

Bertin, Léon. *Eels: A Biological Study.* Trans. Betty Roquerbe. New York: Philosophical Library, 1957.

Birnbaum, Pierre. "Grégoire, Dreyfus, Drancy, and the Rue Copernic: Jews at the Heart of French History." In Nora, ed., *Realms of Memory,* 1:379–423.

Black, Joel. *The Aesthetics of Murder: A Study in Romantic Literature and Contemporary Culture.* Baltimore: Johns Hopkins University Press, 1991.

Blau, Herbert. *The Audience.* Baltimore: Johns Hopkins University Press, 1990.

————. *Blooded Thought: Occasions of Theater.* New York: Performing Arts Journal, 1982.

Bloch, R. Howard. "New Philology and Old French." *Speculum* 65 (1990): 38–58.

Bloch, R. Howard, and Stephen G. Nichols, eds. *Medievalism and the Modernist Temper.* Baltimore: Johns Hopkins University Press, 1996.

Boal, Augusto. *Theater of the Oppressed.* Trans. Charles A. McBride and Maria-Odilia Leal McBride. New York: Urizen, 1979.

Boland, Paschal. *The Concept of* Discretio spirituum *in John Gerson's "De probatione spirituum" and "De distinctione verarum visionum a falsis.* Washington, D.C.: Catholic University Press, 1959.

Bordier, Jean-Pierre. *Le Jeu de la Passion: Le Message chrétien et le théâtre français (XIIIe–XVIe s.).* Paris: Champion, 1998.

Bourdieu, Pierre. *Outline of Theory of Practice.* Trans. Richard Nice. Cambridge: Cambridge University Press, 1977.

Boureau, Alain. *The Lord's First Night: The Myth of the Droit de Cuissage.* Trans. Lydia G. Cochrane. Chicago: University of Chicago Press, 1998.

————. *The Myth of Pope Joan.* Trans. Lydia G. Cochrane. Chicago: University of Chicago Press, 2001.

Boutiot, Théophile. *Recherches sur le théâtre à Troyes au XVe siècle.* Troyes: Bouquot, 1854.

Brecht, Bertolt. *Brecht on Theatre: The Development of an Aesthetic.* Ed. and trans. John Willett. New York: Hill and Wang, 1964.

————. *The Messingkauf Dialogues.* Trans. John Willet. London: Methuen, 1965.

Breisach, Ernst. *Historiography: Ancient, Medieval, and Modern.* Chicago: University of Chicago Press, 1983.

Bremmer, Jan, and Herman Roodenburg, eds. *A Cultural History of Gesture: From Antiquity to the Present Day.* Cambridge: Polity Press, 1991.

Briscoe, Marianne G., and John C. Coldewey, eds. *Contexts for Early English Drama.* Bloomington: Indiana University Press, 1989.

Bristol, Michael. *Carnival and Theater: Plebeian Culture and the Structure of Authority in Renaissance England.* New York: Methuen, 1985.

————. "Theater and Popular Culture." In Cox and Kastan, eds., *New History of Early English Drama,* 231–48.

Brook, Peter. *The Empty Space.* New York: Atheneum, 1968.

Brooks, Peter, and Paul Gewirtz. *Law's Stories: Narrative and Rhetoric in the Law.* New Haven: Yale University Press, 1996.

Brown, Frederick. *Theater and Revolution: The Culture of the French Stage.* New York: Viking Press, 1980.

Brown, Peter. *The Cult of the Saints: Its Rise and Function in Latin Christianity.* Chicago: University of Chicago Press, 1981.

Brunvand, Jan Harold. *The Study of American Folklore: An Introduction.* New York: W. W. Norton, 1968.

————. "Urban Legends." In *Traditional Storytelling Today: An International Sourcebook,* ed. Margaret Read MacDonald, 572–76. Chicago: Fitzroy Dearborn, 1999.

Buckley, William F. "Dressed to Kill." *National Review,* 21 December 1998, 16.

————. "Killer Doc." *National Review,* 21 December 1998, 70.

Burke, Kenneth. *The Philosophy of Literary Form: Studies in Symbolic Action.* 3rd ed. 1941. Rpt. Berkeley: University of California Press, 1973.

Burrow, J. A. "'Young Saint, Old Devil': Reflections on a Medieval Proverb." *Review of English Studies* 30 (1979): 385–96.

Butterfield, Bradley. "Ethical Value and Negative Aesthetics: Reconsidering the Baudrillard-Ballard Connection." *PMLA* 114 (1999): 64–77.

Butterworth, Philip. *Theatre of Fire: Special Effects in Early English and Scottish Theatre.* London: Society for Theatre Research, 1998.

Bynum, Caroline Walker. *Fragmentation and Redemption: Essays on Gender and the Human Body in Medieval Religion.* New York: Zone, 1992.

————. *Holy Feast and Holy Fast: The Religious Significance of Food to Medieval Women.* Berkeley: University of California Press, 1987.

————. *The Resurrection of the Body in Western Christianity, 200–1336.* New York: Columbia University Press, 1995.

Callahan, John M. "The Ultimate in Theatre Violence." In Redmond, ed., *Violence in Drama,* 165–76.

Callahan, Leslie Abend. "Ambiguity and Appropriation: The Story of Judith in Medieval Narrative and Iconographic Traditions." In Sautman, Conchado, and Di Scipio, eds., *Telling Tales,* 79–99.

Campbell, Thomas P. "Cathedral Chapter and Town Council: Ceremony and Drama in Medieval Rouen." *Comparative Drama* 27 (1993): 100–113.

Campion-Vincent, Véronique, and Jean-Bruno Renard. *Légendes urbaines: Rumeurs d'aujourd'hui.* Paris: Payot, 1992.

Canetti, Elias. *Crowds and Power.* Trans. Carol Stewart. New York: Farrar, Strauss, and Giroux, 1962.

Carlson, Marvin. *Performance: A Critical Introduction.* London: Routledge, 1996.

————. *Places of Performance: The Semiotics of Theatre Architecture.* Ithaca: Cornell University Press, 1989.

————. *Theatre Semiotics: Signs of Life.* Bloomington: Indiana University Press, 1990.

Carro, A. *Histoire de Meaux.* 1865. Rpt. Paris: Res Universis, 1989.

Carroll, William C., ed. *"Macbeth": Texts and Contexts.* By William Shakespeare. Boston and New York: Bedford and St. Martin's Press, 1999.

Carruthers, Mary. *The Book of Memory.* Cambridge: Cambridge University Press, 1990.

Caruth, Cathy. *Unclaimed Experience: Trauma, Narrative, and History.* Baltimore: Johns Hopkins University Press, 1996.

Case, Sue-Ellen. "Classic Drag: The Greek Creation of Female Parts." *Theatre Journal* 37 (1985): 317–27.

————. "Toward a Butch-Femme Aesthetic." In *Making a Spectacle: Feminist Essays on Contem-*

porary Women's Theatre, ed. Lynda Hart, 282–99. Ann Arbor: University of Michigan Press, 1989.

Cavell, Stanley. *Must We Mean What We Say? A Book of Essays*. New York: Scribner's, 1969.

de Certeau, Michel. *The Practice of Everyday Life*. Trans. Steven Rendall. Berkeley: University of California Press, 1988.

————. *The Writing of History*. Trans. Tom Conley. New York: Columbia University Press, 1988.

Chaikin, Joseph. *The Presence of the Actor*. New York: Atheneum, 1974.

Chambers, E. K. *The Mediaeval Stage*. 2 vols. Oxford: Oxford University Press, 1903.

Chandler, Alice. *A Dream of Order: The Medieval Ideal in Nineteenth-Century English Literature*. Lincoln: University of Nebraska Press, 1970.

Chateaux de la Loire. Guide de Tourisme Michelin 9. 4th ed. Paris: Pneu Michelin, 1996.

Chotin, A.-G. *Histoire de Tournai et du Tournésis, depuis les temps les plus reculés jusqu'à nos jours*. Vol. 1. 1840. Rpt. Brussels: Éditions Culture et Civilisation, 1982.

Ciletti, Elena. "Patriarchal Ideology in the Renaissance Iconography of Judith." In *Refiguring Woman: Perspectives on Gender and the Italian Renaissance*, ed. Marilyn Migiel and Juliana Schiesari, 35–70. Ithaca: Cornell University Press, 1991.

Clark, Priscilla Parkhurst. *Literary France: The Making of a Culture*. Berkeley: University of California Press, 1987.

Clark, Robert L. A., and Claire Sponsler. "Othered Bodies: Racial Cross-Dressing in the *Mistere de la Sainte Hostie* and the Croxton *Play of the Sacrament*." *Journal of Medieval and Early Modern Studies* 29, no. 1 (1999): 61–75.

Clément-Hémery, Mme Albertine. *Histoire des fêtes civiles et religieuses*. Avesnes: C. Viroux, 1846.

Cloquet, Louis. *Guide de Tournai et du Tournaisis*. Bruges: Desclée, De Brouwer et Cie., 1884.

Cohen, Esther. *The Crossroads of Justice*. Leiden: Brill, 1993.

————. "'To Die a Criminal for the Public Good': The Execution Ritual in Late Medieval Paris." In *Law, Custom and the Social Fabric in Medieval Europe*, ed. Bernard S. Bachrach and David Nicholas, 285–304. Studies in Medieval Culture 28. Kalamazoo, Mich.: Medieval Institute Publications, 1990.

Cohen, Gustave. *Études d'histoire du théâtre en France au Moyen-âge et à la Renaissance*. 7th ed. Paris: Gallimard, 1956.

————. *Histoire de la mise en scène dans le théâtre religieux français du moyen-âge*. 2nd ed. Paris: Champion, 1951.

Cohen, Walter. *Drama of a Nation: Public Theater in Renaissance England and Spain*. Ithaca: Cornell University Press, 1985.

Coldewey, John C. "Thrice-Told Tales: Renegotiating Early English Drama." In *European Medieval Drama 1996: Papers from the First International Conference on Aspects of European Medieval Drama. Camerino, 28–30 June, 1996*, ed. Sydney Higgins, 17–34. Camerino: Università degli Studi di Camerino, Centro Linguistico di Ateneo, 1996.

Coleman, Janet. *Ancient and Medieval Memories*. Cambridge: Cambridge University Press, 1992.

Coleman, Kathleen. "Fatal Charades: Roman Executions Staged as Mythological Enactments." *JRS* 80 (1900): 44–73.

Cornagliotti, A. "Apocryphes et mystères." In *Le Théâtre au Moyen Age*, ed. Muller, 67–78.

Côté, Diane Saint-Jacques. "Réalisations matérielles et techniques de représentations dramatiques à la fin du Moyen Age." In *Les Arts mécaniques au Moyen Age*, ed. G. H. Allard and S. Lusignan, 75–90. Cahiers d'études médiévales 7. Montreal and Paris: Bellarmin and Vrin, 1982.

Cox, John D. "The Devil and Society in the English Mystery Plays." *Comparative Drama* 28 (1994–95): 407–38.

————. *The Devil and the Sacred in English Drama, 1350–1642.* Cambridge: Cambridge University Press, 2001.

Cox, John D., and David Scott Kastan, eds. *A New History of Early English Drama.* New York: Columbia University Press, 1997.

Cunningham, Karen. "Renaissance Execution and Marlovian Elocution: The Drama of Death." *PMLA* 105 (1990): 209–22.

Dakyns, Janine. *The Middle Ages in French Literature, 1851–1900.* London: Oxford University Press, 1973.

Darnton, Robert. *The Great Cat Massacre and Other Episodes in French Cultural History.* 1984. Rpt. New York: Vintage, 1985.

Davidson, Clifford. "The Anti-Visual Prejudice." In *Iconoclasm vs. Art and Drama,* ed. Clifford Davidson and Ann Eljenholm Nichols, 33–46. Early Drama, Art, and Music 11. Kalamazoo, Mich.: Medieval Institute, 1989.

Davis, Derek Russell. *Scenes of Madness: A Psychiatrist at the Theatre.* London: Routledge, 1992.

Davis, Natalie Zemon. *Fiction in the Archives: Pardon Tales and Their Tellers in Sixteenth-Century France.* Stanford: Stanford University Press, 1987.

————. *The Return of Martin Guerre.* Cambridge, Mass.: Harvard University Press, 1983.

Deelder, C. L. *Synopsis of Biological Data on the Eel* Anguilla anguilla *(Linnaeus, 1758).* Rome: Food and Agriculture Organization of the United Nations, 1984.

Dégh, Linda. "What Is a Belief Legend?" *Folklore* 107 (1996): 33–46.

Delangre, A. *Le Théâtre et l'art dramatique à Tournai.* Tournai: Vasseur-Delmée, 1905.

Diderot, Denis. *Paradoxe sur le Comédien.* In *Oeuvres esthétiques,* ed. Paul Vernière, 299–381. Paris: Garnier, 1968.

Diehl, Huston. *Staging Reform, Reforming the Stage: Protestantism and Popular Theater in Early Modern England.* Ithaca: Cornell University Press, 1997.

Dollimore, Jonathan. *Radical Tragedy: Religion, Ideology, and Power in the Drama of Shakespeare and His Contemporaries.* Brighton: Harvester, 1984.

Dominguez, Véronique. "Le Corps dans les mystères de la Passion français du XVe siècle: Discours théologiques et esthétique théâtrale." Diss., Université de Paris IV Sorbonne, 1999.

Dougherty, Carol. *The Poetics of Colonization: From City to Text in Archaic Greece.* Oxford: Oxford University Press, 1993.

Dox, Donnalee. "Medieval Drama as Documentation: 'Real Presence' in the Croxton *Conversion of Ser Jonathas the Jewe by the Myracle of the Blissed Sacrament.*" *Theatre Survey* 38 (1997): 97–115.

Duffy, Eamon. *The Stripping of the Altars: Traditional Religion in England c. 1400–1580.* New Haven: Yale University Press, 1992.

Dundes, Alan. *Folklore Matters.* Knoxville: University of Tennessee Press, 1989.

Dundes, Alan, ed. *The Study of Folklore.* Englewood Cliffs, N.J.: Prentice-Hall, 1965.

Dupont, Léopold. "Denis Coppée: Tradition religieuse, actualité politique et exotisme dans le théâtre à Liège au temps du baroque." *Revue Belge de philologie et d'histoire* 55 (1977): 791–840.

Dutton, Richard. "Censorship." In Cox and Kastan, eds., *New History of Early English Drama,* 287–304.

Eco, Umberto. "Interpreting Drama." In Eco, *The Limits of Interpretation,* 101–10. Reprinted from "Semiotics of Theatrical Performance," *The Drama Review* 21 (1977): 107–17.

————. *The Limits of Interpretation.* Bloomington: Indiana University Press, 1990.

————. *The Name of the Rose.* Trans. William Weaver. San Diego: Harcourt Brace Jovanovich, 1983.

————. *The Open Work.* Trans. Anna Cancogni. Cambridge, Mass.: Harvard University Press, 1989.

Edwards, Christine. *The Stanislavsky Heritage: Its Contribution to the Russian and American Theatre.* New York: New York University Press, 1965.

Eliot, T. S. *Selected Essays.* New York: Harcourt Brace, 1932.

Elliot, Dyan. *Spiritual Marriage: Sexual Abstinence in Medieval Wedlock.* Princeton: Princeton University Press, 1993.

Elliott, John R., Jr. "Medieval Acting." In *Contexts for Early English Drama,* ed. Marianne G. Briscoe and John C. Coldewey, 243–44. Bloomington: Indiana University Press, 1989.

————. *Playing God: Medieval Mysteries on the Modern Stage.* Toronto: University of Toronto Press, 1989.

Enders, Jody. "Delivering Delivery: Theatricality and the Emasculation of Eloquence." *Rhetorica* 15 (1997): 253–78.

————. "Dramatic Memories and Tortured Spaces in the *Mistere de la Sainte Hostie.*" In Hanawalt and Kobialka, eds., *The Medieval Practices of Space,* 199–222.

————. "Emotion Memory and the Medieval Performance of Violence." Special issue: "Medieval Studies." *Theatre Survey* 38 (1997): 139–60.

————. "Homicidal Pigs and the Antisemitic Imagination." *Exemplaria* 14, no. 1 (2002): 201–38.

————. "Medieval Death, Modern Morality, and the Fallacies of Intention." *New Medieval Literatures* 5: 87–114.

————. "Medieval Snuff Drama." *Exemplaria* 10, no. 1 (1998): 171–206.

————. "Of Miming and Signing: The Dramatic Rhetoric of Gesture." In *Gesture in Medieval Drama and Art,* ed. Clifford Davidson, 1–25. Early Drama, Art, and Music 28. Kalamazoo, Mich.: Medieval Institute Publications, 2001.

————. "Of Protestantism, Performativity, and the Threat of Theater." Special issue: "Figuring Protest and Lament in the Sixteenth Century," ed. Dora Polachek. *Medievalia* (1999): 53–72.

————. *The Medieval Theater of Cruelty: Rhetoric, Memory, Violence.* Ithaca: Cornell University Press, 1998.

————. *Rhetoric and the Origins of Medieval Drama.* Rhetoric and Society 1. Ithaca: Cornell University Press, 1992.

————. "Violence, Silence, and the Memory of Witches." In *Violence against Women in Medieval Texts,* ed. Anna Roberts, 210–32. Gainesville: University of Florida Press, 1998.

Epp, Garrett P. J. "John Foxe and the Circumcised Stage." *Exemplaria* 9 (1997): 281–313.

Evans, E. P. *The Criminal Prosecution and Capital Punishment of Animals: The Lost History of Europe's Animal Trials.* 1906. Rpt. London: Faber and Faber, 1988.

Evans, Ruth. "When a Body Meets a Body: Fergus and Mary in the York Cycle." *New Medieval Literatures* 1 (1997): 193–212.

Faber, Frédéric. *Histoire du théâtre en Belgique depuis son origine jusqu'à nos jours: D'après les documents inédits reposant aux Archives Générales du Royaume.* Vol. 1. Brussels: Olivier; Paris: Tresse, 1878.

Fabre, Adolphe. *Études historiques sur les clercs de la Bazoche.* Paris: Potier, 1856.

Fabre-Vassas, Claudine. *The Singular Beast: Jews, Christians, and the Pig.* Trans. Carol Volk. New York: Columbia University Press, 1997.

Faivre, Bernard. "La Piété et la fête (des origines à 1548)." Part 1 of *Le Théâtre en France,* vol. 1: *Du Moyen âge à 1789,* ed. Jacqueline de Jomaron, 15–85. Paris: Armand Colin, 1988.

Farmer, Sharon. *Communities of Saint Martin: Legend and Ritual in Medieval Tours.* Ithaca: Cornell University Press, 1991.

Ferguson, Suzanne, and Barbara Groseclose, eds. *Literature and the Visual Arts in Contemporary Society.* Columbus: Ohio State University Press, 1985.

Flahault, François. *L'Interprétation des contes.* Paris: Denoël, 1988.

Flanigan, C. Clifford. "Liminality, Carnival, and Social Structure: The Case of Late Medieval Biblical Drama." In Ashley, ed., *Victor Turner and the Construction of Cultural Criticism,* 42–63.

Forrest, David M. *Eel Capture, Culture, Processing, and Marketing.* Surrey, England: Fishing News Books, Ltd., 1976.

Foucault, Michel. *Discipline and Punish: The Birth of the Prison.* Trans. Alan Sheridan. New York: Pantheon, 1977.

Foulet, Alfred. "Is Roland Guilty of *Desmesure?*" *Romance Philology* 10 (1957): 145–48.

Freud, Sigmund. *Introductory Lectures on Psycho-Analysis.* Ed. and trans. James Strachey. New York: W. W. Norton, 1966.

Futrell, Alison. *Blood in the Arena: The Spectacle of Roman Power.* Austin: University of Texas Press, 1997.

Gallagher, Catherine, and Stephen Greenblatt. *Practicing New Historicism.* Chicago: University of Chicago Press, 2000.

Gardiner, Harold C. *Mysteries' End: An Investigation of the Last Days of the Medieval Religious Stage.* New Haven: Yale University Press, 1946.

Garner, Stanton B., Jr. *Bodied Spaces: Phenomenology and Performance in Contemporary Drama.* Ithaca: Cornell University Press, 1994.

Gatton, John Spalding. "'There Must Be Blood': Mutilation and Martyrdom on the Medieval Stage." In Redmond, ed., *Violence in Drama,* 79–92.

Gelderen, Martin van. *The Dutch Revolt.* Cambridge: Cambridge University Press, 1993.

Gibson, Charles, ed. *The Black Legend: Anti-Spanish Attitudes in the Old World and the New.* New York: Alfred A. Knopf, 1971.

Gilder, Rosamond. *Enter the Actress: The First Women in the Theatre.* London: George G. Harrap, 1931.

Girard, René. *Violence and the Sacred.* Trans. Patrick Gregory Baltimore: Johns Hopkins University Press, 1977.

Goebel, Julius, Jr. *Felony and Misdemeanor: A Study in the History of Criminal Law.* Philadelphia: University of Pennsylvania Press, 1976.

Goffman, Erving. *Frame Analysis: An Essay on the Organization of Experience.* 1974. Rpt. Boston: Northeastern University Press, 1986.

Goldberg, Jonathan. *Sodometries: Renaissance Texts, Modern Sexualities.* Stanford: Stanford University Press, 1992.

Goodich, Michael E. *Violence and Miracle in the Fourteenth Century: Private Grief and Public Salvation.* Chicago: University of Chicago Press, 1995.

Goodman, Walter. "TV Shows Make Fantasy the Nation's Reality." *New York Times,* 14 July 2000.

Goodwin, Sarah Webster, and Elisabeth Bronfen, eds. *Death and Representation.* Baltimore: Johns Hopkins University Press, 1993.

Gordon, Mel. *The Grand Guignol: Theatre of Fear and Terror.* Rev. ed. New York: Da Capo, 1997.

Gosselin, E. *Recherches sur les origines et l'histoire du théâtre à Rouen avant Pierre Corneille.* Rouen, 1868.

Gould, Timothy. "The Unhappy Performative." In Parker and Sedgwick, eds., *Performativity and Performance,* 19–44.

Grafton, Anthony. *The Footnote: A Curious History.* Cambridge, Mass.: Harvard University Press, 1997.

Graver, David. "The Actor's Bodies." *Text and Performance Quarterly* 17 (1997): 221–35.

Gray, Floyd. "Ambiguity and Point of View in the Prologue to *Gargantua*." *Romanic Review* 56 (1965): 12–21.

Gray, Paul. "A Critical Chronology." In *Stanislavski and America: An Anthology from the Tulane Drama Review*, ed. Erika Munk, 137–77. New York: Hill and Wang, 1966.

Green, Richard Firth. *A Crisis of Truth: Literature and Law in Ricardian England*. Philadelphia: University of Pennsylvania Press, 1999.

Greenblatt, Stephen. *Shakespearean Negotiations: The Circulation of Social Energy in Renaissance England*. Berkeley: University of California Press, 1988.

Greetham, David. "Facts, Truefacts, Factoids; or, Why Are They Still Saying Those Nasty Things about Epistemology?" *Yearbook of English Studies* 29 (1999): 1–29.

Gregg, Joan Young. *Devils, Women, and Jews: Reflections of the Other in Medieval Sermon Stories*. SUNY Series of Medieval Studies. Albany: State University of New York Press, 1997.

Gruber, William. Review of Francis Barker, *The Culture of Violence. Comparative Drama* 28 (1994–95): 527–33.

Guilfoyle, Cherell. "The Staging of the First Murder in the Mystery Plays in England." *Comparative Drama* 25 (1991): 42–51.

Gurevich, Aron. *Medieval Popular Culture: Problems of Belief and Perception*. Trans. Jànos M. Bak and Paul A. Hollingsworth. Cambridge Studies in Oral and Literate Culture 14. Cambridge: Cambridge University Press, 1988.

Habermas, Jürgen. *Structural Transformation of the Public Sphere*. Trans. Thomas Burger and Frederick Lawrence. Cambridge, Mass.: MIT Press, 1989.

Haidu, Peter. *The Subject of Violence:* The Song of Roland *and the Birth of the State*. Bloomington: Indiana University Press, 1993.

Hallays-Dabot, Victor. *Histoire de la censure théâtrale en France*. 1862. Rpt. Geneva: Slatkine, 1970.

Halperin, David M., John J. Winkler, and Froma I. Zeitlin, eds. *Before Sexuality: The Construction of Erotic Experience in the Ancient Greek World*. Princeton: Princeton University Press, 1990.

Hanawalt, Barbara. "Violent Death in Fourteenth- and Early Fifteenth-Century England." *Comparative Studies in Society and History* 18 (1976): 297–320.

Hanawalt, Barbara, and Michal Kobialka, eds. *The Medieval Practices of Space*. Minneapolis: University of Minnesota Press, 1999.

Hardison, O. B., Jr. *Christian Rite and Christian Drama in the Middle Ages: Essays in the Origin and Early History of Modern Drama*. Baltimore: Johns Hopkins University Press, 1965.

Harris, Hilary. "Toward a Lesbian Theory of Performance: Refunctioning Gender." In *Acting Out: Feminist Performances*, ed. Lynda Hart and Peggy Phelan, 257–76. Ann Arbor: University of Michigan Press, 1993.

Harvey, Howard Graham. *The Theatre of the Basoche: The Contribution of the Law Societies to French Mediaeval Comedy*. Cambridge, Mass.: Harvard University Press, 1941.

Hashim, James. "Notes toward a Reconstruction of the *Mystère des Actes des Apôtres* as Represented at Bourges, 1536." *Theatre Research* 12 (1972): 29–73.

Hillairet, Jacques. *Connaissance du Vieux Paris*. 1951. Rpt. Paris: Princesse, 1956.

Hillgarth, J. N. *The Conversion of Western Europe, 350–750*. Englewood Cliffs, N.J.: Prentice-Hall, 1969.

Hindley, Alan. "Preaching and Plays: The Sermon in the Late Medieval French *Moralités. Le Moyen Français* (1998): 71–85.

Hocquet, Adolphe. *Tournai et le Tournaisis au XVIe siècle au point de vue politique et social*. Tournai, 1906.

Holl, Fritz. *Das politische und religose Tendenzdrama des 16. Jahrhunderts in Frankreich.* Erlangen: A. Deichert, 1903.

Holquist, Michael. "Corrupt Originals: The Paradox of Censorship." Introduction to special topic, "Literature and Censorship." *PMLA* 109 (1994): 14–25.

Holsinger, Bruce Wood. *Music, Body, and Desire in Medieval Culture: Hildegard of Bingen to Chaucer.* Stanford: Stanford University Press, 2001.

Homan, Richard L. "Mixed Feelings about Violence in the Corpus Christi Plays." In Redmond, ed., *Violence in Drama,* 93–100.

Huizinga, Johan. *Homo Ludens: A Study of the Play Element in Culture.* 1950. Rpt. Boston: Beacon Press, 1972.

Hummelen, W. M. H. "The Boundaries of the Rhetoricians' Stage." *Comparative Drama* 28 (1994–95): 235–51.

Hüsken, Wim. "Politics and Drama: The City of Bruges as Organizer of Drama Festivals." In Knight, ed., *The Stage as Mirror,* 165–87.

Jacquot, Jean, with Elie Konigson and Marcel Oddon, eds. *Dramaturgie et société: Rapports entre l'oeuvre théâtrale, son interprétation et son public aux XVIe et XVIIe siècles.* Nancy, 14–21 April 1967. 2 vols. Paris: Éditions du Centre National de la Recherche Scientifique, 1968.

Janes, Regina. "Beheadings." In Goodwin, Webster, and Bronfen, eds., *Death and Representation,* 242–62.

Janov, Arthur. *The Primal Scream: Primal Therapy, the Cure for Neurosis.* New York: G. P. Putnam's Sons, 1970.

Jardine, Lisa. "Boy Actors, Female Roles, and Elizabethan Eroticism." In Kastan and Stallybrass, eds., *Staging the Renaissance,* 57–67.

Jauss, Hans-Robert. "The Alterity and Modernity of Medieval Literature." *NLH* 10 (1979): 181–227.

———. *Question and Answer: Forms of Dialogic Understanding.* Ed. and trans. Michael Hays. Theory and History of Literature 68. Minneapolis: University of Minnesota Press, 1989.

Johnson, Eithne, and Eric Schaefer. "Soft Core / Hard Gore: *Snuff* as a Crisis in Meaning." *Journal of Film and Video* 45 (1993): 40–59.

Jolibois, Émile. *La Diablerie de Chaumont.* Chaumont, 1838.

Jonker, Gerard Dirk. *Le Protestantisme et le théâtre de langue française au XVIe siècle.* Groningen: J. B. Wolters, 1939.

Jordan, Mark. *The Invention of Sodomy in Christian Theology.* Chicago: University of Chicago Press, 1997.

Joynes, Andrew. *Medieval Ghost Stories.* Cambridge: Boydell and Brewer, 2001.

Kastan, David Scott, and Peter Stallybrass, eds. *Staging the Renaissance: Reinterpretations of Elizabethan and Jacobean Drama.* New York: Routledge, 1991.

Kelly, Henry Ansgar. *Ideas and Forms of Tragedy from Aristotle to the Middle Ages.* Cambridge: Cambridge University Press, 1993.

Kennedy, George A. *Classical Rhetoric and Its Christian and Secular Tradition from Ancient to Modern Times.* Chapel Hill: University of North Carolina Press, 1980.

Kerekes, David, and David Slater. *Killing for Culture: An Illustrated History of Death Film from Mondo to Snuff.* London: Creation Books, 1995.

Kerr, Walter. *Tragedy and Comedy.* New York: Simon and Schuster, 1967.

Kipling, Gordon. *Enter the King: Theatre, Liturgy, and Ritual in Medieval Civic Triumph.* Oxford: Clarendon Press, 1998.

Kirby, Michael. *A Formalist Theatre.* Philadelphia: University of Pennsylvania Press, 1992.

Knapp, Steven, and Walter Benn Michaels. "Against Theory." In Mitchell, ed., *Against Theory*, 11–30.

Knight, Alan E. *Aspects of Genre in Late Medieval French Drama*. Manchester: Manchester University Press, 1983.

———. "Beyond Misrule: Theater and the Socialization of Youth in Lille." *Research Opportunities in Renaissance Drama* 35 (1996): 73–84.

Knight, Alan E., ed. *The Stage as Mirror: Civic Theatre in Late Medieval Europe*. Cambridge: D. S. Brewer, 1997.

Kobialka, Michal. *This Is My Body: Representational Practices in the Early Middle Ages*. Ann Arbor: University of Michigan Press, 1999.

Kolve, V. A. *The Play Called Corpus Christi*. Stanford: Stanford University Press, 1966.

Konigson, Elie. *L'Espace théâtral médiéval*. Paris: CNRS, 1975.

———. *La Représentation d'un mystère de la Passion à Valenciennes en 1547*. Paris: CNRS, 1969.

Koopmans, Jelle. *Le Théâtre des exclus au Moyen Age: Hérétiques, sorcières et marginaux*. Paris: Imago, 1997.

Kristeller, Paul Oskar. *Renaissance Thought: The Classic, Scholastic, and Humanist Strains*. 1955. Rpt. New York: Harper and Row, 1961.

Kruger, Loren. *The National Stage: Theatre and Cultural Legitimation in England, France, and America*. Chicago: University of Chicago Press, 1992.

Kruger, Steven F. "The Spectral Jew." *New Medieval Literatures* 2: 9–35.

Kubiak, Anthony. *Stages of Terror: Terrorism, Ideology, and Coercion as Theatre History*. Bloomington: Indiana University Press, 1991.

Kyle, Donald G. *Spectacles of Death in Ancient Rome*. London: Routledge, 1998.

Lacan, Jacques. *Écrits: A Selection*. Trans. Alan Sheridan. New York: W. W. Norton, 1977.

LaCapra, Dominick. *Representing the Holocaust: History, Theory, Trauma*. Ithaca: Cornell University Press, 1994.

Lamarque, Peter, and Stein Haugom Olsen. *Truth, Fiction and Literature: A Philosophical Perspective*. Oxford: Clarendon Press, 1994.

Landess, Thomas. "The 'Snuff Film' and the Limits of Modern Aesthetics." In Ferguson and Groseclose, eds., *Literature and the Visual Arts*, 197–210.

Langer, Lawrence L. *The Holocaust and the Literary Imagination*. New Haven: Yale University Press, 1975.

———. *Holocaust Testimonies: The Ruins of Memory*. New Haven: Yale University Press, 1991.

Lebègue, Raymond. *Le Mystère des actes des apôtres: Contribution à l'étude de l'humanisme et du protestantisme français au XVIe siècle*. Paris: Champion, 1929.

———. *La Tragédie religieuse en France. Les débuts (1514– 1573)*. Bibliothèque Littéraire de la Renaissance, n.s. 17. Paris: Champion, 1929.

Lebert, C. "Le Théâtre à Meaux au XV, XVI et XVII siècles." Cited in *Bulletin historique et philologique (jusqu'à 1715) du Comité des Travaux historiques et scientifiques. Années 1955 et 1956*, xviii–xx. Paris: PUF, 1957.

Le Goff, Jacques. *History and Memory*. Trans. Steven Rendall and Elizabeth Claman. New York: Columbia University Press, 1992.

———. *Medieval Civilization, 400–1500*. Trans. Julia Barrow. 1988. Oxford: Blackwell, 1995.

———. *The Medieval Imagination*. Trans. Arthur Goldhammer. Chicago: University of Chicago Press, 1988.

Lerer, Seth. "Making Mimesis: Eric Auerbach and the Institutions of Medieval Studies." In Bloch and Nichols, eds., *Medievalism and the Modernist Temper*, 308–33.

Le Roy Ladurie, Emmanuel. *The Beggar and the Professor: A Sixteenth-Century Family Saga.* Trans. Arthur Goldhammer. 1995. Chicago: University of Chicago Press, 1997.

————. *Carnival in Romans.* Trans. Mary Feeney. New York: George Braziller, 1979.

Lesser, Wendy. *Pictures at an Execution: An Inquiry into the Subject of Murder.* Cambridge, Mass.: Harvard University Press, 1993.

Lestringant, Frank. *Une Sainte horreur ou le voyage en Eucharistie XVIe–XVIIIe.* Paris: PUF, 1996.

Levine, Laura. *Men in Women's Clothing: Anti-Theatricality and Effeminization 1579–1642.* Cambridge: Cambridge University Press, 1994.

Lewis, Robert. *Method or Madness?* New York: French, 1958.

"Looking Out for Mrs. Berwid." Producer, Norman Gorin. *60 Minutes* 13, no. 43 (12 July 1981).

de Lorde, André. *Théâtre de la mort. Les Charcuteurs.—Le Vaisseau de la Mort.—L'Homme Mystérieux.* Paris: Eugène Figuière, 1928.

Lyotard, Jean François, and Jean-Loup Thebaud. *Just Gaming.* Trans. Wlad Godzich. Minneapolis: University of Minnesota Press, 1985.

MacKinnon, Catharine A. *Toward a Feminist Theory of the State.* Cambridge, Mass.: Harvard University Press, 1989.

Mandel, Jerome, and Bruce A. Rosenberg. *Medieval Literature and Folklore Studies: Essays in Honor of Francis Lee Utley.* New Brunswick, N.J.: Rutgers University Press, 1970.

Manselli, R. *La Religion populaire au Moyen Age. Problèmes de méthode et d'histoire.* Paris: Vrin, 1975.

Marshall, David. *The Surprising Effects of Sympathy: Marivaux, Diderot, Rousseau, and Mary Shelley.* Chicago: University of Chicago Press, 1988.

Martin, Hervé. *Le Métier du prédicateur à la fin du Moyen Age en France septentrionale.* Paris: Le Cerf, 1988.

Martinez, J. D. "The Fallacy of Contextual Analysis as a Means of Evaluating Dramatized Violence." *Theatre Symposium* 7 (1999): 76–85.

Maugras, Gaston. *Les Comédiens hors la loi.* Paris: Calmann Lévy, 1887.

Mazouer, Charles. "La Prédication populaire et le théâtre du XVIe siècle: Le cas de Michel Menot." In *Le Jeu théâtral, ses marges, ses frontières: Actes de la deuxième rencontre sur l'ancien théâtre Européen de 1997,* ed. Jean-Pierre Bordier, 79–90. Paris: Champion, 1999.

McConahay, John. "Pornography: The Symbolic Politics of Fantasy." *Law and Contemporary Problems* 51 (1988): 31–69.

Miles, Margaret R. *Image as Insight: Visual Understanding in Western Christianity and Secular Culture.* Boston: Beacon Press, 1985.

Minois, Georges. *History of Suicide: Voluntary Death in Western Culture.* Trans. Lydia G. Cochrane. 1995. Baltimore: Johns Hopkins University Press, 1999.

Mollat, Michel. *Les Pauvres au moyen âge: Étude sociale.* Paris: Hachette, 1978.

Monson, Craig A., ed. *The Crannied Wall: Women, Religion, and the Arts in Early Modern Europe.* Ann Arbor: University of Michigan Press, 1992.

Moreau, Gérard. *Histoire du Protestantisme à Tournai jusqu'à la veille de la Révolution des Pays-Bas.* Bibliothèque de la Faculté de Philosophie et Lettres de l'Université de Liège 167. Paris: Belles Lettres, 1962.

Morse, Ruth. *Truth and Convention in the Middle Ages: Rhetoric, Representations, and Reality.* Cambridge: Cambridge University Press, 1991.

Muir, Lynette R. "Apocryphal Writings and the Mystery Plays." In *Le Théâtre au Moyen Age,* ed. Muller, 79–83.

————. *The Biblical Drama of Medieval Europe.* Cambridge: Cambridge University Press, 1995.

Mullaney, Steven. *The Place of the Stage: License, Play, and Power in Renaissance England.* Chicago: University of Chicago Press, 1988.

Murphy, James J. *Rhetoric in the Middle Ages: A History of Rhetorical Theory from Saint Augustine to the Renaissance.* 1974. Rpt. Berkeley: University of California Press, 1981.

Murray, Alexander. *Suicide in the Middle Ages.* Vol. 1, *The Violent against Themselves.* Oxford: Oxford University Press, 1998.

———. *Suicide in the Middle Ages.* Vol. 2, *The Curse on Self-Murder.* Oxford: Oxford University Press, 2000.

Nichols, Stephen G. "Modernism and the Politics of Medieval Studies." In Bloch and Nichols, eds., *Medievalism and the Modernist Temper,* 25–56.

———. *Rire et théâtralité à l'époque prémoderne.* Geneva: Droz, forthcoming.

Nicoll, Allardyce. *World Drama from Aeschylus to Anouilh.* New York: Harcourt, Brace and World, 1949.

Nirenberg, David. *Communities of Violence: Persecution of Minorities in the Middle Ages.* Princeton: Princeton University Press, 1996.

Nora, Pierre. "From *Lieux de Mémoire* to *Realms of Memory:* Preface to the English-Language Edition." In Nora, ed., *Realms of Memory,* 1:xv–xxiv.

———. "General Introduction: Between Memory and History." In Nora, ed., *Realms of Memory,* 1:1–20.

Nora, Pierre, ed. *Realms of Memory: The Construction of the French Past.* English-language editor, Lawrence D. Kritzman. Trans. Arthur Goldhammer. 3 vols. 1992. New York: Columbia University Press, 1997.

Nussbaum, Martha. *Poetic Justice: The Literary Imagination and Public Life.* Boston: Beacon Press, 1995.

O'Connell, Michael. *The Idolatrous Eye: Iconoclasm and Theater in Early-Modern England.* New York: Oxford University Press, 2000.

Olson, Glending. "Plays as Play: A Medieval Ethical Theory of Performance and the Intellectual Context of the *Tretise of Miraclis Pleyinge.*" *Viator* 26 (1995): 195–221.

O'Malley, John W. "Content and Rhetorical Forms in Sixteenth-Century Treatises on Preaching." In *Renaissance Eloquence: Studies in the Theory and Practice of Renaissance Rhetoric,* ed. James J. Murphy, 238–52. Berkeley: University of California Press, 1983.

Orgel, Stephen. *Impersonations: The Performance of Gender in Shakespeare's England.* Cambridge: Cambridge University Press, 1996.

Otter, Monika. *Inventiones: Fiction and Referentiality in Twelfth-Century English Historical Writing.* Chapel Hill: University of North Carolina Press, 1996.

d'Outreman, Henry. *Histoire de la ville et comté de Valenciennes.* Douai, 1639. Rpt. Marseilles: Laffitte, 1975.

Ozment, Steven. *The Age of Reform, 1250–1550: An Intellectual and Religious History of Late Medieval and Reformation Europe.* New Haven: Yale University Press, 1980.

———. *Protestants: The Birth of a Revolution.* New York: Doubleday, 1992.

———. *The Reformation in the Cities: The Appeal of Protestantism to Sixteenth-Century Germany and Switzerland.* New Haven: Yale University Press, 1975.

Ozment, Steven, ed. *The Reformation in Medieval Perspective.* Chicago: Quadrangle Books, 1971.

Parfaict, François, and Parfaict, Claude. *Histoire du théâtre françois depuis son origine jusqu'à présent, avec la vie des plus célébres poëtes dramatiques, un catalogue exact de leurs pièces, & des notes historiques et critiques.* 15 vols. Paris, 1745–49. Rpt. New York: Burt Franklin, 1968.

Parker, Andrew, and Eve Kosofsky Sedgwick, eds. *Performativity and Performance.* New York: Routledge, 1995.

Parker, Geoffrey. *The Dutch Revolt*. Ithaca: Cornell University Press, 1977.

————. *Philip II*. London: Hutchinson, 1979.

Paxson, James J. "Personification's Gender." *Rhetorica* 16 (1998): 149–79.

————. "The Structure of Anachronism and the Middle English Mystery Plays." *Mediaevalia* 18 (1995): 321–40.

Penn, Dorothy. "The Staging of the 'Miracles de Nostre Dame par personnages of Ms. Cange." French Institute Publications. New York: Columbia University Press, 1933.

Pentzell, Raymond J. "The Medieval Theatre in the Streets." *Theatre Survey* 14 (1973): 1–21.

Peters, Edward. *Torture*. New York: Basil Blackwell, 1986.

Petit de Julleville, L. *Les Mystères*. Vols. 1 and 2 of *Histoire du théâtre en France*. 1880. Rpt. Geneva: Slatkine, 1968.

————. *Le Théâtre en France: Histoire de la littérature dramatique*. Paris: Armand Colin, 1923.

Phillips, Henry. *Church and Culture in Seventeenth-Century France*. Cambridge: Cambridge University Press, 1997.

Philo, Greg. *Seeing and Believing: The Influence of Television*. London: Routledge, 1990.

Piaget, Jean. *The Essential Piaget*. Ed. Howard E. Gruber and J. Jacques Vonèche. London: Routledge and Kegan Paul, 1977.

Plass, Paul. *The Game of Death in Ancient Rome: Arena Spirit and Political Suicide*. Madison: University of Wisconsin Press, 1995.

Po-chia Hsia, R. *The Myth of Ritual Murder: Jews and Magic in Reformation Germany*. New Haven: Yale University Press, 1988.

Postlewait, Thomas. "Writing History Today." *Theatre Survey* 41 (2000): 83–106.

Propp, Vladimir. *Theory and History of Folklore*. Ed. Anatoly Liberman, trans. Ariadna Y. Martin and Richard P. Martin. Theory and History of Literature 5. Minneapolis: University of Minnesota Press, 1984.

Prosser, Eleanor. *Drama and Religion in the English Mystery Plays: A Re-Evaluation*. Stanford: Stanford University Press, 1961.

Pywell, Geoff. *Staging Real Things: The Performance of Ordinary Events*. Lewisburg, Pa.: Bucknell University Press, 1994.

Rackin, Phyllis. "Androgyny, Mimesis, and the Marriage of the Boy Heroine on the English Renaissance Stage." *PMLA* 102 (1987): 29–41.

Ravez, Walter. *Le Folklore de Tournai et du Tournaisis*. Tournai: Casterman, 1949.

Read, Alan. *Theatre and Everyday Life: An Ethics of Performance*. London: Routledge, 1993.

Redmond, James, ed. *Violence in Drama*. Themes in Drama 13. Cambridge: Cambridge University Press, 1991.

Renaudet, Augustin. *Préréforme et Humanisme à Paris pendant les premières guerres d'Italie (1494–1517)*. 2nd ed. Paris: Librairie d'Argences, 1953.

Rey-Flaud, Henri. *Le Cercle magique: Essai sur le théâtre en rond à la fin du moyen âge*. Paris: Gallimard, 1973.

————. *Le Charivari: Les rituels fondamentaux de la sexualité*. Paris: Payot, 1985.

————. *Pour une Dramaturgie du moyen-âge*. Paris: Presses Universitaires de France, 1980.

Riffaterre, Michael. *Fictional Truth*. Baltimore: Johns Hopkins University Press, 1990.

Ringer, Mark. *Electra and the Empty Urn: Metatheater and Role Playing in Sophocles*. Chapel Hill: University of North Carolina Press, 1998.

Robins, J. Max. "When Is the News Just Too 'Horrific?'" The Robins Report. *TV Guide*, 21–27 November 1999, 53.

Roelker, Nancy Lyman. *One King, One Faith: The Parlement of Paris and the Religious Reformations of the Sixteenth Century*. Berkeley: University of California Press, 1996.

Rogoff, Gordon. *Theatre Is Not Safe: Theatre Criticism, 1962–1986.* Evanston, Ill.: Northwestern University Press, 1987.

Rolland, Romain. "L'Oeuvre des trente ans de théâtre et les galas populaires." *Revue* (July 1903): 212–13.

———. *Le Théâtre du peuple: Essai d'esthétique d'un théâtre nouveau.* 3rd ed. Paris: Hachette, 1913.

Roy, Emile. *Le Mystère de la Passion en France du XIVe au XVIe siècle: Étude sur les sources et le classement des mystères de la Passion.* Dijon: Damidot Frères and Champion, n.d.

Rubin, Miri. *Corpus Christi: The Eucharist in Late Medieval Culture.* Cambridge: Cambridge University Press, 1991.

———. *Gentile Tales: The Narrative Assault on Late Medieval Jews.* New Haven: Yale University Press, 1999.

Runnalls, Graham. *Études sur les mystères.* Paris: Champion, 1998.

———. *Les Mystères français imprimés.* Paris: Champion, 1999.

———. "Were They Listening or Watching? Text and Spectacle at the 1510 Châteaudun *Passion Play.*" In *Spectacle in Early Theatre, England and France,* ed. Jean-Paul Debaux et Yves Peyre, 25–36. Lancaster: Lancaster University Press, 1994.

Russell, Jeffrey Burton. *The Devil: Perceptions of Evil from Antiquity to Primitive Christianity.* Ithaca: Cornell University Press, 1977.

———. *Lucifer: The Devil in the Middle Ages.* Ithaca: Cornell University Press, 1984.

———. *Mephistopheles: The Devil in the Modern World.* Ithaca: Cornell University Press, 1986.

———. *The Prince of Darkness: Radical Evil and the Power of Good in History.* Ithaca: Cornell University Press, 1988.

———. *Satan: The Early Christian Tradition.* Ithaca: Cornell University Press, 1981.

Said, Edward. *Culture and Imperialism.* New York: Alfred A. Knopf, 1993.

Sainte-Beuve, Charles Augustin. *Tableau historique et critique de la poésie française et du théâtre français au seizième siècle.* Rev. ed. Paris: Charpentier, 1869.

Sartre, Jean-Paul. *Sartre on Theater.* Documents assembled, edited, introduced, and annotated by Michel Contat and Michel Rybalka; trans. Frank Jellinek. New York: Pantheon, 1976.

Sautman, Francesca Canadé, Diana Conchado, and Giuseppe Carlo Di Scipio, eds. *Telling Tales: Medieval Narratives and the Folk Tradition.* New York: St. Martin's Press, 1998.

Scarry, Elaine. *The Body in Pain: The Making and Unmaking of the World.* 1985. Rpt. New York: Oxford University Press, 1987.

Schechner, Richard. *Between Theater and Anthropology.* Philadelphia: University of Pennsylvania Press, 1985.

———. "Collective Reflexivity: Restoration of Behavior." In *A Crack in the Mirror: Reflexive Perspectives in Anthropology,* Ed. Jay Ruby, 39–81. Philadelphia: University of Pennsylvania Press, 1982.

———. "Introduction: Exit Thirties, Enter Sixties." In *Stanislavski and America: An Anthology from the Tulane Drama Review,* ed. Erika Munk, 13–23. New York: Hill and Wang, 1966.

———. *Performance Theory.* 2nd ed. New York: Routledge, 1988.

Scherb, Victor I. "Violence and the Social Body in the Croxton *Play of the Sacrament.*" In Redmond, ed., *Violence in Drama,* 69–78.

Schmitt, Jean-Claude. *The Holy Greyhound: Guinefort, Healer of Children since the Thirteenth Century.* Trans. Martin Thom. Cambridge: Cambridge University Press, 1983.

———. *La Raison des gestes dans l'Occident médiéval.* Paris: NRF, 1990.

———. "Le Suicide au Moyen Age." *Annales, Économies, Sociétés, Civilisations* 31 (1976): 3–28.

Schmitt, Natalie Crohn. "Was There a Medieval Theatre in the Round? A Re-examination of the Evidence." In Taylor and Nelson, eds., *Medieval Drama,* 292–315.

Schneider, P. E. "Fading Horrors of the Grand Guignol." *New York Times Magazine,* 17 March 1957.

Schulenburg, Jane Tibbetts. "Female Sanctity: Public and Private Roles, ca. 500–1100." In *Women and Power in the Middle Ages,* ed. Mary Erler and Maryanne Kowaleski, 102–25. Athens: University of Georgia Press, 1988.

Schwartz, Regina M. "Teaching a Sacred Text as Literature, Teaching Literature as a Sacred Text." In *Profession 1998,* 186–98. New York: Modern Language Association, 1998.

Shuger, Deborah. *Habits of Thought in the English Renaissance.* Berkeley: University of California Press, 1990.

Siebers, Tobin. *Morals and Stories.* New York: Columbia University Press, 1992.

Siraisi, Nancy G. *Medieval and Early Renaissance Medicine: An Introduction to Knowledge and Practice.* Chicago: University of Chicago Press, 1990.

Snyder, Susan B. *The Paradox of Despair: Studies on the Despair Theme in Medieval and Renaissance Literature.* New York: Columbia University Press, 1963.

Sokal, Alan D. "A Physicist Experiments with Cultural Studies." *Lingua Franca* (May–June 1996): 62–64.

Solterer, Helen. "The Waking of Medieval Theatricality: Paris—1995." *NLH* 27 (1996): 357–90.

Southern, Richard. *The Medieval Theatre in the Round.* London: Faber and Faber, 1957.

Spector, Ethel, ed. *On Freud's "A Child Is Being Beaten."* New Haven: Yale University Press, 1997.

Spector, Stephen. "Anti-Semitism and the English Mystery Plays." In *Drama in the Middle Ages: Comparative and Critical Essays,* ed. Clifford Davidson, C. J. Gianakaris, and John H. Stroupe, 328–41. New York: AMS, 1982.

———. "Time, Space and Identity in the *Play of the Sacrament.* In Knight, ed., *The Stage as Mirror,* 189–200.

Spiegel, Gabrielle M. *Romancing the Past: The Rise of Vernacular Prose Historiography in Thirteenth-Century France.* Berkeley: University of California Press, 1993.

Sponsler, Claire. *Drama and Resistance: Bodies, Goods, and Theatricality in Late Medieval England.* Medieval Cultures 10. Minneapolis: University of Minnesota Press, 1997.

Stanislavski, Constantin. *An Actor Prepares.* Trans. Elizabeth Reynolds Hapgood. New York: Theatre Arts, 1936.

———. *Building a Character.* Trans. Elizabeth Reynolds Hapgood. New York: Theatre Arts, 1949.

———. *Creating a Role.* Trans. Elizabeth Reynolds Hapgood. 1961. Rpt. New York: Routledge, Theatre Arts, 1988.

States, Bert O. *Great Reckonings in Little Rooms: On the Phenomenology of Theatre.* Berkeley: University of California Press, 1985.

Statman, Daniel, ed. *Moral Luck.* Albany: SUNY Press, 1993.

Steen, Charlie R. *A Chronicle of Conflict: Tournai, 1559–1567.* Utrecht: HES Publishers, 1985.

Steiner, George. *The Death of Tragedy.* New York: Alfred A. Knopf, 1961.

Steiner, Wendy. *The Scandal of Pleasure: Art in an Age of Fundamentalism.* Chicago: University of Chicago Press, 1995.

Straeten, Edmond Vander. *Le Théâtre villageois en Flandre: Histoire, littérature, musique, religion, politiques, moeurs, d'après des documents entièrement inédits.* 2nd ed. Brussels: Alex Tillot, 1881.

Sullivan, Karen. *The Interrogation of Joan of Arc.* Medieval Cultures 20. Minneapolis: University of Minnesota Press, 1999.

Tallis, Raymond. *In Defence of Realism.* London: Edward Arnold, 1985.

Taylor, Archer. "The Anecdote: A Neglected Genre." In Mandel and Rosenberg, eds., *Medieval Literature and Folklore,* 223–28.

Taylor, Jerome, and Alan Nelson, eds. *Medieval Drama: Essays Critical and Contextual.* Chicago: University of Chicago Press, 1972.

Tentler, Thomas N. *Sin and Confession on the Eve of the Reformation.* Princeton: Princeton University Press, 1977.

de Terwangue, M. C. *Le Personnage de Judas dans les mystères français.* Mémoire de l'Université Catholique de Louvain. Louvain, 1949.

Le Théâtre au moyen âge. Actes du deuxième colloque de la SITM . . . Alençon, 11–14 juillet 1997. Ed. G. R. Muller. Montreal: L'Aurore, 1981.

Theiner, Paul. "Medieval English Literature." In *Medieval Studies,* ed. James M. Powell, 239–75. Syracuse: Syracuse University Press, 1976.

Thomas, Antoine. "Le Théâtre à Paris et aux environs." *Romania* 21 (1892): 606–12.

Thompson, Stith. "Unfinished Business: The Folktale." In Mandel and Rosenberg, eds., *Medieval Literature and Folklore,* 213–21.

Turner, Victor. *Dramas, Fields, and Metaphors: Symbolic Action in Human Society.* Ithaca: Cornell University Press, 1974.

———. *From Ritual to Theatre: The Human Seriousness of Play.* 1982. Rpt. New York: PAJ, 1992.

Tydeman, William. *The Theatre in the Middle Ages: Western European Stage Conditions, c. 800–1576.* Cambridge: Cambridge University Press, 1978.

Van Dam, Raymond. *Saints and Their Miracles in Late Antique Gaul.* Princeton: Princeton University Press, 1993.

Waite, Gary K. "Vernacular Drama and Early Urban Reformation: The Chambers of Rhetoric in Amsterdam, 1520–1550. *Journal of Medieval and Renaissance Studies* 21 (1991): 187–206.

Walter, Philippe. "Myth and Text in the Middle Ages: Folklore as Literary 'Source.'" In Sautman, Conchado, and Di Scipio, eds., *Telling Tales,* 59–75.

Walton, Kendall L. *Mimesis as Make-Believe.* Cambridge, Mass.: Harvard University Press, 1990.

Ward, John O. "Quintilian and the Rhetorical Revolution of the Middle Ages." *Rhetorica* 13 (1995): 231–84.

Warning, Rainer. "On the Alterity of Medieval Religious Drama." *New Literary History* 10 (1979): 265–92.

Weaver, Elissa B. "The Convent Wall in Tuscan Convent Drama." In Monson, ed., *Crannied Wall,* 73–86.

Weisberg, Richard. *Poethics, and Other Strategies of Law and Literature.* New York: Columbia University Press, 1992.

White, Hayden. *Metahistory: The Historical Imagination in Nineteenth-Century Europe.* Baltimore: Johns Hopkins University Press, 1973.

Wickham, Glynne. *A History of the Theatre.* 2nd ed. Cambridge: Cambridge University Press, 1992.

———. *The Medieval Theatre.* 3rd ed. Cambridge: Cambridge University Press, 1987.

Wiley, W. L. *The Early Public Theatre in France.* Cambridge, Mass.: Harvard University Press, 1960.

Wilkinson, James. "A Choice of Fictions: Historians, Memory, and Evidence." *PMLA* 111 (1996): 80–92.

Will, George. "Naive Hopes and Real Decadence." *Washington Post,* 28 March 1976, C7.

Williams, Bernard. *Moral Luck.* Cambridge: Cambridge University Press, 1981.

Williams, John A. *The Cost of Deception: The Seduction of Modern Myths and Urban Legends.* Nashville: Broadman and Holman, 2001.

Wilshire, Bruce. *Role Playing and Identity: The Limits of Theatre as Metaphor.* 1982. Rpt. Bloomington: Indiana University Press, 1991.

Wilson, Katharina M. "The Saxon Canoness: Hrotsvit of Gandersheim." In Wilson, ed., *Medieval Women Writers*, 30–63.

Wilson, Katharina M., ed. *Medieval Women Writers*. Athens: University of Georgia Press, 1984.

Wilson, Luke. *Theaters of Intention: Drama and the Law in Early Modern England*. Stanford: Stanford University Press, 2001.

Wolkomir, Richard. "If Those Cobras Don't Get You, the Alligators Will." *Smithsonian* 23, no. 8 (November 1992): 166–77.

Woods, Leigh. "Actors' Biography and Mythmaking: The Example of Edmund Kean." In *Interpreting the Theatrical Past: Essays in the Historiography of Performance*, ed. Thomas Postlewait and Bruce A. McConachie, 230–47. Iowa City: University of Iowa Press, 1989.

Woodward, Geoffrey. *Philip II*. London: Longman, 1992.

Worthen, W. B. "Drama, Performativity, and Performance." *PMLA* 113 (1998): 1093–1107.

Wright, Stephen. "Joseph as Mother, Jutta as Pope: Gender and Transgression in Medieval German Drama." *Theatre Journal* 51 (1999): 149–66.

Yates, Frances. *The Art of Memory*. Chicago: University of Chicago Press, 1966.

Young, Karl. *The Drama of the Medieval Church*. 2 vols. Oxford: Clarendon Press, 1933.

Zeitlin, Froma I. "Playing the Other: Theater, Theatricality, and the Feminine in Greek Drama." In *Nothing to do with Dionysos? Athenian Drama in Its Social Context*, ed. John J. Winkler and Froma Zeitlin, 63–96. Princeton: Princeton University Press, 1990.

Zink, Michel. *La Prédication en langue romane*. Paris: Champion, 1976.

Zumthor, Paul. *Essai de poétique médiévale*. Paris: Seuil, 1972.

———. "From Hi(story) to Poem, or the Paths of Pun: The *Grands Rhétoriqueurs* of Fifteenth-Century France." *NLH* 10 (1979): 231–63.

INDEX

Note: Boldface page numbers refer to original documents